A Bicycle Journey to the Bottom of the Americas

Edith
Thanks.
Enjoy George H

A Bicycle Journey to the Bottom of the Americas

Being a true account of a bicycle adventure
from Alaska to Tierra Del Fuego

George J. Hawkins

Writer's Showcase
New York Lincoln Shanghai

A Bicycle Journey to the Bottom of the Americas
Being a true account of a bicycle adventure from Alaska to
Tierra Del Fuego

Writer's Showcase
an imprint of iUniverse, Inc.

For information address:
iUniverse, Inc.
2021 Pine Lake Road, Suite 100
Lincoln, NE 68512
www.iuniverse.com

ISBN: 0-595-13238-3

Printed in the United States of America

Contents

Part One

Top of the Americas

Chapter 1

North America

"The life in us is like the water in the river. It may rise this year higher than man has ever known it, and flood the parched uplands; even this may be the eventful year, which will drown out all our muskrats."

-Henry David Thoreau

Departure

Next thing I knew I was aboard Alaska Airlines flight #91 bound for Anchorage, Alaska. When boarding the plane I found myself seated next to a college-age Japanese fellow with a tennis racket across his lap. From the looks of things I thought perhaps he'd boarded the wrong plane. He had the aisle seat and I had the window seat. Minutes after I'd made myself comfortable a woman carrying two small babies stopped beside the Japanese tennis player. An alert stewardess sensing a problem checked the fellow's ticket to discover he was in the wrong seat. I soon had not one, but three seatmates: two burping, slobbering toddlers and their 30ish mother, whose nerves appeared to be on the ragged edge. By comparison, I was calm and collected. Though the babies were napping, they had all the earmarks of time bombs, ready to activate soon after a noisy takeoff.

Once airborne, I glanced back and forth from my book to the window, remembering little of what I read or saw. Thirty minutes before landing in Seattle, Crystal, the 22-month baby girl closest to me, spit up a ghastly mixture of what must have been cookies, cereal, and juice, at least those were some of the items I saw her push into her gaping maw with saliva-coated fists. At that very moment, mother Wilma was trying to squelch an outburst from Crystal's 4-month old sister, Goldie. Uncharacteristically, I volunteered to mop up the "accident" on Crystal's sweater. Airborne again, the girls fell into a stupor, much to mother Wilma's and my relief.

Somewhere off the coast of Alaska I looked down at what appeared to be thousands of miles of snow-capped mountains and twisting glaciers. The vista filled me with so much dread and anxiety I thought I'd wind up with an "accident" similar to Crystal's, but before I had time to exaggerate and distort the many fear-filled thoughts going through my mind, the plane landed in Anchorage on a runway, I was pleased to observe, free of ice and snow.

"Hello Anchorage, Good-bye Dream," is the title of an article I read in the March 1988, *National Geographic* long after that fateful day of July 1, 1988 when I pedaled out of Anchorage, inaugurating my hemistour. I laughed out loud when I first read the title, knowing full well the disappointment of its author when arriving in Anchorage. Although not the capital of Alaska, it could easily be characterized as the financial and population center. In 1986 it boasted a populace of 250,000, which at the time was nearly half the state's total population, but with the tapering off of the oil boom, Anchorage lost some 20,000 residents, a substantial number by any city's standards.

My first glimpse of Anchorage and its surroundings was from the window of Lance Nowland's Van on our way to the youth hostel where I spent the night. That "first glimpse" was one of skyscrapers, glass monoliths and a skyline comparable to many cities in the lower 48. I was expecting log cabins chinked with whitewashed cement, dirt streets, and wildlife cropping bunch grass beside a one-room school-house in the center of town. More than disappointed, the disparity of my expectations and the real world of Anchorage confounded me. But as Lance told me on the way into the city, Anchorage is only an hour away from the real Alaska, and he was accurate to a degree, but on a bicycle it's more like a day's ride away from Anchorage.

Another, not too humorous joke Lance told me on the way to the hostel was about Alaska's weather. According to local folk Alaska has nine months of winter and three months of bad weather. Ironically, that is a fairly accurate picture of Alaskan weather.

After landing and reassuring myself that I wouldn't need snow chains or a winter parka to bike through Alaska, I made my way to the Alaska Airlines baggage claim area which was deserted by the time I got there. There on the unmoving baggage carousel were my panniers, backpack, bike box and two huge metal trunks of a suspicious nature. To say I was pumped with adrenaline would be an understatement. I literally attacked my baggage as though it were an enemy fortification. When at last I tore my bike and assorted gear from the bike box I found myself staring senselessly at the ripped and shredded container I had just decimated. I was panting as though I'd run a marathon. With the idea of straightening the bike's handlebars, I somehow found my tools, grabbed an Allen wrench and applied it to the fitting on the front brake guide attached to the handlebar stem. I watched with displeasure and fear as the cable guide cracked. It took only a few seconds to realize that the guide cracked because I'd needlessly and recklessly over-tightened it. I put the wrench aside and forced myself to take several deep breaths. After achieving a condition of semi-hyperactivity, I finished making adjustments to the bike, sorted gear, and generally made myself useful. Finally, with at least 1/3 of the baggage claim area filled with torn cardboard, rope, newspaper and packing material of all kinds, I discovered my Orvis flyrod, encased in its 8-foot aluminum protective tube, was missing. I rummaged amongst the packing debris around my bike and gear, but found not a trace. I was furious and found myself raging around the baggage claim area like a wild animal.

I was ready to call the president of Alaska Airlines to personally make him aware of the bold thievery running rampant in his company, when I noticed someone lifting the suspicious trunks off the luggage carousel. When the gentlemen hefted the trunks onto a luggage cart, he reached down and picked up an 8-foot aluminum tube with my name inked on the cylinder in three conspicuous places. The bearded man of about my age held the tube aloft and called to me.

"Say, is this yours?"

"Ah, yes, yes it is, for a minute I thought I'd lost it," I said sheepishly.

"Looks like you're going to do some fishing. This your first time up to Alaska?"

About two hours later, when Lance dropped me and my bike off in downtown Anchorage in front of the youth hostel, I told him all about myself and the great bicycle adventure commencing the very next morning. By way of thanking Lance for the ride I gave him the aluminum cylinder that housed my Orvis flyrod. How I would attach or secure the two four-foot sections of the flyrod to my bike I hadn't given much thought to, but I knew that Alaska was the sport fishing capital of the world. That being the case, I thought I'd stop each night beside crystal clear, glacial-fed rivers and streams, make a few dexterous presentations with my flyrod, then haul the behemoth salmon or steelhead from its aquatic home and relocate it to the aromatic bacon grease of my frying pan. Dreams die hard.

The massive clouds hovering above the city looked a few degrees friendlier, but far from benign. With my gear and bike parked off to the side of the military-like cement block hostel dormitory, I checked my watch to discover I'd have to wait outside the youth hostel for an hour until it opened at 5 p.m. As a new International youth hostel member it would take awhile to get used to the hostels being closed between the hours of 9 a.m. and 5 p.m. daily. I used the hour wait to outfit my bike and load and reload gear and generally fine tune my touring profile developed during test rides in California. Funny, now that I was in this gloomy, moist climate I thought of my home as "sunny" California where people in shorts and sunglasses strolled under palm trees, stopping only occasionally to rub tanning lotion on their bronze skin. Of course, this mental picture was not even close to the reality of where I used to live, but more a product of a mind that would conjure up an Anchorage populated with caribou, moose, reindeer, eagles, Eskimos, sourdoughs, trappers, hunters, and dog sled mushers. Of course, all of the above would somehow be concentrated, at least in my mind, in the few blocks that the log cabin frontier town consisted of. At least in my mind.

I worked and waited outside the hostel trying to rein in a mind that was stuck in a rerun mode of all the "bear and bandido" stories extant. With panniers, sleeping bag, rucksack, and assorted gear lashed and anchored to my touring bike I was at a loss with what to do with the mound of remaining gear covering the ground between me and the bike. While I plugged holes and spaces in the already bulging panniers, a young bicyclist pulled up on the lawn nearby, laid his mountain bike down and lighted a cigarette. I guessed he was no more than 16 years old. For all of his youth, he seemed to lack any interest in my grossly overloaded touring bike.

"Where you been riding?" I asked.

Bart was returning from work at a nearby supermarket, where he'd been employed for the past two weeks. Prior to this job, he'd been bike riding down the Kenai Peninsula, up to Denali, out to Kodiak Island, and to a dozen other exotic-sounding places I assumed were suburbs of the north pole. At the end of the month he and his new girlfriend were going to work at one of the backcountry fishing-hunting resorts in the Wrangell Mountains. The one bit of advice I'll never forget, was Bart's insistence on carrying a 2 lb. jar of "goober jelly" as a staple in one's bike touring food stores. If you're not familiar with this item, it's a mixture of peanut butter and jelly mixed together and packaged in a single jar. My experience was that this concoction's bizarre taste was only exceeded by its looks. I assured Bart I would procure a supply of this item at the earliest opportunity.

Shortly, another biker wheeled up to the small well-used patch of green grass outside the hostel. This gentleman was Peter, a solo bike tourer from London. Bearded and wearing glasses, this unobtrusive Englishmen had obviously been influenced by some of the great explorer's like Shipton, Livingston, and Whymper, of his homeland. While I tweaked and fussed with my gear, Peter regaled Bart and I with a recitation of his harrowing bicycle tour from Vancouver to Dawson to Fairbanks to Denali to Anchorage. As many parts of his route were on my itinerary I paid close attention as he described the dirt roads and highways of the Yukon and Alaska.

I couldn't believe my eyes when I inspected his bike. I suspected it was a prototype of the first two-wheeled, multi-geared bicycle ever made. Although the tubing was of a respectable diameter, it wasn't made of lightweight, chrome moly, but of cast or hand-forged steel. At least that was my guess after hefting it. Unladen, I estimated Peter's bike weighed close to 50 lbs. The bike had a rear luggage rack from which two canvas panniers of uncertain vintage were suspended. He explained that all the necessities and a few luxuries (flask of scotch, cigars) were stuffed into those bags. Everything else was tied or strapped on to the rear rack. I felt like a space shuttle astronaut confronting one of the Wright brothers.

I was amazed that Peter and his two-wheeled anachronism survived the arduous journey he'd just described. Outside of a few broken spokes and bent rim repaired along the way, the velocipede "performed flawlessly" according to Peter. His only complaint was not seeing much animal wildlife. In an effort to provoke wildlife sightings he disregarded all common sense and precaution, but without incident.

Minutes before the 5 p.m. hostel opening, two more bikers wheeled up in the front yard. Immediately, Peter and I impaled them with the usual opening questions about where they came from and where they were going. Phil and brother Ed were from Washington State; they'd just completed a short bike ride from Fairbanks to Anchorage, stopping off at Denali. As we talked, the front door opened and we all kind of flowed into the hostel talking as we moved. We got registered, then started moving bikes and gear inside. As it turned out, the four of us, Peter, Phil, Ed and I shared a living area complete with two bedrooms, living room, bath, and kitchen. The bedrooms were small and made even smaller with two sets of bunkbeds squeezed in. When we spread out our sleeping bags, panniers and extra duffel it was difficult to move between the bunks. Eventually, everyone settled in and had something to eat. Lighting one of his many cigars, Peter announced he was going out in search of Anchorage nightlife, at least what was available within walking distance.

~ ~ ~

Darwin's Theory

Somewhere around 7 p.m. Phil, Ed, and I also found ourselves marching up and down the streets of downtown Anchorage. The city had a strange feeling about it, like everyone had left town for the evening and hadn't told anyone else. There didn't seem to be any restaurants, bars, or stores that had people in them. In a way it reminded me of an Edward Hopper cityscape—quiet, lonely, forsaken. We turned a corner and saw a shingle sign hanging over the sidewalk. It was an elaborately carved wood sign, depicting a seated monkey contemplating a human skull held in its hand. Below this was the name of the establishment—Darwin's Theory. We made our way inside to sample the ambiance and libations of the pub and discover, if possible, how the bar had been christened with such a cryptic rubric.

The cramped little pub with horseshoe-shaped bar had a good crowd seated and standing about. Everyone seemed to be chain-smoking and from the looks of it drinking mostly beer. We spotted Peter at the far end of the bar and made our way to him, squeezing our way past clusters of people. Once seated and served with a glass of beer, we ceremoniously toasted each other's travel adventures. Shortly thereafter, Peter lighted a fresh cigarillo and began a recap of his bike tour from Vancouver to Anchorage. Though I heard much of the story before, I had to laugh out loud almost to the point of exhaustion when he regaled us with his attempts at attracting wildlife, especially bears. Like all of us he had been inundated with bear stories before his departure from England from well meaning, though callow, friends and relatives. In fact, Peter declaimed, he was so inculcated with tales of savage beasts, he expected to be greeted at the Vancouver airport by a welcoming committee of them. Much to his chagrin, he had seen very little wildlife and had no close encounters of the wild kind. Halfway through his bike tour, some-where in the Yukon, he started ignoring camper's etiquette regarding the security of food. Soon he fell into the routine of storing all his food in his tent, considered by most "wild life" experts as tantamount to suicide. Taking this type of behavior to the extreme, Peter began cooking his bacon and eggs "in" his tent. The most he got out of this rash behavior was a visit or two from ground squirrels. He thought, Peter continued, he had finally attracted a bear to his digs when camping in Denali Park. Whilst preparing his usual breakfast of bacon and eggs inside his tent, he heard a loud smashing and crashing in the brush nearby. Hurrying out to investigate, he "thought" he saw a patch of brownish fur disappear into the dense bushes and pines. Further inves-tigation turned up paw prints of a goodly size, but for the remainder of his two-day camp at Denali his sightings were limited to homo sapiens and park buses.

Occasionally, as we recounted our favorite travel stories and swilled beer, someone would glance outside through two large plate glass front windows and comment on how early it was. At one point, we had the owner of the pub telling us how and why the place was named "Darwin's Theory." Very simply the owner's name was Fred Darwin. He didn't claim any kinship to THE Darwin, but after a number of years as proprietor of the pub he came to share Darwin's belief that man descended from apes. We were all a bit disappointed with this rather pedestrian explanation, preferring our own private, grandiose speculations.

Somewhere around midnight, we again commented on how the evening seemed to linger-it was not quite as light as it was at 9 p.m. Checking our watches in unison, we allowed that perhaps we had seen enough of Anchorage nightlife and began our trek back to the hostel. I don't recall that anyone one of us had trouble falling into a deep sleep that night, or day as the case may be, light or no light. Although this was my first experience with 24-hours of light I don't remember having trouble getting a good night's sleep, especially after a day of bike touring.

~ ~ ~

Bears and Robinson Crusoe

In the morning, after Peter, Phil, and Ed said goodbye and headed for the airport, I gathered up my panniers and gear and began to reassemble everything on my bike. With the bike leaning up against the railing in front of the hostel, things were moving along nicely when a young Japanese fellow cutting the small strip of grass in front of the hostel put his mower aside and approached. After the usual introductory questions, he launched into one of the most bizarre and horrific accounts of a bear attack known to man. The odd thing about his scenario, which ended with the death of two innocent campers, is he got his information from a film he had evidently seen. I've always wondered if the two campers, a male and female, knew in advance that they were to be sacrificed for the sake of an educational film or if the film in question was a horror film "gone wrong." ✱

Looking back now on all the advice, written, verbal, and otherwise, accumulated before, during, and after my trip, the best information I found (oddly enough) regarding a confrontation with a bear was in

✱ An amateur bear observer who had no major problems with the brown bears (coastal grizzlies) the 1st few seasons he was in nearby contact with them, invited a girlfriend up for his last season. They were attacked by a rogue bear & killed. No one knew anything in advance.

Daniel DeFoe's novel, **Robinson Crusoe.** Towards the end of the book, when Crusoe and Friday are crossing the Pyrenees between Spain and France, they confront, or at least Friday confronts, a bear in the forest. Robinson Crusoe says, *"As the bear is a heavy, clumsy creature, and does not gallop as the wolf does who is swift and light so he has two particular qualities, which generally are the rule of his actions; first, as to men, who are not his proper prey; I say, not his proper prey because though I can't say what excessive hunger might do which was now their case, the ground being all covered with snow; but as to men, he does not usually attempt them, unless they first attack him. On the contrary, if you meet him in the woods, if you don't meddle with him, he won't meddle with you; but then you must take care to be very civil to him, and give him the road, for he is a very nice gentleman, he won't go a step out of his way for a prince; nay, if you are really afraid, your best way is to look another way and keep going on; for some times if you stop, and stand still, and look steadfastly at him, he takes it for an affront; but if you throw or toss anything at him, and it hits him, though it were but a bit of a stick as big as your finger, he takes it for an affront and sets all his other business aside to pursue his revenge; for he will have satisfaction in point of honor; that is his first quality. The next is, that if he be once affronted he will never leave you, night or day, till he has his revenge; but follows at a good round rate till he overtakes you."*

With those final thoughts simmering on the front burner of my seething brain, I began pedaling out of Anchorage, hopefully in a northerly direction. At first, the loaded bike felt awkward and sluggish, but after several blocks, and gear changes, things began to settle in. Though the weather was less than inspirational, I managed to smile with inner pride and joy as I made my way along the highway headed north towards Denali. The time was probably 9 or 10 a.m. on Friday, July 1. My initial route was a modern freeway system, with multiple lanes and center dividers and exit and on ramps. In fact this was so close to everything I was trying to get away from, I stopped, looked at my map and found a secondary road that appeared to parallel the freeway for at least 10 miles. Pedaling down the two-lane road without any sign of civilization, I soon outdistanced the icons of "modern" civilization and settled into a peaceful tour of the Alaskan countryside. At least for the first two hours I half-expected to round a bend in the road and be confronted by a behemoth bear who had an especial dislike for bicycle riders. Which reminds me, the night before while finishing off a cup of coffee after dinner at the hostel I happened to be browsing through the local newspaper, when my eye zeroed in on a cartoon of interest to me. In it, a bear fresh from hibernation is pictured spitting out the stick-figure of a bicycle rider and complaining bitterly that because of low body fat bikers were not his favorite meal, he preferred a body with a lot more meat and fat on the bone.

After a number of miles of pleasant riding, I found myself in the small town of Willow where the secondary road joined with Alaska Highways 1 and 3. This being about 30-miles from Anchorage, I found I'd developed an appetite. While eating a snack, I watched the steady stream of traffic head west to Hwy 1, to join hundreds of other vehicles speeding north. It suddenly dawned on me that this was the Fourth of July weekend, so I presumed everyone who had spent that long 9-month winter in and around Anchorage was out on the road hell-bent for someplace else. After eating I cycled east on a two-lane road with little traffic, eventually returning me and my bike to Palmer and the same McDonald's where I'd breakfasted that morning. To say I was disappointed with Alaska would be an understatement. There I was in a typical McDonald's, grousing about traffic and crowded roads. All this and the weather wasn't terrific either. After my Big Mac and fries, I cycled around Palmer looking for a campground or even a field where I could pitch my tent, but soon growing tired and disgusted, I checked into a cheap motel. That night while watching movies on cable TV I recorded my first day's mileage, 78.2, in my journal along with my first day's commentary. *"I came to Alaska for the great outdoors, so where do I end up my first day—a motel."*

~ ~ ~

In Search Of An Excellent Campsite

But next day the sun was mostly out and it was warm and for the first time I saw blue sky. Another thing visible was the mountains, not just the bottom half with the top half obscured by clouds. I decided to cycle east on the Glenn Highway. The traffic, at least judging from what I saw the day before was tolerable. My map showed mountains not far down the road. More than ever, I was determined to find a picturesque, quiet campsite for my second night in the wilds of Alaska.

Not far out of Palmer a cyclist on a road bike pulled alongside and we chatted. He recommended a campground on the shore of Long Lake, a few hours away. Topping out on a hill about 25 miles farther, there below me was Long Lake and it was picturesque. Though it was only 3 p.m. I decided to set up camp and enjoy the peace and quiet, as the campground looked empty. The occupants of the lone pickup in the parking lot appeared to be fishing along the shoreline. Under fairly sunny skies I set up camp, cleaned myself up, and then hiked around the shore looking for a possible fishing spot. Not finding anything of immediate interest, I retired to my tent for a nap. About 5 p.m. I was awakened by an incredibly loud engine noise that seemed to be headed directly for my tent. I groped my way out of the tent to watch as an amphibious plane swooped low over the campground, banked at the end of the lake then made a smooth landing on the water. Not only did the plane land on the lake; it proceeded to taxi out of the water and into the parking lot at the lakeshore, coming to a halt about 50-yards from my tent. As soon as the engine was silenced, three waiting men began loading the plane with supplies. By now, I had pulled on my sweats and shoes and was on my way across the parking lot to see what was going on. Halfway to the plane I saw that most of the campsites were now occupied by campers and motorhomes. I was still the only tenter there.

Alongside the floatplane, I struck up a conversation with one of the fellows putting things into the small cargo area. The cargo was a month's supply of groceries headed for a fishing and hunting lodge accessible only by floatplane. I also learned that floatplane pilots all over Alaska used the thousands of lakes near highways and roads as landing strips. In the winter the planes were fitted with skis enabling the planes to land on the frozen, snow-covered lakes.

Within an hour the plane was loaded to the ceiling, bulkier items were lashed to the pontoons. I watched as the plane rolled into the water, taxied to the far end of the lake, turned, then came roaring back toward the campground. Halfway down the lake, it lifted off and gained altitude quickly before banking and disappearing over the treeline at the far side of the lake.

I returned to Chez Hawkins to prepare a dinner of Alpine-Aire freeze-dried Mountain Chili. The first of over two hundred such meals I would consume over the next three years.

Journal entries for that 41.1-mile day included: *"Believe it or not, just saw my first Alaskan mosquito, didn't bite though...hate to look at my maps, especially to gage distance, these maps don't seem to have any relationship to the real world. Nothing I've seen or ridden by, e.g. rivers, mountains, is on map. Like some geography has mysteriously disappeared."*

~ ~ ~

A Piece of Pie In Hand

One of the wonderful things that happened with frequency during my trip was discovering unexpected things and places, especially places to eat. Next morning, not more than ten miles east of Long Lake, through beautiful mountains, I coasted down a hill and saw the Eureka Creek Lodge. According to my stomach clock it was time to eat a second breakfast. I propped my bike against the log wall and walked inside to find the cafe empty of people, but judging from my twitching nostrils there was at least one prolific cook somewhere close by, for on the cash register counter were a half-dozen newly baked pies. Not just regular sized pies either; these were Alaska-size pies-big, sprawling, two-fisted pies.

While making a quick visual inventory of the stuffed Moose heads, Caribou antlers, various animal pelts and skins, a girl of about 10-years old appeared. She coughed to get my attention, then pushed a menu up at me. She took me by the hand and led me to one of a dozen tables where I dutifully took a seat. After carefully filling my cup to the very rim with coffee she announced that her mother would be in shortly take my order. Though the menu itself drove me to distraction, the savory aromas emanating from the kitchen made my mouth water. I could swear I smelled pumpkin pie or was it mincemeat? Momentarily, an aproned woman with long red hair, set two more pies on the counter, then made her way over to me.

"Sorry to keep you waiting, but today is my pie day and I'm running a bit late."

"That's fine with me. Looks like my lucky day. I've never smelled so many pies in one place at one time."

In a flash, I ordered a ham and cheese omelet, home fries, toast, and juice. I'd have bet money my red-haired waitress and pie baker was also the head chef. In no time at all, she reappeared with heaping platters containing my breakfast, her daughter following close behind with a coffeepot. I was instructed to "just yell" if I required anything else.

While shoveling away my morning feast, a middle-aged couple entered the restaurant and seated themselves at a table across from me. After breakfast and a third cup of coffee, I opened my journal and began making an entry, but was distracted by the lingering fragrance of the cooling pies. As soon as I could get the attention of my hostess I ordered up a thick slice of apple pie. Afterward while paying my bill, I couldn't resist ordering a piece of pumpkin pie for the road. Needless

to say I exited the lodge with a swollen stomach and a smile on my face. More than just a stop for food and rest, the Eureka Creek Lodge became a paradigm for the future. Fortunately, I learned early on never to pass up a good food or rest stop like Eureka Creek, regardless of time or mileage. It has been my experience that those places over the next hill or down the road another 30 minutes never materialize, or when they do they're closed. My golden rule, starting in Alaska was "a piece of pie in the hand is worth two in the bush."

This might be a hard lesson to learn for destination-oriented people, but it can keep you sane, healthy, and happy while touring, not to mention well fed. Let me explain. During my preparation stage, I would sometimes set an arbitrary time or number of miles to pedal before stopping for rest or food. I'd pass one or more cafes and a half dozen scenic spots all for the sake of an odometer or watch. Generally, when I'd achieved the mileage goal or the necessary elapsed time I found myself in an unattractive place, but I was too damn hungry or tired to pedal on to anything more satisfying. So I came to rely on my personalized version of "a bird in hand is worth two in the bush."

If there's any advice I'd offer to the fledging bike tourer it would be to **forget the numbers**—i.e. time and miles. My most unforgettable experiences have come about because I stopped to investigate something or someplace. On the other hand I've been disappointed, more often than not, when I forced myself to reach a destination.

~ ~ ~

Sheep Mountain

"Just after climbing a particularly long grade, saw a sign for food, gas, and lodging, so pulled off with the idea of filling my water bottles.

So there's this neat little lodge, cafe, bar, log cabins-all this at the base of a spectacular mountain."

That's how I described my first impressions of Sheep Mountain Lodge in my journal, truly an oasis of beauty, warmth, and friendliness in the Alaskan wilderness. It was only 3 or 4 p.m. on a 26-mile day, when I pulled off the road to fill my water bottles, but once inside the cozy log cafe and bar, with spectacular views of the mountains, a wood fire burning in the stove, I couldn't extricate myself. Only a handful of people lingered around the hand-hewn wood tables. Waiting for my bottles to be filled, I noticed a corner library bulging with paperbacks and magazines.

It was extremely easy to convince myself I needed a cup of coffee. Once seated at the table near the library, I figured I might as well look at the menu while sipping my coffee. I put the menu aside to watch the waitress serve the couple in front of me what looked like a steaming loaf of homemade bread, but a closer look revealed a loaf of bread with the center hollowed out and filled with homemade chili. To sweeten the deal the "missing" piece of bread was used as a tool for soaking up the chili juice.

It took only a second to order up a similar portion for myself. While waiting for my chili I got acquainted with my neighbors, Jerry and his girlfriend June, school teachers from Anchorage. By the time I consumed my homemade bread with chili, plus an Anchor Steam beer, there was no way I was going to pedal another foot. Dave the owner of the cafe/lodge told me I could camp there for the night.

"Just pick out any spot behind the cabins," he advised. That took in roughly 800,000 square miles. I found something a lot closer under a few tall pine trees. I had my tent pitched, gear stowed and was headed for the shower before 4 p.m. After cleaning up I made myself comfortable in the cafe. Over a cup of coffee I made a journal entry, recounting a chance encounter with the driver of a motorhome earlier that day. There the sight of my first glacier—the Matanuska Glacier, off to the side of the Highway captivated me. I stood there mesmerized, when a huge motorhome, rolled into the rest area and stopped about 20 feet from me. It just sat there, engine throbbing. I was about to ask the owner to shut the engine off so I could enjoy the peace and quiet of Mother Nature, when all of a sudden the driver's window rolled down. The driver sat there, cigarette in one hand and camera in the other. He proceeded to take a picture from his seat.

"Hey, come on out an look at this, this is beautiful." I called to him.

"We've been looking at it for the last five minutes," he replied. The window closed and away they went.

Yeah, I bet you saw it, I said to myself, from inside your land barge doing 60 m.p.h. *The American tourist is an enigma, a mystery, a puzzle,* I wrote in my journal.

Later that night, about 8 p.m., I wandered back down to the lodge, pulled up a tree trunk-stool to the bar and ordered a beer. While sipping the brew I noticed a telescope mounted on a tripod out on the porch. With one eye glued to the eyepiece of the telescope I could scan the mountains and river valley now clear of clouds and mist. Back in the lodge I ransacked the bookshelves next to the corner table, finally selecting Herman Melville's, *Typee.* This was one of 67 paperbacks I would enjoy during the next three years of my tour.

Enjoying the view from the lodge, I made this journal entry. *"Feeling quite good now. Naturally was a bit off center back in Anchorage. Seemed like I had twice as much gear as I needed or could use. Everyone at the hostel was commenting on the size of my load, including the young Japanese fellow who told me the bear story."*

Next morning enjoying a breakfast of hotcakes I was extremely happy so I decided to stay over an extra day as it commenced raining. With nothing much to do but stay out of the rain, I found myself quartered in my tent much of the time. If you're wondering what one does in a tent while waiting out an Alaskan rainstorm here's the answer: read, write letters or postcards, floss teeth, think, count mosquitos outside mosquito net, count mosquitos inside tent, speculate on how mosquitos got inside tent, sew, think about food, trim moustache and beard (if any), speculate on when and if the rain will stop.

That evening over a bowl of soup and homemade bread, I talked with Dave, an architect from New Jersey and his wife Lydia. They were ending their first week of a two-week Alaskan vacation. They were also thinking of flying to someplace like New Mexico or Arizona where it was warm and dry.

~ ~ ~

Has Anyone Here Seen Slana

Next morning I started down the highway headed east in a thick ground fog. As it had rained most of the night much of my gear was soaking wet, but I was glad to be back on the road. Now that the Fourth of July weekend was over the traffic was light. After a few hours of pedaling, I pulled over into one of the few designated rest areas I saw in Alaska, this being a patch of dirt and gravel with a 50-gallon barrel chained to a stake in the ground. I'd just raised my water bottle to my mouth when in rolled a Honda Goldwing motorcycle pulling a small trailer. Spence and Bea Pennington from Minnesota climbed from their huge motorcycle, then proceeded to remove helmets, gloves, and assorted rain gear. After introductions, they asked me where I was headed. I learned they'd passed through Dawson in the Canadian Yukon about a week ago. Heavy rains had turned dirt roads into quagmires; some places were impassable for the motorcycle and trailer. Like me, they hadn't expected so much foul weather. As for myself, I was from the Bay area of northern California where we were experiencing a third year of drought conditions.

After 57 miles of easy pedaling I pulled in to a deserted campground alongside the highway. Lucky for me across the road was a lodge and restaurant. Not as warm and friendly as Sheep Mountain

Lodge, but I was able to take a shower in the men's room before enjoying a dinner of beef stew. The only thing I can remember about the dining room was that it featured what must have been the world's largest collection of Caribou antlers, which are one of the most prodigious growths of antlers in the animal kingdom. Being the solitary patron I felt like I was dining in a caribou graveyard. I would not have been surprised if I were eating Caribou stew.

Although only day five with a mere 208 miles under my belt I'd begun a cycling routine that would be an ingrained habit by the end of the year. The foul weather notwithstanding, I was enjoying the nomadic life of striking my tent every morning and looking for some commodious oasis every night, especially one that would provide the essentials of campsite, water, and possibly wood for a campfire.

Two things I noticed here in Alaska were that distances between human habitations got bigger and bigger, while the human habitations got smaller and smaller. Perhaps the most significant thing I noticed was myself; I was getting stronger and feeling better each day. The weather no longer seemed to be such a critical factor in my overall appreciation.

I was looking forward to reaching Tok Junction, where Alaska Highways 1 and 2 joined about 200 miles south of Fairbanks. There I would find another youth hostel. Tok was also a jumping off point for the Taylor Highway, the dirt road that would take me into Dawson in the Canadian Yukon.

Somewhere west of Tok I made this journal entry. *"Wildlife. A lady on a tour bus at rest stop asked me how much wildlife I'd seen. So far, I told her, I'd seen a chipmunk, a rabbit, and two black birds (one alive, one dead). Actually, I got within 50 feet of the rabbit, but dared not penetrate its attack zone. Figuring it was an Alaskan Grizzly Rabbit it would have reared up on its hind legs, growled, then ala 'Search For the Holy Grail' it would have zapped me with a laser or some such diabolical weapon. The lady tourist told me I'd been on the road too long. Not long enough, I retorted"*

Somewhere down the not-so-straight and narrow highway was Christochina, at least it was on my map. But I discovered just because a settlement was on a map didn't necessarily mean it was "really" on the ground. Let me explain. One morning when I was still a destination-oriented biker I picked out the town of Slana on the map as the place I would stop for lunch, being some 25 miles down the highway. After pedaling 25 miles according to my cycle computer, I should have arrived at Slana or at least have seen some evidence of Slana. There wasn't any Slana on or near the highway so I pedaled another few hundred yards until I saw two guys doing survey work.

"Hey, where's Slana," I asked.

A rather taciturn gent pointed to a telephone pole alongside the road. I pedaled close enough to read the small wooden sign, with faded lettering—Slana. Okay, I'd reached Slana alright, but instead of a quaint outpost of civilization with a cafe, lodge, gas station and maybe a bakery, it was just a sign nailed to a telephone pole. Disappointed, I continued pedaling east, but not more than a mile down the road I experienced my first flat tire, one of 17 on my trip. Wouldn't you know it, it was my rear tire. I'd no sooner laid the bike on its side and was pulling tools from the panier when it started to rain. Not a heavy rain either, but a drizzly rain that gets everything wet and messy and makes you madder than hell at a map that shows there's suppose to be a town where there isn't one. Finally, realizing my stupidity and the fact that I was getting wet, I started laughing, howling until tears mixed with raindrops rolled down my cheeks. The absurdity of my situation finally came home to me. Still laughing, I pulled on my rain parka and started fixing the flat tire. I was in the middle of nowhere; not a vehicle had passed by in an hour. I could laugh, sing, cry, talk to myself and no one would ever know. So for some unknown reason I began singing " Heartbreak Hotel." When I stopped my feeble rendition of this Elvis classic, I noticed how quiet it was, except for the gentle patter of rain on my hooded parka. Still in a good spirits, I finished replacing the tube and reassembling the rear wheel. Yes, the point of this chataugua is mainly to alert the budding bike tourer to some of the realities of touring, i.e. sometimes the weather ain't so good, sometimes the scenery ain't so pretty and sometimes things go wrong, real wrong, but and this is a big but, you're living your own great adventure.

~ ~ ~

Hans Eugen

Just outside Christochina at mile 208 I was cycling along minding my own business when out of nowhere an ~~Indian~~ Native* with long black hair, plaid shirt and jeans and a sawed-off, pump-action shotgun slung over shoulder materialized out of the thick forest alongside the highway. I looked up from my meditation to see him standing there scrutinizing me.

"Say, where in hell do you think you're going," he said.

I stopped and looked around fearful I was trespassing on sacred ceremonial grounds. Looking over at him the only thing I could think of by way of a reply to his question was, "South America."

"The hell you say. Well, have a good trip." He said smiling. He waved then stomped back into the woods.

Not far from there I spotted the typical Alaskan roadhouse—cafe, bar, gas station, general store. Inside the log structure I found a restaurant-bar that also served as a community TV room. There were four or five men and women huddled at the end of the bar close to the TV watching some type of soap opera. The proprietress behind the bar told me that I could pitch my tent in back at no charge. She said all this while glued to the tube. She also informed me I could use their shower for 50 cents if I provided my own towel or $1 if I used one of theirs. All this without looking away from the TV.

*Indians are from India.

In back of the lodge I found I was sharing a generous strip of green grass with someone on a huge 1000cc BMW motorcycle. Additionally, not more than 50-feet away was a large, noisy diesel generator that supplied the lodge with electricity to keep the TV and other electrical appliances going, night and day.

Figure 1: Hans Nusser and his BMW motorcycle.

While putting up my tent, the owner of the BMW motorcycle emerged from his tent from what appeared to be a pleasant nap. I introduced myself to Hans Eugen Nusser from Germany and learned he was finishing up a 12-week trip that took him all over the West Coast of the U.S. to include Baja California. He had ridden as far north as Prudhoe Bay on the Beaufort Sea in northern Alaska. From what I could understand of his English, he had stopped at all the scenic places between Baja and Alaska to include Yosemite and Yellowstone Parks. He was now on his way south to Vancouver, British Columbia where he and his motorcycle would catch a airplane back to Germany, there to finish his last year of college.

Figure 2: Author setting up camp at Christochina, Alaska

After my shower and a dinner of freeze-dried chicken primavera, I retired to my tent to read. But at 9 p.m. nearly full daylight made the reading easy, however I found it a bit difficult to concentrate with the roar of the generator so close by. I finally gave up and went into the lodge for a late night snack. While there I met four cyclists from the Anchorage area off on a two-week vacation. They had elaborate plans of fishing, biking, and rafting their way to Tok where they had a vehicle waiting for them. I must admit I admired their confidence and enthusiasm, especially regarding their touring bikes, converted from old ten speeds. These were what you would call "low tech" touring machines. A bag was tied here and a sleeping bag there, a fish pole bungeed here, a tent there. One hardcore biker had actually duct taped canned food to his handlebars and front fork. This intrepid fellow had among his selection of canned goods a 1-lb. can of Dinty Moore beef stew taped to the headset. Rather than camping behind the lodge in relative comfort, they planned to pedal down the road to a river to do some fishing before setting up camp. I wished them good luck as they cycled away.

When I finally crawled back into my tent, I noticed Hans Eugen was snoring away in hot competition with the generator.

In the morning he joined me in the cafe for breakfast, that is once we were able to coax the cook away from the TV long enough to scramble our eggs and toast our toast.

No more than 20 miles from Christochina I came to a bridge spanning Indian Creek where off to my right I saw the bikes and tents of the cyclists from Anchorage. It looked like everyone was sound asleep even though it was almost 10 a.m. and the fact that at least 7 people were fishing from the bank of the creek directly behind their tents.

I couldn't pass up the opportunity to stop and yell out, "Hey, you guys are missing out on some of the best fishing in Alaska."

I heard a few grumbles, but no one hustled out of a tent with a fish pole.

~ ~ ~

Fragrance

Late that afternoon I discovered a neat campground in a small grove of cedar pines. The fragrance of the trees overwhelmed me as I pedaled slowly around the campground looking for a quiet tent site. In addition to picnic table and fireplace, my space came equipped with a thick carpet of cedar pine needles and felt quite like I was walking on a thick, padded carpet. This extra natural padding made my night's sleep one of the most comfortable on my journey. Of course, the smell of my evening cook fire and campfire were so fragrant I stayed up late to stare into the undulating flames and sniff the aroma of burning cedar wood.

When I crawled out of my tent next morning about 8 a.m. I was amazed to see the campground cleared out leaving me the lone custodian of the cedar forest campground. The pattern of motorized camping seemed to be arriving late and leaving early making my routine of arriving early and departing late advantageous.

After a breakfast of oatmeal, coffee and a week old bagel, I departed reluctantly.

~ ~ ~

Tok

Tok at the junction of Alaska highways 1 and 2 is a fair-sized settlement catering to tourists and tour buses. For me it marked the end of my first week on the road. There were a handful of cafes, restaurants, even two bakeries, but I was only concerned with finding the youth hostel, where I supposed I could stow my gear, take a shower and get a bed for the night. As Tok was small, I figured the hostel would be two or three blocks away. Asking around for directions to the hostel proved frustrating and merely served to reinforce my belief that asking locals for directions is mainly a risky proposition. Most of the local folk just shook their head or shrugged their shoulders. A few had a vague idea it was north of town. A waitress in one of the restaurants said, "I'm sure it's around here somewhere." She was right to some extent anyway, for in addition to being eight miles north of Tok, it was also two miles west down a dirt road that forced me to push my bike most of that two miles.

To characterize the hostel as "Spartan" would be understatement. It consisted of two large, stained, aging Army tents pitched in a muddy, mosquito infested-bog. The floor of the main tent was hard-packed dirt, which made it easy to tidy up, but difficult to find anything dropped on the floor, especially at night. There wasn't any indoor plumbing or toilet, which would have been okay, but there wasn't much outdoor plumbing or bathroom facilities either. On top of that there wasn't anybody around, except a Japanese motorcyclist who didn't speak much English. But regardless of aesthetics and amenities, this was going to be my home for the night, unless the proprietor informed me I had to pay more than two dollars for my accommodations.

Much later, the proprietress arrived carrying a young child in a backpack to find four occupants in her olive drab hostel. After collecting fees of two dollars per person, she assigned chores. I believe I fared best, as it was my duty to sweep the dirt floor. Although never a paragon of cleanliness around the house I can safely boast of sweeping the hostel floor to perfection. In fact, my comrades even commented on what a marked difference my efforts achieved, exclaiming it was perhaps the cleanest dirt floor in all of Alaska.

Next morning in Tok I enjoyed a breakfast of hotcakes and eggs, before strolling next door to the bakery where I wolfed down two Danish pastries and carried away a bag containing a half dozen goodies for the road.

~ ~ ~

Do-It-Yourself Dentistry

Twelve miles south of Tok was the junction of the Taylor Highway, about 200 miles of dirt road leading to the Canadian Yukon and the fabled city of Dawson on the banks of the Yukon River.

Only a few miles down this primitive thoroughfare in the wilderness I was glad I had my dirt tires on, instead of the treadless street tires I had planned to put on my rims in Anchorage.

I made 72.66 miles that day, ending my ride at a pleasant campground on the banks of the Denelson River. The next day I was sure I would reach the metropolis of Chicken, but a massive construction zone forced me to push my bike four miles through mud, over piles of stone and rock and through unbridged creeks. My only consolation during this death march, was that vehicular traffic was slowed to a snail's pace or came to a complete standstill until the lead vehicle could be towed free of a quagmire. On one particularly nasty, steep hill, a pickup stopped long enough to offer to transport me through the construction zone, but at this point in my tour I was still a purist and insisted on pushing my bike until the track was rideable. Although declining the offer, I gave silent praise for Alaskan hospitality, at least until the truck passed and I observed it had a California license plate.

The road conditions might have degenerated, but there was a vast improvement in the scenery, complimented by an improvement in the weather. After a grueling 34.28 miles in 8 hours and 14 minutes, averaging a mere 4.1 mph I gladly pulled into a campground on the Walker River there to inhale a freeze-dry meal and retire to a warm, dry sleeping bag and tent.

Before dinner I took a quick, extremely quick, dip in the rust-colored river, high with the combined runoff of rain and glacial melt. I also found it necessary to use my Katadyn pocket filter for the first time. Later when cleaning the filter I was surprised to find the silver-impregnated ceramic filter laden with silt from the river water.

Once again my Northface Tadpole tent proved a haven of dryness, warmth and security, albeit false security. In the months and years to come I would often refer to my tent as my womb, for on many a night, both near and far afield, I would curl up inside, tired and sometimes hungry, and fall into a peaceful, restorative sleep. Or after a hearty meal, a campfire, and an hour of meditation, I would crawl into my tent, light my candle lantern and read for an hour or two before succumbing to a deep sleep. My tent was (and still is) one of the most valuable pieces of gear in my kit. I paid a good price for it, but it never let me down and small though it may be, it was my home-away-from-home in 16 countries. It enabled me to establish a sense of "homeness" no matter where I was or whatever diverse circumstances I found myself in: i.e. rain, shine, wind, cold, day, night. This might strike an odd note, but the tent also afforded me a degree of privacy, a place to be alone with my thoughts, a book, or my journal and on more than one occasion it became a storage room for all or part of my gear.

Chicken wasn't exactly what I had in mind. A settlement of a mere dozen log houses and shacks, services were nonexistent, except for a bar. While stopped in the dirt street in front of the bar to rest and revise my travel plan, a man clothed in wool, plaid flannel, and denim caromed out of the bar, tripped, and stumbled his way toward me, finally falling face down in the dirt five feet from me. In his wake came a short, rotund woman similarly garbed. In passing the inert body at my feet, she told me not to worry about her husband that he wouldn't bother me. Or, in his present condition, anybody else, I surmised.

I stopped at the newly constructed general store-gas station on the main road to discover it was also lacking in provisions, save for unwanted items like chewing gum, potato chips, pretzels, chewing tobacco, 50-lb bags of dog food, and nearly every brand, size, and container of beer imaginable. The beer and liquor supplies in this "wide spot in the road" could rival competition in New York, Chicago, or Dallas. The owner of the store, who was also the Mayor (unofficial I believe), told me that I would find a good cafe at Boundary, the next stop along the highway. Perhaps for the hundredth time that day he patiently explained how Chicken got its name. At a town meeting at which residents gathered to decide on naming their community, a requirement of the Post Office Department, a motion was made to call the place Ptarmigan (a type of grouse). Few people could pronounce the name,* let alone spell it, prompting an old sourdough to suggest they call their home chicken. Most everyone could pronounce and spell chicken.

* The "P" is silent.

And no one could come up with a better idea. Thus the town of Chicken was born and duly recognized by the U.S. Postal Department and the rest of the world.

I'll never forget the day I wheeled into Boundary, Alaska. To be uncharacteristically precise it was Monday, July 11, 1988 at 2:27 p.m. I believe the sun was out. The first thing I saw was a handpainted sign above a log cabin—CAFE. Pedaling slowly into this collection of dilapidated buildings of log and tarpaper after a long uphill grind was similar to a person lost in the desert for weeks finally seeing the green of date palms marking an oasis.

I made a beeline for the cafe where I quickly dispatched two servings of stew, homemade bread, milk, and two pieces of pie a la mode. The cook and waitress, conveniently husband and wife, ran the little cafe only during the summer months. They didn't seem particularly surprised at my appetite or my trip. In fact, they looked like very little surprised them. They were gracious, but like many Alaskans they go out of their way to leave people alone, and expect the same in return. My guess is there is a common "type" of person who immigrates to Alaska to escape the constant people hassles of large metropolitan areas in the U.S. They all have a deep respect for privacy.

Boundary consisted of a gas station, cafe, and saloon. It got its name because of its close proximity to the U.S./Canadian border, approximately ten miles distant.

After my pig out at the cafe, I strolled next door to the "Action Jackson Saloon" a humble, ramshackle structure of diverse materials, including wood, tin, shingles, and no small amount of contrasting paints. Decor aside, the huge rack of Moose antlers over the front door was what really attracted my attention. Only one customer, a scruffy, old fellow fresh from the mines or traplines, sat at the ten-stool bar. Behind the bar a huge fellow with black beard and black L.A. Raider T-shirt was stroking the contents of a crock pot with a wooden spoon. He introduced himself as "Boulder" and his solitary patron as "Mountain Mule." When Boulder learned where I was from and where I was going he bought me a beer. As I sipped my brew I learned a bit about what life was like in the wilds of Alaska. The Mountain Mule or "Mule" as Boulder called him, a man of about 30-odd years, with blond hair falling to his shoulders, an untrimmed beard, a sparkling gold front tooth, claimed he made a living, "not gettin' rich ya understand," mining gold and running a trap line. He was extremely cryptic regarding his gold mining activities. I found out later it was considered impolite, possibly dangerous, to pry for details regarding a mining operation. I also learned most of these "miners" only reported a small percentage, if at all, of their gold finds to avoid paying taxes and more importantly to avoid contact with government bureaucracies. Many fellows like the Mountain Mule were after nuggets that are preferred by jewelers who are willing to pay a premium price, with the idea of incorporating the nuggets into belt buckles, tie clasps, or other jewelry items. Poking around someone's mining claim or digs without invitation was a sure way of getting a case of lead poisoning, warned the Mule.

Figure 3: L-R, Boulder, Saigon Jim, Mountain Mule. Seated, Shorty.

Working on my second beer, I asked the Mule what he'd do if he got sick in the middle of winter. What with medical help being hundreds of miles away and only accessible by air, not withstanding a blizzard, things could be a bit dicey. He told me he had a god-awful tooth ache the previous winter and knew he would have to do something about it sooner or later. So one night he drank a bottle of whiskey then proceeded, as best as he remembers, to pull the infected tooth with a pair of vice grip pliers. Next morning when he came to, he discovered two extracted teeth by his bedside.

"I was damn glad at least one of 'em was the bad tooth," the Mule smiled, pointing at a cavernous space in his lower jaw.

Soon, two more locals wandered into the bar to "wet their whistles" and to check up on the news. These gentlemen went by the names of Shorty and Saigon Jim. At barely 5 ft., Shorty's moniker was more than appropriate, but I was never to learn the story behind Saigon Jim's name. On the point of names I quickly wised up to local protocol of not asking about surnames. As I listened to their stories of hunting, trapping, of weeklong drunks, and narrow escapes with death and marriage, I became aware of the tempting aromas wafting from Boulder's crock pot. Judging from the data being received by my educated nose, I guessed Boulder would have himself an excellent dinner of Spaghetti and meatballs that evening.

Feeling a bit too relaxed after my second beer, I asked Boulder if there was a spot to pitch my tent. "Any old place," was his reply. I was also welcome to stay in the Boundary Hilton, an old 10' x 10' tarpaper shack abandoned by the road construction crew a few years ago. It was located on the southeast side of the bar. Also, I could take a shower located just in back of the Cafe. "But don't expect anything fancy," Boulder cautioned. "Oh and don't forget to come back about 8 o'clock for some of this spaghetti," he added.

Even with a full stomach, I promised I'd be back to help polish off the spaghetti.

After pitching my tent near the Boundary Hilton, I gathered my toilet kit and towel together and went off in search of the shower. To call it a shower was a generous description. In reality it was a combination shower, laundry room, bathroom, and birthplace for a dozen or so kittens. The shower stall itself could be best characterized as the ultimate Rube Goldberg contraption. Suspended on the roof were five 50-gallon drums of water. Water from a nearby stream was pumped into barrels. The electricity of course is provided by a nearby diesel generator, which according to Boulder "has problems." Shower pipes, both metal and plastic, snaked down through the ceiling, like the tentacles of a Jules Verne octopus, ending in a shower head so high a person of average height, like myself, had to climb up on a water-logged, soap-slippery wooden box in the corner to adjust the angle of water erupting from the shower nozzle. About chest level a collection of pipes and plumbing fixtures escaped from the buckling, rotting plywood wall. Opening both faucets I was pleased to feel warm water cascade over my body, only to be superseded moments later with frigid water, perhaps piped directly from a nearby glacier. But the results are what counts and my body was soon clean. Now, some three years after this experience, I would consider the Boundary shower as one of the more "high tech" versions of shower facilities it was my fate to experience during my trip.

Back in my tent, I was stretched out and on the brink of a 30-minute nap, when all of a sudden I heard the distinctive clicking of a bicycle freewheel. My first thought was that someone was making off with my bike, but a quick look outside proved this invalid. The clicking continued to get closer. I crawled out of the tent to see a cyclist of about my age pushing his tour-equipped bike in my direction.

"Hello," he said, "the big fellow in the bar told me you were camped up here and said if it was OK with you I could pitch my tent around here too."

"Sure, just pick a spot," I said, pointing to an unoccupied wedge of grass and weeds fenced in by abandoned road graders, rusting mining equipment, stacks of lumber, and the Boundary Hilton.

While he pitched his tent, Mike Blackwell, a geologist from Seattle, Washington, told me he was headed for Dawson, where he planned to meet his friend Jim Thompson. Together they were going to bike the Dempster Highway to Inuvik above the Arctic Circle. Mike had done substantial geophysical work there in the 60's and was anxious to return.

After he got settled in, we repaired to the saloon for beer and Boulder's Alaskan spaghetti and meatballs and a lengthy conversation about bikes and bikes tours—past, present, and future.

Chapter 2

Yukon Ho!

"There is a law of the Yukon and ever she makes it plain send not your foolish and feeble; send me your strong and sane."

-Robert Service

The Law of the Yukon

Paris of the North

On Tuesday, July 12, 1988 I cycled across my first international border. On the "Top of the World Highway" a few miles southeast of Boundary, Alaska, Mike Blackwell and I pedaled into the Canadian Yukon. Easy though the border crossing was it was a long pull on the dirt road from Boundary up to the Canadian customs station at the top of the hill. From there on Mike and I cruised steadily up and down the two-lane dirt highway that snaked along a ridgeline leading to Dawson 72.05 miles away. Breathtaking views of mountains and river valleys were made even more memorable under mostly clear skies. Although the Top of the World Highway is unpaved, the dirt is compacted and scraped to a hard surface mostly free of potholes and gravel. When we stopped to rest or eat Mike would explain the geology of the area. I was pleasantly surprised with having Mike to cycle with. Our pace was closely matched on the flats and hills, though I had a slight advantage on the downhills with my heavier mountain bike frame geometry combined with wider, stronger wheels and tires. On some of the descents I was clocking close to 30 mph, while Mike had to slow down considerably because he had the traditional touring bike frame with narrow rims. One of the things that "made" our ride that day was a 15-mile descent to the banks of the Yukon River. From that vantage point we could see Dawson. Here we found two campgrounds: an official one and unofficial one. The official campground, large and crowded, was part of the Canadian Provincial Park system. Mike and I managed to find a campsite along the riverbank close to the park entrance. The unofficial campground, located in the hills west of the official campground, was a squatters tent city filled with a diverse populace of backpackers from around the world who were either working in Dawson for the summer or staying in the area for a few weeks. The campers here were able to avoid paying the five-dollar per day fee collected at the government campground.

After setting up camp and stowing our gear, we gathered our towels and toilet kits, anxious to get across the river to Dawson and find a hot shower and a pub. With no connecting bridge over the river, we pedaled down to the ferry crossing below the campground to wait for the next available ferry boat that would carry us across the 200-yard wide river in approximately 15 minutes. The huge boats, running 24-hours a day, accommodated both pedestrians and vehicular traffic, to include large trucks and buses. Fortunately, there was no charge for pedestrians and bicyclists. During the ferry ride Mike explained that building a bridge over the Yukon River would be a multi-million dollar project, connecting a secondary road that was open to traffic only four or five months of the year and used by a relatively small number of vehicles even in the summer. In a nutshell, it would not be cost effective.

Pushing our bikes up the ramp into the boat, we prepared for our first Yukon River crossing and a visit to what was called in 1896 the

"Paris of the North." Of particular interest to me was the fact that Dawson was at various times in the late 1800's home to both Jack London and Robert Service. The homes of both these writers have been preserved, as in Service's case or reconstructed in London's case. The Service cabin has been declared a Canadian historic site. During the summer months a resident actor, dressed in period clothing, recites a sampling of Service poetry twice daily to crowds of tourists gathered in the front yard. During my stay I was able to attend recitals of both *"The Cremation of Sam McGee"* and *"The Shooting of Dan McGrew."*

After a short voyage across the brown, turbulent river to Dawson the ferry docked and disgorged a mixed cargo of cars, trucks and foot traffic.

One of the best descriptions of Dawson during its gold rush days, one I found I could relate to the most, is in a letter written by Alfred G. McMichael, a 40-year old photographer from Detroit, Michigan, who traveled to Dawson in 1898 in search of gold.

"At last we are in the Mecca of all gold seekers. We arrived yesterday about noon...We are camped on the side of a hill...This is a strange place and my first experience in a mining camp...The hillsides are white with tents and the streets black with a crowd of men. It is said there are 40,000 people here, but I do not believe it."

After taking a shower at a local laundromat for 50 cents, Mike and I cycled about town sightseeing, eating, and stopping to sample the atmosphere at some of the local saloons before taking the boat back across the river to our campsite.

Next day, we met with Mike's friend, Jim Thompson. They planned to leave Dawson in a few days for their tour up the Dempster Highway to Inuvik. Jim's brother Dave had a good-sized placer mining operation up on Bonanza Creek outside Dawson. We were all invited up to the operation later that day for a tour and dinner. Over the years placer mines along the creek have yielded millions of dollars in gold.

But placer mining is not a pretty thing to see. Basically, placer miners use high pressure water hoses to wash away tons of earth down into the creek bed where it is bulldozed into processing machinery that extracts the gold, what little there is. The ratio of gold to sediment is almost incalculable. It would probably be 100 times easier to find the proverbial needle in the haystack. Predating the placer era was the dredge era (30's and 40's) when apartment-house sized dredges, looking like landlocked paddlewheelers, would propel themselves up a creek or riverbed, consuming everything in their path. After internally digesting the river or creek and removing the gold, they would excrete the wastes in the general area where it was consumed, only this time forming a man-made creek bed. In reality it is environmental devastation. During our tour of Bonanza Creek, Jim Thompson told me that every rock, stone, and pebble along the creek had been consumed and excreted in this fashion at least five times

The day before Mike and Jim pedaled south for the Dempster Highway we met two other bikers headed for Inuvik. Will and Gisela Cronyn of San Diego, California, newly arrived in Dawson from Skagway, Alaska, were headed up the Dempster two days after Mike and Jim. I agreed to ride along with them to the junction of the Dempster, about 25 miles south of Dawson. The night before Mike and Jim departed all five of us had a small banquet to celebrate our individual bike touring efforts.

The ride from Dawson south was doubly enjoyable for me, as I'd replaced my dirt tires with my high pressure, treadless road tires. For the first time in weeks I was pedaling on pavement. I felt like I was supercharged, pedaling twice as fast with half the effort, a few times reaching speeds of 20 to 25 mph on the flats.

We reached the Dempster junction just in time to have a second breakfast at the restaurant located there. Afterward, we exchanged addresses, took pictures of each other, then said goodbye, wishing each other good luck and safe biking. I promised the Cronyns I'd stop over in San Diego for a visit on my way south to Baja.

~ ~ ~

On Being Alone

Biking down the Klondike Highway felt different-for the first time in a week I was cycling alone. And it took a few hours to adjust to this aloneness. Though I missed the pleasant company of Mike Blackwell and Will and Gisela Cronyn, I appreciated once again the feeling of solo touring. One of the most asked questions during my trip to Tierra del Fuego was, "Don't you get lonely all by yourself?"

Here's an essay I composed to answer, as fully and intelligently as possible, that question. I composed this essay while laid up in my hotel room in La Paz, Bolivia suffering from "soroche" or high altitude sickness.

~ ~ ~

Even along those long, desolate stretches of road in Alaska I had sufficient companionship. Was it not Henry David Thoreau himself who sat next to me by a roaring campfire encouraging me to live simply and deliberately. I've tried to heed his advice as I pedaled ever southward. I've fallen asleep many a night in my tent while Hemingway, Faulkner, or Kipling spun one of their memorable yarns.

During one particularly long and solitary ride through central California, I slipped off my bike to join my old friend John Steinbeck in the front seat of his camper Rocinante and watch, along with Charley, as the ever changing American countryside passed by. Camped on a sandy beach on the shore of the Pacific Ocean in Mexico, where I hadn't encountered another human being for days, I clung to the coattails of Sherlock Holmes as he sleuthed the narrow, cobbled streets of London or raced across the rainswept moors of Scotland pursuing some fiendish blackguard like Moriarty.

Have I been lonely? Why I laugh at the question and its implications. I've visited hundreds of countries, real and unreal, past, present and future with scores of fellow travelers, as you no doubt have done yourself. These book-comrades remain forever, while the books themselves go from hand-to-hand and eventually disappear. But, at a second's notice my friends will come for a visit, to delight, to philosophize, to entertain, again and again.

Have I not as recently as a day ago, in my sick bed in La Paz stood in the stern of a whaling boat, beside pipe-smoking Mr. Stubb and held on for dear life as his boat sped after Leviathan? Fascinated, I watched as Queequeg thrust his harpoon into their prey.

Loneliness be damned! If anything, I've done too much socializing. I've been surrounded by too many comrades. This is not to say that human companionship along the way was not appreciated, nor in any way held less valuable than my book-comrades. Moreover, the human contacts amongst the Americas gained added value because of their timeliness or circumstance, enabling me to appreciate them more.

No, no, no, I will never be lonely. I've comrades, fellow travelers, guides, and trail mates for ten lifetimes. The solitary man is never alone; the lonely man, most often, is surrounded by his cronies.

~ ~ ~

The Hottest Shower I Never Had

Today, for a change, I had a destination in mind. Will and Gisela raved about a cafe/lodge they stayed at on their ride up to Dawson from Whitehorse. According to the Cronyns, Moose Creek Lodge not only offered good food, coffee and beer, additionally there were hot showers to be had.

After 101.41 miles of pedaling I arrived at Moose Creek at 8 p.m. with a ravenous appetite and a tired, sweaty body. A scenic spot it was, with a campground across the highway from the lodge, a gushing creek beside the lodge, and plenty of tall, thick pine trees, which in themselves were a welcome relief from the skinny pine forests of northern Alaska. After setting up camp, I cycled over to the lodge only to learn from a young lady that the showers, along with the rest of the plumbing, were "out of order." Anne, the friendly lodge-person, suggested I go down to the creek, not more than 50-yards away, and take a bath there. Reasonable suggestion, I thought, so with my towel and toilet kit I proceeded there. With no one in sight, I stripped off my sweats and waded into the creek, only to quickly retreat from the icy waters. Deciding there was only one way to accomplish my task, I dove into the water, submerging my body, then made a run for the creek bank, where I dried myself off. Clean and incredibly refreshed, not to mention awake, I returned to the lodge for a large bowl of beef stew, homemade bread, pie, and two beers.

That night while curled up in my sleeping bag it occurred to me that I learned two valuable things in only 17 days of travel.

1. **Directions**. Whenever asking directions take a survey of at least three people, especially when asking distance in miles. Inevitably, you'll get three different answers, so total the mileage estimates and divide by three, then disregard the answer and navigate by gut instinct. Regardless of what you do, you'll be 5 miles off, generally 5 miles short of your destination.

2. **Maps and Newspapers**. Always carry a map. It's the biker's version of a clipboard or attaché case. A map will give you credibility. And a map is a prop everyone can identify with, while carrying around a small book of poetry makes one suspect. I prefer a map and/or a copy of USA Today. Especially after a 50—60 mile ride without a break. A map or newspaper are useful things to stare at while you recuperate. Just sitting and staring at a counter in a cafe will draw raised eyebrows from waitresses and other diners. When you sit down in a cafe overcome with endorphins, instead of staring at a blank wall, the person in front of you, or the cook's back, you can stare at your road map or newspaper and at least look productive.

I prefer a USA Today newspaper, especially a two-week old edition. In a crowded cafe people who would otherwise shoot skeptical looks at you because of your funny clothes and haggard appearance, think you're catching up on world events, checking stock market quotes, or reviewing sports scores. After you've snapped out of your trance you can actually read those neat little blurbs about tractor pulls in Tennessee or about a farmer in Kansas who grew a 10-lb ear of corn.

Additionally, maps and newspapers can be used to swat flies and mosquitos, fan a campfire, as an impromptu tablecloth, and, last but not least, as emergency toilet paper.

~ ~ ~

An Invitation

While enjoying a huge breakfast of eggs, pancakes, fruit and some of the best coffee I had north of a San Francisco, I got to talking with a lady and her daughter who just returned from Dawson where they had participated in a 10K run. Having seen my heavily laden bike outside the lodge they inquired about my tour. We spent the next hour talking about the pleasures of camping and bike touring. I learned that Mary Whitley, her husband Gerry and daughters, Moriah and Rebecca, were also mountain bikers. As my plans included a stop in Whitehorse where they lived, Mary invited me to stay with them when I passed through there.

~ ~ ~

At Pelly Crossing, 61 miles south of Moose Creek I met two Canadian bike tourers headed north. Phil and Karen Shiel of Calgary were on their way to Inuvik. I began to wonder if some kind of harmonic convergence was supposed to happen there. Months later I received a letter from the Shiels telling of their trek up the Dempster Highway and of their decision to stay in Inuvik and spend the winter above the Arctic Circle. After a peaceful camp on the bank of the Pelly River, we cycled over to the Native settlement across the highway in search of water. There wasn't any drinking water available at the campground and all of our bottles were empty. We got directions from a man working on a bulldozer. Following his instructions we found ourselves, a few blocks away, staring at a wooden building that resembled an outhouse without an entry door. A plastic pipe poked out of a hole in a board in the front of the wooden shanty. Judging from the puddle of water on the ground below the pipe, we suspected this was the well, but couldn't figure out how to coax water from the pipe. After further investigation, Phil discovered a switch on the side of the shack. He pushed a button and a few seconds later water gushed from the plastic pipe in the wall. Not quite the same as Abraham smiting a rock in the desert, but with the same miraculous results. We filled our bottles, took a swig for good measure, then pedaled back to the highway, where Phil and Karen headed north and I pedaled south.

A few days later, north of Whitehorse, I passed a beautiful, pristine lake beside the highway. As it was evening, I pulled over to review the situation. The sun had dipped low over the horizon, giving the smooth surface of the lake that rich, deep color one sees in the landscape paintings of Albert Bierstadt. There wasn't a sign of human life along the shore of the lake, making it more appealing. Directly below the guardrail where I stood, halfway down the gentle slope, was a level spot ideal for pitching a tent.

After setting up camp, I made my way down to the lakeshore with towel and soap in hand. Finding my way with difficulty through thick bushes and small trees, I emerged onto a shoreline packed with driftwood. The accumulated flotsam of hundreds of years had with natures help been fashioned into a natural wooden dock at lake's edge. Placing my towel and clothes on the "dock" I plunged into the water with my bar of soap in hand. I was relieved to find the water temperate compared to that of Moose Creek. Following a restorative swim and bath, I climbed back onto the driftwood dock to dry myself and survey my private lake, whose name I am still ignorant of. Out of nowhere, a huge beaver came cruising by, making a distinctive "V" on the water's surface not ten feet in front of me. I continued drying myself while following the slow progress of the beaver. Directly in front of me, the beaver, a good four-feet long from nose to tail, stopped, slapped its tail on the lake's surface, then plunged out of sight, while the water exploded to a height of five or six feet. I looked around to see if anyone else was witness to this incredible performance, but found I was still utterly and completely alone. Momentarily, the beaver resurfaced to perform this singular feat again and again, until I withdrew to my camp about 20 yards above the shoreline.

At first, I assumed the beaver's aquatic display was a form of showing off, but later learned from a trapper that the beaver was actually challenging me as I had invaded its territory and was most likely standing on top of its lodge. Whatever the case, I did notice that as soon as I vacated the driftwood dock the beaver ceased its tail slapping.

I believe it was the next day while cycling further south on the Klondike Highway, passing pristine lake after lake, that I felt tears streaming down my face. It took a few seconds to realize I was crying tears of joy. This sensation or condition being new to me, I didn't know what to make of it. I was feeling so peaceful and happy I suspected the tears were a release of the joy I was feeling from experiencing nature at its finest.

Next day, I cycled past the "marge of Lake Lebarge" where according to Robert Service, Sam MeGee was cremated. A few miles north of Whitehorse on the verge of bonking I was forced to stop repeatedly to gulp trail mix and cookies. So it was, when coasting down the highway into Whitehorse with great difficulty I looked up to see what I thought was a jogger running straight at me. I thought, wow this is the first jogger I've seen since leaving California. When the runner got close enough I recognized her as Mary Whitley the lady I'd met at Moose Creek lodge a few days earlier. I wondered what she was doing out jogging along the highway. Of course she wasn't jogging, but had driven past me on the road into town. She stopped to say hello and give me directions to her house, then off she sped in her station wagon. A mile from Whitehorse, Mary appeared again, this time on her mountain bike, to personally guide me to the Whitley residence.

I was incredibly glad to be a guest of the Whitleys, a luxury comparable to a suite in a five-star hotel. Even my bike got the VIP treatment stabled in the Whitley garage with nine other bikes. Later that afternoon I met the rest of the family, including their frisbee-playing dog, Sky. While Mary went off on a training run with her running group, Gerry took me on a tour of Whitehorse. Having worked for the Provincial government for many years Gerry gave me an excellent overview of life in the Canadian north, which was not as idyllic as one would think. Even this small, rural community was faced with many problems common to much larger cities in the United States, i.e. unemployment, alcoholism, even drugs.

After the tour we returned to a huge spaghetti dinner, with fresh salad from Mary's garden. During the next two days I was able to take care of some much-needed maintenance and cleaning of my bike and gear, not to mention myself. I was also able to stock up on a number of bulk food items at the local market and gorge myself on things like cheeseburgers and fries. Things I hadn't tasted in weeks.

I recorded in my journal that at day 23 of my trip I'd cycled 949.6 miles. When I reached Skagway, in a day or two, I would break the first 1,000-mile marker.

As a small gesture of appreciation for the Whitley's hospitality, I treated them to dinner at Whitehorse's only Mexican restaurant, Rosa's Cantina. The next morning I rolled out of Whitehorse bound for Skagway, Alaska, approximately 110 miles southwest.

~ ~ ~

Gold Fever

Two days later I found myself in the historically infamous town of Skagway, Alaska, the jumping off point for the Klondike gold rush of 1898 and also the final resting place of Jefferson R. "Soapy" Smith, the frontier version of Chicago gangster Al Capone. Smith terrorized Skagway before being killed in a gunfight with vigilante Frank Reid. My first day in Skagway was warm and sunny, an unusual occurrence I soon found out. I located a campsite in a private campground on the edge of town, next to the railroad tracks. With my tent pitched and most of my gear stowed away, I headed into town for a two-wheel tour of Skagway. The main street leads straight down to the wharf on the Lyn Canal, a fiord connecting Skagway with the Pacific Ocean and where the Alaskan Ferries load and unload a steady stream of visitors to southwest Alaska and Canada.

Perhaps the highlight of my stay in Skagway was the opportunity to hike the "Trail of '98", better known as the Chilkoot Trail. The trailhead, just a few miles from Skagway, saw upwards of 50,000 stampeders make the 33-mile trek over the Chilkoot Pass to Lake Bennett, eventually to Dawson between 1897-98. To make things more difficult, most of the gold seekers accomplished this feat during the winter of 1898. These days, during the summer months, hundreds of backpackers retrace the steps of the stampeders enjoying a trail that passes through settlements that no longer exist, but still retain evidence of the Klondike Gold Rush.

My problem was what to do with my bike and gear while I spent three days tramping over the trail. Riding back to the campground my first day in Skagway I noticed a sign on a garage next to a house across from the campground. The sign read, "Knapp Bros. Bicycles for Rent." I waded through a sea of used bicycles into a garage cluttered with bikes, cars, and snowmobile parts to find Paul Knapp half-submerged in the engine compartment of a vintage 1927 Franklin automobile. After explaining my plans to hike the Chilkoot and the need of a storage place for my bike Paul told me I could store the bike safely inside his shop right beside his prized motorcar. The next morning I rolled my bike beside the Franklin, confident it would be safe for years to come, if need be.

With my tent, sleeping bag, rain gear and backpack crammed with extra food, clothes, and cooking gear, I walked out of Skagway headed for the trailhead at Dyea in much the same fashion as the stampeders did in 1898. Under cloudy, rain-threatening skies, I began the trek over the Klondike Trail. My first destination was Canyon City at mile 7.8. I hiked in complete solitude for over an hour before catching up to a group of trekkers resting at a creek crossing near Finnegan's Point. Arriving at Canyon City at 6:30 p.m., I discovered a log cabin with a wood stove. It hadn't rained, but with threatening skies I figured this would be a good first night camp spot. True to its name the log cabin was nestled in a canyon filled with pine and firtrees. An energetic creek gushed down a nearby hillside and under a wooden footbridge not far from the log cabin. Although the camp area was deserted when I arrived, I guessed I would see other trekkers stopping there before the night was over.

Shortly after eating my dinner of freeze-dried chicken primavera, Gerhard Götzendorfer of Austria, trudged into camp shouldering what appeared to be a 75-lb. backpack. As we sipped fresh coffee brewed on the wood stove in the cabin, Gerhard told me in faltering English, of his canoe trip through the upper lakes of the Yukon River to Dawson. According to Gerhard, he had never paddled a canoe before his solo trip down the Yukon. Now, he was a true voyageur.

About 8 p.m., Josef and Lisa Lors of Calgary, Canada wandered into camp, tired and hungry. Like myself they were headed for Lake Bennett, while Gerhard was on his way to Skagway. While sitting around the table in the cabin, I cooked up another freeze-dried dinner and ate with Josef and Lisa. Josef asked if I'd seen any bears around Finnegan's Point. Besides a tired group of backpackers, I told him I hadn't seen anything except a lot of overturned stones. Josef surmised that I scared a bear away, as he observed a number of paw prints around the overturned stones when he and Lisa passed by there. He guessed the bear was probably grubbing for insects or bugs. Though it was hard to believe I scared a bear, instead of the opposite, I was more observant on the trail in days to come. I also learned the art of making noise while hiking in the Alaskan woods. Talking, whistling, or singing are handy ways of making noise, at least in my case, that gives bears advanced warning that someone or something is approaching. Any bear with an ounce of common sense will take to the hills when it hears these types of noise. At least that's the theory.

Next day, Josef, Lisa and I hiked the next leg of the trail to Sheep Camp at mile 13. Up until now the trail had been moderately steep with no difficult ascents. Here at Sheep Camp we were at the base of the pass. There were good campsites scattered about another log cabin. The weather had been rainy on and off all day, with a promise of more rain that night, making the cabin an excellent place to warm up, dry wet clothes over the wood fire, and cook dinner. Unlike Canyon City, there were dozens of campers here.

Though only a log cabin warming hut now, during the winter of 1898, merchants, saloon keepers, hotel, and restaurant owners and gamblers had set up shop here to cater to a shifting population of approximately 8,000 gold seekers. That night it became a temporary home to about 50 campers, including 20 Canadian scouts and a group of eight Japanese high school girls. Multicolored tents of all shapes and sizes dotted the forest like mushrooms.

Once a wood fire got blazing in the cabin long about dinnertime a friendly crowd gathered there to dry out sodden socks and boots, brew tea, cook dinner, and socialize. It was there that I met perky, red-headed French Canadian, Helena Ray from Quebec. About 8 p.m. that night in the crowded cabin, I found myself seated across the table from Helena. We were both writing in our journals, but soon I was telling her and a few of the Japanese schoolgirls about my bike trip. Though English proved to be the common language, I had to stop many times to act out what I was saying or to draw crude sketches of by bike or maps of where I had been and planned to go.

Helena and I made plans to leave camp the next morning about 7 a.m. hoping to get over the infamous Chilkoot Pass before it started to rain or snow. Though it was drizzling when we left camp, we were among the first hikers on the trail next morning. One of the first things to catch my eye on the trail above Sheep Camp was an area about the size of two football fields where an avalanche had swept down the precipitous mountainside that spring, decimating everything in its path. Huge trees were split like matchsticks; enormous boulders lay side-by-side in the ravine below us as though some giant had pitched them down the mountain like bowling balls. I remembered reading that in the spring of 1898, an enormous avalanche had cut loose from those same peaks and covered a ten-acre area to depths of ten feet. Dozens of stampeders had perished; their bodies recovered weeks and months later when temperatures rose and snow melted.

The trail got much steeper as we worked our way above treeline. Soon we were crossing drifts of snow, then nearer to the Scales at the top of the pass we hiked across glacial ice fields. The snow and a dense fog made it difficult to follow the trail. Visibility at best was only 50 feet. Mostly, we relied on the serpentine groove worn in the snow by previous trekkers, that and an occasional red wand stuck in the snow marking the trail. At the 3,000-foot level, the cold air forced Helena and I to put on additional layers of clothing. The fog got even thicker near the top of the pass. I wandered off the trail, but thanks to Helena's bloodhound instincts was quickly directed back to the correct route. At the top of the pass we were forced to climb hand-over-hand over rocks and boulders. Cold and foggy though it may have been, I was glad it wasn't raining. Rain would have made our slow progress treacherous.

Once over the pass, we stumbled down a hundred yards to Stone Crib, crossing the Canadian border in the process, where the Canadian Park Service maintained an A-frame warming hut. Helena and I were more than happy to drop our packs and squeeze into the hut where a park ranger served us hot tea and lemonade. After a pleasant respite we headed down the trail towards Lakes Lindeman and Bennett. About this time the clouds began to break up, allowing the warming rays of sunlight to ignite the alpine landscape like a crystal diorama. We immediately put on our sunglasses to protect against the blinding glare reflecting off glacial snowfields, lakes, and rivers surrounding us. Marching down the trail with renewed strength and enthusiasm, we began stripping off layers of clothing.

From our vantage point we could see the trail, paralleling a stream created by glacial melt off, as it wound its way down the gently sloping valley before us, adding dozens of streams and creeks to its liquid mass along the way until it emptied into Lake Lindeman a full fledged river. Later that day while passing Deep Lake and down among the pines again, Josef and Lisa caught up with us, then passed us, promising to meet at Lake Lindeman.

Less than an hour later, we were seated around a woodstove at the log cabin on the shore of Lake Lindeman. While resting our weary feet we swapped stories about the tough but beautiful climb over the Chilkoot Pass. I also got reacquainted with a few of the Canadian Reservists in charge of the scouts I'd seen at Sheep Camp. A particularly memorable fellow, both for his sense of humor and yarns, was Captain Lee Drover, a retired Special Forces officer, in charge of the scouts.

Next morning we woke to a sunny, warm day, one not conducive to haste or hurry, especially with a body full of complaining muscles. After taking pictures of Captain Drover and his cadets, I hiked over to the tent museum not far from our camp. On display were dozens of pictures and related memorabilia, books, and news clippings about the gold seekers who passed through there in 1897-98. Although tranquil and uninhabited now, Lindeman had once been a tent city of 10,000 during the height of the gold rush. The population at Lake Bennett swelled to 20,000 during this same period. While camped on the shores of Lindeman and Bennett during the winter of 1898 the stampeders cut trees, sawed planks, and constructed crude boats and rafts for their perilous voyage down the Yukon River to Dawson about 600-miles away.

Helena joined me as I entered the last tent housing gold rush artifacts. I must applaud the efforts of the Canadian Park Service for establishing this fascinating piece of interpretive history. For one thing, it's accessible only to backpackers and hikers. The displays must be packed in by horse, mule, or boat. For another, this was a seasonal exhibit, so everything would have to be packed out at the end of summer. As far as I know this might be the only wilderness museum of its kind in the world.

By mid-morning we were back on the trail to Lake Bennett, looking for the tracks of the Yukon and White Pass Railroad that we would follow to the highway, where we would hopefully hitch a ride back into Skagway. Thanks to sunny, warm weather the hike out to the highway was swift and enjoyable. When we reached the highway we rendezvoused again with Josef and Lisa and Captain Drover and his band of trail weary cadets.

Lucky for us there was a construction zone where the railroad tracks joined the highway, forcing traffic to come to a standstill until a pilot car was available to escort vehicles through the road work. In minutes, we were able to pile in the back of a truck that took all of us into Skagway.

As we drove away, we saluted Captain Drover and the scouts, who were left to wait at the roadside for buses that would transport them back to Whitehorse, but for some unknown reason were delayed.

Back in town, we all headed to the campground to pitch our tents, then en masse, hurried downtown to the Chevron station for a hot shower. Strange as this may seem, many gas stations in Alaska offer coin-operated showers where travelers and scruffy trekkers alike can wash off trail grime for $1.00. Afterward, we all met at the Red Onion Saloon, a few blocks away, to celebrate our successful hike over the Chilkoot Pass and commiserate with those hearty gold seekers who navigated the Chilkoot Trail during the winter of 1898. The Chinook draft beer I savored was the sweetest liquid to pass my lips in many a day. The following day we exchanged addresses, took a few group pictures, then everyone including my new friend Helena, headed off in separate directions.

~ ~ ~

Chilkoot Stew

I was alone at my campsite writing in my journal when a dust-covered Toyota pulled up. Out piled two young fellows I'd met at Canyon City on the trail. Aaron Reyes and Jim Patton, college students from Tucson, Arizona asked if they could use my picnic table to cook up a meal. Learning they were about to concoct something they called Chilkoot Stew, I not only encouraged its speedy preparation, but offered to be the unbiased judge of their individual results as each of these gentlemen had his own version of the recipe. For those interested, listed below is a composite of both "secret" recipes, or at least what I was able to document during the gourmand dueling match.

~ ~ ~

Recipe for Chilkoot Stew

by
Aaron Reyes and Jim Patton

1 lb. reindeer sausage

3 eggs

1 onion diced with a K-bar knife

1 potato sliced thinly

Bunch of mushrooms—diced, sliced, whatever

Mrs. Dash to taste

White wine, if available

Pinch of tobasco sauce

Fry up in a skillet on an MSR stove

As the cooks bustled about the table, they explained they'd taken a few months off from school and work to do some trekking and climbing in Canada and Alaska.

When the results of their Epicurean labors were ready I found it necessary to sample each delicacy numerous times before arriving at my decision that both were of such high quality I would have to call it a tie.

~ ~ ~

Later that day I made a pilgrimage to the grave of the infamous Jefferson R. "Soapy" Smith, once the undisputed ruler of the criminal element in Skagway. The irony of his final resting place was not lost on me, for his ghost is forced to listen to the perpetual crashing and gurgling of nearby Reid Falls, named after Soapy's nemesis and killer, the stout hearted vigilante Frank Reid. To make the irony cut even closer to the bone, the headstone of Reid's plot, within spitting distance of Smith's, has the following inscription carved on it. "He gave his life for the honor of Skagway."

The worst casualties of the Chilkoot trek were my feet, which were blistered and sore for a couple of days afterward. Fortunately, I had two full days to recuperate before boarding the Alaska ferry boat, Malaspina, for an inland passage to Prince Rupert, B.C. where I would pedal across the Yellowhead Highway to Jasper. I also used this opportunity to visit Juneau, Sitka and Ketchikan. While waiting for the boat, I nursed my sore feet and calf muscles while journalizing and relaxing with pint or two at the Red Onion Saloon. Here is a sampling of the philosophical inquiries I made during my Skagway respite.

~ ~ ~

Concerning Outhouses

Whether at home or on the road, we frequent a toilet at least once a day. Generally, these visits are in commodious,[*] functional cubicles, tributes to modern plumbing and building technology, representing the zenith of man's technological battle with the disposal of bodily wastes. Though the modern bathroom has become highly functional and efficient, it likewise has become quite boring. Frontier America, however, had an efficient, ecologically sound, structurally rustic icon called an "outhouse," also colloquially called a chicksales, one-holer or privy. This piece of Americana can still be found in a few remote wilderness areas, but with alarming infrequency. The single negative element associated with the outhouse is a slight, but pungent, odor that pervades this edifice on a warm day.

The wooden outhouse devotee gets a bit of fresh air and exercise as he or she hikes the short distance from his dwelling to the wooden privy located approximately 20 to 25 yards behind his domicile or place of business. A typical one-holer has a circular aperture fashioned in a slab of wood large enough to accommodate the fully developed adult buttocks, yet not so big that it would endanger an unattended child. Typically, a wooden outhouse is about 5 feet wide by 5 feet long and 7 feet in height with a slightly sloping ceiling or roof to shed rain. Generally, it is constructed of rough-hewn planks nailed onto a frame of 2x4's or dressed lodgepole pines. Its single plank door is generally hung on squeaky hinges and secured with a wooden hasp, allowing entry and exit. Traditionally, a crescent moon is cut into the door for added ventilation and to designate that structure's singular function. Plank siding is spaced 1/2 to 1 inch apart to promote generous circulation of air and the entry of a certain amount of light. This spacing also allows the occupant of the inner-sanctum to observe any person approaching the privy. Custom requires that one call out, "Be out in a few minutes." Etiquette prescribes that the person approaching and

*Not all commodes are commodious.

hearing this salutation stop and reply, "Don't take all day," or "Don't fall asleep in there," or even, "Don't fall in." ✳

Benefits of the outhouse are manifold. For one, the occupant is semi-connected with nature, i.e. there is plenty of fresh air, especially during inclement or windy weather, and also one can listen to birds, squirrels and other small animals frolicking in nearby fields and woods. Time allowing, the occupant can indulge in educational pursuits like reading a book or newspaper or more typically perusing a Monkey Wards or Sears catalog. In years past, men would take this opportunity to smoke a cigar or cigarette whilst occupied. Of the pursuits of women while thus occupied, I have no knowledge. With the biological task completed, the occupant would stroll leisurely back to his dwelling or place of business, once again reaping the benefits of fresh air and exercise.

The drawbacks of this type of accommodation are: cold and dark visits during the winter months or flies and mosquitos during the summer.

Though wooden outhouses were standard facilities in most state and national parks, during the past ten years they have been steadily replaced with fiberglass and plastic privies or full-sized cement buildings equipped with plumbing, hot showers and electrical outlets for shavers and hair dryers. As strange as it may seem, I even observed a person using the electrical outlet in this type of facility to pop popcorn. All of these modern improvements have served to depersonalize the experience and change the vernacular to the point where we now refer to this time-honored fixture as a "comfort station" or "restroom."

So in your travels if you happen upon an authentic wooden outhouse try to take advantage of the opportunity if only to sit awhile and enjoy the rustic ambiance.

✳ Polite people not in a hurry say, "Take your time." Those who don't are usually "full of shit."

More on Newspapers

As I mentioned earlier, newspapers are useful as props. Additionally, they have many practical purposes:

1. **Insulation**—You can create a vapor barrier by placing newspapers between the ground and bottom of your tent or between your ground cloth and bottom of tent.
2. **Bathmats**—papers, especially Sunday papers make great bathmats on cold, usually damp, cement floors in campground shower stalls. Additionally, they are useful beside streams and lakes, allowing the bather to avoid stepping on broken glass, prickers, or sharp stones and keeping feet free of sand.
3. **Tablecloths**—for campground picnic tables or even directly on the ground for an improvised luncheon along the road.
4. **Incendiary Device**—great for starting campfires.
5. **Cushions**—for a padded seat at a picnic table or on the ground.
6. **Body Insulation**—great for emergency body insulation during those long, chilly mountain descents. Just place one or more layers of newspaper between shirt and sweater or jacket. Conserves upper-body heat and protects against wind-chill.

~ ~ ~

Another Roadside Distraction

If there's one thing I learned early on my cycling adventure it was the importance, better yet, the necessity of relieving oneself at regular intervals while bike touring, especially on extended trips like mine. I discovered that many people, including me, suffer from either anxiety constipation or diarrhea, i.e. we become so obsessed with the importance of elimination we either can't get started or can't stop. Either condition can jeopardize any bike tour, short or long.

During the preparation period of my trip I read many articles about the necessity of eating copious and varied meals and drinking generous amounts of water and other liquids, but nowhere have I read a single sentence about the importance of eliminating the end result of all this eating and drinking. Procrastination may cause an uncomfortable, possibly painful, condition of irregularity.

The Basics. When I first started touring I got in the habit of putting off nature's calls, especially bowel movements, telling myself I would wait until I found a gas station or public restroom. But in Alaska and many places in Central and South America a biker can go a day or more without seeing a restroom. On more than a few days I rode until my eyes were yellow. The consequences of delaying a bowel movement and urination are an overloaded bladder or colon, which can create serious discomfort and possible health problems, causing you to pedal faster and longer, miss meals and rest stops-all resulting in spoiling your bike tour, or worse.

After a few hundred miles of touring, I developed this strategy. For a quick urination break I'd pull off to the side of the road and stop. With feet on the ground and straddling my bike I'd pull down my shorts and take a leak. If there was a lot of traffic, I'd lean over and study, or pretend to study, the map on my handlebar bag while emptying my bladder.

For bowel movements and emergency situations, I simply lay my bike down at the side of the road, as far from traffic as possible, seek privacy behind a tree, bush, or rock, drop my drawers and blast off. If there are no trees, bushes, or rocks to hide behind, as is often the case, I walk as far from the road as practical, drop my drawers, and hopefully move my bowels. For the sake of appearances, I usually face traffic while thus engaged. If perchance a passing motorist beeps his horn or waves, I smile and wave back. There were a few times in Alaska and many times in the deserts of Baja California, Peru, and Chile where I had to do just that.

At first you'll be reticent to adopt this method, but faced with the possibility of hundreds of miles, or more, of incredible discomfort, you'll get used to it in a hurry. Of some possible help is this rationalization, i.e. deer, moose, bear, even the neighborhood dog can get away with this (or worse) on a daily basis, so why can't we, when necessity dictates, do the same?

It goes without saying the experienced bike tourer will have one or more stashes of toilet paper handy (in handlebar bag, shirt pocket, wallet) at all times. Also, I carry clean-wipes or saniwipes with me for those times when a bit more cleansing action is needed. These handy reserves are carried not only for roadside distractions, but for all occasions. There's nothing worse than finding a great restroom, taking care of business, only to discover there is no toilet paper. This can happen, as I'm sure you already know, at the best restaurants and worst gas stations. For that matter, it can even happen at home.

As an added safeguard, as already noted, I carry a paperback book or newspaper with me for restroom respites. Here again, newspapers and paperbacks serve more than one purpose. You can read them while waiting, then tear out a page or two for emergency use if there isn't any toilet paper. In many primitive restrooms or banos in South America squares of newspaper are spindled on a nail driven into the wall close to the toilet. This is their version of a toilet paper dispenser. What better way for the environmentally conscious traveler to recyle the staggering guantities of obsolete newsprint. Whether strips of newspaper or triple layered, designer tissue, the results are all the same.

When available I encourage travelers to use restroom facilities. In addition to being functional, public restrooms can be an educational experience, especially those in bars and pubs. It is here the tourist can witness firsthand another vanishing form of folklore—restroom graffiti. Although one occasionally sees an elaborate piece of poetry, traditional wall graffiti takes the form of the limerick. These bits of doggerel and verse are penned on walls and ceilings with pencil, pen, and increasingly with magic markers. In all of my travels over the years the two most interesting and prolific graffiti walls were in Creede, Colorado and Skagway, Alaska. Ironically, these small towns are sister cities.

Here's an example of wall graffiti I observed in the men's room of the Red Onion Saloon in Skagway, Alaska.

> *"Here's to the women who do*
>
> *here's to the women who don't*
>
> *here's to the women who say they might*
>
> *here's to the women who won't.*
>
> *Here's to women in bright of day*
>
> *to the very dark of night*
>
> *who say I never have before*
>
> *but just for you I might."*

The odd thing about all restroom graffiti is that I have never once observed a person actually scribbling any on a restroom wall. Getting back to restrooms, perhaps the cleanest, most commodious can be found in Tourist Offices or Visitor Centers at National Parks in the United States. They are models of comfort and cleanliness and exude an ambiance that impresses even the most fastidious visitor. In addition to urinals there are usually two or three sit down toilets with enclosed stalls outfitted with one or more toilet paper dispensers, seat covers, and coat hooks. Also available are sinks with hot and cold running water, soap dispensers, paper towels, mirrors, and electrical outlets. In many cases the air is heavy with pine or lemon-scented air freshener. If time allows and circumstance dictates, these are perfect places to indulge in a quick upper-body sponge bath. I keep a wash cloth and small towel handy in my kit for this type of situation.

The most dreaded of all restroom situations is the infamous "pay toilet." Fortunately, I never came across any of these during my trip. I would rather urinate in the street than pay 25 cents to relieve myself in a pay toilet. My feeling is that man has reached a new low when he makes money off of other people's bodily wastes.

~ ~ ~

Propriety While Camping

If you're like me, you wake up at least once in the middle of the night to "empty your tank." When camping this presents a problem as restrooms, if any, may be yards or miles away. What does one do on a dark and stormy night of tent camping when nature insists on being dealt with? Outside the campground environment the simplest thing is to crawl out of your tent, walk a few yards and relieve yourself. But for worst-case scenario conditions I keep an empty #10 soup can handy. Rather than lying awake for hours with a bursting bladder, I get out of my sleeping bag, kneel, and piss in the can. I have never overfilled my can and consider myself above average in the quantity department. When done, set the can outside the tent, because of the potential mess that could result if overturned inside. In the morning remove the can to a suitable location for emptying and cleaning. Remember not to use the can to drink out of or cook in as it might take the edge off your appetite for a few days. Then again maybe not.

As this commentary is written from the male perspective I cannot honestly or accurately address the special needs of the female biker and camper. However, I can recommend a book titled, *How To Shit In The Woods*, by Kathleen Meyer. This volume contains a wealth of informative and instructional material on the subject, plus a chapter addressing the subject of female hygiene in the outdoors.

~ ~ ~

The Inland Passage

Late on the night of August 2nd, I was packed and ready to board the Malaspina and head south to Juneau. Having never sailed on a ship before I was looking forward to the voyage. On my way to the wharf that night about 10 p.m. I stopped by the Red Onion Saloon for a glass of beer and to say goodbye to a few of the locals I had the pleasure of meeting during my stay in Skagway. Afterward, with streets dark and quiet, I pedaled the few blocks to the wharf where the huge ship was anchored. Lights shining from all levels and parts of the boat made it look like an amphibious hotel. In a way it was. The front loading hold was open and cars and trucks were being driven into the cavernous interior of the ship. After getting my ticket inspected, I pedaled into the hold down a narrow aisle toward the front of the boat. There I secured my bike, removed the gear necessary for the overnight passage, and then made my way to the upper deck solarium to stake out a reclining deck chair. Like other backpackers and travelers, I spread my sleeping bag on a deck chair and made myself at home. After taking an investigatory hike about the ship, noting locations of cafes, bars, snack bars, hot shower points, I returned to my chair and crawled into the sleeping bag. Thanks to overhead heat lamps in the solarium, I remained warm despite it being open to the sea air on three sides.

As the Malaspina pulled into the wharf at Juneau, I was down in the storage hold putting the last of my gear on the bike. Shortly after the cargo hold was opened I pedaled down the ramp and off to visit Juneau, probably the most inaccessible capital in the United States, except Honolulu. It started drizzling soon after heading to town and lashed out with a few downpours before I arrived.

I pulled up at the youth hostel just before it closed for the morning, enabling me to check in and stow my gear before being turned out into the soggy streets of the city. But with my bike stored in a shed and the rest of my gear in the men's dorm at the hostel, I was free to roam about the city unencumbered. In fact, the rain in Juneau proved to be so constant one of the first things I did in the capital city was to purchase a pair of rain pants. My rain parka was not sufficient to keep me warm and dry under those extremely wet conditions. The sales clerk wondered if I would also like a pair of "Alaskan sneakers." Upon asking the obvious question, I learned he meant a pair of rubber rain boots. The gregarious clerk added that it rained so much in Juneau that when they finally got a sunny day the Governor would declare it a holiday for state government workers knowing if he didn't the majority would call in sick. Still smiling, he added that it rains approximately 120 inches per year, that's ten feet of rain.

Next day at 4 p.m., I boarded another ferry for an overnight trip to Sitka, one of the earliest Russian outposts in North America. Knowledgeable about the routine of boarding, especially with a bicycle, I had my bike stowed safely and deck chair staked out before most of the passengers boarded. Although the night passage was smooth and I enjoyed a whole day of sunshine in Sitka, I was getting irritable and sluggish from not riding my bike. The daily routine of biking and camping established over the past two months, had been broken and I was sorely missing it. Plus, I was getting tired of the pedestrian tourist circuit.

Sitting in the lounge on the return trip to Juneau, I was ruminating on my lack of exercise and generally blah mentality, when I got to talking with Marylou Cooper and Kim Elton, both from Juneau. The three of us sat for hours talking and playing endless games of Boggle, in addition to drinking a few beers. Hours later, when returning to the solarium I discovered I was camped next to two Californians, Vince Streano and Carol Havens from Laguna Beach. Both were professional stock photographers traveling all over Alaska in search of scenic images of all kinds. They suggested taking pictures of me at the Mendenhall Glacier. We made plans to meet at the campground near the glacier.

The boat docked at the ferry terminal, a few miles out of Juneau, at 8:30 a.m. I rolled off and waited for Kim and Marylou, who wanted to take a few pictures of me. I reciprocated with pictures of them for my scrapbook. Yes, it was raining, so I was encased in rain gear from head to foot. I also took the precaution to cover my panniers with large plastic garbage bags, securing them to the gear with some of the extra bungees I carry. Then off I wheeled to the Mendenhall Glacier Campground to rendezvous with Vince and Carol. Finding them proved much simpler than I suspected, as the campground was sparsely populated. The first road I turned down I saw Vince and Carol and a third photographer, Cradoc Bagshaw in the process of erecting Vince's camper-tent. This according to Vince was a simple and straightforward task when it's not raining. But in fact it was pouring, making the operation a soggy, muddy nightmare. Having been subjected to this type of weather condition for the past two months it didn't bother me at all, especially since I was garbed in a full set of rain gear. Finally, with the camper securely erected and my bike stowed in a dry place, we piled into Vince's Isuzu Trooper for a quick tour around the city. South of Juneau we stopped to observe a salmon run. Thousands of 10 to 25 lb. salmon packed cheek to jowl in the stream, not more than 15 ft. wide, fought the current and each other to advance to some mysterious spot upstream to spawn where they had been spawned and die where their progenitors had died. The carnage resulting from this catastrophe was particularly evident where the creek fed into the bay. The rocky shallow area around the inlet was littered with hundreds of salmon in various stages of death and debilitation. Also in evidence were the eagles that feasted on the carnage like vultures. Ravenous bears would join them that evening to share in the spoils. A rainbow of colors from red to deathly white could be seen on the flesh of the salmon as they surged up the creek.

Instead of being a fisherman's dream, it was a nightmare. The quantity of fish in such a restricted, vulnerable location was visually unpleasant. A hundred yards or so up the creek, the Fish and Game Department had installed weirs or traps beside the creek bank to temporarily capture some of the fish and remove their roe for hatchery spawning purposes. I looked into the depths of the diversion weirs to see huge salmon undulate in the current, waiting their turn (much like lines of cars at freeway tollgates) to get back in the river and continue their mission to oblivion.

None of this did anything to improve my lust for catching salmon, nor did it stimulate my appetite for their delectable flesh. Quite the opposite, it left me with a hollow feeling in my stomach and the taste of copper in my mouth. It took almost two years and 18,000 miles to overcome my phobia for salmon. At Puerta Natales in Tierra del Fuego* I had my first salmon dinner since witnessing nature's version of mass suicide in that Alaskan stream.

That evening we drove into town for dinner and a walking tour of Juneau nightlife, such as it is. Back at the campground about midnight, I got ready to leave for the Ferry terminal to board a ship to Prince Rupert. Huddled under the trailer canopy exchanging telephone numbers and addresses, Cradoc disappeared into his VW camper to emerge moments later with arms bulging with freeze-dried food, all 21 meals of them, all for me. I readily and gratefully accepted his offerings. My only problem was finding room in my already overstuffed panniers for the food, but with Vince and Carol's help we somehow crammed every last meal on the bike.

I cycled out of the campground into one of the blackest, rainiest nights I'd ever experienced. I was on my way to the terminal for a final boat passage south to Prince Rupert, British Columbia where I planned to pedal across the Yellowhead Highway to Jasper, then slowly make my way southwest to the United States. With my yellow flasher clipped to by rear pannier and a mini-mag flashlight attached to the handlebar bag I cycled tentatively through the darkness, made even more precarious because of the rain. At the main highway a lone streetlight and the scattered lights of businesses at the intersection greeted me. After a four-mile ride down the deserted highway I coasted up to the terminal glad to see a number of people already queued up at the door waiting for it to open.

"Goodmorning, " I called to the people watching me roll up to the covered entry way. " Staying dry?"

* Tierra (Land) del (of) Fuego (Fire) after the fires on shore observed by Magellan's crew when they passed through on their circumnavigation

Someone in line called back, "How about you?"

"Oh, I'm just wet on the outside. Inside I'm as dry and warm as a woodfire."

That seemed to be the magic formula, for in another two minutes, all the people were gathered around my bike asking questions. We even had a contest to see who could guess the weight of my bike and gear.

At 1 p.m. the doors of the terminal opened allowing everyone waiting to flock inside and queue up in new lines. As I had already purchased my ticket, I could relax, remove my wet clothes and go to the bathroom for a quick sponge bath. Two hours later we were allowed to board the Malaspina.

I was up in the solarium sound asleep before the ferry cast off. I awoke, or better yet was awoken about 8:30 a.m. by the ship's public address system calling all passenger's attention to a humpback whale off the starboard bow. Along with dozens of other sleepy passengers in the solarium, I slithered out of my bag, pulled on my jeans, grabbed my camera, and scrambled still half-asleep to portside, only to see half the camera-toting landlubbers rushing to starboard, while the rest of us rushed back to the portside. Then with exuberant cries of "whale, whale" coming from the starboard bow, everyone headed in that direction. There, sure enough I saw a whale spouting not more than 25 yards away from the boat. I watched the enormous flukes rhythmically stroke the calm, ink black water as it pushed itself into the depths, only to emerge minutes later, with an explosion of air and water shooting skyward from its blowhole.

After the cool, misty ocean air gently slapped me awake I came to my senses and left the tourists to stare at the whale while I made my way to the cafeteria for coffee.

Chapter 3

The Crucible

The Malaspina docked at Prince Rupert on a gray, drizzly Tuesday, August 9,1988 at 5:30 a.m. Amidst the clanking of tie down chains being released, the whine of ignitions, and throb of mufflers, I pushed my bike to the open hold at the front of the boat. I was as skittish as a racehorse in the starting gate, ready to get back on the road and cycle, regardless of weather conditions.

As I pedaled though the dismal streets of Prince Rupert I smiled with delight at being back on my bike and moving under my own power in the direction of my own choice. The tall smoke stacks of the pulp mills belched white, noxious clouds skyward to mix with a cloud ceiling so low that it looked like I could reach up and touch it. Within an hour I was out of town and headed due east on Canadian Highway 16—the Yellowhead Highway. The rolling, thickly forested hills of British Columbia seemed to reach out their soaking, green arms to welcome me and wish me a safe and pleasant journey. The road was good, there wasn't much traffic to bother me, so I made good time, finally stopping for a break at Prudhomme Lake Campground, to rest and change out of my soggy Levis and into sweats and rain pants. The rain at this point could be characterized as "cats and dogs."

Crowded up under a partially roofed information sign, I was re-organizing my gear and tightening down the plastic garbage bags used to "help" keep things dry, when I was startled by a noise behind me. I spun around to see a man pumping water into a plastic jug. We exchanged greetings. Joining me under the roof, we started off talking about the weather, but I soon found myself seated in a camp chair under a waterproof canopy sipping hot coffee with Frank and Gloria Scigliano from Pacifica, California, only a few miles from my home in Menlo Park. They were on their way, in a roundabout fashion, to Sitka for Frank's 20th High School reunion. After a second cup of coffee, I encased myself in rain gear and pedaled back to the highway, which I soon discovered winds its scenic way along the banks of the Skeena River. Not far away is the railroad track that also winds its way along the banks of the Skeena. One need only look at these three ribbons of commerce to understand a bit of western Canadian history.

By the time I reached the Exchamsiks River Campground, 62.33 miles out of Prince Rupert, I was exhausted and starving. My slothful days and nights in Skagway and aboard the Malaspina had taken their toll.

Although this was a typical Canadian campground, i.e. beautiful location, spacious and clean, with cords of free firewood (needing only to be split) it was expensive. The camping fee was $8 per camper, no discounts for bikers or backpackers. I guess I'd been spoiled rotten by the $2 biker/hiker camping fee in California State campgrounds.

~ ~ ~

The Fellowship of Wood

After the usual routine of pitching my tent, stabling my bike, and pulling out toiletry articles, and cooking gear, I discovered a small cache of dry, split wood under the picnic table. It was like finding a giant present under a Christmas tree. I felt like I was collecting on a long-term investment. It's my habit of always leaving some kindling or firewood in a campsite I've used. I do this for two reasons: 1. It's like a welcome mat outside a door, a greeting to the new occupant. 2. Generally, the next camper will be road weary, cold, and hungry, so a little cache of wood will not only cheer him up, but also help him get his fire going quickly and food cooked, thereby renewing his bodily strength and (hopefully) faith in his fellow man. All this, plus warming and drying the body. If more people did this it would be a positive way of spreading the camaraderie of camping, outdoor life, and the fellowship of wood.

So with my own cookfire blazing, I mixed up a freeze-dried six-egg omelet. It probably contained enough protein and cholesterol for a pack of boy scouts. Though I'm sure I followed the directions scrupulously, when cooked it was the consistency of silly putty and about as tasty. I even tried doctoring it with a dash or two of Tabasco sauce, which did nothing to improve it. After gagging down half of it, I dispatched the remains to a nearby trash can.

Shortly after my unrequited meal, a neighboring camper, Judy, walked over and presented me with some fried chicken she'd prepared for her husband and father who were out fishing. Since they were three hours late, she surmised, they must be catching a "mess" of fish and would surely prefer fresh broiled salmon to cold, fried chicken "any old day."

Before I could voice my hearty agreement, my mouth was stuffed with delicious broasted chicken, so I merely grunted and nodded my approval. In the midst of her monologue on the importance and benefits of home cooked meals, she stopped suddenly and looked at my bike, then back at me with saucer-like eyes.

"Where's your car," she asked.

I swallowed and licked my lips and fingers, then admitted I didn't have an automobile.

"Nooo, don't tell me all this stuff fits on that bicycle. Don't you tell me that."

I shrugged my shoulder and smiled sheepishly. "It all fits on the bike."

Then I dropped the big one on her, telling her I was on a bike trip from Alaska to the tip of South America.

Judy pressed a fist to her mouth, her eyes swelled to the size of dinner plates. "No, nooo, you poor boy. You've got to eat more than a few tiny pieces of chicken (actually two breasts and two thighs) she said in no uncertain terms as she marched off to her camper trailer. Not more than ten minutes passed when she returned with arms loaded with packages, zip lock bags, and Tupperware bowls. In seconds my picnic table was laden with an assortment of food that would have tempted the pallet of Henry the Eighth.

As I dove into salads, biscuits and gravy, sirloin steak, mashed potatoes and apple pie, I silently prayed that Judy's husband and father caught a big "mess" of fish. Judy stood above me like a coach or concerned parent urging me not to be bashful and to clean my plate.

I certainly did justice to her impromptu banquet, surprising myself with my capacity and complete disregard for anything close to table manners. Gluttony would be an appropriate description.

When Judy finally packed up her empty bowls, dishes, and casseroles, she asked if, maybe, I'd like something to snack on later that night. Holding my stomach with both hands, I assured her I wouldn't have to eat again until the middle of next week. She said good evening and returned to her camper with a feeling of a job well done.

An hour or two later, as my fire burned down to flickering red coals and a half moon rose over the tops of fir trees, a pair of headlights cut through the black night. A pickup truck stopped in front of Judy's camper. I watched in fear as two Bunyonesque men, the husband and father I guessed, emerged to carry a bulky ice chest into the trailer. As I crawled into my tent I whispered a prayer that they had extremely good luck on the river that day. With those thoughts filling my mind and Judy's food filling my stomach I fell into a deep, sound sleep.

While topping off my water bottles the next morning before leaving, Judy's husband came over, introduced himself, and presented me with a huge piece of smoked salmon for the road. Reluctant to explain my antipathy to salmon and possibly incur his wrath, I thanked him profusely while placing the fish in my handlebar bag. With an abundance of food in my larder, I wheeled out onto the rain slick highway and headed east.

~ ~ ~

My Very Own Bear Story

After a short day of cycling in scattered rain showers, I pulled into Kleanzas Creek campground with welcome rays of sunlight warming the landscape. I selected one of the many fine campsites along the nearby creek, then leaned my bike against a picnic table. After sorting my gear and pitching my tent, I covertly slipped the package of salmon into a bear-proof trash container. I walked across a carpet of pine needles toward a VW camper with a green canoe lashed on the roof at the next campsite. A man of about my age was bustling about the picnic table preparing a meal, while a young boy fed sticks of wood into a fire.

"Hello, how are you tonight," I hailed them.

The man looked up from a two-burner Coleman stove "Just fine, now that the sun has finally come out."

"I was wondering if you have an axe I could borrow to split up some kindling. I'm on the bike over there and don't have a way of chopping up those big chunks of wood."

"Sure. Hey Lauren. Bring the axe over here, will you. Say, my name's Ron Walker and that's my son Lauren. We're up here from Vancouver for a week of camping and fishing."

I introduced myself and told him a little about my plans to bike to South America. Ron was so impressed he called over to his son, "Hey, Lauren this guy's pedaling all the way to the tip of South America."

As usual the adult half of the Walker clan was more impressed with the bike trip. I took the axe from Lauren and shook his hand.

"My son's got a bike, but he's more interested in fly fishing right now. Ties his own flies too. I'm cooking the 2 lb. salmon he caught this afternoon."

"Well, I'll let you get back to cooking. Soon as I split some wood I'll bring the axe back."

About an hour later I returned the axe. As we stood about the firepit, Ron gave me a bottle of beer.

Later, after I'd finished up my dinner of pasta, Ron and Lauren came over to look at my bike and gear. Ron also wanted to give me a hatchet so that I would be able to chop kindling at future campsites. As much as I wanted to accept his generous offer, I felt I was over my weight limit already. Sometime during our conversation Ron asked the most popular question of the North Country.

"You see any bears?"

I replied with this incident that occurred on the road earlier that day. About 20 miles east of Exchamsiks River I was pedaling along minding my own business. The sun was out, making for a pleasant, scenic ride when out of nowhere a Royal Canadian Mounted Policeman (R.C.M.P.) pulled over in the middle of the highway. He rolled down the window of his patrol car and called to me. "Say, have you seen a dead bear along the road?"

"No, sure haven't."

"Well, keep your eyes open for one. We got a report that a trucker hit and killed a cub bear, so naturally the sow bear went on the rampage. Be careful now," the Mountie cautioned as he sped off down the highway.

That's great, I thought, a sow bear on the rampage and the guy with the car, the guns, and the two-way radio takes off and leaves me in the middle of nowhere. And me on a bicycle, no less. To make matters worse I had the piece of smoked salmon, compliments of Judy's husband, in my handlebar bag.

Cautiously, I pedaled on. All of a sudden clouds blocked the sun. The dark green forest seemed to encroach on the road like two malevolent walls trapping me. About one hundred yards further east I saw the black hump of a bear emerge from the treeline on the south side of the highway. It looked like a 4-wheel drive pickup truck as it smashed through the bushes and trees close to the road. Without a moment's hesitation, I did a U-turn and pedaled back west as fast as I could. With knees pumping away I kept looking in my rear view mirror for a "sow on the rampage." Luckily the bear had not pursued me. When a few motor vehicles had passed me, I pulled up for a rest and to eat an early lunch. After a leisurely lunch with more traffic passing in both directions, I figured the coast was clear. With no alternative, I got back on the bike and forged straight ahead, retracing my route. I cycled along slowly with a lump the size of a baseball in my throat scanning the woods on both sides of the highway for telltale signs of a bear. Everytime a car or truck disappeared from view I felt like a castaway adrift in the ocean watching as a ship disappears over the horizon. I sped by the spot where I'd seen the bear earlier, but the only evidence that remained was the shredded trunks and branches of trees and bushes. With no inclination to investigate further, I kept pedaling energetically down the road until I arrived at Kleansa Creek Campground.

Early the next morning, while packing the bike preparing to leave, Ron Walker stopped by to wish me luck and to give me a bag containing new potatoes, carrots, and green beans; all from his wife's garden at home. We shook hands and he went back to his VW camper, only to return a few minutes later with a foiled wrapped package.

"Why don't you take some of this salmon along with you. Lauren and I will be catching more today."

Smiling nervously, I reluctantly stowed the salmon in my bulging panniers, but did so with visions of sow bears waiting by the side of the highway, sniffing the air heavy with the aroma of fresh salmon. I wondered if I was some type of human sacrifice, then made a mental note to discard the fish at the earliest opportunity. The odd thing is that from then on I spotted a number of bears on the riverbank alongside the highway, all fishing for salmon with such single-minded concentration a freight train could have run them over and they would never have known it.

~ ~ ~

The Homestead

A few miles east of Kleansa Campground the sky opened up with a rain shower forcing me, once again, to stop and pull on my rain suit. For what seemed like hours I rode along in a stupor trying to think of anything and everything but the precipitation that seemed to be following me like a plague. I was staring down at the slick surface of blacktop, when I felt unusually warm. Miraculously, the clouds had parted allowing great shafts of sunlight to splash down on me like searchlights. Looking up I saw a magnificent rainbow arching over the dark glistening forest ahead. I fully expected to hear a choir of angels accompanied by a symphony orchestra. I stopped on a bridge crossing a turbulent creek gushing down from the mountains beside the road. A small sign near the bridge informed me I was crossing Hell's Bells Creek. Leaning my bike against the bridge railing, I began to peal off my wet rain gear. With my parka and rain pants draped over the bike to dry, I hiked down to the creek to fill two of my water bottles. The creek cascaded over huge rocks forming crystal clear pools, arranged like tiers, as it cut its way down a steep ravine. The water was clear and sweet. I sat down on a rock beside the creek, turned my face up to the sun, closed my eyes, and let the sunlight massage my weathered, unshaven face. In a trance-like state, I leaned back against another rock, feeling the warmth of its surface penetrate my back. The bubbling and churning of the water were the only sounds I was aware of. Totally relaxed and at peace, I drifted off for what seemed like hours, but could only have been five or ten minutes. After I awoke I knelt down over the pool. Splashing water on my face, I tried to wake up. Realizing few places on this earth could offer such privacy and intimacy with nature, I decided to eat my lunch there and prolong the solitary, nurturing experience.

After concealing my bike in a grove of alder bushes, I took my cooking gear and food kit back to creekside, where I made a few sandwiches and brewed a hot cup of coffee. Afterwards, I returned to get my toilet kit and towel. Hiking up the creek a dozen yards, I found a completely concealed pool of water, deep enough to submerge my body for a luxurious bath. By no means warm, my bath felt tepid, or at least it did to a body used to being constantly in the cool, damp out-of-doors. After bathing and washing my hair, I repaired to a nearby flat rock in the sun to dry off and contemplate my wilderness retreat.

Back on the road, I felt like I'd just returned from a two-week vacation on a deserted south sea island. It could have been a mile or a hundred miles for that matter when I stopped again. The sun was still shining; my spirits were soaring like the falcons that seemed suspended in space over the ridge north of the highway. Below me, nestled amidst newly mown hay fields was an ancient log cabin with white chinking between squared off logs. A pole fence separated a grass lawn from the hayfields bordering the cabin on three sides. North of a treeline, the Skeena River undulated and surged energetically westward. A thin ribbon of smoke rose from the cabin chimney. South of the highway I could see the top half of the Seven Sisters Mountains glistening in the sun. The sky was a deep, vibrant blue.

It was only 3 p.m. but I couldn't pass up this scene of classic pastoral beauty. Down a dirt road leading to the cabin I was greeted by the enthusiastic barking of an old dog, signaling my approach more out of duty than desire. Soon after, a young man of about 16 years emerged from the log cabin and walked toward me.

Tom Ainscow and dog, Ginger, were watching the homestead farm for his Uncle, who was away on a fishing trip. Tom's grandfather had purchased the farm in 1929. It had been a cherry orchard back then. Today, in addition to hay, there were cows, chickens, and goats.

At the edge of the field, I leaned my bike against the pole fence. Tom said I was welcome to camp in the field. Both Tom and Ginger watched studiously while I set up my tent and rearranged my gear. The snow-capped peaks of the Seven Sisters looked down on us in all their splendor.

Figure 4: Yours truly at the Ainscow homestead, BC.

When our conversation turned to fishing, Tom suggested we get some poles and tackle and hike down to the river in back of the farm. Down on the riverbank, I could see that a tremendous run of sockeye salmon was in progress. Fish were surfacing everywhere. We wasted no time rigging our spinning rods. I cast out into an area dense with circles. I envisioned a day of fishing surpassing all others. I cast and retrieved, cast and retrieved like a robot, but without results. Fish were actually rising a few feet away from me as if I was just another dead tree trunk flanking the river. Thousands of salmon were migrating up river. I changed lures and changed again, but with the same result-not even a nibble, let alone a bite. When I glanced at Tom some 20 yards away, he shrugged his shoulders. In frustration he went up to the cabin and returned with salmon roe for bait. A delicacy that would tempt even the most jaded of sockeyes, we hoped. The roe was also a failure. If we had nets we could have scooped up fish, but true sportsmen, we merely shook our heads and talked to ourselves. After an hour or two of impersonating fishermen, we gave up. Tom woke up Ginger, who sniffed the air once or twice, then scampered up the trail, leading us safely, but with empty creels, back to the farmhouse.

After stowing the fishing gear, Tom announced that one of his chores for the day was to kill a chicken, not for dinner, but to put it out of its misery. Seems this chicken had broken the pecking order in the hen house and had fallen victim to the deadly wrath of the other hens, who in their haste to enforce group behavior had pecked the offender so badly it was close to death's door. Tom, the humanitarian, was going to assist the badly wounded chicken over the threshold.

With a loaded 22 cal. rifle, Tom gloomily marched off to the hen house to perform his duty of reluctant executioner. The tattered, de-feathered body of the chicken lay panting on the ground just inside the fence. Tom took aim. With twitching finger, he pulled the trigger but nothing happened. He re-cocked the rifle and tried again, but still no death dealing report. He tried a fresh cartridge. Again the rifle misfired. Finally, Tom put the rifle aside and went to the woodshed for an axe. I was left to watch the battered body of the chicken breathe its last fitful breaths. It had literally been pecked half to death. I never realized chickens could be so uptight about conformity.

Looking more awkward with axe than rifle, Tom returned to complete his duty. Trembling slightly, he picked the chicken up by the legs, carried it to the chopping block and dispatched it, hopefully to a more tolerant world. We retreated to the log cabin in silence.

Since fishing had been so unproductive and the thought of chicken dinner was intolerable to both of us, Tom decided on some steaks from a newly slaughtered cow. I gladly contributed the salmon and garden produce given to me by Ron Walker. In addition to homegrown steak, potatoes and vegetables, we quenched our thirst with fresh milk from the Ainscow dairy herd.

At 10:30 p.m. I retired to my tent in the hayfield, there to sleep and dream of sockeye salmon and a non-conformist chicken.

~ ~ ~

George's Mosquito Bite Remedy

Pour 1/4-inch brandy into a cup. Dip finger in brandy; rub on mosquito bites in circular motion. If itching does not subside within 5 seconds, consume remaining brandy. If itching still persists consume additional doses of brandy until itching ceases.

~ ~ ~

Chocolate Covered Raisins

Sunday, August 14th. Goodbye homestead, hello rain. I stopped at another farmhouse along the Yellowhead. The two-story house shingled from top to bottom with composition shingles looked abandoned. No pickups or cars could be seen. No lights were on. No smoke puffed from the chimney. No one home, I guessed. Gone to town to shop, maybe. But just in case, I decided to give it a try. About ten yards from the house, out of nowhere, a mongrel dog missing its tail came running and barking at me. It looked and sounded for all the world like it had just escaped from hell. I dismounted and used my bike as a shield between the dog and me. It growled and howled, salivated and snarled until I thought it would have a cardiac seizure. This went on for ten minutes, perhaps longer. I had intended to knock on the door, but that was out of the question. Now, the only thing I wanted to do was escape to the highway. Just then the front door swung open. An old man in jeans and blue flannel shirt came out and called the dog off. The old fellow didn't look happy to see me. I asked if I could pitch my tent in his field. Looking me up and down for a few seconds, he jerked his head toward the road and grumbled something about going across the highway. Great I thought, maybe I'll escape without teeth bites on my leg.

I thanked him and turned to leave, but as soon as I turned my back on the dog, he leaped at my ankles. It snapped and snarled until the old guy called him off again. "Damn you Dub, sure, you get back here before I, I…" the farmer threatened with a trace of a Swedish accent.

Across the highway and railroad tracks I found another hay field newly mown. Although the sun made a late appearance that day, it did an excellent job of drying my gear out and warming things up. After setting my tent up and stowing my gear I rode down to the river along a track made by the farm equipment that cut the hay. Below the riverbank was a sandbar that appeared to be ideal for getting into the smooth river passing slowly by. With soap and towel in hand I scrambled down to the sandbar, stripped off my clothes, and began wading into the current. The water was so excruciatingly cold, I backed out, took a deep breath, and flung myself into the current, only to emerge seconds later huffing and puffing. After quickly soaping up, I made another quick dip into the river to rinse off, but this time found I was better able to deal with the frigid water.

Clean and incredibly refreshed, I cooked up a freeze dried meal. After dinner, I stretched out in the hay field to enjoy the lingering twilight. An incredibly deep, restful sleep was interrupted only once, when a Canadian Pacific freight train with what seemed like a thousand cars passed by about 3 a.m. shaking the ground under me like an aftershock of an earthquake. Other than that I slept like a baby.

When leaving next morn about 8:30 a.m. I figured I was duty bound to go across the highway and thank the old farmer for letting me camp in his field. Once past the hound of the Baskervilles, the old fellow invited me in for a cup of coffee. Over Paul Larsen's coffee and a breakfast of eggs, bacon, and toast, he told me how he'd come to settle down on the farm. Although the low-ceilinged kitchen seemed to be as hot as a sauna to me, Paul Larsen shuffled about in layers of wool shirts and sweaters that made him look like a stuffed potato from the waist up.

Larsen immigrated to Canada in 1925 at age 17. The small family farm in Sweden could not support the burgeoning Larsen family. Paul was the oldest of seven children. He came alone. He could not speak a word of English. Strong and healthy, he got a job in western Canada building the railroad, the very same railroad that passed by his farm on the way to the West Coast. He was working on a steel gang, setting rails on the existing roadbed and cross ties. When they reached the valley around Smithers, he decided that was where he wanted to live. At last when the work crew reached the end of the line in Prince Rupert, Paul returned to the valley, bought supplies and equipment, and homesteaded the ground he now occupied. Sure, by golly, it was hard, but he'd been raised on a farm in a country and climate less forgiving than British Columbia. That was a long time ago, sure, he chuckled. In a few months he'd be 80-years old. Dub, the snarling mongrel hellhound would soon be twelve. He'd kept a big dairy herd for 25 years, but got too old to take care of it, so sold it off. These days he even leased out his hay fields to neighboring farmers.

There wasn't any evidence of a Mrs. Larsen about, so I guessed she must have passed away or been chased off by Dub. When Paul finally settled in a chair across the table from me, he admitted to being a bachelor all his life. By the time he'd turned his homestead into a prosperous farm and got some spare time and money, he figured he was too old and set in his ways to get married.

For one reason or another, he started telling me a story about a husband and wife who gave their 6-year old son a pet rabbit for a birthday present. The telling is made slightly comical for even though Paul has lived in Canada for over 60 years he still talked with a Swedish accent. Along about Easter, the boy took a special interest in the rabbit and was extremely attentive to the animal, making sure he was fed, watered, his box clean, etc. The boy was so excited and dutiful his parents got a bit concerned. Boys will be boys. But a few days before Easter, the boy started sulking and loosing all interest in his rabbit. He forgot to feed the animal and wasn't eating normally himself. Now the parents were more concerned than ever. The father took the boy aside one night and asked him what the matter was. The boy hemmed and hawed, then finally blurted out, "I've been taking great care of my rabbit 'n all, but every time I check to see if he's laid any Easter eggs all I find is a bunch of chocolate-covered raisins!" With this Paul slapped his knee and guffawed until I thought he was going to pass out.

All of a sudden we heard Dub fly into a rage outside the house. Paul shuffled to the door to call off Dub and admit another biker. In came Klaus Bitter of Bonn, Germany. He'd seen my bike propped up against the side of the house so stopped to investigate. The three of us sat down at the table to enjoy more of Paul's coffee. Klaus was on a two-week holiday that would take him down to Vancouver, where he would fly back to Germany. When I told him my travel plans he was speechless.

After another cup of coffee and more local history from Paul Larsen, Klaus and I stepped out into a light drizzle, hopped on our bikes and pedaled away, but not without a rousing send off from Dub.

Two or three miles down the road it became evident that Klaus was a much faster rider than I was. Calling himself a credit card bike tourer, he eschewed such things as tent, sleeping bag, cooking gear and extra clothes, preferring to travel ultra light and fast. Before riding ahead, we stopped at a roadside store and cafe to exchange addresses, take pictures, and buy some goodies for the road. Not more than a hundred yards from the general store, I had a flat tire, my third since the trip began. Naturally, it was the rear tire and it was raining.

As I replaced the tube with a fresh one, I gave some thought to my short ride with Klaus. I guess I was a bit jealous of his speed and would have liked to have tagged along with him most of the day, but I had promised myself in the preparation stage of my tour that I would never speed up my pace to keep up with another rider. My philosophy then and now is that my pace is perfect and my route is the perfect route. My tour is the perfect tour. My ride, my rules. If someone, like Mike Blackwell, pedals at my pace, all well and good, I'll have company, otherwise I'll do it solo enjoying every minute by myself.

~ ~ ~

Raindrops Keep Falling On My Head

It rained all that day. Luckily toward evening I spotted an enormous hay barn by the side of the road. I cycled down to the large structure to seek permission to camp there, but found nobody about. The barn must have been 25 yards long and 20 wide. Steel posts at the corners and on the sides every ten yards supported the slanted tin roof. I guessed it was 25 feet high at the sides, sloping up to 30 feet in the center. The interesting thing about the hay stored inside was its shape. It was compressed into rolls 6 feet wide, 8 feet long and 6 feet high, instead of in small rectangular bales. Paul Larsen had explained it was cheaper to bale the hay in this fashion. One half of the hay barn was full of these large rolls.

I leaned my bike against one of the huge bales of hay to wait; hoping someone would come along and give me permission to camp. I lay down on a pile of loose hay on the ground, there to rest and wait. All the while the rain beat a pleasant tattoo on the metal roof. Out in the fields near the shed were enormous rolls of hay waiting to be transported to the security of the barn. Tractors and other farm machinery stood idle in the fields waiting, I presumed, for their attendants to return when the rain stopped to complete their chores. But the rain continued unabated. I made a lunch of sandwiches and brewed a hot cup of tea. The time passed pleasantly enough. I read and napped. Occasionally a pickup truck rattled down the gravel road going past the shed, but none stopped. One of the drivers even waved to me as he drove by.

At dusk, about 9 p.m., I decided to make camp, but rather than pitch my tent I opted to spread my sleeping bag in the bed of a pickup truck loaded with loose hay. If I were asked to vacate the premises I would be able to do so quickly. In this way, snug in the back of the truck, warm and dry in my sleeping bag I passed the night in total comfort.

Next day, more rain. Still no one stopped by to question me, so after breakfast I packed up and cycled away into the wet. During the past few days I'd emerged from the mountain forests of pine and fir into a gently rolling landscape of farmland fringed with alder and aspen trees.

It rained at Fraser Lake. It rained at Prince George. It rained at Beaver Creek and it poured at Purden Lake. If I had been a student of the bible I would have stopped and begun construction of an Ark.

On Tuesday, August 16th., at a Fraser Lake campground I made this journal entry. *"Wanted to write a short essay about maintaining morale during wet weather, but too tired and depressed to do so. One last note. Since my weather predictions have been so bad, i.e. always calling for sunny, warm days, I'm going to go against the grain and forecast cloudy skies with more rain, possibly accompanied by a tidal wave or two. Good night and keep your gear dry."*

Next morning I discovered leaches attached to the underside of my rainfly—ah, the little boogers.

~ ~ ~

Riding In The Rain: A Primer

The wet can get you down, drain your physical and mental energy, erode morale, plus it's dangerous out on the road in rainy weather. Drivers have a difficult time seeing you. Your visibility is reduced, but sometimes you have to ride. So be cautious. You must have the best rain gear available, top and bottom, gloves, layers, no skimpy plastic poncho here, especially in the North Country where temperatures plummet during storms, increasing the wind-chill factor. Your worst enemy is hypothermia. You must stay warm and dry. Think riding safety. Wear high visibility clothing. In addition to reflectors I have a flashing yellow safety light I attach to the left side of my rear pannier. I rely on a helmet-mounted rear view mirror to keep a watchful eye on traffic approaching from behind.

If you get soaked, stop cycling. Find shelter; change into dry clothing, especially socks and shoes. Make a cup of hot tea or soup to maintain core temperature. If you get wet and chilled and don't stop you're inviting hypothermia, which tends to feed on itself, i.e. you don't think straight, you make judgment errors, possibly a critical one.

I carry a flask of brandy for worst case scenarios. I stop, pitch my tent, brew a hot cup of tea, laced with brandy, and relax. I usually eat something weather I'm hungry or not. After a few sips of hot tea and brandy I think about all those desk jockeys and housecats back home with piles of bills they'll never pay in two lifetimes, who will never in their entire life experience the great outdoors as I have. Besides a few rainy days will make the sunny ones that much sweeter.

Also, save plastic bags of all sizes. They're great for keeping clothes, food, etc. dry. Use double plastic bags for bulk foods, film and cameras. I collected so many plastic bags along the way that I had a plastic bag for my plastic bags.

Sage advice notwithstanding, prolonged wet weather will take its toll, as evidenced in another journal entry, this one at Purden Lake.

"Good morning campers! It's one wet, sonofabitch out there. Raining so hard it woke me up about 4 a.m. That's saying a lot. Lay awake waxing philosophical about the rain. A camper's tent is like a solo sailor's boat at sea. It must be water tight, impregnable to the elements through the sea of wet with that single candle lantern providing the light, the beacon, in the dark wetness. For it is better to light one little candle lantern than to freeze one's tail off in the dark at 4 a.m. So you look around the tent checking for leaks, and thank God, finding none, you continue to wax philosophical in comfort. Shall I now gather the animals two by two? No, not yet, first a sip of brandy. This is a test of endurance, mental endurance, with no grades, just pass/fail.

"Must continue to maintain morale. Consider riding and camping in the rain like a siege. The strong shall survive, no, no, the dry shall survive. Fantasize about sunny, warm tropical beaches, Baja California, sun tan lotion, sipping Dos Equis while swinging in a hammock. More tortillas and giant shrimp, Jose. And be quick about it. Doesn't pay to keep Sahib waiting. There lads, more beer in the cooler and check the lobster pots, that's a good lad. And slice a few more limes before you vamanos old boy. Gracias."

And then I heard a weird scratching or scraping outside the tent. Not a bear I hoped. I went back to my journal, but the scraping continued. It was close, real close. The rain slacked off. So getting a case of tent fever, I unzipped the mosquito net and rainfly and crawled outside. It was light now, about 6 a.m. I looked around cautiously. God! It was a humongus black RAVEN. It barely fit under the picnic table. He flopped around, his one outstretched wing scraping the ground. I noticed it had only one claw. The other leg looked like a tiny wooden pegleg. So it gimped around using the wing to hop and flop. When it saw me it started making that hideous cawing noise that Ravens make-aaawk, aawk, something like that. The sound sent goose bumps up and down my spine. I stared at it bleary-eyed expecting it to blurt out NEVERMORE any second. It managed to extricate itself from under the table and did a bit of a gimp-dance around the firepit. I figured it was looking for a handout. Aaawk, aawk. I can't stand it. I've got to get out of here.

I began packing my gear, keeping a wary eye on the gimper. I had the tent down and almost rolled up when it started raining again. Damn. I put the tent up and hauled my panniers in with everything else to keep them dry. Once settled in the rain stopped as suddenly as it started. I peeked outside and looked around. The gimper was on top of the picnic table watching me. Its beady eyes seemed to beg for food, drink, mercy, anything. It started raining again. The hell with it. I've got to get out of here rain or no rain. So I packed up. Everything was wet. I didn't care. I pedaled out of the campsite, leaving the gimper to flap and flop around. Good riddance. It was raining like hell now, but I didn't care, I was just glad to get away. Aaawk, aawk.

I had 85 miles between McBride and me. After 12 days of the wet and cold I needed a hot meal, a hot shower, a soft bed, and no evil-eye, gimp-leg, black RAVEN. Just your average ravenous raven.

Looking back, I realize my mistake was not having coverings for my riding shoes. All this speechifying about top quality rain gear, parkas, gloves, pants and I did not have coverings for my shoes. Result: wet shoes and socks for eight days. Cold, wet feet for ten days. Somewhere outside of McBride I started shivering uncontrollably. I pulled off in a picnic area and immediately fired up my stove to make a cup of hot soup. I was definitely flirting with hypothermia. I took off the wet shoes and socks. My feet were stone cold. I found one pair of dry wool socks and put them on. After my hot soup, I saddled up and headed for McBride, about 20 miles farther on. Still, I know I wasn't too sharp. I could barely pump my legs. Low energy. I was bonking, but had to make it to McBride. Rolling in about 5 p.m., I found the only hotel in town and booked a room at $26. The manager let me carry my bike and gear up to my room on the second floor, no mean feat considering the shape I was in. My heated room had its own bath, a color TV, a soft bed, and a view of the softball field across the street where a game was in progress. The rain had stopped. I took my first sit-down-in-a-tub bath in 20 years. It was pure luxury. I soaked in the scalding bath, sipping hot lemonade and brandy. After another hot lemon brandy and a nap, I dragged myself downstairs to the restaurant for dinner. Can't remember what it was exactly, only that it was hot, delicious, and not freeze dried. Up in my room again, I devoured three pieces of carrot cake purchased at the grocery store across the street. My wet tent and clothes were hung around the room drying. I filled my cup with brandy, lay back on the bed, turned on the TV, and watched one of my all time favorite movies-*Jeremiah Johnson* with Robert Redford. I was a supremely happy camper.

Thus ended my 12-day siege of rain on the Tete Juane (Yellowhead Highway). Next day the sky cleared and the sun came out. It stayed sunny and warm for the next three months. I passed the survival test.

The weather and scenery were so beautiful the next day, I pulled off after only 30 miles to set up camp in a hayfield. I spent most of the afternoon sitting outside my tent Indian style, soaking up the sun and contemplating my recent ordeal.

Journal entry: Monday, August 22, 1988, 8:05 a.m. Hayfield 30 miles east of McBride.

"First morning on trip, about seven weeks now, I woke up to completely clear blue sky. Sun slowly, ever so slowly, inching its way up over the mountains to the east. Just starting to splash sunlight into the field. A long, golden swath of freshly cut golden greenness. Greenness layered with dew. Peaceful and quiet now, just the sound of a few birds off in the trees, trill of cicadas and grasshoppers.

Everything celebrating the sun. Trees tipped with golden light. Quite breathtaking. Hands cold.

"I feel 100% better this morning. Now sun up over the ridgeline, lighting me up, warming me. So bright I can't look directly at it. I feel it on my hands and face, like turning up a thermostat. This is a special day, mark it well. Feels like a dark, damp cloud has been lifted off me. With eyes closed I face the sun while sitting in front of my tent. As far as I can tell I'm the only one on earth this morn. Must sit here a bit and soak up the warmth. Thanks."

About 30 miles east I rounded a curve and saw a snow-capped peak. Farther on more peaks, then suddenly I was riding directly toward Mt. Robson with a clear blue sky as a backdrop and wreath of white clouds capping the peak. It was mesmerizing. Mesmerizing, in that I rode for approximately four miles getting closer and closer until I was overwhelmed by the majesty of the mountain in front of me. With tears of joy in my eyes I pulled off the road and visually drank in the beauty. I believe my journal entry later that day best captured the spirit of the scene.

"Here the biker has the advantage, for he drinks the natural spirit as a drunkard quaffs his pints-two fisted. It is intoxicating. The motorist, speeding by at 60 mph, gets a mere sip, barely enough to wet the lips, let alone drown the senses."

~ ~ ~

The Gam

Closer to Mt. Robson I saw another biker headed toward me. He pulled over to my side of the road and stopped. We introduced our-selves. I shook hands with George Klacsansky of Seattle,

Washington. Neither of us being in any great hurry, we repaired to a nearby cafe.

This type of chance meeting with other cyclists happened several times during my trip. It was a special time, more of an event than merely a social meeting. The best way of describing it is to call it a "Gam," which is an old whaling term used by Herman Melville in *Moby Dick.* On page 343 he offers this definition. "GAM, noun, a social meeting of two (or more) whale ships, generally on a cruising ground when, after exchanging hails, they exchange visits by boats crews: the two captains remaining, for a time, on board one ship and two chiefs mates on the other."

As Klacsansky was headed over the Yellowhead to Prince Rupert, I was able to share information regarding camping spots, restaurants and cafes, stores, and other information that would be useful to him along the way. Likewise, he gave me tips regarding the Icefields Parkway and points south. He was on a six-week vacation out of Seattle. Having already biked east to Glacier National Park, he was bound for Prince Rupert via the Yellowhead, then south by ferry to Victoria Island, before cycling home. After an hour of conversation and two cups of coffee, we paid our bill, said goodbye, and pedaled off in opposite directions.

~ ~ ~

Vengeance is mine, sayeth the Lord

I believe most of us have a naive perception of animals and birds. We treat them like Disney characters performing a list of bird-like and animal-like things, i.e. barking, singing, hiding bones, and picking worms. True, they do all these things, but have a bag of tricks humans seldom see, unless like Thoreau, you spend a lot of time in the woods observing them.

I've discovered nature's creatures have personalities too. Also, they have a sense of humor, lots of curiosity, and even a mean streak. I was rudely awakened at 6 a.m. during my camp at Mt. Robson. I thought it was hailing. When I hurried outside of my tent, half asleep, I discovered the "hail" was really the handiwork of squirrels in the pine trees above the tent. Chattering and scurrying among the branches they would knock pinecones off, then stop to watch as these missiles dropped with incredible accuracy onto my rain fly, there to bounce onto the ground and be gathered up. After a bombardment, they would race higher into the tree and renew their efforts. If this had been merely part of their yearly foraging ritual of gathering pine nuts for the long, hard winter, then why had they picked the trees over my tent when there were hundreds, thousands, of similar trees offering bumper crops of pine cones? The only explanation, or at least my only explanation, is that they wanted to have a bit of fun while doing a necessary, but boring job. From the sound of things they were having one hell of a good time.

An upstart in the bird world is the Jaybird, a notorious noisemaker and disturber of the peace. When you've settled down for a siesta along comes a Jaybird to perch on a nearby picnic table or branch above your tent, there to bleat and yammer pointlessly until you crawl outside and throw something at it, only to watch it fly away giving you the horse laugh. He will return again and again to disturb you until you're so worked up you can no longer sleep.

Campground chipmunks and squirrels are also notorious for disturbing the peace and quiet of a campground, but more of that in a later chapter.

~ ~ ~

Mind Games

Never tell another biker about a hill or mountain pass they're about to negotiate. And never, ever tell a biker their choice of bike routes is wrong.

The day I left the hostel at Whistler, outside of Jasper, I got in a conversation, mostly one-sided, with a lady just beginning a bike tour with three other cyclists. I happened to mention my planned route through Idaho, eastern Washington, and Oregon. She informed me I had chosen the worst possible bike route. According to her I should have cycled down the coast of Washington and Oregon. She never considered that "maybe" I'd already seen a lot of the Pacific coast and during the next two years would see 3,000 plus additional miles of it. Besides, I was anxious to explore the farming country of eastern Washington and Oregon, especially the wheat belt of the Palouse.

Never try to second-guess somebody else's route. It's totally subjective. Once you've chosen your route and started down the road, it's the best route available.

If you meet a biker headed down the road toward a steep mountain pass don't ruin their day by telling them how incredibly difficult it's going to be. First, they will undoubtedly know about it anyway. Secondly, if they don't know and you break the news to them they'll be thinking about that gut-busting climb until they get there. In their mind they'll turn a moderate ascent into a death march over a Himalayan-type mountain range. Keep the bad news to yourself.

~ ~ ~

Les Promenade des Champs Glace

The French have a way with words, as evidenced by the signs along the Icefields Parkway or Les Promenade des Champs Glace. My favorite was the sign cautioning tourists not to feed the wildlife, or Les Animaux Sauvage.

From Jasper south I began a 150-mile tour of the most scenic country on my entire trip. A few places came close, like Machu Picchu in Peru and Torres del Paine in Chile, but the Canadian Rockies between Jasper and Banff will always have a special place in my heart.

In Jasper, I stocked up on bulk foods at Nutter's Health Food store. I bought supplies of pancake mix, granola, raisins, dried apples, bananas, apricots, pasta, fig bars, rice, and a few other sundries— enough to last at least a week on my trek down the Icefields Parkway. While in Jasper I also purchased a lightweight, telescoping fishing rod to replace my fly rod, lost along the road between Tok and Dawson.

After a few days in the bustling tourist Mecca of Jasper I was looking forward to getting out in the mountains and camping. During my brief layover I did some maintenance on my bike, discovering it needed only minor adjustments to the derailleur and brakes.

I find it difficult to adequately describe the magnitude of sensory delights awaiting the traveler along the Icefields Parkway. Perhaps David Douglas, a Scottish botanist for whom the Douglas Fir tree is named, best describes the natural beauty to be found there. Exploring the Canadian Rockies in 1827, he wrote:

"How familiar soever high snowy mountains may have been to us...yet on beholding the grand dividing ridge of the continent all that we have seen before disappears from the mind and is forgotten, by the height, the sharp and indescribably rugged peaks, the darkness of the rocks, the glaciers and eternal snow."

While resting and sightseeing at Athabasca Falls, approximately 18-miles south of Jasper, I met photographer David Barnes from Seattle, Washington. Strolling by with a tripod on his shoulder and loaded with camera gear, he stopped to ask about my tour. In addition to being a professional photographer he was also an avid cyclist, having done extensive touring in the U.S. and Europe.

We started out talking bikes, but soon Dave was taking pictures of my bike and me at the falls and a half dozen other nearby scenic locations. About 7 p.m. with the sun dropping behind Mt. Fryatt, we pulled into Kerkeslin Campground. As I prepared a dinner of Chili and rice, Dave told me he was on a photo trip that would take him, over the course of the next two months, as far south as New Mexico. The next morning, after a breakfast of blueberry pancakes and oatmeal, Dave headed south to Banff, while I pedaled a mere 11.28 miles to Honeymoon Lake where I set up camp. Though I'd only been on the road for about two hours, I couldn't pass up the scenery of the lake. During the next two days I discovered that pulling into a campground around 2 p.m. enabled the slothful biker to take his pick of campsites. At Honeymoon Lake, recommended by George Klacsansky, I selected the most scenic spot above the shoreline, then went about my chores of pitching the tent, gathering fire wood from a huge pile provided by the park service, washing clothes, then with chores completed I indulged in a siesta. Arising at 4 p.m. I gathered up my fishing tackle and walked down to the lake for a bit of fishing.

While sitting around the campfire that evening, I was inspired to compose this verse as testimonial to the utility of the bungee cord:

Ode To A Bungee Cord

You stretch, bend and lash
my abundant packs, bags and stash.
You even make a fine clothesline
from which to hang these rags of mine.
I beat you, I flail you, I stretch you
into all manner of shape and form.
I thank the Lord

for you're made of more resilient material
than I old bungee cord.

Steer clear from a grungy, spongy bungee.

Travel Advisory

Never lay a gloom and doom story on another biker. Most of what we know is half-truth tempered by our own prejudice and bias. Save the bear and bandido stories for the hardsiders (camper trucks, motorhomes), scare the hell out of them they love it.

Always, I repeat, always keep your water bottles filled, no matter how far you plan on riding. Sooner or later you're going to "need" that water for cooking or drinking.

Always keep your panniers zipped closed, especially in campgrounds. Squirrels and chipmunks will wreak havoc on your food stores if you disregard this advice. Besides plundering, these rascally rodents carry a potential threat of disease, particularly bubonic plague. Considering the quantities of food they can consume, they are notoriously bad tippers.

Always lock your bike, even in your garage at home. Do this so it becomes a habit. In my case, if my bike were stolen I would lose my home, family, and transportation in "one swell foop."

~ ~ ~

Chocolate Moose

At Jonas Creek Campground, 17 miles south of Honeymoon Lake, I again had my pick of the choicest campsite. The campground filled up to capacity that night. I even let a fellow pulling a camper trailer use the driveway in front of my tent as a temporary campsite. As a gesture of gratitude he even paid the $8 fee.

After setting up camp at 2:30 p.m. I took a hike along a path leading up a ravine in back of the campground. I thought I'd find a small lake teeming with voracious trout, but succeeded only in getting thoroughly lost and tired. I got so energy low during my hike I had to stop and rest several times along the way. Putting one foot in front of the other became a major effort. As I plodded on, I munched chocolate bars kept handy in my fanny pack for just such occasions. Fortunately, the trail back to camp was downhill. Somewhere during my retreat I stopped by a good size pool in the creek by the trail. After an ice cold bath I dried off in the sun. Still, I was sluggish.

By the time I got back to my campsite I was exhausted, barely managing to crawl into my tent for a nap. I was a bit concerned about my lack of energy, but figured it was due to the altitude, which was only 4,500 ft. at road level. Regardless, I delved into my food stores to find a giant chocolate bar I'd purchased back in Jasper. Without thinking I consumed the whole thing.

While starting a cookfire after my nap, a neighbor camper strolled over to chat and drink his mug of coffee. A gentleman from the Calgary area, he asked if I'd ever eaten Moose meat. I hadn't, but being the inveterate meat eater that I am, said I would welcome the opportunity to do so. He hurried back to his pickup camper, returning minutes later with a thick Moose steak, which I put right on the grille. As it cooked over the wood coals, I kept cutting off pieces to taste for doneness, but before I had a chance to prepare soup or vegetables, the entire Moose steak was eaten. Without question, it was one of the tastiest pieces of meat I'd ever had. Next morning, I woke up feeling completely energized. Over my breakfast coffee I came to the conclusion I'd been low on animal protein, the Moose meat had brought me up to speed. In their own way, the calories from the chocolate bar also helped to speed my recovery.

That evening three bikers pedaled into the campground and set up their tents a few campsites away from mine. We got together for brandy and coffee and bike talk after they had dinner. Bruce and Gail Hunt and Alan Torgerson were from Spokane, Washington. Their two-week tour, starting in Jasper would end back in Spokane. Before they left next morning, Bruce and Gail gave me their address and telephone number. I would be a welcome guest, they promised, if my route took me through the Spokane area.

A Walk On The Wildside

With renewed energy, thanks to a anonymous Moose meat donor, I began packing up and mentally preparing myself for an attack on Sunwapta Pass, approximately 27-miles south and 6,500 feet*elevation.

As the pass offers a shorter climb when cycling north to south, I achieved the summit in 4.5 hours, including stops at all three scenic overlooks. That night I managed to eat dinner and enjoy half a campfire before rain forced me into my tent. Under fair skies next day, I relished a speedy, long descent into Banff National Park. Cruising along gawking at the scenery for 24 miles, I looked up to see a spectacular series of waterfalls cascading down the mountain on the east side of the road and forming a creek that passed under the highway and eventually emptied into the Sunwapta River. I stopped for a drink of water and a closer look at the falls. Digging my camera out of my handlebar bag, I spent about ten minutes composing shots of what I think was Panther Falls. I enjoyed the view so much I pushed my bike off the road and prepared lunch. Afterward, I decided this was one of those must-stop-and-investigate-spots.

* 1.23 miles.

I pedaled back up the highway about 50 yards to a place where I could push my bike into the woods where it wouldn't be seen. Back in the trees and well hidden, I loaded my backpack with enough food and gear for an overnighter, then changed into my hiking boots. As an added precaution, against what I don't know, I locked my bike to an aspen tree. Shouldering my backpack, I began the steep climb up the side of the mountain to the falls. Every step was its own reward. I worked my way over to the cascading creek, then up through the bushes and rocks at creekside. Fortunately, the weather was magnificent-blue skies, white puffy clouds, and warm temperatures. I stopped many times during the ascent to drink the deliciously cold water from the creek.

The higher I climbed, the steeper the terrain got, forcing me to traverse the upper slopes. Three quarters of the way up I passed two magnificent falls where glacial melt off, on warm days like this, appeared to explode over rock ledges, then roar down into pools of frothy water. The noise produced by so much thunderous hydraulics was deafening, but invigorating. From those majestic heights I could look out across the valley at white-peaked, glaciated mountains.

Just below the uppermost falls, squeezed between huge granite boulders, I found my way blocked, forcing me to hike carefully along narrow mountain sheep trails. The wall of rock was just too high to scale without a climbing rope. Raging water pouring down from above made it impossible to cross the creek to where a possible route led up to the summit. Regardless, the view I had was breathtaking. The sluiceway above and beside me appeared to be crafted by an expert stone carver. I hungered to scale those last 20-feet of solid rock to see what incredible vistas were to be had, but I was blocked. From a point at the edge of the creek where the water plummeted to a pool fifty feet below, I could look straight down. My eyes followed the raging water as it plunged and dove down and over ledge after ledge. I soon realized how precarious my position was and made haste to lower myself carefully hand-over-hand to a level area at the base of the highest falls where I'd left my pack.

After a photo session, I refilled my water bottles and descended 300 feet to a level area scooped out of the mountainside where I pitched my rain fly and made camp for the night. Every so often I'd look down into the valley to see a small dot of a car or truck move noiselessly up or down the highway. While eating my dinner I watched in silence as the sun dipped below the mountain range across the valley, its golden rays turning the glacial peaks various shades of crimson.

I awoke at 3 a.m. to see a nearly full moon light up the valley below me. An occasional cloud would temporarily pass in front of the moon creating a surreal nightscape. Splashing water from the nearby creek looked like an explosion of diamonds in the moonlight. Except for the baffled sound of bubbling, churning water all was silent and peaceful. I awoke again a few hours later to watch in awe as the morning sun rose behind the granite peaks above me, slowly painting the valley in hues of pink, magenta, and red. Sitting there in the cold, frosty morn, warming my hands in my armpits I felt a spiritual closeness with nature. I gave thanks to whatever powers were responsible for allowing me to share this extraordinary experience.

Later that morning after sliding down the mountainside, I found my bike still safely locked to the aspen tree. What I would have done if it weren't there, I often wonder. Considering the copious amounts of food stored in them, I was relieved to find my panniers unmolested by bears. After a few hours and 18 miles of cycling, I rolled into a nearly deserted campground at Waterfowl Lake. Somewhere along the way I broke the 2,000-mile mark on my land voyage. Back then it seemed like an incredible distance. But as I noted in my journal later that day, *"All that stuff, miles, speeds, times, is not important. The important things are yesterday's trek to the falls and today's ride to Waterfowl Lake. When I saw this emerald green lake in a basin below glacial peaks I knew I had to stay here a few days."*

~ ~ ~

Another Travel Advisory

Always zipper the mosquito fly of your tent or, like me, you'll have unwelcome guests supping on your chocolate bars, snacking on your trail mix, shredding your mountain money (toilet paper), and generally raising holy hell in your tent. Of course, it goes without saying these food items should not be in your tent in the first place, but somehow they seem to migrate there.

~ ~ ~

The Ubiquitous Disposable Diaper

Ever since Anchorage I'd been noticing something along the highway with alarming regularity. A presence more noticeable than bottles and cans, it was nonexistent only a few years ago. It was a white plastic bundle filled with excrement and is popularly known as a disposable diaper. They look like a pound of hamburger wrapped in butcher's paper, but don't even have the dubious distinction of being garbage. I cannot understand why mothers pitch these sacks of crap onto the shoulder of our roads. Why can't they wait until they reach a rest area, or gas station, or some such place equipped to handle these reeking bundles? Even in the remotest parts of Alaska I've seen them doting the side of the road like giant mushrooms. I've seen them in Canada, the lower 48, Mexico, Central and South America, even the windswept, barren wastes of Tierra del Fuego. Admittedly, there were fewer in evidence south of the border, but they were there. All of them, hundreds, like 20th century mileage markers, could still be there and might remain there for thousands of years unless some highway road crew removes them. Or, God forbid, some motorist or cyclist gets rid of them.

One wonders how these children turned out, having parents that are the same thing they tossed — trash.

A Coyote

Thursday, September 1, 1988, I rolled into Lake Louise. After a little grocery shopping and exploring, I pedaled a few miles out of town to the Corral Creek Hostel.

That evening while eating in the communal kitchen/dining room I got to chatting with Christine Lieb from Coburg, Germany. She was on an extensive solo tour that would take her as far south as Guatemala and as far east as New York before returning to her home. Early next day, we started out on a hike around Lake Louise, one of the most memorable hikes of my life. Not only did we have excellent trekking weather; additionally the tourist season had wound down leaving the trails with little traffic. A little over two miles from Lake Louise, Christine and I found ourselves looking down at Lake Agnes, a small glacial lake nestled in a bowl at the base of steep mountain peaks. Below us on the shoreline near the outlet of the lake was a log structure with shingled, peaked roof. A few minutes of hiking brought us to the building which we discovered was a tea house, providing refreshment, snacks, and sandwiches to ravenous hikers. After coffee and a confection, we followed the trail west around Lake Agnes, making a short detour to explore severely glaciated rock formations northwest of the lake. Afterward, we climbed an extremely steep trail along the southwest end of the lake that took us up to a saddle, with observation area, affording a spectacular view down at Lake Louise and Chateau Louise. We descended to a connecting trail that brought us higher into the mountains and eventually to another Tea House situated just below the plain of six glaciers. Here we rested and enjoyed spectacular views of Victoria glacier looming above us. Following a short hike to an observation point just below the glacier, we turned back and followed the scenic trail down the valley back to Lack Louise. Back on level ground again, we enjoyed a slow and pleasant walk on the shoreline trail to the huge hotel, Chateau Louise that dominates the east end of the lake.

Two days later I was cycling to Banff with all intentions of meeting Christine Lieb at the Banff youth hostel, but when I found myself at the crossroads of Hwy. 93 at Castle Junction I headed south for Radium Hot Springs. About six months later I received a letter from Christine in which I learned the details of the remainder of her sojourn. Once over Vermillion Pass at 5,415 feet I made a long, slow descent. The weather had warmed so much I made the mistake of riding with my shirt off. A mistake I would pay for later on. When I finally bottomed out I enjoyed a leisurely pedal along the rolling highway flanking a river. Stopping by the river for a rest, I checked my thermometer to see the temperature was in the mid-eighties, the warmest weather I'd experienced since leaving California months ago. About 3 p.m. I pulled into a rest area suffering from dehydration and too much sun. Fortunately, a water pump and shaded picnic area were available. Much to my discomfort the temps had soared to the low 90's. I soaked my head and body under the water pump, then retired to the shade to rest and mop my head with a towel soaked in water. After a two-hour rest period I managed to pedal a few miles to a campground crowded with Labor Day campers.

I was up and on the road next morning trying to beat the heat. It was cool and the highway was deserted. I plateaued about halfway up Sinclair Pass. Pedaling slowly and enjoying a quiet morning, I looked up on the hill to my right. There sat a good-sized coyote looking down at me. I pedaled and watched it. The coyote moved closer to the edge of the hill, continuing to stare down at me, more out of curiosity than appetite. It looked the way a dog does with head cocked to one side
*1.03 miles.

wondering what you're up to. I figured it was out for the morning sun or was just about to cross the highway when I came along. I finally stopped and looked it in the eye. It sat there equally engrossed in the staring contest. This mutual admiration went on for five minutes when we heard an approaching truck. It sprang to its feet and headed into the woods behind it. Goodbye coyote.

~ ~ ~

More Travel Advisories

When passing a stream, creek, or river in hot weather stop and take a swim or just soak your shirt and head. This will help keep your core temperature down and prevent dehydration. It's also a great energy booster, not to mention a golden opportunity to fill water bottles.

~ ~ ~

Smoke Gets In Your Eyes

South of Fairmont Hot Springs, I noticed a couple of butterflies resting on the shoulder of the road and jerked my handlebars to avoid running over them. I was surprised they didn't fly away. I couldn't believe my eyes when I looked up to see hundreds, perhaps thousands of butterflies massed on the shoulder of the road like decorations. None attempted to fly away as I cycled by. For a minute I thought the sun was getting to me again or I was hallucinating, or both. I stopped to take a closer look. After an inspection I discovered what had happened to them. The hot weather was responsible on two counts: first it caused a late butterfly hatch. Also, the heat had caused the tar on the shoulder of the road to heat up and become sticky. The butterflies landed on the sticky tar to become terminally stuck, creating a natural butterfly collection.

At Ft. Steele I stopped at a roadside cafe for some pancakes. There I learned from a couple out of Calgary that a big forest fire was raging at Yellowstone National Park in the States. Additionally, there were forest fires burning in parts of Montana and Idaho. Over my pancakes I consulted my map. I was approximately 45 miles from the U.S. border and I was anxious to get to Coeur d'Alene, Idaho, hopefully to pick up mail and replenish my bankroll, which had shrunk to $105. With any luck I guessed I'd make it in two or three days.

~ ~ ~

George's Spider Bite Remedy

Same as mosquito bite remedy, except double dose of Brandy, both externally and internally.

After my first windy ride in weeks, I crossed the U.S.-Canadian border near Kingsgate on Wednesday, September 7th. The Canadian customs inspector held up traffic to question me about my trip, I suspect more out of curiosity than duty. A few minutes later I was back in the States.

Chapter 4

Lower Forty Eight

North of Bonner's Ferry, Idaho I ran out of energy and had to pull over for a rest in a field beside the road. As I pedaled south, the smell of smoke got stronger and the sun looked like an orange disk behind translucent glass. In addition to being tired I felt sick to my stomach, so I stopped to rest. After propping my bike against the side of a barn, I spread my ground cloth out and lay down, then soaked my bandana with water and draped it over my face to help cool my head. I was out like a light seconds after lying down. When I came to an hour later the smoke was so thick it looked like fog. By now I realized the smoke was responsible for my queasy stomach and wasn't doing my lungs any good either. The smell of smoke was so strong I was afraid the forest fire was headed my way, but there were no emergency vehicles on the road. I guessed if there were danger in the immediate area I would see police and fire trucks or at least hear sirens, but everything was eerily quiet. Just when I concluded the area had been evacuated and I was left behind, I was reassured when a few cars and pickups passed by. Rather than backtrack, I decided to forge ahead. Some five or six miles down the road I stopped at a cafe for a cold drink and the latest information regarding the fires.

In Bonner's Ferry, Idaho I stopped to ask directions to a campground from Mark Engler. He not only directed me to a KOA just south of town, but also invited me to stop over at his house in Sandpoint when I cycled through the next day. Mark said he'd call ahead to his housemates and let them know I was coming. He gave me the telephone number to call when I arrived.

Although it was barely 30 miles to Sandpoint, the road and scenery were so pleasant I took my time, stopping several times along the way. About eight miles north of Sandpoint I felt compelled to stop at a roadside tavern named *Duffy's Saloon*. Sure enough inside were Irish flags and memorabilia from the "old sod." The red-haired barmaid recommended I sample a microbrew named Hale's Ale. Brewed, she told me, in the Spokane area. While sampling a glass of this superb beer I proposed a toast to W.B. Yeats.*A broad smile on her freckled face, Mrs. Duffy declared it did her heart so much good to hear the name of one of Ireland's finest poets she would buy the house a drink. Though a magnanimous gesture on Mrs. Duffy's part, I was her sole patron, so she joined me for a wee bit of the suds in a juice glass. Upon departing, I saluted buxom Mrs. Duffy and called out "Erin Gobraugh."

In Sandpoint I dialed the number Mark had given me. Brian Lojek answered. He told me I was but three blocks from their home and was expected. He mentioned that there weren't any extra rooms, but I was welcome to pitch my tent in their spacious backyard. I arrived to find Brian gone, but wife Julie, in the midst of canning peaches and baking banana bread, showed me to the backyard and introduced me to my yardmate, Tasha, a 90 lb. German shepherd.

Assisted by Tasha, I began making my bivouac and was nearly completed when Julie brought me a huge bowl of fresh peaches with cream. We sat at the picnic table nearby and talked about camping, skiing and bicycling. Julie told me Brian and her were going to a salmon bake that evening and I was invited. After hearing my story about the Alaskan salmon run, she laughed and assured me there would be plenty of hamburgers too. In addition to three hamburgers, I was allowed a sip of 8-year old, homemade corn liquor.

*Education is not the filling of a pail but the lighting of a fire.

Yeats

Before leaving the next morning, Julie supplied me with a sack of fresh peaches and a small loaf of her banana bread. If memory serves me right, both were eaten before I stopped to make camp that night.

~ ~ ~

A Financial Crisis

Fortunately, the winds of the past few days had blown the smoke out. The sky was clear blue as I pedaled south along the shore of Lake Pend d'Orielle. I must admit for a few days after leaving the Icefields Parkway in Canada everything my eyes beheld seemed prosaic, but as I passed slowly through the woodlands and bountiful agricultural areas of Idaho my interest and appreciation were rekindled. It has always been interesting and gratifying for me to see the 5% who produce the food for the 95%.

Coeur d'Alene proved to be a disappointment on two counts: 1. there wasn't any mail waiting for me at the Post Office. 2. I wasn't able to cash a check to bolster my dwindling finances. When I called my father the message on the answering machine informed me he was away on a golfing trip. Sitting on a bench outside the main Post Office I counted my money to find I had a grand total of $60.35. Now the question was how far could I go before being penniless. At least I had a two-week supply of freeze-dried food to see me through. So, only a chip shot away from Spokane, Washington, I called Bruce and Gail Hunt, the two bikers I met along the Icefields Parkway. No one answered the phone. A little depressed and frustrated with the money situation I cycled out of Coeur d'Alene headed west for Spokane, but didn't get far before the sun dropped below the horizon forcing me to

beat a hasty retreat to a field alongside the two-lane road I was traveling. As a consolation I enjoyed a peaceful, undisturbed camp in a field.

Stopping for breakfast outside Spokane at the Three B's restaurant
I questioned the friendly waitress about the meaning of the name
Coeur d'Alene. She thought it had something to do with the heart of
an owl, but after a conference with the other waitresses and the cook,
I was told it meant, "Heart of Awl." An awl being a small tool for
punching holes in leather. That's how the local Indians described
early traders or at least their practice of driving hard bargains, i.e.
men with hearts like an awl.

First thing in Spokane I called Bruce and Gail. This time Gail
answered and assured me their invite was still good, adding they were
anxious to hear more about my trip. Bruce got on the line to say hello
and give me directions to their home. I'd pedaled but a few blocks
before a station wagon passed. "Hey George," someone yelled. I
looked up to see Bruce at the wheel of the wagon. For a second I
thought they'd reconsidered, but Bruce emerged from the vehicle all
smiles. He said that after hanging up he remembered there was a
detour because of road construction. To avoid the possibility of me
getting lost he came to offer a ride. We quickly stowed my bike and
gear in the back of the wagon, then off we went. Can't beat that, pick
up and delivery, I joked. My bike was stored in Bruce's basement
workshop, equipped with all the tools needed to repair or even build a
bike. Afterwards, we sat around their kitchen table, sipping coffee,
munching Gail's chocolate chip cookies, and recounting our separate
routes from the Canadian Rockies to Spokane. After looking at the
phone book, I was disappointed to discover there wasn't a branch of
my bank in Spokane, so I was still in a bind as far as money went.
Numerous collect calls to my father in Reno, Nevada produced the
same message about his golf trip.

Putting money concerns aside for awhile, we repaired to Bruce's
shop to do a thorough tune-up on my bike. Later that afternoon, Bruce
drove me to a bike store owned by a friend of his. The proprietor
gladly accepted my out of state check for the tire I bought.

The only downside to my stay in Spokane was the constant reminder of my dwindling finances and my inability to deal with it. The irony was I had plenty of money in the bank, but no way of getting it out. I realized I should have bought an emergency supply of travelers checks. But this provided food for thought about my finances south of the border. In Mexico, Central, and South America I wouldn't be able to pedal up to an ATM for a quick cash fix. What would I do in South America if I was robbed or lost my money? Here in the U.S. I was close to help, but what would it be like in a foreign country if I were suddenly penniless. Additionally, here I didn't have to grapple with another language. I told myself I would have to be prepared to travel without credit cards, travelers checks, or a big wad of U.S. dollars. I had to learn to be creative, to use my brain to overcome setbacks, financial or otherwise. Afterall, I could always work in exchange for a meal or a place to pitch my tent.

Early Sunday morning, Bruce and his friend from the bike shop escorted me through the nearly deserted streets of Spokane to the monotonously straight, but spacious Highway 195 south. After they peeled off onto a secondary road I was left to pedal solo. I soon found I was bored to tears with the straight and not-so-narrow. Turning off at a junction I discovered a magnificent twisty, turny two-lane county road that passed by farmhouses, barns, and fields that stretched to the horizon. Every hour or two I'd find myself at a crossroads settlement consisting of an agricultural emporium selling everything from birdseed to posthole diggers. A gas station, grocery store, church, and sometimes a cafe were usually close by. If the little town also happened to be the county seat I'd stop to inspect the old-timey brick or stone courthouse with a sheriff's department or volunteer fire department attached. Depending on the prosperity of the region, I'd also see such rural icons as a John Deere farm equipment store or perhaps a Ford Agency selling trucks, automobiles and farm machinery, both new and used. As often as not, an American flag signaled a small post office. A cluster of 6 to 10-story grain silos, visible from miles away, would inevitably signal the approach of one of these hamlets.

Of course on Sunday these crossroads settlements were like ghost towns. A stray dog or a pickup truck parked with engine idling were sometimes the only signs of life. Somewhere in the midst of all the farms, fields, and silos I discovered I was exploring one of the richest agricultural areas in the U.S.—the Palouse, birthplace of the Appaloosa horse, known for its sturdiness and black and white markings. Surrounding these pastoral settlements for hundreds of miles in all directions were golden wheat fields, with an occasional dark brown square or rectangle of fallow land. Out amongst the fields, sitting like sugar bowls on kitchen tables, were white clapboard farmhouses.

~ ~ ~

The Mystery of Fritz

Somewhere along this zigzag county road while passing one of many farms, I pedaled by an apple tree laden with fruit. Though a wire fence separated the tree from the roadside, bushels of windfall apples lay in the ditch beside the road. A goodly amount had rolled onto the pavement forcing me to steer a precarious course amongst them. Suddenly recognizing this was an opportunity to stock up on fresh fruit I stopped and returned to the tree. A quick inspection and taste test proved the apples were ripe and juicy. At least two bushels were lying in the grass on my side of the fence. I selected a half dozen or so to stow in my panniers, then with a bit of gymnastic agility knocked down a few more from branches overhanging the fence. I filled my bags and mouth with as many apples as possible before resuming my ride. For all I knew this might be the only apple tree I'd see for hundreds of miles. Besides, there's something infinitely more tasty about a purloined apple right off the tree than a store bought one.

That afternoon while cycling through the rolling hills of wheat eating apples it dawned on me that I wouldn't be seeing any campgrounds along this route. Far from being a negative conclusion, I welcomed the opportunity to stop at one of the many farms along the way and ask permission to pitch my tent in a field or sleep in a hayloft. The only flaw in this scenario was that the farmhouses I could see from the road were situated a goodly distance down gated, gravel roads. In some instances these gates had industrial grade locks on them. Large dogs could be seen lurking behind a few fence gates. Consumed with these thoughts I came wheeling down a hill and there before me was a clump of trees, the only swatch of green in a sea of brown and gold. I could see neat, plowed, undulating furrows curving around the trees forming a semi-circle and creating an oasis in the desert of wheat. Closer, I could see a two-story white, wood-frame house hunkering back in the trees. There was even a white picket fence out front, though many of the pickets were missing. I stopped to investigate. The house not only looked abandoned, it looked haunted. Leaning my bike against a Poplar tree in the front yard, I turned around to see if anyone was watching me, then walked slowly up to the screened-in front porch where a door hung precariously from one hinge. I believe I even whistled a tune as a subtle warning to any trigger-fingered occupants. At the steps of the front porch, I stopped and called out, "Anybody at home." I repeated this a few times, but received only dead silence in reply. Perhaps an old retired farmer was living in squalor, a prisoner in a wheelchair dependent on an old friend to stop by once a week with groceries. The front door was ajar. I walked slowly to it, calling out again, "Anybody at home." Pulling the door open slowly, I was met with an explosion from within. Dozens of nesting pigeons erupted from the living room rafters, dive-bombing past me through the doorway and escaping out broken windows. Scared spitless, I stepped quickly outside and waited until everything was quiet again, then walked cautiously into the living room. It was empty of furnishings. The floor was covered with broken glass, old newspapers, assorted trash and copious amounts of pigeon droppings. Certainly, no one could be living here, I told myself as I walked around the empty room into the kitchen and out the back door. An old water pump stood rusting next to an empty root cellar.

After looking around for "No Trespassing" and "Posted" signs and finding none, I decided to make camp there for the night. I pushed my bike around to the back of the house, there to set up my tent on a small patch of grass between the house and a root cellar. Using the pantry inside the back door as my field kitchen, I set up my stove and began preparing dinner. While searching the kitchen drawers for matches I discovered a handwritten note, possibly left behind by the family who once lived there. I carefully unfolded the note and read it.

"Enclosed is $20 for expenses. Sorry to hear about Fritz. Yesterday on my way to Babe's I told Mom that I was worried about Fritz. Then Babe told me what happened. E.S.P. I guess. Write and tell me when harvest on the Green place is completed. Be sure (to) move two sixes on the old house porch. They were in the barn. See you partner.

Love, Dad."

I carefully refolded the note and placed it back in the drawer, like placing a piece of memorabilia in a time capsule. In a way, I felt like a latter-day Sherlock Holmes ensnared in a complex mystery. Who was Fritz, a husband, child, or pet? What had happened to him, her or it? Was Babe a relative or friend? And what did E.S.P. have to do with it? Was the note addressed to a son or daughter?

Finishing off my dinner in the deserted house I kept thinking about the note and the former occupants, wondering if a catastrophe had anything to do with the abandoned farm. Everytime I heard the infrequent sound of a truck or car pass on the road, I half expected it to pull up and stop in the driveway. The driver, an unshaven, aging farmer dressed in bib overalls and boots would enter the house and provide the missing clues that would solve the mystery and close the case. Except for the pigeons, no one returned. The peace and quiet pervading the farm was like a sedative. I crawled into my tent at sunset to sleep soundly and undisturbed beneath a sky with a million stars, next to a house with a million secrets.

~ ~ ~

In Praise of Luddites

That night I dreamed of Ned Ludd, mythical leader and reactionary who believed the emerging industrial revolution was anathema to the English way of life. With a growing group of like-minded people they stormed factories and sweatshops, there to bash and pommel the heartless, bloodless machines and looms that were replacing human workers. I was one of his fanatical lieutenants. The Luddites had a mission. We failed in the early 1800's. But through the magic of time travel, I was jettisoned into the 20th century. Just me and my bike-the last of the Luddites. I couldn't believe what I was seeing and experiencing. The world was machine-driven, except for me the semi-zealot, for even bicycles are machines. I didn't know where to start. I was overwhelmed. I hammered out a simple plan. I would recruit a band of new-age Luddites, probably from California. We'd arm ourselves with chains, pumps, and lengths of chrome-moly and carbon fiber tubing. Late of an evening we'd storm down on a KOA or Good Neighbor Sam RV park to batter and bludgeon the road monsters to Kingdom come. I woke with a start, before the mayhem started. A huge diesel truck had just passed over the horizon of the hill in front of the farmhouse. I washed my face with cold water from the nearby pump. I've had enough of this place, I counseled myself, time to go.

~ ~ ~

A Finishing School for Heifers

Walla Walla, according to a survey of local folk, had a number of meanings: Water-Water, Meeting-of-Waters, Father-of-Waters, or Big-Waters-that-Flow-to-the-Father-of-Waters.* The only point of agreement was that the name derived from local ~~Indians~~ Natives. Anyway, I was more concerned with finances than word origins. I had $2 to my name. I found the Western Union office on Main Street, called home, and was pleased to finally talk to the wandering golfer. He promised to wire $500 to me before his 11 a.m. tee off time. Much relieved, I pushed my bike across the street to a sidewalk cafe where I purchased a $1.50 cappuccino. The balance sheet now showed a mere 50 cents. A couple at the table next to me, noticing my laden bike asked if I was afraid someone would steal it. I told them it was securely locked, but even if it weren't I'd enjoy the comic relief provided by the unlucky thief who attempted to leap on the saddle of my 110 lb. behemoth and speed off, only to immediately fall over and be crushed to death beneath the load; or pedal a few yards, realize the folly of his larceny, abandon the bike, and run off on foot in search of better prospects.

Joining them at their table I learned Tom and Penny Williams lived in Walla Walla. In addition to being a breeder of heifer cows, Tom was also a city councilman. After a recap of my trip to date and previews of coming attractions, I explained my current situation and asked if they could put me up for the night if my money didn't arrive that day. A real possibility, I added, considering the distorted priorities of golfers. They immediately proclaimed that I would be welcome whether my money arrived or not. While enjoying another cappuccino, courtesy of Tom, Penny drew me a map that would direct me to their nearby home.

A couple of hours later with a new infusion of capital and armed with Penny's map, I pedaled up a tree-lined street, right out of the 30's, flanked on both sides by meticulously cared for Victorian homes. The Williams' house, in the middle of the block, was a stately, two-story

* The Gualala (pronounced Wa·la·la) River in Mendocino County, California means, in the local Native tongue, Where The Waters Meet. How did 2 separate Tribes arrive at almost the same word & its meaning over 1000 miles apart?

lady adorned with much oak, brass, and beveled, stained glass. I coasted down the two-strip cement drive to the back of the house. A few knocks on the screen door on the back porch, summoned both Tom and Penny. They lead me to the two-car detached garage, where I parked my bike and with their help carried a few items back to the house, with Suzie, a "Heinz 57" cow dog in the lead. After I settled in my upstairs room, I rejoined the Williams' at the kitchen table for conversation and a snack.

Following some preventive maintenance on my bike, Penny called me to an early dinner of Pasta, vegetables, and salad. Over dinner, Tom explained his unique business. He described himself as one of the largest dairy farmers in the west without a dairy herd and characterized his business as a finishing school for heifers (young cows that have not calved). Holstein heifers were trucked to his spacious farm outside Walla Walla from all the western states. There Tom and his farmhands fattened them up on a special diet, then artificially inseminated the cows.

After birth, the calves and cows were shipped back to their respective dairy farms there to lead productive, cost effective lives. Tom suggested a tour of his "finishing school" the next day, if time allowed. I eagerly accepted the invitation. After dinner, Tom and Penny excused themselves to attend a city council meeting, leaving me and Suzie to fend for ourselves.

After breakfast the next morning we loaded my bike into the back of Tom's vintage 1953 International pickup. With Suzie on the seat between us we drove out to Tom's spread to visit 2,500 Holstein heifers, each with a numbered identification tag in its ear, enabling Tom to track its history of care and feeding on a computer. After a brief, but aromatic tour, I mounted my bike and cycled away, whistling "Good Morning America How Are you," southwest toward the Columbia River, stopping in the little town of Touchet for a blueberry pancake breakfast that proved to be the best pancakes I'd eat on my entire trip.

But, I had doubts about how my day would go. Just before sitting down to my pancakes I used the restroom to relieve myself. Somehow, during this usually mundane task, I managed to drop my wallet into the urinal giving it a thorough baptism in the process. Instead of blowing a fuse, I calmly retrieved the wallet and washed it off under the tap. I'm not sure what kind of moral, if any, can be drawn from the incident? The wallet baptism notwithstanding, my second breakfast was superb. The two ladies running the cafe knew Tom and Penny, who recommended the place. They kept my coffee cup full during our chat about life in rural America.

~ ~ ~

Victor The Pedaling Preacher

Not far out of Touchet I left the rolling farm country behind, exchanging golden fields of wheat and green pastures dotted with dairy herds for the more prosaic landscape of earth tones dominated by sagebrush.

I got my first glimpse of the Columbia River at Wallala. I was astonished at its size, looking more like an inland sea than a river. I judged its width at 10 to 15 miles in places, perhaps more. The Columbia drains 259,000 square miles in northwest U.S. and Canada: 219,000 square miles in the U.S. alone. Rising in British Columbia it works its way south some 1210 miles through Washington State and Oregon, eventually to the Pacific Ocean. Its watery voyage is second only to the Mississippi. Far below my vista point huge ships and barges pushed packets of flatbottom cargo boats up and down its length and breadth.

With an Oregon bicycle map, compliments of Penny Williams, I chose Highway 84 on the south side of the river for my route through the Columbia gorge. Some miles east on Hwy 84 I stopped for a rest at the junction of Hwy 37. A no man's land, save for a grove of shade trees.

While eating a peanut butter and jelly sandwich and engrossed in my map, a cyclist pulled up and stopped in the shade. His bike an ancient, though serviceable Schwinn. A large assortment of bags and boxes were fastened at various places on the bike frame without the help of racks or panniers. The gentlemen had long hair and a beard. A straw hat provided protection from the sun. A shiny blue serge sports coat was worn over faded, blue bib overalls. After leaning his bike against a tree, he walked over and sat on a log across from me. He introduced himself as Victor the Pedaling Preacher. He said he wasn't affiliated with any particular church or religion, as he didn't like to play favorites; he was just a traveling two-wheeled evangelist. As it was warm, he took off his coat, allowing me to make a quick inventory of the tattoos on his arms. Of particular interest was a long-tailed devil holding a spear, this on his right forearm. All, I guessed, were the crude work of an amateur tattoo artist. To say the least, Victor did not look like your garden-variety preacher. After rummaging in a plastic bag hanging from the handlebars of his bike, he returned to the log with an 8 x 10 manila envelope. He carefully withdrew a sheet of paper and handed it to me. It was a certificate of divinity, obtained by correspondence courses, verifying that Victor was an ordained minister and graduate of the Reformed Bible Ministry in Florida.

Victor returned the certificate to the envelope, telling me he had been spreading the word along the highways and byways for the past four years. He didn't have any money, food, or water. God will provide, he assured me. In this instance anyway, George provided—a P & J sandwich and cup of water. For all his wild and crazy appearance, he seemed to be sincere. In exchange for the sandwich and water, Victor read passages from the Bible, this while chewing the sandwich and slurping water. After our luncheon, he closed the bible and announced that I had been "chosen." But he never fully explained what I'd been chosen for. He looked like a dehydrated scarecrow, so I gave him two cookies and an apple.

"Praise the Lord." He crooned.

"I'm curious, Victor, what have I been chosen to do?"

"You've been anointed."

"Okay, but for what?"

"It doesn't matter, He'll show you. Look for signs."

"You mean metaphorical signs, like burning bushes say."

"The ways of the Lord are mysterious," he said then threw his apple core into the bushes.

I was about to tell him about my dream of Luddites and smashed up motorhomes, but thought better of it. For all of his cryptic palaver, he had me convinced I just might have been chosen. Perhaps I was "chosen" to donate a couple of bucks to his ministry, but I never found out. As we sat in silence, I watched a station wagon pull off the road on the other side of the highway and come to a stop in a cloud of dust. The driver removed a cardboard box from the back of the wagon, then marched with it to the base of a sandy ledge 20 yards or so from the station wagon. He set the box on the ground and returned to the back of the wagon, where he removed a rifle from a scabbard. Draped over the hood with the rifle, he began firing at the box. I winced. I hoped there wasn't anything alive in the box. I was about to comment on the disturbance, when Victor jumped up, got on his bike, and started pedaling furiously toward Walla Walla. The rifle fire continued so I quickly packed up and headed west for Umatilla, not knowing what the riflemen might train his sights on next. I wanted to be long gone when he lost interest in shooting at the box.

From Umatilla west it felt like I was riding in a wind tunnel with some unseen sadistic hand turning the power up all day. At one point I was in my granny gear clocking a mere 5-mph. I estimated the constant headwind was blowing at 30-40 mph. Whenever I stopped at a rest area or service station some helpful motorist would tell me I should be headed east. To make matters worse the surrounding country was flat, devoid of anything resembling a windbreak that I could get behind to enjoy a few minutes rest out of the wind. At mid-afternoon I spotted a train trestle over a dirt road headed down to the river. I stopped under the trestle for a rest from both the wind and the road. To pass the time I paged through a book of essays I'd purchased in Walla Walla for 25 cents. I began reading an essay, appropriately titled, "On Going a Journey," by William Hazlitt (1778—1830). It begins, *"One of the pleasentest things in the world is going a journey; but I like to go by myself. I can enjoy society in a room; but out of doors nature is company enough for me. I am then never less alone than when alone."* (From Great Essays, Washington Square Press, New York, 1954, Houston Peterson, Ed.)

~ ~ ~

Still More Travel Advisories

Wind is the biker's worst enemy. It saps your strength and energy, both physical and mental. It turns you into a raving bad tempered, maniac. The only suggestion I have for relieving the misery of riding in the wind is to swear out loud, the louder the better. Be creative no one will hear you. You'll soon find yourself laughing at yourself. For awhile anyway.

~ ~ ~

The Old Curiosity Shop

In Madras, Oregon I secured a room for $15 at the "Historic Madras Hotel, Bed & Breakfast, and Antique Shop." At least that's how the business card characterized the place. It was like something out of a Charles Dickens novel. In addition to the above, it was a retirement hotel and home for migrant farm workers. In order to get to my room on the first floor I had to squeeze my bike carefully through aisles of "antiques." A better description of the "memorabilia" scattered liberally around the lobby would be: old furniture piled high with magazines, coke bottles, newspapers, used clothing, thousands of 45 and 78 rpm records, assorted farm equipment and tools, dozens of 8 track tapes, dishes, pots and pans, plus hundreds of other items that have passed into the twilight zone between curios and junk.

Ozzie, the owner of the hotel, blamed his wife for the clutter. Groaning and shaking his head, he declared that hell would freeze over before he'd touch the "antiques." From the looks of things, neither Ozzie nor his wife had touched them for a very long time.

While settling into my room without bath, I got a visit from my neighbor across the hall, 80-yr old Jenny Pruitt who was recuperating from a bleeding ulcer. Always the patient listener, Jenny told me, among other things, that the 50-foot long motorhome blocking the hotel front entrance was hers and she was going to drive over to Portland when she felt better and pick up her boyfriend, then they were off to Mexico for the winter. I never did get a chance to ask her why she was renting a room in the hotel when she had a palatial motorhome. Before leaving she invited me to watch the Olympics on color TV in her room.

After dinner at the Stag restaurant across the street, I repaired to the bar for a glass of beer and a chance to watch some of the Olympics. Just as the big swimming race between Matt Biondi and the Albatross was about to start the guy sitting next to me at the bar decided he wanted to talk. While chain smoking, he launched into a monologue about smoking. When he was a young buck he used to roll his own cigarettes, then he started buying store bought cigarettes. He even chewed tobacco for awhile, before changing to cigars. His grandpa was a pipe smoker. Died at age 97 with a pipe in his mouth. Actually, the pipe fell out of his mouth when he breathed his last breath. That's how grandma knew he was dead. She wrapped the pipe up in tissue paper and buried it along with grandpa. With my beer glass drained, I excused myself. So much for the Olympics.

~ ~ ~

A Down Home Haircut

I rolled into Bend, Oregon late in the evening. One of the first things that caught my eye on main street was a neon lit pizza parlor. While eating my first pizza in months I got to chatting with Brent Laws, regional director of Ducks Unlimited. He told me one of the best bike rides in the area was the century loop around Mt. Batchelor. I would find plenty of campgrounds, beautiful scenery, and good fishing, he promised. At some point in our conversation I told Brent I'd made the decision to do my biking odyssey on April 1st. He was quick to point out that April 1st was also known as April Fools Day. Before I had a chance to ponder the significance of that piece of information another local, Kevin McDonald, joined us at our table. Kevin was an engineer with an electronics firm near Bend. He liked the small town atmosphere of Bend and the many opportunities for enjoying the outdoors. His passion these days was sailing a catamaran. While getting an update on the Olympics from Kevin, Brent excused himself to attend a meeting.

Over a second glass of beer, Kevin asked where I planned to camp that night. After admitting I hadn't even thought about it, he suggested I stay at a house he shared with another engineer at his company. His housemate was away so there was plenty of room. He gave me directions, pointing out that his place was just on the edge of town.

Camp McDonald was one of the plushest campsites on my trip. Not only did I have a roof over my head and mattress on a carpeted floor, additionally I was surrounded by a hi-tech entertainment center bristling with giant screen TV, state-of-the-art stereo system; plus standard amenities, like a hot shower, refrigerator, and kitchen, plus a hot tub on the back porch. But the icing on the cake was the "no fee" camping policy. We sat up talking and watching TV until the Olympic coverage ended for the night.

Next day, I cycled into Bend to restock my food stores and find a used paperback bookstore recommended by Kevin. Frost on the lawn that morning signaled the beginning of autumn, as did low-flying wedges of Canadian honkers headed south for warmer climes. Watching those flapping V's pass in review, I wondered if they'd beat me to Mexico.

Attired in sweats, windbreaker, gloves and wool socks, I cycled a circuitous route through quiet neighborhoods trying to get a feel for the town. Smoke curling from chimneys scented the crisp air with the smell of burning pine whilst a warming sun rose slowly in an azure sky.

While negotiating the side streets of Bend I found myself in front of Jim's Barbershop. As good a place as any to ask for directions to the bookstore, I guessed. From the sidewalk I could see "Jim" snipping away at the head of a white-smocked customer ensconced in the traditional nickel-plated, porcelain barber's chair.

Inside, I felt awkward. A half dozen middle-aged men, most in plaid wool shirts and jeans, sat reading or talking back and forth to Jim. No one seemed to notice me. Suddenly, I felt the shagginess of my hair and beard untouched by human hands for two and a half months. Instead of asking directions to the bookstore, I walked slowly across worn and crinkling linoleum to the far end of the room and slipped quietly into a chair. Cigarette and pipe smoke hung in the air like a cloud. Noticing the table beside my chair was piled with hunting and fishing magazines, I picked a *Sports Afield* up and leafed through it. I made furtive looks around the room, noticing the absence of hair dryers and slick pictures of pouting, sulking European men and women sporting avant-garde hairdos, often found in trendy hair salons. What I did see were calendars showing huge buck deer with enormous antlers or fat trout leaping out of pools of water with artificial flies or spinners stuck in their jaws. There were even a few "girlie" calendars with the name and address of a local auto parts store. I also spied a hand-lettered sign in back of Jim advertising haircuts for $5. And there was music. The strangled sounds of guitars and fiddles oozed from a small plastic Philco radio on the shelf in back of Jim. Occasionally, a chuckle, cough, or curse escaped from behind a newspaper blocking the upper torso of the reader. No *New York Times* or *Wall Street Journal* here, the front pages of these papers had photos of award winning bulls, quarter horses, or group shots of Rotarians and Legionnaires.

Between haircuts I watched as Jim pitched quarters against the baseboard with departing customers for tips. Judging from the jingle in his side pocket, Jim was a consistent winner.

In the barber chair at last, Jim pinned a white sheet around my neck.

"How would you like it?"

"Just a trim."

Engrossed in a *Field and Stream* story about rampaging Grizzlies, I listened to the snip of scissors and hum of electric clippers. Soon the sheet was unpinned, my collar turned up, and the chair swiveled around to the mirror. For the first time in months I could see my ears; they looked and felt elephantine. Certainly no Samson, I did however feel vulnerable and defenseless. While I stared at myself in the mirror, Jim brushed off my shirt with a small whiskbroom.

"Say, where's that used bookstore," I said handing Jim a five dollar bill.

"Down to the corner and half block over." He answered placing the bill in the cash register drawer.

I stepped outside to suffer what I thought would be the finger-pointing ridicule of the locals, but no one even looked twice at me. Except for the beard, I felt like a young recruit ready for basic training. As I was about to straddle my bike, I heard the galonking of geese overhead and stopped to watch as a broken V circled overhead then proceeded to land in a park alongside the Deschutes River. Smart honkers these, no shotgun totting hunters here to greet them with buckshot, just bread-crust throwing toddlers with mothers warning them not to sit in the doodoo.

The air was clear and crisp as I pedaled out to Mt. Bachelor the next day after an early breakfast with Kevin McDonald before he headed off to work. A bit disoriented on my way out of town, I stopped at a small grocery store to ask for help. The cashier had me turning in so many directions I felt like a blindfolded person in a game of "pin the tail on the donkey." However, only a half block from the store I almost ran into a sign pointing the way to Mt. Bachelor. The road was excellent, with little traffic, but with a long, gradual climb, all 23 miles to the summit. With the sun warming my back and clear skies ahead, I geared down proceeding at 5—6 mph.

Checking my rearview mirror occasionally, I noticed another biker coming up behind me. Minutes later a young lady rolled alongside and said good morning. Julie Winokur, a writer for *Travel & Leisure Magazine* in New York City was on a trip west scouting stories. An enthusiastic cyclist, she naturally brought her road bike with her. We rode together for about 45 minutes before I had to stop and catch my breath. We used the time to chat and exchange addresses. Julie wished me luck, then turned around and headed back to Bend. About an hour later I achieved the 5,000-ft.* pass. From the summit I began a gradual descent through meadows sparkling with crystal clear streams.

As soon as I saw Devil's Lake I knew I had to camp there. A piece of shimmering glass set in a green trough of pines, it looked like the

*.94 mile.

cover of a magazine. Rolling into the camp on a dirt and gravel road I was pleased to see it was a walk-in campsite. As the place was nearly deserted, I rolled my bike to the most picturesque spot close to the lakeshore and set up camp. Nearby, an icy cold stream flowed into the lake. The warming sun made me sleepy so I crawled into my tent for a nap.

~ ~ ~

Punk Munks at Devil's Lake

I heard the all too familiar sounds of scrabbling, clawing, and scratching. Reluctantly, I pried my eyes open. Peering out of my tent I saw not one, not two, but a gang of punk chipmunks ravaging my panniers and generally raising hell with the things I'd left on the picnic table. Mind you, these were not your run-of-the-mill chipmunks; they were an advanced strain of state campground, end of the summer, pigged out, 20% body fat freeloaders with bizarre haircuts, sunglasses, black tank tops and itty-bitty earrings.

I scrambled out of the tent to save my threatened larder. I was shocked and repulsed by the scene before me. A handful of punk-munks were lounging on the rocks at the edge of my campsite, soaking up the sun and listening to a micro-ghetto blaster, most likely purloined from an unsuspecting summer camper. They barely noticed me. Instead they brazenly mocked me, bobbing their heads and snapping their fingers in time to rap music.

Tired and irritable, I chased a bunch of the rogues off my bike then re-zipped the panniers they had opened and plundered. Trail mix, chocolate covered raisins, and dried fruit lay scattered on the ground.

Feeling a bit intimidated, I crawled back into my tent to resume my nap. Slowly drifting off I was rousted again by the sound of pebbles hitting my tent and the unmistakable clicking of a freewheel. FREE-WHEEL! I poked my head from the tent again to see two burly, steroid pumped punk-munks trying to make off with my bike while a few of their comrades were in the process of unzipping the panniers again.

Sonsofbitches, I yelled, bolting from the tent, scattering the punk-munks to the rocks and the security of their gang. There, they ridiculed and jeered me. I grabbed a slender tree branch and took a few steps forward. Suddenly, the rap music stopped. They jumped to their feet bristling with defiance. I took a few tentative steps forward, slashing the air with a tree branch like a swordsman. Undaunted, they formed ranks and slunk toward me. I froze. I was badly outnumbered. Sure, they were just punk-munks, but…A gravelly voice, exactly like John Wayne's, shattered the ominous silence, like a rock striking a plate glass window.

"Well, pilgrim, got yerself in quite a fix."

I wheeled about to see a park ranger, 6' 8", if an inch and a broad as a Winnebago. He ambled up alongside me, his right hand hanging loose at his side. Out of the corner of my eye I saw a punk-munk make a move. Blam, blam, blam. The air filled instantly with gun smoke. He'd cut down a baker's dozen, the rest turned tail and ran for their lives.

I stood there with mouth gaping. With a practiced twirl the ranger holstered his 45.

"Been after that pack of varmints all summer," he drawled.

Tipping his Stetson, he wheeled quickly about, jumped in his four-wheel drive jeep and rode off into the blazing ball of afternoon sun. Peace, quiet, and justice descended on Devil's Lake like a curtain.

I jolted awake and shook my head, then looked cautiously outside. My bike was unmolested. From that day forward I've never looked at a chipmunk quite the same again.

Next morning there was ice in my water bottles and a thin skim of ice clinging to the shore of the lake. Cool, crisp air notwithstanding, the sun gradually warmed me. It was so quiet I could hear pinecones drop through the branches of trees and hit the ground with a muffled thump.

After a breakfast of oatmeal, I settled down with my journal and a second cup of coffee.

~ ~ ~

The Wayward Couch

For no reason in particular I remembered a story Kevin McDonald recently told me. We were talking about traveling in general, then touched on the subject of hitchhiking, a mode of travel I had some experience with when in college. He said that sometimes it seemed impossible to get a lift even though you were in a great location and hundreds of vehicles passed by. During his college days, Kevin had two friends who set out to hitch from Logan, Utah to Chicago. It was the end of the spring semester 1987. With backpacks and sleeping bags, Mike and Jim struck out on a trip across the states, stopping here and there to camp, sightsee, and explore.

On a beautiful, warm Spring morning, Kevin gave his buddies a lift to the edge of town where the interstate passed by heading east. With smiles on their faces and adventure in their hearts they stuck out their thumbs, convinced they'd be hunkered down in the back of a pickup in five or ten minutes. Traffic sped by as though they were invisible. Time ground to a halt. They turned into stone pillars with extended thumbs. Smiles turned to anxious, tight frowns. Hours passed and still no ride. They were now hungry and tired. While eating their tuna fish sandwiches, they came up with a plan. One person would hitch, while the other rested, read a paperback, or dozed. After a few hours of the "plan" a disagreement developed over "who" was doing most of the hitching and "who" was doing most of the reading and dozing. As a compromise they agreed to shoulder their packs and start walking and hitching. Perhaps the karma wasn't right in that spot, one of the collegians suggested.

They walked and walked, hitched and hitched. Ten miles down the road they were once again hungry. Also, their feet were hot, tired, and blistered from new hiking boots. The romance of the open road was wearing thin. They ate more tuna fish sandwiches and finished off the last of their drinking water. It was hot too. Neither had thought to bring along any sunscreen. Wearing his Oakland A's baseball cap, Mike chided Jim for not having enough sense to remember headgear. Jim did not take kindly to this barb. They walked along now in silence, not even lifting their arms to thumb passing cars. Up ahead by the side of the road they spied an abandoned couch. Approaching it warily, they commented on its near-new condition and wondered why it had been left there. Mike and Jim set their packs down and sunk into the inviting softness of the cushions. Removing their hiking boots they massaged complaining feet and rethought their ambitious travel plans. Jim shared his last Snicker's bar with Mike. After a few minutes they talked about their luckless day. They even laughed about it. As they talked and relaxed, a big pickup truck pulled over and stopped not far from them. They suspected the owner of the couch had returned to claim it. Hastily, they pulled on their boots as the pickup backed slowly toward them. The driver looked out the window on the passenger side and yelled, "How far you going?"

The two young men looked at each other gleefully. Jim ran to the side of the truck. "We're headed for Chicago."

"Come on get in," the driver said.

They stowed their packs in the back of the truck and clambered into the cab.

The driver looked over his shoulder. "Hey, ain't you going to take your couch?"

Smiling at each other, Mike and Jim got out of the truck and quickly loaded the couch into the back of the pickup. Off they went, two college guys and a couch. Nine rides and two weeks later they arrived in Chicago. On the outskirts of the "windy city" they sold the couch to the proprietor of a fruit stand who used it to watch ball-games on a portable TV when not waiting on customers.

~ ~ ~

Yellow Canoe on Blue Water

After two days of hiking and camping at Devil's Lake I worked up enough energy to pedal 11.04 miles farther to Hosmer Lake, my second shortest day on the entire trip. It was worth the effort. A few miles down a dirt road, I found a lake surrounded by a thick pine forest. A fringe of cato'nine tails along the shoreline on the west side of the lake provided shelter and forage for migrating ducks and geese. Again, the lakeside campground was sparsely populated. The main attraction was its status as a fly fishing only lake. Canoeists armed with rods and reels dotted the lake like a picture on a calendar. Once again I could taste the succulent flesh of trout cooked over a wood fire.

After setting up camp beside the lake, I assembled my fishing gear then hiked around the shoreline looking for a likely spot. Except for the hum of a few hardy cicadas and the occasional quacking of ducks, it was mountain quiet. Out on the lake I watched a few fishermen floating up to their chests in rubber inner tubes, their arms whipping back and forth sending long fly lines out on the water.

After battling my way through marsh and thicket, over rocks and under logs I found the perfect spot affording me enough room to back-haul my flyline. Given the fact that all the signs were ideal, I still wonder why I didn't get a bite, let alone a trout dinner. At any rate, I supped on freeze dried Chili, instead of the much preferred grilled trout.

While idling about the campfire after dinner, my neighbor came over with two beers. Dave Kelly of Oregon City, Oregon was the owner of one of the canoes I'd seen skimming silently across the lake earlier that day. He offered a test ride in his one-person canoe. With an hour or two of daylight left, we made our way to the boat launch where Dave's green canoe was beached. After a briefing on the basics of paddling, I helped push it into the shallow water at the boat ramp. I was amazed at the lightness of the canoe, figuring it weighed less than my fully loaded bike. Dave explained the narrow, short hull was designed with the advanced canoeist in mind. With a pair of Dave's knee-high boots on I made the precarious transition from land to canoe. After adjusting the bucket-style seat I took the super lightweight paddle in hand and zipped across the water effortlessly. After an exhilarating tour of the lake I returned to the launch area, where Dave waited to assist me in extricating myself from the canoe without mishap.

We returned to my camp to enjoy a blazing campfire, two more beers and a lengthy conversation about fishing and life in general.

Two days later I completed the century loop around Mt. Bachelor, breaking the 3,000-mile mark in the process. In the small town of Chemult, Oregon I found a $2 campsite in a trailer park, complete with hot shower and laundromat; two amenities I was in much need of. At a dinner/map session at the cafe across the road, I decided to proceed west through Crater Lake* National Park, then southwest through the Rogue River Valley.

A week or so later I was back in California. At McBride Springs Campground on the forested flank of Mt. Shasta I made camp and looked with anticipation to meeting two biking comrades from home. Pete Peterson and his wife Vangie were to rendezvous with me at Mt. Shasta for a tour down to Lassen National Park.

* The deepest lake in the U.S.
Lake Tahoe is 2nd.

The Sacred Mountain

After biking 3,371.9 miles from Alaska to northern California on my way to Tierra Del Fuego I needed a place to rest and recharge my cerebral batteries. I was in the town of Mount Shasta, California to meet two friends for a bike tour to Mt. Lassen, but found myself in the awkward position of being ahead of schedule (I had approximately five days to kill before my friends arrived) therefore I needed a place to set up a base camp and find some things to do. Two not so demanding requirements by anyone's standards. Being a bit road weary and trying to fight off feelings of alienation and rootlessness one sometimes experiences on solo treks, I was searching, and had been searching for weeks, for a magical, comfortable camp, that special place both in the woods, but close to town, with good water, toilets, firewood, and yet close to the road and not more than a 30-minute ride to a pub.

Knowing full well this Oz-like spot didn't exist, but nevertheless searching for it, I stopped at the tourist information center when I pedaled into Shasta and picked up a map and information packet. Among this assortment of brochures, flyers, and pamphlets, was a curious five-page mimeographed handout titled *"The Sacred Mountain."* On the lawn beside the Chamber of Commerce I rested, munched trail mix, and skimmed over the handout. According to the author, Shasta was one of seven "sacred mountains." Who designated Mt. Shasta as such was never explained, but I learned a dozen religious cults, sects, and philosophical societies had established communities on the slopes or nearby environs to be within close proximity to Shasta's spiritual force field. Beside the more conventional organizations like Buddhists and Yogis, there were a number of lesser known groups none of which I had the slightest knowledge of, to include: Knights of the White Rose, Radiant School of Seekers and Servers, Sanada and Sanat Kumara, League of Voluntary Effort (LOVE), Blue Flamers, Saint Germain Foundation, and Brotherhood of the White Temple.

Also included in the Chamber information packet was a Forest Service guide that, to my delight, listed two campgrounds on the mountain. One was on the lower slope, the second closer to the top of the 14,162′ mountain.* To my further delight, the closest campground, McBride Springs, was only 3 miles from town. McBride Springs could be my abbreviated Walden, my healing place, my R & R center. Eagerly, I leaped on my heavily laden bike and began the trek to the holy mountain.

Barely a mile from town I was drenched with sweat and gulping water from my dwindling supply. It was hot, close to 85 degrees, and the road to McBride Springs was, naturally, uphill. The 3-mile climb wouldn't have been bad, but for the fact that I'd climbed close to 23 miles of hills already that day. I chugged onwards and upwards with glacial speed, stopping occasionally to drink water and wipe my dripping brow. Ah, but the sacred one was looming closer, its peaks patched with snow, its ice fields glistening like jewels in the afternoon sun. Soon, I thought, I would be able to make obeisance to the holy one in the privacy of my own camp. As I rounded a curve, the entrance to McBride Springs came into view motivating me to pedal harder. I noticed my bike computer showed the campground was actually 4.6 miles from town not 3.0 miles, but that was just a small oversight, still to a cyclist that extra 1.6 miles is a considerable distance, especially at the end of a long day.

Hot, tired, and thirsty, I pulled slowly into the campground with visions of spiritual and physical renewal, tranquility and succor dancing in my head. I was eager to encounter the Holy One's mystical ambiance, perhaps experience some kind of vision, however modest.

What do I hear as I pedal into the campground? Celestial voices? Prayer bells? No, I swear I hear music. Yes. It got louder and louder. The wind had shifted bringing its full effect to me. It was Dire Straits exploding from some unseen stereo mega-blaster hidden in the depths of the forest and seemingly wired to every tree and bush. If it

* 2.68 miles high & only 320 feet shorter than Mt. Whitney, the tallest peak in the lower 48.

had been any other music besides Dire Straits I believe I would have pulled my Swiss Army knife, charged into the forest and plucked out the very heart of the diabolical monster producing those sounds. Sounds I might add that seemed so out of context with time and place. But Dire Straits was a favorite. As I looked around I became even more confused and disoriented. From all appearances the campground was empty, save for one lone dome tent pitched up the hill among scattered Ponderosa pines.

As an alternative to a possible confrontation, I decided to find a campsite as far away from the source of the music as possible, thereby diluting it to a kind of wilderness Musak. I pushed my bike into campsite #2; a secluded spot surrounded by towering fir, hemlock, and pine and propped the bike against the picnic table. It was a beautiful site, not only did I have an unobstructed view of the western slope of the mountain, but also the site was carpeted with pine needles and had two fireplaces. Water and restrooms were only a few yards away. I was a happy camper. BUT, I decided to recon the area JUST in case there was a more commodious campsite available.

In my wanderings about the campground I drew closer and closer to the source of the music. Checking out the sites along the way and not finding anything better than my first choice, I stopped at a water spigot for a drink and chance to soak my handkerchief. As I looked around, my eyes came to rest on what I believed to be the source of the rock music—a beat up Van, half-concealed under the pine and fir trees, doors flung wide open. I could hear people, at least faint murmurs, when the wind shifted or a song ended, but I couldn't see anyone. For a few seconds I thought about marching up to the Van and demanding they lower the volume of the music, arguing that it was neither compatible nor conducive to the wilderness experience. But on second thought I realized that any demand, no matter how justified, would only serve to increase the volume instead of the reverse effect—sort of a Newtonian law of volume. Additionally, there might have been an ugly scene filled with profanity, threats, counter-threats, and possibly even bloodshed. Besides all this, the purpose of my retreating to the mountain was to relax and renew my inner being amidst the natural beauty and spiritual power of the mountain. Fisticuffs and split lips were not part of the renewal process.

Satisfied I'd found the ideal campsite, I returned to #2 and began setting up camp.

Not 30 minutes later, while sipping freshly brewed coffee, I heard a voice call in back of me.

"Hello there. Enjoying the mountain?"

I turned and faced a man of about 40-years old. Strapped to his back was a vintage, shabby aluminum-frame backpack. Webbing, useless straps, and strings dangled from it like the tentacles of a giant squid. For all of its scarred and well-used appearance the pack looked empty.

"Yes, how 'bout yourself," I said.

The interloper approached with a bouncy step. The first thing I noticed was his conspicuous smile. Though broad and friendly, it was nevertheless empty of teeth, at least the well formed, glistening teeth I'd come to associate with healthy outdoor people. What I observed between his grinning lips was a series of battered, discolored stumps that looked like they'd been brutally punched or kicked out. My own tongue automatically searched out and caressed the side of a gold crown installed only days before leaving for Alaska. In complete contrast to this scene of dental devastation was a single, intact tooth jutting out of the left side of his mouth like a broken picket. His Polo shirt was so sweat stained and dirty I couldn't tell what color it was. Blue gabardine pants were wrinkled, worn, and equally dirty. He had tennis shoes on that looked two sizes too big and were laced with green twine. Although he wasn't wearing socks, the darkness of the skin showing between tennis shoe and hiked pant cuffs suggested beige or light brown. Salt and pepper hair was cut back short, but with such unevenness and randomness I suspected he cut it himself or had a visually impaired friend cut it for him. He was unshaven, unwashed, unkept, but did not smell, though all visual signs suggested gross foul odor. Dark eyes were buried in a brow slanted and twisted by years of nearsightedness. Two black caterpillar eyebrows heightened the effect.

He was about 5' 8" tall, 150 lbs. and for all the critical and negative aspects of his appearance, he looked quite healthy and happy. He moved closer, clutching a plastic shopping bag to his shirt. He asked where I'd come from and was both amazed and impressed with my bike story. He talked fast, spewing out words that formed statements, questions, and exclamations—none of which seemed to have any relationship to the other. I had difficulty getting a word in edgewise. After a minute I gave up.

From the plastic bag clasped to his chest he pulled a handful of something he called Pennyroyal, a bouquet of scented wildflowers. He offered me a handful for $1.50, then before I could say a word, pulled out four pinecones available at $1 each. As the ground around my campsite was littered with pinecones of larger dimensions than the ones he displayed I declined his offer, adding that unfortunately for both of us, I was nearly broke. He was not disappointed. I had a feeling he'd been turned down before, many times.

His name was Jack Scharf. Shaking hands, I introduced myself. I returned to my chores of starting a fire and heating up corn dogs. Jack plugged the breach of silence with an endless monologue involving economics, metaphysics, scientific-positivism, Einstein, Bohr, Descartes, Muir, Emerson-his list of subject material seemed infinite. Eventually he somehow segued to the subject of Darwin and the voyage of the H.M.S. Beagle, *The Origin of Species*, tectonic plate theory, travel in Patagonia, yadada, yadada.

Figure 5: The enigmatic Jack Scharf

Jack was sitting on my picnic table by now, backpack still on, talking a mile-a-minute. I attended the corn dogs. While trying to listen to
him and respond the campfire went out. Jack kept calling me
Hawkins, like it was a title or rank—Captain, Sir, whatever. Relighting
the fire, I was suddenly aware the rock music had ceased. I handed
Jack a corn dog. He stripped the batter casing off and ate it, leaving a
naked uncooked hot dog on a stick. In the midst of reciting Gerard
Manley Hopkins' poem, "*Spring and Fall*," he started roasting the hot
dog over the flames. I did likewise. Somehow we got on the subject of
literature. Contemporary—Jack felt Stephen King was a genius, his
style was junk but underneath all those words was pure genius. He
recommended Jackie Collins and Danielle Steele. I winced, confessing
I'd not read either writer. The hot dogs were severely burned, inciner-
ated, but we ate them like candy. Jack recommended **Death on The
Installment Plan**, by Celine. Herman Melville was the greatest
American writer, according to Jack. He bombarded me with a melange
of names and titles—Sartre, Thoreau, **Return of The Native**, Erica Jong,
James Joyce, **Les Miserables**, D.H. Lawrence. While passing through
Taos, New Mexico a few years back, Jack discovered a collection of
modernistic paintings by D.H. Lawrence in a Lodge owned by a lisp-
ing Austrian. As he babbled, Jack managed to eat half a bag of my
Chips Ahoy. I consumed the other half. Suddenly, Jack remembered he
was supposed to be somewhere to help someone cook a big dinner. He
must leave. He must cook. He must "vibe a contact." Now! He was
going to the Mojave Desert, but not RIGHT now, when the time was
right, only then would he leave. The mountain will channel the vibes,
he whispered. As he stood up and prepared to go, we heard bellowing
from the trees near my camp. A guy about 30ish, bearded, long hair,
naked from waist up, arms, chest, and back covered with tattoos
(Harley-Davidson eagles, snakes, macho messages) crashed out of the
trees and stomped toward us. He looked pissed. "Hell with
Columbus," he spat. At least he knew it was Columbus Day, I thought.
He yelled at Jack as though he were in the next county. He yelled at his

wife who was somewhere, I gather, tending a fire. He yelled everything as though he were cast adrift in a world of deaf people.

Jack apologized for being late for the cooking appointment. Tattoos
yelled, "forget about cooking." His Van batteries were dead. No more
sounds. No more beer. Need jumper cables, man. Get us some jumper
cables now! The way he stated things gave them all the intensity and
immediacy of a life and death situation. Jack started telling Tattoos
about my bike trip, but was rudely interrupted. I feared for his life and
mine. Jack introduced me to Tattoos. Brian this is Hawkins. Brian
yelled something about his Harley Knucklehead and mistakenly
called me Homer. I didn't correct the miscue. Brian invited me to dinner—ribs, chicken, Tatter Tots, Scotch, beer, Pepsi. Jack wanted to
cook. Brian wanted him to shut up and get some jumper cables. We
need jumper cables. NOW! NOW!

A blue pickup truck with a camper cruised by, probably looking for
peace and quiet and a campsite. Brian spun around and yelled. The
truck kept going. Brian yelled louder. The truck skidded to a stop and
backed up.

Next thing I knew we were all gathered around a fire pit at Brian's
campsite, the former source of the music. He had run down the batteries
in his Van. No music. No music because batteries are dead, Brian diagnosed. If Jack was a drunken sailor with words, Brian was a teetotaler.
Again, the war cry—WE NEED JUMPER CABLES! Brian bellowed this
to the mountain. No one seemed to be listening to him. Brian's wife
Susan, encased in sweatshirts and overalls, had the charcoal fire piled
with foil-wrapped packages of ribs, chicken, and Tatter Tots. Jack
wanted to cook. Jack wanted to put wood on the fire. Susan ignored
him. Brian yelled for jumper cables, beer, Scotch, for real men to stand
up and be counted. Richard, the driver of the truck with the camper,
apologized profusely for not carrying jumper cables. Brian suggested
that Richard drive him to town for the jumper cables so he could
recharge his Van batteries, play his tunes, eat his ribs, talk his shit. Ha,
ha! Richard leaped in his truck and was almost gone before Brian cried
that he wanted to drive. He knew where to go. Richard didn't argue, but

reluctantly relinquished the wheel of his new pickup to a raving, tattooed man he'd known scarcely five minutes.

As the truck roared away, a skinny, spectacled lady in jeans, denim jacket, black cowboy hat with feathers hanging from the hatband, wobbled her way toward the cookfire. Jack greeted Terry. Bear bells tied to her hiking boots jingled as she swayed toward us. She knew where there was plenty of wood, she announced. Where? In the forest. Jack insisted there wasn't any wood in the forest. He knows. He lives there. Been camping there since June. No wood. Yes there is, says Terry, calmly pointing to the surrounding trees. Susan announced, to no one in particular, that she had salad, Pepsi, Mr. Tuffy paper towels, a gallon of Scotch, orange juice, but no beer. Jack was drinking the last beer. For no reason whatsoever, Terry, Jack, and I decided to split up in three directions and go looking for firewood. Out of sight, I went back to camp for my boots.

An hour later, back at Brian's campsite, Susan was tending the cookfire. Jack was sitting on a log. Terry was fast asleep on the picnic table. None of us had uncovered one stick of wood. Leaping to his feet, Jack declared he knew where there was a "shitload" of firewood. Jack and I wandered into the trees and encroaching manzanita. Jack, in a confessional tone of voice, told me he had been fasting for a week and was looking forward to tonight's feast. I suspected the fast had not been of his own volition. Jack confessed further that pennyroyal and pinecone sales had been soft. I prepared myself for the inevitable bite, but it didn't come.

"Fasting cleanses the body and mind," Jack said with complete candor.

I looked at him and wondered.

"Shasta could be a world-class, new-age religio-philosophical community," Jack declared. He ticked off the names of all the sects, cults, disciplines, and groups that I read about earlier, plus a few not included in the mimeographed handout. Jack was particularly high on Morningstar, a struggling commune a few hundred yards down the highway from the campground. Tomorrow, he would take me there to meet his friends, Brother Timothy and Timothy's wife, Wisteria. Rhymes with hysteria, Jack chuckled. We'd been walking in circles. I noticed this because we had circumnavigated the same dead coyote for the third time. I looked at Jack curious about Brother Timothy and his wife, but knew he'd probably digress about Kerouac or Maugham if I asked.

Spotting some dead manzanita, I started pulling it free from the tangled roots hoping Jack will follow suit. He removed his pack and started burrowing inside.

"But the locals are too divisive, too polemic, too capitalistic to achieve the necessary unification that would establish the required power base. You understand, Hawkins?" He muttered while rummaging in the backpack.

Of course, but how about helping with the wood gathering, I suggested. When I looked, he was slowly pulling on work gloves. While doing so he confessed he was anti-establishment, moreover he wanted to "vibe a contact" and get off the mountain. Mojave will be more centered and balanced, he assured me. By the time Jack had his gloves on and ready to help me, it was too late. I had a huge pile of manageable wood ready to be carried back to Brian's campsite. Filling my arms with wood I hoped Jack would do the same; to the contrary, he began the laborious procedure of taking the gloves off and returning them to the backpack. As I walked away I called over my shoulder to grab a few pieces of wood on the way back. That's exactly what he did, two small pieces of wood were clutched under his arm when he walked into camp.

Jack woke up Terry and gave her hell for not helping us gather wood. Both assisted in the splitting and stacking of kindling next to the firepit, but did it like method actors or mimes simulating the splitting and stacking of wood. Typically, they babbled on and on, neither one listening to what the other was saying. Susan warned she didn't want any wood on "her" cookfire. I asked myself, as much as anyone else, why we bothered to gather wood in the first place. We will celebrate our feast with a huge campfire after dinner, not before, she proclaimed.

It was pitch black now. The meat sizzling on the coals smelled delicious. A truck pulled up behind the Van. Brian leaped from the truck holding a set of jumper cables aloft, like he single-handedly captured a boa constrictor. "We gots some jumper cables, man," he shouted needlessly. Everyone within a three-mile radius could hear his tale of motherin' gas station attendants, $50 deposits, more beer, more music.

In the glare of the truck's headlights I watched as Brian and Richard worked at odds connecting the cables to the batteries. Sparks flew. Brian bellowed profanity to the four corners of the earth. Amidst more yelling, a flashlight appeared out of the dark. The cone of light splashed over our faces, trees, and the ground. Renewed cursing boiled from Brian. Under the scrutiny of five people the cables were finally connected. Brian jumped into his Van and switched on the ignition. Nothing. More yelling and cursing. Brian stormed back to the open hood of the Van and blindly reached inside, yanking and pulling at wires and cables. Bolts of electricity arced and crackled. Everyone jumped back. Susan screamed at Brian to "watch out." Somebody, I think Terry, asked if I was a Libra. I turned to my right and saw Terry shining the flashlight on her beaded moccasins. Before I could answer, Brian howled again, amidst an explosion of arcing and flying sparks. The next thing I knew the Van was started and almost simultaneously the stereo began cranking out more Dire Straits. Somebody, maybe Richard, suggested it might be a good idea to let the batteries charge a bit before turning on the stereo. Brian screamed something about food. He wanted to eat. He stood in the firelight, still naked from the waist up, tattoos dancing and gyrating. Brian yelled at the top of his lungs that he wanted to eat right now! Susan and Brian got into a heated exchange about the main course; while nearby, Jack suggested to Terry that she add some wood to the fire. The music finally drowned out everyone.

I wondered if the few other campers I noticed earlier had fled down the mountain and reported us to the Shasta police.

We all watched eagerly as Susan began pulling packages of food off the fire. Chugging from a gallon of Scotch, Brian warned the food better be good. Susan told him to butt out and leave the cooking to her. Mark Knofler sang about a river deep and wi-a-ide and somebody waiting on the other si-a-ide. Any second, I expected to hear the wail of sirens, or worse the tramp of National Guard infantry. Jack was armed with plastic knife and fork and a tin plate he obviously carried in his backpack. He was salivating. His fast would soon be over. Stalking closer to the food, he continued babbling incoherently about Melville, Bertram Russell, Satan, and Conan Doyle.

The smells of succulent ribs, chicken, and Tatter Tots had me lathered into a frenzy of hunger as well. Help yourself, Susan called at last. Arms shot forward in the dark, food was torn from grasping hands, plates clattered, a bottle was spilled. More yelling, cursing, swearing. Then at long last—silence. Everyone, except Mark Knofler, was stuffing his or her face. Knofler lamented about " lawyers and rules." A hand appeared out of the dark and deposited a mound of Tatter Tots on my plate. I snarled and pounced on a juicy rib like a drowning man at a life ring. More salad and chicken. Mr. Tuffy paper towels were passed around.

Wood was thrown on the fire-branches, limbs piled on haphazardly, and some missed the fire completely. The blaze intensified, forcing us farther and farther away. There was much yelling about heat. Brian's tattooed back looked like MTV. Jack was silent, still gnawing a bone. Ah yes, the fast was definitely over. Now, Mark Knofler chortled about "industrial disease." Slowly the fire died down. Yelling. The huge log Jack was sitting on was tossed on the fire by Brian. Three feet of log overhung the fire pit on both sides. Smoke got in Brian's eyes, triggering another outburst. Jack disappeared. Terry shuffled off into the darkness waving her flashlight like a laser sword. I thanked our host and hostess for a delicious meal, said goodnight, and then stumbled into the pitch black to my campsite. An invitation to a breakfast of bacon and eggs at 8 a.m. echoed through the campground. Everyone come, Brian commanded. **Hear me, everyone!** Wife cook bacon and eggs.

I dissolved into the darkness, feeling my way uncertainly along the road. Perhaps a seven-foot tall Lemurian would appear from its home deep in the bowels of the mountain, its luminous aura lighting the way to my campsite. Or maybe I'd "vibe a contact" and wangle a ride aboard one of their spaceships that allegedly made scheduled trips between Mt. Shasta and some mysterious island in the South Pacific, or so goes the legend of the disciples of Saint Germain.

But no, no visitations or spiritual experiences that night, thank God. I tripped, stumbled, and eventually found my way back to camp where I eagerly crawled into my sleeping bag. While lightning flashed and thunder rolled, I fell fast asleep wondering about the power of sacred Mt. Shasta.

Next morning, the guttural exhaust of a Harley Davidson motorcycle startled me from a sound sleep. I figured Brian, the tattooed sybarite, was off in search of more beer, more tapes, possibly more jumper cables.

I'd barely poured my first cup of coffee when Jack Schaarf materialized, his backpack still on. I wondered if he ever took it off. Not wanting to get a reputation as an inattentive host, especially after last night's feast, I offered Jack coffee and a stale bagel. The caffeine seemed to ignite intellectual fires. He erupted in a monologue on contemporary fiction, his alma mater the Iowa Writer's Workshop, the rebirth of the short story, and on and on. This one-sided conversation soon wore me down, but I was saved in the nick of time by Terry who came bouncing up to the picnic table like a samba dancer. Before I could say good morning, she and Jack got into an argument over her "missing" espresso maker. Terry, by the way, was camped two spaces away in a tepee. While the verbal fisticuffs raged, I speculated that perhaps a sacred mountain is not the best place to find peace and harmony. Without rival, Mt. Shasta was the noisiest, busiest, zaniest place I camped during my entire trip. I got on my bike and announced I was going to ride into town. During my tour around the village, I made a telephone call to Pete Peterson to confirm our forthcoming meeting and tour.

I returned to camp with all good intentions of enjoying a peaceful afternoon working on my journal and relaxing. No sooner had I settled down at the picnic table, than Jack and Terry dropped by to announce they'd found the "missing" espresso maker. If I wouldn't mind, they'd like to use my fireplace to brew espresso. I was about to suggest a wood gathering trip, but realized the futility of it, especially since Jack was already kneeling before the firepit lighting my kindling. Sometime later, as I watched Jack pour syrupy, black liquid into Terry's cup, I got out my stove to prepare coffee.

In the midst of my coffee preparation a green Forest Service pickup pulled into the gravel drive at my campsite. An attractive Rangerette got out of the truck. She had the look of a slumlord with a pocket full of eviction notices. Jack was on a first name basis with her. Before she opened her mouth, he grilled her about construction of a proposed ski area further up the mountain. Sandy told him she couldn't comment, directing him to speak to the district ranger in town. Shortly, she took me aside and asked discreetly if "those" people were bothering me. Earlier in the season some campers had complained about Jack and his pennyroyal. I raised my hands palms up and shrugged my shoulders—no problem. Satisfied I was in no immediate danger, Sandy got in her truck and drove away.

~ ~ ~

California Dreaming

After a two-day rock climbing side trip to Castle Crags, south of Shasta, I returned to meet tandem bikers Pete and Vangie Peterson.

That night over a spaghetti dinner washed down with pitchers of beer we discussed our tour south to Mt. Lassen. For the first time in days I enjoyed a normal conversation.

Logging trucks notwithstanding, we enjoyed a superb trip south, made more enjoyable by lingering Indian summer weather. Temperatures sometimes creeped up into the low 80's. While camped at the town of Mineral just outside the south entrance to Lassen Volcanic National Park I looked over my maps to discover I was closer to Reno, where my Father lived, than to the San Francisco Bay area. Before our trails forked, I made plans to meet Pete and Vangie at their home in Palo Alto on my way to Mexico.

On Thursday, October 20, 1988 I rolled into the driveway of my father's house in Sparks, Nevada with a flat rear tire. During two-weeks of rest, recuperation, and bike maintenance I had a chance to reflect on the 3,724-mile tour from Alaska. I felt like I'd successfully completed basic training. Now I had the confidence and desire to deal with the nebulous uncertainties of travel in third world countries—language, currencies, culture, dietary problems, and political instability. Once across the Mexican border I knew I'd be swimming at the deep end of the pool. Also, I was determined not to turn back until I cycled into Ushuaia, Tierra Del Fuego, 13,776 miles later. That is, barring any major disaster. Unfortunately, there would not be any pleasant respites with friends and family along the way.

My bike and gear passed the test with flying colors too. Besides a few minor adjustments the bike had proven itself to be a workhorse. I had complete confidence it could meet the demands of the journey, but if I did encounter mechanical problems, large or small, I knew I could deal with them.

Perhaps the most important discovery dealt with inner biking. Somewhere on the road between Anchorage and Reno I'd undergone a transition. After months of living so close to nature, of living a life unen-cumbered by conveniences, gadgets, and toys, I realized how healing and restorative solo travel could be. My experiences both on and off the bike cleansed my mind and soul. I reckoned my three-month bike trip was worth three years of life in the mainstream. Rediscovering the hinterland, especially mountain wilderness, not only eradicated unhealthy influences, it also energized and strengthened the "individual" element of my psyche, an aspect of inner-life unfortunately neglected in day-to-day living.

I was amazed at my eating habits. I was consuming food like a machine out of control. With a 20-lb deficit, I guessed my body was intuitively replenishing and stocking up on nutrients for the long haul. Although I felt in excellent health, I figured a few additional pounds wouldn't hurt, in fact they would be quickly shed once the second leg of my trip began. I also believe my mind had secretly communicated to my body that once across the border it wouldn't be supplied with cheeseburgers and fries, milkshakes, pie a la mode, and pizza.

After a session with the calculator, I discovered my daily trip expense so far averaged $13.73 per day, for a total outlay of $1,525. Although this was more than I thought I'd spend (it always is) I'd traveled conservatively, succumbing to only a few luxuries and indulgences along the way. An encouraging thought was that I'd completed the most expensive part of the trip. From Mexico south I guessed my expenses would be 40 to 50% less.

One of my main concerns was how I could safely carry my money, i.e. traveler's checks and cash. On the advice of a friend working in the international department of a major banking institution I decided not to have money transfers sent to me along the way. This approach, I was advised, was rife with potential problems ranging from language to implacable bureaucracy.

After a few days of visiting and cycling with the Petersons in Palo Alto, California, I headed west over the coastal mountain range to the Pacific Ocean, stopping the first night at the Pigeon Point youth hostel near Pesquedero. Though sunny, the December temperatures were averaging 55 degrees during the day. Combined with limited daylight hours, my cycling routine was severely curtailed. But I was never a mileage glutton anyway.

About the only negative aspect of cycling the coast during winter months was the abbreviated hours of daylight. I had only eight and a half hours of daylight, compared to as many as 15 or more during the summer. Three of those 8 1/2 hours were used setting up and breaking camp, leaving me with a mere five hours of road time. This did not take into account rest stops, lunch stops, or additional breaks to gawk at scenery and take pictures. My cycling day during that period averaged a mere four hours, as I did not ride at night, unless forced to. It also meant I spent a lot of time in my tent reading or journalizing, an added bonus in my opinion. Daily trip mileage ranged from 14 to 66 miles with an average daily distance of 20 miles. Which isn't all that bad considering my average daily distance from Alaska to California was 55 miles.

I'd usually have camp set up by 4:30 p.m. What with sundry camp chores I'd end up eating by candlelight.

On Thursday, December 8th I arrived at one of my all time favorite campgrounds—Pfiefer State Park at Big Sur. This is part of my journal entry on my first night in Big Sur.

"Here I go again-beautiful warm, sunny days. Hey, I'm sorry but this is superb cycling along the most beautiful coastline in the world. Man, I really apologize for having such a great time."

In addition to a $2 fee, Pfieffer had a special camping area set aside for bikers and hikers. Thankfully, it was located in a grove of magnificent redwoods close to the park entrance. Nearby was a spacious restroom with hot showers. I camped for three whole days. Except for a few hardy squirrels I had it completely to myself.

~ ~ ~

The Fellowship of Books

Something I've made a habit of during my trip, and hope others will emulate, is sharing my books with unknown travelers. After I finished reading Edward Abbey's, *Desert Solitaire*, I wrote this note inside the cover.

"Dear friend,

Hope you enjoy this book. When you're done, please pass it on.

Hawk"

Before departing, I wrapped the book in one of my many plastic bags and left it on the picnic table with a rock on it. If there's a food locker available I put it in there. The idea is similar to the "fellowship of wood." Leave something for the next person. It's a small gesture that reaffirms our humanity.

Oddly enough, I felt miserable the day I left Big Sur. Shows you what three days of rest can do. Regardless, pedaling along the coast that day was a once-in-a-lifetime experience. All day I saw cars pulled off on the side of the road, their occupants outside gawking at magnificent vistas. The ocean was like a sheet of glass. A deep blue sky was branded with a Titian sun. Three miles offshore a fleecy fog bank lay shimmering in sunlight. The icing though was swarms of migrating Monarch butterflies filling the air like an orange and black cloud or covering Eucalyptus trees like colorful wrapping paper. A few years earlier one would have described the scene as "psychedelic."

Chapter 5

California Hedonism

"Sometimes you're the windshield, sometimes the bug."

-Mark Knofler

Dire Straits

Cats

Late that afternoon I set up camp at Kirk Meadows south of Big Sur, a green swath bordered by 10-foot high pampas grass and perched on the edge of a cliff overlooking the Pacific. Feeling a bit groggy and sore, I crawled in my tent for a nap, emerging 30-minutes later. I had to rub my eyes to believe what I was seeing. The low angle sun beat down on emerald green grass, but what really caught my attention were a half dozen black cats slinking around my bike and parading across the picnic table. They trooped over the grass like a conga line, then broke formation to play what looked like a game of touch football. Black cats on a green background. After five minutes of sporting about they disappeared in the towering pampas grass as mysteriously as they appeared. Black ballet cats doing slow motion improvisation.

Afterward, I walked to the edge of the cliff and stood there awestruck. A magnificent orange ball of sun disappeared in the milky fog bank offshore. Several other campers joined me on the edge of the cliff to watch and take pictures of this spectacular show in silence. When it was over we clapped spontaneously to show our appreciation. The curtain fell, the show was over.

~ ~ ~

Biography of A Motor Car

During the 4,000 miles I'd spent on the road so far I'd found some interesting items lying on the side of the highway waiting for me to stop and pick up. Besides a dozen bungee cords, a jackknife, a pair of scissors and a sewing kit, my most interesting road find was a small notebook. It was somebody's maintenance record of their automobile from 1968-88. A biography of a motor car. I found it at the entrance to the Esalon Institute on Hwy. 1 south of Carmel, California. Judging from the entries in the notebook I guessed the automobile was a diesel Mercedes. In addition to mileage entries, it appeared to contain all maintenance and repairs performed on the automobile, e.g. "oil filter, 1/20/74, 99,250," and "new front end, suspension, Oct. '81, 186,050."

The entry on the last page was regarding a trip from Esalon to British Columbia, August 29 thru Sept. 21, 1980. "Left Esalon about 3 p.m. with Hugh. Arrived Esalon Sept. 21, Sun., 6:45 p.m., 170, 040."

Is this guy a record keeper or what?

~ ~ ~

Butterfly Soup

I felt progressively worse the next few days, until my physical condition gradually affected my mental condition. I guessed I had the flu. Rain and cold weather were constant companions on the way to Moro Bay Campground. While in the midst of setting up camp, I bent over to pick something up only to pull muscles in my lower back. Exhausted by my bout with the flu, I gobbled a handful of aspirin and crawled into my tent to rest and ease the lower back pain. With no appetite for food or energy to prepare it, I lay in my tent listening to the rain. During the cold, rainy, sleepless night I began to doubt I had the necessary strength and resilience to pedal to the bottom of the Americas. If I couldn't handle the temperate winter weather of California how was I going to deal with the numbing cold and high altitudes of the Andes or the heat and humidity of Central America.

I felt weak and depressed the next morning. My back was so stiff and sore I couldn't stand up straight. The only ray of sunshine on that wet, miserable morning was a growing appetite. I had a craving for hot soup. After hobbling around a bit to loosen up, I managed to get on my bike and pedal slowly into town in search of a bowl of soup. Once I got going and warmed up my back seemed to feel better. Although the rain had stopped it was still quite damp and chilly. In town, I cycled down mainstreet. Like a pot of gold at the end of a rainbow I discovered Kitty's Kitchen. Inside, the waitress took one look at me and said, "Listen why don't you let me bring you some of our chicken soup."

I inhaled the steaming, hot broth and ordered a second bowl. Wolfing that down along with a piece of hot pie, I ordered a third cup of soup to go. Feeling halfway decent, I took a stroll around town before heading back to the campground. To my amazement, the ground around my campsite was littered with the fragile bodies of monarch butterflies. God, I thought, not them too. I stooped down to inspect one of the butterflies at close range to find it was still alive, but barely so. I picked it up, sheltered it in the palm of my hand and breathed on it. My warm breath seemed to revive it for its orange and black wings flapped sporadically. I also noticed a miniscule tag on one of its wings. While engrossed in my inspection, a green truck pulled up. The park ranger joined me amidst the butterfly carnage. He explained that monarchs migrated to the temperate climes of coastal California from the Sierras and as far away as the Canadian Rockies. The longest documented flight, 1,870 miles, was from Toronto, Canada to San Luis Potosi, Mexico. Here they sought the protection of Eucalyptus groves where they formed dome-shaped clusters on the trees. This communal effort provided a sanctuary against the cold. They can't fly in temperatures much lower than 40 degrees, the Ranger offered, looking around at dozens of monarchs scattered around my tent. From the looks of it they could barely survive. When the sun warms them, he continued, they leave the security of the cluster to feed on nearby flora. At last when Spring arrives and temperatures increase they mate and return to their far-flung alpine habitat. With an estimated lifespan of perhaps a year, most would have to endure only one arduous migration. The tags on their wings, the ranger pointed out, are a way of tracking their migratory patterns, adding that if I found a deceased butterfly with a tagged wing to return it to the nearest forest service office or campground.

Now I felt responsible for the twitching monarch in the palm of my hand. In the tent I lit my candle lantern and held the butterfly as close as was prudent. When it recovered sufficiently, I set it on the lid of a go cup of Kitty's soup. Maybe it was the warmth, maybe the vapor from the soup, but it started moving its wings rhythmically. When it appeared to be in stable condition, I relocated it to the vestibule of my tent. Next morning it was gone.

After two days of rest and shuttling back and forth to Kitty's Kitchen I felt healthy enough to move on. But somewhere along the road south of Moro Bay I took a wrong turn, winding up at Montana D'Oro State Park.

~ ~ ~

Shoot the Moon

Before I had my tent pitched, raccoons were swarming over my bike, opening panniers, sampling food items, and generally making a damn nuisance of themselves. Given enough time I'm sure they would have pedaled off with my bike! Enraged at their boldness, I ran at them wielding, for lack of anything more effective, a paperback copy of James Herriot's, *All Creatures Great and Small.* Oh they departed alright, but with much reluctance on their part and much coaxing on mine. As soon as I had my camp in order, I lighted my stove to prepare my favorite Alpine Aire freeze-dried meal—Chicken Primavera. I barely had the package open when a gang of eight raccoons materialized. Slinking arrogantly, they approached my camp. Enraged, I picked up a rock and chucked it, scattering the varmints into the hills. To insure my own sanity and the security of my bike and gear I gathered a small pile of rocks in preparation for a return engagement. And return they did like a band of marauding, renegade savages. Each time their number grew larger. When it got dark I swear there were about a dozen raccoons circling my camp waiting for the right time to spring their next offensive. Smelling something in the wind, beside myself, I removed the panniers from my bike and stowed them in the tent along with all my other equipment, then burrowed in amongst it. As I zipped the rainfly, I saw the tip of a full moon rising over a nearby ridge.

Trying to follow my usual evening routine I stripped naked, crawled into my sleeping bag, lit my candle lantern, and proceeded to make entries in my journal. No sooner had pen touched paper than I heard scampering and scurrying around the tent. Being a deserted campground on a calm December night, the raccoons sounded like a herd of stampeding buffalo. Then silence. I suspected they were discussing how to divvy up my equipment. Next thing I knew my tent was shaking and the zipper of my rainfly was being unzipped. Then I saw a claw reach under the rainfly and grab my MSR stove. It disappeared before my eyes. Enough is enough, I yelled and cursed at the top of my lungs. "You sonsofbitches have gone too far," I bellowed as I backed out of the tent. I grabbed a handful of rocks from my nearby cache and flung them with the speed and accuracy of a Nolan Ryan, sending the raccoons packing once again. "You bastardly vermin. Come back again and I'll kick your asses from here to breakfast," I yelled after them.

As I stood there panting and staring into the darkness, a voice called from behind me. "Those 'coons a little pesky tonight, are they?"

I jumped and wheeled around. As the moon had risen much higher I could clearly see a Park Ranger complete with Smokey Bear hat, gun, and badge. Not only was I making a complete naked fool out of myself in front of a park ranger, this ranger was a female ranger. I stood there paralyzed for what seemed like hours before feeling the chill night air and realizing I was in the buff. I looked around for some kind of covering, but it was no use, so I walked as casually as I could over to my tent and pulled on my sweat pants.

"Nice moon tonight, isn't it, " I stammered.

"Yes, you might say that, " the Rangerette smiled.

"Well listen, those raccoons were out of control. I wasn't trying to hurt them with the rocks, just trying to scare them off," I babbled pulling on my wool sweater.

"Oh, we know we have a problem, that's why I stopped by. I noticed you were the only camper when I made my 6 o'clock check. Thought I'd warn you about the 'coons, but I see they've introduced themselves. By the way my name's Ranger Johnson."

After shaking hands and saying goodnight I crawled back into my tent, this time however I kept my sweats on. The band of raccoons returned twice that night in futile attempts to steal my food. Ranger Johnson stopped by only one more time. In all, I guess I got six hours sleep. Next morning while packing my gear I vowed I'd buy a sling-shot at the first opportunity. I did and now consider myself an expert marksmen with a Whamo deluxe.

~ ~ ~

I Love Lucy

I leaned my bike against the plate glass window advertising Franky's Cafe. This was on main street in Ventura, California. My back was killing me, my muscles were sore, and my bones ached. It was Thursday, December 22nd. Merry Christmas. I felt like the cycling version of a cold remedy commercial. I staggered inside to a table near the window so I could keep an eye on my bike. While eating a bowl of thick vegetable soup a guy rushed in, surveyed the nearly empty restaurant, and then headed straight for me.

"Say, it that your bike outside?"

"Sure is," I replied wiping soup from my chin.

"Are you really headed for Tierra Del Fuego?" Evidently he noticed the sign on the back of my bike.

"Sure am."

"Well, I have some friends here in town who did that same tour a few years ago. I'm going to call them. I'm sure they'd love to talk to you. Oh, by the way my name's Bill Haldane, I'm the owner of this restaurant."

Bill raced over to the cashier's counter and dialed the phone. Slurping soup, I watched him. A few minutes later he returned to join me at my table.

"Listen, I just talked to John Powell. He and his wife Ilona cycled down to the tip of South America in 1976. Here's the directions to his shop. It's only a few blocks away, he's expecting you," Bill said as he drew a crude map on the back of his business card.

Ten minutes later I pedaled through the gate of a chain link fence into a small compound housing two foreign car repair shops. At the back end of the shop area was a diverse collection of bicycles, tricycles, and other human-powered vehicles. A handpainted sign above the doorway to the shop proclaimed this to be "The Bike and Bird Shop." For a few seconds I wondered if I'd gone astray. I checked the directions on the business card, then pedaled over to the side of the building and there, standing next to an outdoor workbench, was a huge fellow dressed in red T-shirt, red shorts, and hiking boots. I guessed he weighed in at 230 lbs. Standing beside a bike clamped in a workstand, he was so involved in what he was doing he didn't notice me. But someone else did. A 300-lb., black pig stormed from beneath a GMC bus parked alongside the shop. It headed straight for me and would have eaten me whole had not the behemoth gentleman in red called it off, booting it in the hindquarters for emphasis.

"Lucy, get back over there," he ordered, pointing toward the bus.

A large black Lab and a Doberman Pinscher, lounging nearby, reluctantly looked at me. Deciding I wasn't worth the effort, they dropped their heads on outstretched paws and went back to sleep.

"Say, I'm looking for John Powell," I said timidly.

"That's me. What can I do for you."

"Bill Haldane sent me over. I'm George Hawkins. I'm on my way to Tierra Del Fuego."

A broad grin slashed across his face, making the black moustache on his upper lip look like the outstretched wings of a crow.

"Well, set your bike up someplace and let's talk."

In addition to the Bike and Bird Shop housing an assortment of exotic birds, including macaws, toucans, and parrots, the area around the shop held a conglomeration of bike frames, wheels, mounds of sprockets, gears, handlebars, tires, saddles, pumps, and spare parts of every description. There was something Dickensien about the place and its proprietor. John and wife Ilona lived in the bus parked near the back fence. They were in the process, he told me, of refitting and refurbishing it. In addition to exotic birds, there was Lucy the pig, Bengie and Fordo the dogs, and a cat named Bunkie, the self-proclaimed CEO of the operation. Everyone and everything inside the compound, including Lucy, came under Bunkie's scrutiny.

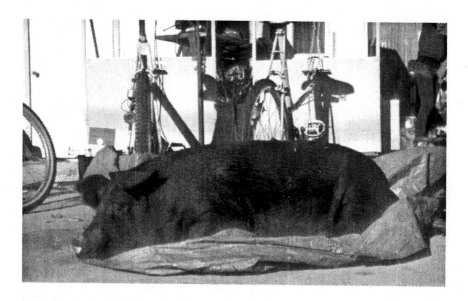

Figure 6: Loveable Lucy.

John was an encyclopedia of bike touring lore. Not only had he completed a hemistour with Ilona in 1976, but also as a tour leader for Bike Centennial he had crossed the U.S. several times. I listened for two hours straight as John talked and worked on various projects. Often, I handed him a tool or spare part needed for the job. Much later, over coffee, John told me his wife was both a Chiropractor and Massage Therapist. She would be returning from her office about 7 p.m. that evening and I was invited to join them for dinner. And if I wasn't too particular about where I camped I could roll out my sleeping bag in the empty storage shack behind the shop.

"Just keep the door closed or Lucy will wander in to keep you company. She's very friendly you know," John said candidly.

That night over a huge spaghetti dinner, John and Ilona regaled me with stories of their hemistour, graphically illustrated with the help of photo albums. Ilona, a vivacious Australian, confessed she'd never did any bike touring before setting out for TDF with her husband, but once underway she blossomed into an accomplished biker and camper. Now, she confessed, she couldn't wait to return to Australia and New Zealand with John for an extended tour.

Sometime later that night, with his pet Macaw, Brandy, perched on his shoulder sipping beer from his glass, John asked me how much money I had for my trip. When I told him I had about $1500, he laughed. John suggested, with Ilona concurring, that if he were to do the hemistour again, he'd have a minimum of $6,000, per person. They had started out with $7500 between them, but had to wire home for more money in Brazil on the way back.

This information set me to thinking. Before retiring that night, with Christmas only a few days away, they invited me to stay over the holidays with them so they could show me their slides and prep me with valuable travel tips they learned along the way. Aware of my lower back pains, Ilona volunteered to give me a free spinal exam and any therapy needed to get me back in top cycling shape. She guessed the back pains could be symptomatic of other health problems and cautioned me not to cross the border unless I was in excellent physical shape.

Next morning when I opened the door of my new quarters behind the shop there was Lucy hunkered down in the weeds at the doorstep like a faithful watchdog. I soon discovered that Lucy had a sweet tooth for chocolate and made the mistake of sharing giant Hershey almond bars with her. From then on, no matter how covertly I tore the paper and foil from the chocolate bar, there was Lucy, grunting and snorting.

I returned to Franky's Cafe to thank Bill Haldane for the introduction to the Powells and enjoy one of his locally famous cappuccinos. After a brief tour of downtown Ventura I stopped at the Public Library. While inside, the single rear pannier I left outside on my bike was stolen. Among the contents were my rain gear, Katadyn water purifier, tools, and miscellaneous spare parts. The first experience with theft on my trip, I took it quite hard, not so much over items lost, but because it made me more aware of my vulnerability. The problem was compounded because I would have to buy a new set of panniers and other expensive items. At least I thought so.

Back at the Bike and Bird Shop, John shook his head and commiserated with me. After a moment of silence, he suggested I get in touch with the Rhode Gear rep to see if I might be able to purchase a single pannier. Luckily Rhode Gear had a warehouse in Santa Barbara, just north of Ventura. I telephoned Ron Guilbault, the West Coast rep, and explained my problem. He said he'd check and call me back. That evening Ron called to inform me that he had located a single left side rear pannier. Not only that, but he would give it to me as a Christmas present. All I had to do was get up to Santa Barbara to pick it up.

With John's help and generosity I was able to replace most of the stolen tools and spare parts and then some. He even handmade a set of freewheel tools for my kit. Better yet, he handcrafted a rear luggage rack out of chrome-moly tubing, assuring me the bike would break before the rack would. At the local Patagonia outlet selling seconds and discontinued items I was able to purchase a new set of rain gear at half price. Now, the only item needed was the missing Katadyn water purifier.

Thanks to Ilona's chiropractic expertise my back was much improved, as were my spirits. On Christmas Eve we gathered around the Powell table, along with a few of their friends, to feast on a 21-lb. turkey with all the trimmings. I contributed a bottle of wine for a toast to friendship.

After dinner, we exchanged gifts. I presented John and Ilona with a basket of cheese and wine with a card attached expressing my gratitude for their hospitality and generosity. They gave me a book with a note wishing me luck and safe biking during my tour. Christmas festivities were capped off with a slide show of the Powells' bike tour to Tierra Del Fuego.

All of my good intentions of departing the next day were for naught, as John and Ilona persuaded me to stay over with them through News Years. That week John gave me an intensive course in bicycle maintenance. Under his expert supervision, he had me strip my bike down, lubricate or grease all parts as needed, then reassemble it. Knowing from personal experience that I wouldn't have access to many bike shops or special tools once south of the border, he showed me how to perform standard repair and maintenance procedures using only the tools in my kit.

In the evenings after dinner, Ilona would advise me on the health and dietary problems I might encounter south of the border and, if the occasion arose, how to deal with them. She also wrote out a list of medicines I could purchase in third world countries to treat various diseases.

During my two-week stay at the Bike and Bird Shop my health improved immeasurably, thanks largely to spinal adjustments from Ilona. I was also armed with a wealth of knowledge regarding the many countries I'd be cycling through during the coming year.

Figure 7: L–R—Humans–Bernie Wright, Ilona & John Powell, L–R— Animals–Bunkie the cat, Brandy the Macaw, Benjie the Doberman and Fordo the Lab.

After a difficult parting with John and Ilona, Bengie and Fordo, Brandy and Sonny, Bunkie the cat, and especially Lucy the pig, I resumed my journey south. On the way to San Diego I planned to re-evaluate my finances.

~ ~ ~

Hiatus

My long awaited reunion with Vince Streano and Carol Havens in Laguna Beach turned into a 17-day working holiday. In the process of spiffing up their house before putting it on the market, they talked me into becoming their live-in painter and carpenter. Between projects, we sampled the local cuisine and watched the sun set over Catalina Island.

By the time I reached San Diego on January 24th. I decided to stay in the U.S. and work long enough to bring my bankroll up to the $6,000 level. My plan was to return to Sparks, Nevada and live at my father's house allowing me the opportunity to save most of the money I earned.

My stay with Will and Gisela Cronyn in San Diego was both enjoyable and educational. Among the many cycling enthusiasts I met there, I became friends with Rusty Runholt and Patty Fares, a couple who had just completed a two-year, around the world bicycle tour. Their cycling stories and slide shows whetted my appetite for future tours.

One of the many bike trips I shared with Will and Gisela and Rusty and Patty took us to the Anza Borego Desert, east of San Diego. At Aguas Caliente* Hot Springs we camped and took day trips in the surrounding desert. Cool nights provided the perfect excuse to soak in the hot waters at the springs.

I returned to Nevada in late January to find work and open a savings account. Far from being a waste, the time I spent there allowed me to do

* Aguas (Waters) Caliente (Hot).

intensive research and reading about the 16 countries I planned to cycle through on my way to Tierra Del Fuego.

The most useful reference book I acquired during my cycling hiatus was the *South American Handbook*, which I purchased as a remainder for $14. The 1989 edition I purchased included Mexico, Central and South America. Currently, three separate volumes cover each geographic area. With the help of the handbook I was able to plot a course that would be both practical and scenic, allowing me to target specific cities and scenic attractions to include in my travel itinerary. In addition to a historical overview of each country, the handbook also provides detailed information and maps on every aspect of travel.

With the help of the handbook I discovered an organization called the South American Explorer's Club, formerly headquartered in Denver, Colorado. Services provided to members include: quarterly magazine with stories and travel updates, library of books and maps, and classified ads, but perhaps the most useful service was a compilation of trip reports authored by members. Hundreds of reports describe excursions to Mexico, Central, and South America and are available to members at 20 cents per page. Most reports run from 1-3 pages. My first order totaled 19 trip reports at the extremely reasonable price of $7.60. Of particular help were descriptions of bicycle tours in many of the countries I planned to visit. The author's address and telephone number are available if additional information is desired.

Other membership benefits I took advantage of during my trip were the use of the clubhouses located in Quito, Ecuador and Lima, Peru. I was able to mail boxes of miscellaneous supplies ahead to be claimed when I arrived there months later. The clubhouses were also a forum for networking with other travelers, as well as a place to study selections from their well-stocked library of books and maps.

Oddly enough, the South American Explorer's Club fills a role many Americans expect, erroneously or not, of their foreign embassies. As many an American has found out while traveling abroad, U.S. embassies are reluctant to acknowledge your existence, let alone provide help or assistance. But embassies are not in the travel business.

Based on my travel experiences in South America, I recommend both the South American Explorer's Club and American Express. American Express traveler's checks were accepted routinely in all the countries I visited. I would guess a traveler would encounter more problems cashing their Amex traveler's checks in the U.S. than any other place in the world. As most people know, Amex traveler's checks are fully reimbursable if lost or stolen. Also, cardholders are able to cash personal checks at international Amex offices providing that service. In Santiago, Chile, for example, I had the option of cashing travelers checks or a personal check at the American Express Bank located there. And I had a choice of local currency or American dollars. This was a favorable option, as most indigenous banking institutions will cash travelers checks in local currency only. The advantage of procuring U.S. dollars is significant. I discovered the American greenback was the most sought after currency throughout all of my third world travels. No matter what country I was in, no matter how small or isolated the place, I was always able to find someone to exchange dollars for pesos, cordobas, quetzals, australes, or whatever. Because of the relative stability of the American dollar, many locals in third world countries actually prefer it as a hedge against the capricious inflationary problems in their own countries, e.g. Argentina, Peru, and Nicaragua. When I was in Argentina, the peso went from 600 to 5,000 in exchange for one dollar, this in a matter of weeks. Be forewarned this does not signify that goods and services will be cheaper as prices are constantly adjusted to keep pace with inflation. However, it does mean that if you exchanged one U.S. dollar at the 600 peso rate, it would be worth 12 cents at the 5,000 peso rate.

Naturally when currency experiences this kind of devaluation prices skyrocket, sometimes changing on an hourly basis. Many cafes and restaurants I visited in Argentina threw away their printed menus and relied on chalkboards for repricing items on a moment's notice. The best advice I can give a traveler in Central and South America is to exchange small sums ($20-40) of U.S. dollars. As mentioned above I was never in a place where the U. S. dollar was not exchanged. I might have had to shop around and exchange on the black market, but that is the rule, not the exception.

Another resource that was particularly helpful was National Geographic Magazine. I was able to buy duplicate copies at 5 cents each at the public library. Over the months that followed I amassed a private library of one hundred plus Geographics, each one with one or more articles about the country I planned to visit.

In retrospect, I realize how much that time of research and study enriched my travels, providing a rich historical background as well as invaluable information, both visual and written. This background helped enormously in appreciating and understanding the countries and cultures I was exposed to.

The time I spent cooling my heels and wheels also enabled me to sharpen my Spanish language skills, another tool that enhanced my travels. Fortunately, I had only one language to deal with during my bike tour. With the help of Berlitz books and tapes, checked out of the library, I was able to ease comfortably and confidently into the Hispanic cultures south of the border.

~ ~ ~

Guidebooks: The Dilemma

For the neophyte or even the experienced traveler I believe the *South American Handbook* will always be an essential resource. There are others available, like the Lonely Planet Guides, but I have no firsthand knowledge of them. During my travels I've heard conflicting reports about their relative merits, but most often (75%) travelers I talked with who have used the S.A. Handbook had good things to say about it. Its ubiquitous presence among travelers in all the countries I visited is silent testimony to its popularity and usefulness. Because of the magnitude of the information provided and increasing popularity of South American travel, the S.A. Handbook, as noted, is now published in three logical volumes—Mexico, Central America, and South America.

Like the majority of fellow travelers I met and networked with I carried the S.A. Handbook like a bible, constantly referring to it. Whether in a cafe, hospedaje, or plaza, I'd always spot one or more trekkers engrossed in their S.A. Handbook. I can only think of a few instances when information regarding prices or addresses was inaccurate. But considering the lead-time involved in publishing such a volume, combined with the volatility of the tourist industry, the inaccuracies were not significant. Keep in mind that I was traveling in the third world where politics and economies were equally fragile and changeable.

If I learned anything in my travels it was that the stability of all aspects of American life we take for granted is experienced only to a limited degree or not at all in third world countries.

The only negative aspect of the S.A. Handbook and similar guides is that many travelers depend on them completely. This creates two problems: 1. a majority of people go to the same places, stay at the same hotels, and eat and drink at the same cafes and bars, thus unintentionally creating a "gringo trail." 2. when a hotel, cafe, or bar becomes popular with tourists prices go up, sometimes to astronomical heights.

Then too, getting locked into the "gringo trail" takes the edge off the spontaneity and sense of discovery that makes travel so adventuresome and rewarding.

A globe trotting American in Chile told me his travel strategy was to find out where the S.A. Handbook recommended to go then head in the opposite direction. S.A. Handbook or not, I found myself getting off the beaten path, discovering new places and people on a regular basis, but that's because my mode of travel allowed me a greater degree of flexibility than would an airplane, train, bus, or automobile.

~ ~ ~

Money Matters

As my departure approached, and time flew by, I was increasingly concerned with how to transport my fat bankroll, which at that time totaled a little over $7,000. I'd already been advised not to rely on bank transfers, so I had to come up with an alternative method. A week before leaving I purchased $5600 in American Express traveler's checks in various amounts, a prodigious pile of paper even in large denominations. Combined with $1,400 in cash, I knew I would never be able to carry that much money on me, so I went to a local hardware store where I bought three feet of one-inch plastic tubing. I cut the tubing into two 7-inch lengths. Into each section I stuffed tightly rolled bundles of travelers checks and cash, sealed both ends with tape then pushed them down into the depths of the seat tube on my bike. They fit snugly and could be easily pulled out with the help of a drawstring. I carried the balance of checks and cash in a small fanny pack along with my wallet and passport.

Although I never heard of any other biker carrying money in this way (it wasn't the most ingenious method) it was the best idea I could come up with. During the first few months on the road I was paranoid about being more than three feet away from my bike, but eventually I became quite cavalier about leaving the bike outside restaurants while I filled my stomach. A few times I left my bike stored at someone's home or at a hotel while I went off exploring for days at a time, returning to find everything in order.

To some this method of transporting money might seem foolhardy or irresponsible. My only comment is that it worked perfectly. I was never robbed and I never lost any money. Besides, I had the security of knowing the travellers checks would be replaced if they were lost or stolen.

Part Two

Mexico

Chapter 6

South of the Border

"The border means more than a customs house, a passport office, a man with a gun. Over there everything is going to be different. Life is never going to be quite the same again after your passport has been stamped."

-Graham Greene

On Friday, May 11, 1990, I pedaled across the Mexican border at Tecate, entering Baja California Norte. I had ambivalent feelings of confidence and dread. My pockets bulged with 86,000 pesos, equivalent to 30 U.S. dollars.* Three men with guns, dressed in dapper military uniforms, looked at me in a funny way. They weren't smiling. One of them motioned me to a nearby office, then lighted a cigar. Here we go, I warned myself, I'll wait in a long line, then at the last minute, a soldier with scrambled eggs on the bill of his cap and gold epaulets on his shoulders will lead me to a back room where I'll be interrogated under a naked light bulb. Smoke will fill the windowless room. I won't be able to see my interrogators. Perhaps 50,000 pesos will ameliorate the situation, I thought slyly.

There was a mob of people alright. But they were mostly Mexicans trying to get into the U.S. Seeing my passport in hand, an attractive

*28.67 pesos = 1 cent

Mexican lady escorted me into a spacious, brightly-lighted office, where she typed up my three-month visa, smiling all the time.

"Welcome to Mexico," she said handing me the completed form.

In a way I was rather disappointed with her efficiency and friendliness. I had steeled myself to expect hours of delay, indifference, and even arrogance, perhaps an insult or two.

As I approached my bike, the cigar-smoking military person motioned for me to approach his outdoor sentry post. Okay, here's where I get shaken down, but hey, no problema, I'll just grease a few palms and I'll be over the border like a gunshot. Before I could even ask, he took my passport and looked at the visa, then with the dexterity of a surgeon he hammered my passport with a beautiful, ink-smeared rubber stamp.

"Bien Viaje," he said returning the passport.

"Muchas gracias." I said in my best Berlitz Spanish.

Pushing my bike clear of the customs station, I looked over my shoulder, half suspecting some last minute command to stop. The three guards waved at me. I saluted them, mounted my bike, and pedaled into the busy streets of Tecate looking for a road sign that would direct me south to Ensenada. My plan was to find a nice camping spot somewhere along the highway and set up for the night.

Tecate itself held no attraction for me. Like so many small border towns I'd pass through during the coming year, it was a bustling, hustling village, filled with bustling, hustling people.

~ ~ ~

Hounds of Hell

On the south edge of Tecate, I was initiated to a ritual that would recur over and over during my bike ride through Baja. A pack of snarling, salivating, emaciated dogs chased me down the highway. Baja appeared to be a hot bed of mad dogs. As I passed through a settlement of crumbling adobe houses I'd be set upon by at least two, sometimes six, vicious mongrels that hadn't had a square meal in years judging from their appearance. I was a moveable feast just for them, "if" they could catch me. They came exceedingly close on more than one occasion, but I always out-sprinted them. After a few days of Baja touring, I kept a stick on my handlebars, available on a second's notice when under siege.

A daily nuisance and threat, I never realized how potentially dangerous they were until I reached Cabo San Lucas at the tip of Baja where I met Eric Ellman, bike tourer and author of "Bicycling Mexico." He gave me the low-down on the dogs of Baja.

First of all they're not pets, like they are in the U.S. They've never seen a can of dog food or a bone. These mongrels are half-starved, some on purpose, most out of necessity. And they are mistreated, neglected, and carry diseases. Some are vicious watchdogs; others are outcasts and scavengers. There is no such thing as table scraps in the Baja.

Eric told me about a lady friend of his who worked at the Rabies Research Foundation at Cornell University. She estimated that 90% of the rabid canine cadavers they studied came from Baja. In a way I was glad I acquired this information at the end of my Baja tour and not in Tecate.

Regardless, these dogs present a double-edged problem for the cyclist. First, it they bite you chances are excellent you'll get rabies. As the availability of rabies serum is problematic in Baja there is a distinct possibility you'll die. Secondly, even if you aren't bitten by a dog there's a chance you'll take a spill, as I nearly did a dozen times, and break a wrist, collarbone, or any number of other fragile body parts.

Worst case scenario is that you'll take a fall and get bitten too. My only defense was a stick or a rock. Whether mace or some other chemical spray would be effective against a dog attack is conjecture, at least on my part.

Eighty-six miles south of Tecate I wheeled into Ensenada and did a real dumb thing. I started this stage of my trip determined not to spend more than $10 per day, so what did I do on my first night in Mexico, I paid $42 for a hotel room in Ensenada. What with dinner and a few beers I spent over $50. So much for the budget. But I swear I didn't see any camping spots along the road and it turned into a long day and I was in a foreign country. And so it goes.

The one thing that became clear as I rode deeper into Baja was that I would have to rely more than ever on my helmet-mounted, rear-view mirror. The two-lane highway without shoulders didn't leave any margin for safety. To make things "muy peligroso", there's heavy truck and bus traffic. Apparently, speed limits are nonexistent or if there are they're disregarded by one and all.

~ ~ ~

The Private Property of Pancho Aguillar

The road passed through sand dunes, then at the top of a "cerro" I looked down at the Pacific Ocean, my old friend. Along the beach below I could see what looked like a small Puebla. It was a warm, sunny afternoon and I wasn't in any particular hurry. At the bottom of the hill, I turned off on a dirt road leading to the ocean. A few hundred yards down the road I stopped to read a sign scrawled in English, "You are entering the private property of Pancho Aguillar, get his permission before going farther at nearby house." I pedaled to the rancho not far away, but did not see a soul, so I propped my bike against a tree. A few minutes after knocking at the front door, an old fellow, probably in his late 60's, shuffled out of the cool interior onto the shaded veranda. I think I interrupted his siesta. Pancho told me I was welcome to camp on his beach; moreover, he would not charge me. He smiled, ran a meaty hand through his gray hair, then shuffled back inside.

I had to push my bike the last 50 yards through deep sand before reaching the beach. Off to my right I saw a truck. Two guys were loading fishing equipment into the back of their camper. I went over and asked how the fishing was, only to discover Rueben and Eduardo were from the San Francisco Bay area. They'd been down here for a week of fishing. Now they were preparing to return home. As he talked, Rueben handed me a freshly cooked cheeseburger and told me I was welcome to use their campsite. This was good news because as far as I could see it was the only campsite on the beach. Moreover, it was half-concealed below the protective side of a sand dune. A rocked-in firepit still smoldered with briquettes. Rueben opened his ice chest and handed me a cold Pepsi. Then he opened another cooler and began filling my arms with eggs, cheese, hamburger, hot dogs, fruit, Pepsis, hot dog and hamburger buns, two instant lunches, and a half-dozen thick slices of ham. I estimated I had enough food to last a week. Then off they went, leaving me as sole occupant of 100 or so miles of beachfront. After setting up my tent I took a refreshing swim in the ocean, then set about whipping up a feast of eggs, ham, cheese, and coffee.

With my belly full, I leaned back on my flatrock easy chair to see what condition my condition was in. I came to the conclusion that I was back in sync with the rhythm of the road, much like the "rhythm" I'd established by the time I'd reached the Icefields Parkway in Canada. In a nutshell, this meant I'd forgotten about time and mileage, schedules and destinations. I was back in tune with body, mind, and spirit.

Later that night while eating a ham and 4-egg omelet under a star-filled sky, I got to thinking about Robinson Crusoe, literary history's most famous castaway. In a small way I shared some of the feelings Crusoe felt when cast up alone on the beach of that unknown island. The feelings were mixed. True, there wasn't anyone to annoy me; then again, there wasn't anybody to talk to either. I had plenty of food, but no one to share it with. I had time to do anything I wanted, but with this bottomless well of time I did very little. I concluded that I admired Crusoe, but pitied him as well.

After two days of gluttony and sloth, I pried myself from my beachfront paradise to head further south.

I wrote this in my journal later that night. *"Climbing, climbing, climbing, and more climbing, with incredible amounts of sweat burning hell out of my eyes, trucks on hills, no shade, hot, hot, and low on water 'cause I didn't want to stop in El Rosario. How about that great advice about always filling your water bottles?"*

That was a tough day. It was also my first encounter with the blistering heat of Baja, something I hadn't reckoned on. When I finally topped out on the last hill about 6 p.m. I pulled off the road into a "rock garden" of various cacti and weathered rocks. Instantly, I had my tent pitched without the rainfly and crawled inside for a siesta. Instead of a restful sleep I sweated and groaned.

I thought back to those days in Alaska and Canada when I cursed the rain and the cold, but that was then, this is now. If I could only have one or two hours of rain and cold I'd feel like a king, I groused. Then and there I vowed I'd never, ever curse rainy weather again, ever.

~ ~ ~

Mas O Menos

Literally translated this Spanish phrase means—more or less. The odd thing is it can be applied to everything in Mexico from distance to time, hours of business, even to the condition of plumbing. Whenever I asked about distance from one point to the other, I'd always get an answer in kilometers, but with the little mas o menos proviso attached.

There didn't seem to be any rhyme or reason why a cafe or mercado was open or closed. If I asked someone if a restaurant was open, I'd be told in all seriousness, "mas or menos."

"My good fellow, is that air hose working?"

"Sure, mas o menos."

"Senorita, is there any drinking water available?"

"Si, mas or menos."

"I say, would it be possible to get a cold beer?"

"Si Senor, mas o menos."

Quite literally this catchall Spanish idiom became my theme song as I biked deeper into the hellaceous Baja desert.

~ ~ ~

Rock Gardens

While trying to mooch a bit of white gas from tourists passing through Catavina, I met Jeff and Yvonne Jamison and two-year old son Earl from Abingdon, England. They had toured across the United States in a rented motorhome and were now in the process of exploring Mexico before returning to their home in England. According to Jeff, they had passed me on the road the day before. We commented on the superb "rock garden" just north of Catavina, which we both stopped to admire. Unfortunately, the huge, sculpted rock formations, underscored by huge barrel cactus, had been defaced with multiple layers of spray paint graffiti. We agreed it was a crime that man could destroy in a matter of hours what had taken nature millions of years to craft.

~ ~ ~

The Longest Day

It was a perfect cycling day. The road had been mostly flat with rollers and the weather had been warm, but not oppressively hot. Much of the ride was done with the welcome assistance of a tail wind. The last ten-mile stretch was a descent into Bajia de Los Angeles on the Sea of Cortez.

The trip mode on my odometer read 117.11 miles. I never intended racking up that much mileage, but aided by favorable conditions I would have felt less than satisfied if I hadn't taken advantage of them.

Dazed and bit dehydrated, I found myself in front of Guillermo's Restaurant. It was 5 p.m. and I had an incredible thirst for a margarita. The dehydrating effects of the alcohol aside, I hungered for crushed ice mixed with lime, all saturated with the subtle taste of tequila. Besides, I'd already consumed nearly two gallons of tepid water that day.

I stumbled into the bar and eased slowly onto a stool, there to watch the mustachioed bartender prepare gallons of that infamous frozen concoction-all before my covetous eyes. Noticing my parched state, he smiled and asked what I wanted to drink. Jimmy Buffet's eulogy notwithstanding, I pointed a shaky finger at the bowl-sized glasses overflowing with creamy, aquamarine liquid.

"Grande?" Guillermo smiled.

"Si, grande, muy grande," I muttered.

After a second margarita, I ordered the seafood combo dinner of shrimp, lobster, and scallops. I sat down with a group of fishermen to eat and swap stories. With a belly full of seafood and grande margaritas I was in no mood or condition to look for a campsite, besides it was late and quite dark. Feeling little pain or anything else, I retrieved my bike from the patio and pushed it some 20 feet onto the beach in front of Guillermo's. Somehow I managed to put my tent up and crawl inside.

Wind and blowing sand woke me up sometime during the night. I was awake long enough to pull on my sweat pants and wool socks. The next thing I remember was turning over to watch a tequila sunrise (literally) over the Sea of Cortez. Minutes later, I looked around to find I was a mere 50 feet away from a trailer court. Pushing my bike through the sand toward the trailer park I noticed an old fellow, gray bearded and wearing a baseball cap, sitting outside his trailer. I stopped to ask if there was someplace I could camp for a few days.

He invited me to sit down and have a cup of coffee. My host, Jim Black, was a retired machinist from Torrance, California. Like many other southern Californians, Jim had been making an annual fishing trip to the Bay of L.A. for many years, so when he retired he decided to move down for good. Trailer court denizens drifted by to chat or sit and drink coffee, exchanging news about fishing and the weather. No one seemed to be in any particular hurry to go anywhere or do anything. Soon it was 10 a.m. and I hadn't moved from the patio table under Jim's trailer awning.

Sometime about noon I noticed it was extremely hot. People slowly drifted away to find a shady spot and I supposed take a siesta. When I finally got around to asking Jim about the camp spot again, he waved his hand toward the back of his trailer where, he said, I'd find enough room to pitch my tent. Luckily there was a six-foot cinder block wall that served as a windbreak and provided a bit of privacy. With camp in order, I strolled down to the beach for a swim and to wash out my sweat-stained biking clothes. The bay was like a piece of glass. That afternoon I made this entry in my journal.

"Sitting on Guillermo's veranda sipping Coke with ice cubes looking out at the bay. Islands dotting the horizon, blue sky, boats moving slowly in and out of the bay. Starting to relate to the manana mentality."

~ ~ ~

Disneyland?

A few days later I was back at the Junction of Hwy 1, where I stopped at the Pemex Gasoline station to top off my water bottles before heading down the road into, from what I could tell from the map, endless desert. Checking the thermometer attached to my handlebar bag I was shocked to see it was already 100 degrees, this at 9 a.m. Nevertheless, I pedaled away hoping to find some shade before noon and rest during the hottest part of the day.

I'd gone but a few miles when I began to feel a bit of intestinal discomfort. After another 1/2-mile I couldn't ignore the problem any longer. Hurriedly, I laid my bike down, scanned the desert for something to hide behind, but except for a few scraggly weeds the land was as flat as a pool table. So with no options available, I walked a few yards to the side of the road, dropped my drawers and squatted, none too soon either. This was my initiation to what is commonly referred to as "Montezuma's revenge." So much for tequila and seafood I thought.

Feeling a bit weak and shaky, I nonetheless remounted my bike and did my best to pedal away. Regardless of discomfort, I knew I had to get out of the sun. I'd stop now and again to drench my head with water, then soak my bandana and drape it over my head. Feeling momentary relief from the heat I secured my helmet and pedaled on.

No more than 45 minutes later my hair and bandana would be dry as a bone, so I'd stop and douse everything again.

To help reduce glare and the burning rays of the sun on my face I attached a visor to my helmet using Velcro strips. Combined with generous amounts of sunblock I avoided a sunburned face. Despite precautions against the sun, by midday I was feeling like a chili pepper. On a particularly desolate stretch of highway, I peered through the heat waves wafting up from the road surface to see what I thought was a roadside cafe, but getting closer I began to have my doubts. I could make out a structure of tin, plywood, and cardboard, but there didn't seem to be anyone around. The dirt parking area out front was empty of vehicles. Inhabited or not, I had to pull off anyway to seek momentary relief in the shade. I couldn't bike any farther.

Wheeling off the highway onto the dirt I headed straight for the building. Getting closer, I detected the odor cooking. It didn't smell like homemade apple pies fresh from the oven, but at least there was someone in there. While leaning my bike against the side of the building two small boys, about 6 or 7 years old, came running out of the ramshackle building, but stopped when they saw me and my bike. Standing there like pillars of stone they stared as though I'd just stepped out of a spaceship. I said hello and asked if the place was open. Possibly not understanding my Spanish, they beat a slow retreat inside with me on their heels. Shade at last, I thought, entering the hard scrabble luncheria.

I sat down at a rickety card table set with the usual condiments of a Mexican cafe—oil, vinegar, salt, salsa, jar of Nescafe coffee, and a glass filled with spoons. Flies buzzed lazily around the table as I soaked my head and face with my water bottle. I wasn't in any hurry. Although the interior of the cafe was in no way cool, just the absence of the burning sun combined with shade made me feel halfway human. Perhaps ten minutes later, a woman about 30-years old walked out of the kitchen area. Forewarned by the two boys, I presumed, she stopped behind the counter to stare at the alien. I did my best to smile and greet her, then asked if she was serving food. She was indeed. What would I like?

I thought for a minute, forget cheeseburgers and fries, forget shrimp salad, forget just about everything.

"Huevos revueltos, por favor."

"Con tortillas?"

"Si, y cafe."

While the Senora scurried to her butane gas stove, my eyes wandered around the cafe, stopping on the wall opposite me. There amongst the ubiquitous pictures of the Virgin of Guadalupe and assorted saints was an old color postcard of Disneyland, featuring those time-honored icons Mickey, Minny, and Goofy. I walked over for a closer inspection. In faltering Spanish I asked the Senora if she had been to Disneyland. She beamed from behind the counter. Yes, yes, she had been there with her husband and their first child. Her husband left her after the second boy was born. He went north to find work. She never heard from him again. Yes, Disneyland was her favorite. Someday she would like to take her boys there. But there is so little money. Who knows, maybe God will smile on her again. Maybe her husband will return with much money. He has been gone a long, long time. While we talked the boys reappeared briefly before hurrying outside to push a broken plastic truck in the dirt.

I sat down at the table and watched as the Senora set a small plate of scrambled eggs and tortillas in front of me. I chewed the eggs cautiously, my tongue finding neither taste nor texture. A plastic cup of boiling water was also set on the table, ready for me to add a heaping spoonful of Nescafe transforming it into a pale imitation of real coffee. Though my stomach, and other parts of my lower anatomy, had not fully recuperated I was compelled to seize the salsa bottle and put a generous coating on my eggs. I guessed the combination of greasy eggs, salsa and Nescafe was a recipe for disaster, but also surmised I'd find myself, further down the road, shoveling more obnoxious food and drink than this down my throat.

While I picked at my food the Senora disappeared into the nether regions of the building. Occasionally, I would hear the sound of a passing vehicle override the noisy companionship of the brothers playing in the dirt just outside the front door.

Relentlessly chewing the last tortilla, the Senora reappeared and asked if I'd like a second cup of coffee. I noticed she had taken the time to wash and brush back her raven hair. It was still wet and glistened. Also she had, for some unknown reason, painted her lips with fire engine red lipstick. I declined the coffee, but asked if she could fill my water bottles for me. She took the plastic bottles over to her fifty gallon drum of drinking water and filled them using a dipper, all the while smiling at me warmly. Leaving a small pile of pesos on the table I accepted the filled bottles and made my way outside, then stopped in the doorway and turned around.

"Disneyland," I said smiling and pointing at the postcard on the wall.

~ ~ ~

Somehow I managed to pedal 90.86 miles that day. It was dark as I approached the lights of what I guessed was Gerrero Negro. Not far from Gerrero Negro I was stopped at a police checkpoint blocking the highway in both directions.

Pedaling into a blinding light, I finally came to a stop beside a vehicle, where a policeman or army officer asked if I was carrying drugs or firearms. Assuring him that I had neither and explaining the nature of my travel plans, he waved me through the checkpoint. It took a good ten minutes for my eyes to adjust to the darkness again, but once acclimated I pedaled slowly and cautiously towards the bright lights of the town not to far in the distance. To help insure that passing motorists would see me I clipped my yellow flashing light to a rear pannier. With the help of a Mini Mag flashlight fixed to my handlebar bag I negotiated the potholed road to the turnoff to Gerrero Negro. Nearly incoherent and ravenous I pulled into a motel and restaurant a few miles from the main highway.

After a meal and a hot shower, I lay in my bed mentally devising a new riding plan. The soaring temperatures of the past two days made midday riding if not dangerous, at least foolhardy. I was already feeling the effects of dehydration and exposure to the broiling sun. Additionally, I was losing my appetite. To avoid further problems I planned to be on the road every morning no later than 5 a.m. Although I would have liked to cycle for a few hours after dark, I realized that would be an invitation to disaster. So biking from dawn until about 11 a.m., taking a rest break and eating during the hottest part of the day, then cycling a few hours before the sun set became my daily routine.

~ ~ ~

Oasis

The dictionary definition hardly does the word justice, i.e.. "a fertile spot in a barren, sandy desert." Well, when I first set eyes on the oasis of San Ignacio, it appeared to be a vision of paradise or the Promised Land. For the first time in weeks my eyes had to get used to colors: greens, reds, blues. It would probably be like an artist working for years in charcoal discovering the possibilities of a full pallet of oil paints.

I approached the village skeptically, suspecting the heat and constant sun had congealed what little gray matter I possessed; I really thought that any minute the whole colorful vision would vanish.

But no, this really was the oasis of San Ignacio. As I cycled down the narrow road into the village my eyes squinted at all the green leaves of palm trees and bushes. Then I passed a small pond filled with greenish, blue water. A most incredible sight, I mean all that water concentrated in one spot and not being used. There were flowers too. Coming around a bend in the road I confronted a magnificent hotel surrounded by equally magnificent landscaping. The driveway glistened with red and blue tiles. A carved wooden sign near the entrance read *La Pinta*

Hotel. It was so quiet and peaceful, the only sounds were those of birds perched in the nearby palm trees and shrubs. Again, there weren't any vehicles or people visible so I thought that perhaps it was closed.

I walked slowly into the cool, quiet lobby. At the registration desk a uniformed man directed me to the restaurant. Massive, carved wooden beams soared to the ceiling, tiled walkways crisscrossed flowerbeds and hedges in the interior courtyard.

The restaurant was more like a medieval banquet hall, with 20-foot ceilings and huge wooden posts and beams. Great windows shot up from floor to ceiling. Handcrafted tables and chairs were scattered about the tiled floor. All was cool and quiet and empty, save for a waiter and waitress pressed against the wall, as if standing at attention. I resisted the urge to look behind me to see if some diplomat or celebrity was about to enter and order breakfast.

The waiter glided toward me bearing a tooled leather menu the size of an attaché case. I was about to tell him I just wanted a cup of coffee, but checked myself, fearing that such a request would get me expeditiously escorted to the street. I wanted to linger here as long as possible, perhaps most of the day. In seconds, I was seated at one of the ponderous wooden tables. Upon a starched white tablecloth were enough cutlery, plates, glasses, cups, saucers, and linen napkins to accommodate a wedding party.

The waiter withdrew a few feet and stood in silence while I reviewed the capacious menu. My eyes literally popped when I saw such items as fresh orange juice, toast, bacon and eggs, pancakes, and sweet rolls. Though prices were higher than those at the tin and plywood luncheria up the road they were not what I would call unreasonable. Considering the ambiance I decided they were more than equitable. I told the waiter I wanted one of everything. Accustomed to dealing with raving gringos, he didn't bat an eye. Before he departed, I asked him if the coffee was freshly brewed. He assured me it was, adding that it was "muy rico."

While still engrossed in the elaborately printed menu, the waiter emerged from the kitchen bearing a tray containing a silver pot. With all the showmanship of a courtier he filled my cup half full encouraging me to taste the coffee. I raised the cup slowly to my lips; my nostrils engorged with the heady aroma, then sipped the liquid in much the same manner of a wine connoisseur. It was beyond my expectations. I smacked my lips, nodded my head agreeably, and watched as he filled my cup. Yes indeed, it was honest to god freshly ground and brewed coffee. Leaving the steaming silver pot beside me, he retreated to the far side of the room, available at the nod of a head or twitch of a finger.

Moments later, I heard footsteps echo off the tiles. I looked up to see the waiter lead a Senorita toward me. Her arm appeared to be impaled in the bottom of the huge tray she was carrying. At tableside, he removed one silver cover after another, placing lacquered plates of food on the tablecloth in front of me. Before departing to his station the waiter poured fresh juice into a glass, then set the decanter beside the filled glass.

Midway through my bacon and eggs, pancakes, and a week-old New York Times two gringos entered the restaurant. Although there were at least two dozen empty tables in an area half the size of a football field the waiter seated the two gentlemen at the table next to me. We acknowledged each other, said good morning, and commented on the weather. When asked how the coffee was, I smiled and gave them the O.K. sign with my thumb and forefinger. With breakfast resting comfortably in my stomach, I joined them at their table to share a pot of coffee and chat. I became fast friends with Bill Gilchrist and Gene Eaton, both from San Diego, California.

They guessed correctly that I was the owner of the laden bicycle outside. While they ate an equally sumptuous breakfast, I recounted my cycle adventures to date and plans to navigate to the tip of South America. They were on their way to Mulege to do some fishing and visit friends. After a second pot of coffee they offered me a ride into Mulege with them. They assured me there was plenty of room in their Toyota Land Cruiser.

A few hours later we pulled into Mulege, on the Sea of Cortez, and secured inexpensive rooms at a Hacienda converted into a hotel. The spacious courtyard, formerly a circular drive accommodating horse drawn carriages, was now dominated by a swimming pool. Bill knew the owner so we got settled in quickly in our second story rooms overlooking the interior courtyard. Before long we found ourselves a few doors down the street sipping margaritas at the Casitas Hotel, where Bill also knew the manager. Later that afternoon, we drove out to the Hotel Serenidad for a round of beer compliments of the owner who, naturally, was also an old friend of Bill's. It seems Bill used to fly his airplane regularly down to Mulege before a double bypass operation to fish and vacation with his wife. He'd been doing this for many years before the operation and subsequent suspension of his pilot's license.

After a dinner of grilled yellowtail at the Casitas Hotel, we sat around drinking beer and listening to guitar music 'til the wee hours.

At 7 a.m. next morning the mercury in my thermometer registered 92 degrees. I spent most of the day sightseeing with Bill and Gene. During the hottest part of the day, we returned to the hacienda. While they enjoyed a siesta, I submerged my body in the cool water of the pool to talk with some German tourists.

That evening the three of us attended a dinner fiesta at the Casitas Hotel, complete with fireworks, mariachis, and a lovely flamenco dancer.

Round about 10 p.m. I excused myself, explaining to Bill and Gene I planned to leave at 5 a.m. next morning. I said goodbye and thanked them for their pleasant company.

A courtyard full of singing, laughing, and drinking people circumvented all of my plans for a good night's sleep. When I cycled away from the hotel early next morning, a handful of revelers were still talking and drinking in the courtyard. On the edge of town I got a flat rear tire. Getting safely away from the highway, I checked my thermometer to discover it was already 90 degrees, but that shouldn't have surprised me as it had probably been 90 degrees, or close to it, all night. I slowly replaced the punctured tube and pedaled away dripping with sweat.

~ ~ ~

The Helados Man

Twenty miles south of Mulege I looked down from the highway at a beautiful horseshoe-shaped beach fringed with palm trees and makeshift thatched huts called "palapas." The water looked clear, cool, and particularly inviting, so I rode down to take a swim and investigate.

Within minutes I had my bike propped up against one of the many empty palapas. Stripped to my shorts I hurried to the water to swim and soak in the coolness. That was the beginning of a five-day stay at El Coyote Beach.

Because of the heat, I found it advantageous to sling my hammock inside the palapa for siestas and nocturnal sleep. Though most times I was clad only in shorts, I usually woke at 3 or 4 a.m. to pull on my sweat pants and a long-sleeved shirt.

I learned from a young Brazilian couple in the palapa next to me that one could dive for scallops off the beach, so I went into town to purchase a couple of days of supplies, a diving mask, and a snorkel. Between snorkeling expeditions I sat on the beach cleaning scallops and watching pelicans drop like bombs into the bay in search of their dinner. Wondering how they could hurl themselves with such force into the water and survive, I was constantly amazed to see them surface with the catch of the day in their cavernous bills.

Every afternoon and evening Danny's Helados truck would cruise down the beach accompanied by jingling bells, to sell popsicles and ice cream to the campers. Just like a kid anywhere, I stopped whatever I was doing when I heard the familiar jingling bells and hurried over to the helados truck. You could ask for any flavor you wished. Danny would always smile and say, "Si, si." But it would always be strawberry or vanilla.

"Chocolate espresso, por favor," I'd say.

"Si, no problema." Danny would say handing me a cup of strawberry.

Onto this little charade almost from the start, I bombarded him with outrageous requests.

"Rocky road and maple walnut, por favor."

"Si, si."

"Banana nut and pistachio with mocha almond fudge, por favor."

"Si, muy hambre."

"Okay, give me chocolate, peach, raspberry marble and top it with a scoop of watermelon sherbert."

"Si senor, gracias," Danny would say handing me a cup of vanilla ice cream.

~ ~ ~

La Paz

It was dark and finally began to cool off. For the first time in weeks I was pedaling amidst motor vehicle traffic and the crazy thing is I didn't have any idea where I was going; it's just that the cool breeze developed by pedaling felt so great I hated to stop and sweat again.

La Paz was a big, bustling city, well comparatively anyway. Out of the dense traffic a small station wagon pulled alongside me. Two mountain bikes were lashed to the roof. I looked through the passenger side window at the driver, a young gringo smiling confidently.

"Hey, where you biking to," he yelled.

"You mean right now?"

"No, where you going."

Glancing nervously back and forth between the station wagon and the cars parked along the sidewalk to my right, I yelled back at the driver to go to the nearest cafe and I'd follow him. A few blocks farther he pulled up to a taqueria and parked. I rolled my bike onto the sidewalk and secured it.

Eric Ellman, the station wagon driver, was writing a book about Mountain biking in Baja. We went in the taqueria and ordered Pacifico beer and a platter of tacos. Eric guaranteed I'd like them. He had been in and around La Paz for the past month. He'd found the best and cheapest taquerias, the best beer, and a reasonably priced and reasonably clean hotel. Well, it wasn't exactly a hotel, Eric paused to sip his beer, it was more like a convent that had been sort of transformed into a hospedaje.

I told Eric about my trip south from Tecate, complaining unnecessarily about the incredible heat and the fact that the incredible heat had sapped my strength and precious bodily fluids. He commented that my body was merely adapting itself to the torrid climate. Also, he suggested that I should buy some liquid electrolytes available at many of the farmacias. In fact, he thought so highly of his prognosis he volunteered to accompany me to a farmacia the next day. For now, he added, drink Pacifico and think about alpine glaciers. Wanting to know my impressions of biking Baja, I told him three things come to mind immediately—hot, hot, and hotter. On a more serious tack, I recounted my extraordinary camping experiences at Pancho Aquillar's and El Coyote Beach.

Born and raised in New York City, Eric had adapted to the culture and climate of Mexico with ease. He and a colleague had spent a few years bike-touring central Mexico gathering information for a book titled, *Bicycling Mexico*. His Spanish was excellent. He loved the culture, the food, and the people. I supposed out loud that he had been a language major in college, perhaps specializing in Spanish, or maybe a social anthropologist with a field of concentration in Mexico. I was way off the mark, for Eric's major was Geology. He was thinking of returning to graduate school to seek an advanced degree in water resource management. Again I wondered out loud about his interest in bicycling. Elementary my dear Hawkins, Eric joked, he'd been a bicycle messenger in Manhattan long before mountain bikes turned it into the stuff movies are made of. He'd done a lot of touring in the U.S. too before pedaling south of the border, but once here he fell in love with everything. He can't understand how Mexico has gotten such a bad reputation in the tourist industry. Judging from my limited experience I wondered too.

"Listen," Eric advised," take a rest, do some sight seeing. La Paz is a beautiful city. Sure it's hot as hell, but there's a lot to do. Tell you what, come over to La Casa Convento, it's cheap, we can split the cost of the room. There's this interesting painter, an American, who lives there, he can fill you in on all the local color and history."

"Why not, I'd like to take a break from the road heat anyway."

"Hey, can you believe the temperature on the road surface during the hottest part of the day is probably 150 degrees or more," Eric said with a smile.

"Thanks for the information."

I followed Eric to the Convento, where I moved my bike and gear into Eric's room, spacious enough to accommodate all my gear and bike, plus an extra bed. As a precaution against theft Eric removed his two mountain bikes from the roof of his wagon and wheeled them into the room. By the time we got settled in I felt like I was living in a bike shop. A ceiling fan did little more than push the humid heat about the room. I fell asleep immediately, but was awakened around midnight to skirmish with a squad of invading cockroaches.

In the morning, before leaving for a meeting with organizers of kayak and mountain bike tours, Eric guided me to the public market not far from the Convento. This was the first of many experiences I'd have with the public markets of Mexico, Central, and South America. The best description I can come up with, inadequate at best, is to call it the organic version of a shopping mall. The market is usually housed in a huge adobe building, sometimes in a tin-roofed shed open on all sides, or in a public square. In La Paz, shops and stalls lined the perimeter and center of the interior, which was about the size and shape of a football field. If it's a popular market there are generally stalls outside as well. In addition to the craftsmen, merchants, and purveyors who pay rent or tax on their stalls, there are numerous street vendors strolling about selling everything from apples to shoelaces. Because inside space is at a premium, the stalls are generally small, but vendors use every available square inch to their advantage, usually cramming so much merchandise into the space it overflows into and over the aisles. In a few markets I visited I had to crouch low to negotiate the narrow warren-like aisles. To make matters worse one also has to squeeze around and between men and women carrying children and shopping bags.

If anything, the cramped quarters add to the ambiance and the experience. Just like any shopping mall in the U.S. you can purchase just about any commodity. Generally, these markets are open every day, but are particularly interesting on one or two days during the week when farmers and crafts people come in from the countryside to sell their produce or crafts.

Once I caught on to the scheme of things, I would always head to the market to eat and browse. In the morning I'd get a fresh fruit juice smoothie with an egg, then follow my nose to the panaderia for baked goods. Strolling about the aisles, munching on a bun or cookie, I'd inspect the hand-woven blankets, rugs, sandals and shoes, leather jackets, pottery, and glassware. When my Spanish reached a certain level of proficiency I'd stop and talk to the artisans or vendors, forever trying to get me to buy something I had absolutely no use for. On my part, I would shake my head, haggle over the price and generally act like I knew what I was doing.

Later that morning Eric took me to a farmacia where I purchased a container of electrolytes fortified with vitamins and minerals. I mixed up a batch in one of my water bottles and carried it with me wherever I went, sipping the tart liquid throughout the day.

Although Eric had to stay around La Paz for a few days, I planned to leave in the morning. I learned from Eric that the ferry I planned to take from Cabo San Lucas at the tip of Baja was no longer in service. In fact, Eric commented, it was sunk in the shallow waters off Cabo slowly turning into a man-made reef. I would have to return to La Paz to board the Ferry for Mazatland on mainland Mexico. A really neat bike route, according to Eric, would be to bike over to Todos Santos, on the pacific coast, then down to Cabo San Lucas. When I returned to La Paz I could complete the loop by cycling up the highway to La Paz on the east coast of Baja. As it was only a few hundred miles from La Paz to Cabo by either route, we made plans to meet at the Mexican Youth Hostel in Cabo San Lucas in three or four days.

~ ~ ~

Hotel California

The thing I liked best about cycling to Todos Santos was that the closer I got to it, the cooler it got. A breeze flowed inland from the Pacific Ocean mitigating the intense desert heat. Coasting down the main street in Todo Santos I couldn't help but notice the Hotel California, a two-story whitewashed adobe building encroaching the road. About 50-yards past the hotel I stopped. I had to go back and investigate. At the very least I had find out how much a room cost. It was cool and quiet inside. I estimated the adobe walls were at least four-foot thick. Wandering though the lobby into a cozy dining room I found Senor Louis, the manager, finishing his lunch.

Not in the least put off by my somewhat scruffy appearance, he proudly showed me around the hotel. I was impressed with the airy rooms on the second floor, all whitewashed, tiled, and immaculately clean. More impressive, however, was the circular, blue-tiled swimming pool off the rear patio. A profusion of blue and white wisteria clung to a brick wall surrounding the patio. Amidst a ledge of colorful plants and flowers, a water fountain spouted a stream of water into the pool. It was quiet and peaceful. As yet, I hadn't seen a single guest.

Even before Sr. Luis told me the room tariff was $27 a night, I'd already made up my mind that I would splurge and stay there. When all the registration formalities were taken care of, Senor Luis showed me to a storage room off the small lobby where I could secure my bike and various gear I didn't want to drag upstairs. I shouldered my pack and filled my arms with the items I wanted and went to my room. After settling in, I took a shower and pulled on my swimsuit. Now, I thought, time to soak in the pool and sip an ice cold soft drink.

At poolside I was amazed to see two women stretched out on lounge chairs sunning themselves. I introduced myself to Pat and Susan, from Seattle, Washington, on a short vacation to Cabo San Lucas. Wanting to escape the tourist bustle of Cabo they had rented a car and driven to Todos Santos for some peace and quiet. The three of us spent the afternoon sunning, soaking in the pool, and sipping Cokes and beer.

That evening we gathered in the dining room for a combination seafood dinner. That's when we began drinking margaritas.

After dinner, in the small bar off the dining room, we unwisely encouraged Jorge the bartender, Senor Luis's 14-year old son, to add just a bit more tequila to a blender full of margarita mix. With more coaxing, Jorge found the Eagles tape with the cut of Hotel California. Feeling relaxed and enjoying the music, we decided to dance. We started by dancing together, then split off into solo performances, gradually reforming into a trio, sometimes bumping into each other, sometimes bumping into the wall.

The next thing I remember, I was dancing alone, the music long since turned off. My final memory of that night, a fuzzy one at that, was of me knocking on Pat and Susan's door, next to mine, and asking them if they would like to go fishing.

First thing next morning I went downstairs to the pool for a tall glass of Pepsi filled with ice cubes. Later, while enjoying a breakfast of coffee and rolls, Pat and Susan, strangely quiet that morning, stopped at my poolside table to say goodbye before checking out and heading over to La Paz.

I kept doing a body check to determine if I'd hurt anything the night before. Thankfully everything was present and accounted for and in serviceable condition. My head and most of what was inside it seemed to be functioning adequately, so I sat by the pool with my sunglasses on trying to piece together a plan for the day, half expecting Senor Luis to confront me with a huge bill for damages and a stern lecture on the proper behavior of hotel guests. Fortunately, there was no lecture and the only additional expense incurred was a $16 bar bill from the previous night's festivities.

Out in front of the Hotel California in the blinding sun, I still could not come up with the day's marching orders. Down the road near the plaza I spotted a watermelon stand and made a beeline for it. I bought a melon and shared it with the seven brothers and sisters tending the stand. The oldest, Teresa, informed me they ranged in age from seven to eighteen. She, the eldest, was in charge in the absence of her father, she said matter-of-factly. Momentarily, the father emerged from the house behind the stand. I asked him if all the kids were really his. Smiling proudly, he said, yes that was true, adding with a wink they were from three different wives. About 60 years old, perhaps a little on the lean side, I guessed the Senor had a strong constitution.

I asked if he could direct me to a beach where I could camp. With a good deal of pointing and waving, he said there was a nice beach just a few miles south of town. Except for the sandy road leading down to the ocean it was a short, sweet ride, 6.79 miles according to the odometer.

Although the campsites were primitive, only a few were occupied. Not far from the bath and shower was a small palapa cafe. With camp quickly set up I strolled to the beach to watch the surfers with my binoculars. The huge surf made it a bit intimidating for swimmers, but offered several hearty surfers a challenge.

~ ~ ~

Cacti and Cockroaches

Months before I ever set foot in Mexico I was deluged with stories and information about cactus: the ocatilla, the barrel cactus, the yadada cactus. I must admit I was looking forward to observing cacti in its many forms and they were a relief against the otherwise bland desert, but day-after-day of cactus and more cactus; short cactus, tall cactus, skinny cactus, young healthy cactus, old rotting cactus, the cactus thing not only lost its appeal, it became a cactus torture chamber. I guess cactus became a symbol of the heat and pain of the desert. I never, ever want to see another cactus as long as I live.

Another thing I don't mind seeing for as long as I live is a cockroach. Before cycling across the border on my way south, I'd never had any real experience with the cockroach. I'd read things about them and heard things about them, but had never confronted one. Well, that certainly changed south of the border. Fact is the cockroach is indestructible, it has been around for about 320 million years. In the U.S. alone there are some 55 species. Complimenting its resiliency is a talent for reproduction. A mated pair can account for as many as 400,000 progeny in a single year. With nothing to eat, a cockroach can survive for a month or more; it can live for about three months on water alone. This world citizen seems to thrive in tropical climates. To my mind at least, one of its least admirable traits is manifesting itself, usually in great numbers, immediately after the lights are turned out.

The La Paz hotel room I shared with Eric Ellman was my initiation to the nocturnal world of the cockroach, for the most part the cockroach is a night person. No sooner had I turned out the lights in our room at La Casa Convento than they emerged from the lower depths to scuttle and scurry about, some actually audacious enough to parade over my body. I'd leap up, turn the lights on, and poof they vanished. Awakened by the light and noise, Eric asked what was the matter. I asked if the cockroaches were bothering him.

"What roaches," he said turning over and falling asleep.

Frustrated and wide awake, I extinguished the lights and returned to my bed with a rolled up magazine. Out they came again. Sometime during the night I stepped into the combination bath and shower, lighting my way with my Mini Mag flashlight. There I found a stout fellow about 4 inches long swilling the water collected near the shower drain. After several thwacks from the magazine it finally died. I was amazed at its stamina. No sooner had I dispatched this intrepid warrior, than several reinforcements emerged to take his place. Somewhere around dawn, I gave up my vigil and lapsed into a fitful sleep.

~ ~ ~

Two Donkeys in the Shade

Returning to my campsite on the beach south of Todos Santos I was surprised to see a blue VW bug parked nearby. While doing some preventive maintenance on my bike, two young ladies came up from the beach. From the crowded interior of the car they pulled out a tent and began pitching it. I strolled over the few paces to their campsite to introduce myself. After their camp was in order we walked over to the cantina for beer. Alexandra Wyss and Judith Emmenegger were on holiday from Switzerland. Their two-month tour of Mexico had started on the Yucatan peninsula. Now, they were heading north to California where they would catch a plane home.

The temperature had been close to 100 degrees all day. I was literally riding in an oven. By midday I was so weak and dehydrated I had to push my bike up hills. The last of my electrolyte supply was used up the day before. I deteriorated to the point where I couldn't even push the bike. Standing beside it trying to work up enough strength to move, I saw what looked like a large shade tree. The only tree I'd seen all day. I stumbled toward it like a sun-crazed desert rat. As I got closer I was disappointed to see two donkeys occupying the shady patch under the tree. Getting even closer, I hoped to scare them away, but no such luck, they stood their ground like sentries guarding a sacred treasure. Adding insult to injury, they bared their teeth and hee-hawed from their shady retreat.

Standing alongside the road I looked ahead to see the shimmering ribbon of blacktop rise up to form another dreaded hill. In my condition it looked insurmountable. Sweat oozed from every pore and crevice of my body. Instinctively, I reached for a water bottle, my last one, and took a sip, almost spitting it out. The water was warm and tasted like brine.

Soaking my head with the luke warm water, I began pushing my bike up the hill. After three tentative steps I heard the donkeys bray again. Whispering obscenities, I continued pushing my bike. An hour later, exhausted but at the top of the hill, I stopped to soak my head and bandana with the last of the tepid water. As I wrapped the dripping bandana on my head, a VW bug pulled off the road and stopped. It was Alexandra and Judith. They emerged from the car with an ice chest. Swarming about me with much concern, they opened the cooler to reveal a liter of Pepsi and bag of ice cubes. They watched as I gulped one glass of cold Pepsi after another, supplemented by long draughts from their jug of cold drinking water.

Concerned about my biking in the heat, they'd decided to backtrack to Cabo San Lucas and head north through La Paz, hoping to see me along the way and make sure I didn't get caught in the heat and sun without water. When I finally came to my senses I thanked them profusely, adding that they came along just in the nick of time. Pulling out their map and studying it for a bit, they said there was a nice beach a few miles down the road where they'd stayed about a week ago. Their plan was, they told me, to drive ahead with some of my gear and find a camping spot. When I got there they'd make hamburgers. With my backpack, tent, and sleeping bag in their car they drove off, but not before filling my bottles with ice cold water.

Later, after a swim in the surf and a few more cold Pepsis, I developed enough of an appetite to eat two cheeseburgers, a banana, sliced pineapple, and some cookies. Sitting around our small campfire that night, talking and playing backgammon, I thanked the ladies for rescuing me from the hellfires of Baja.

Somewhat rejuvenated the next day, I managed to pedal into Cabo San Lucas. There in downtown Cabo I pulled over to the first open-air cafe I saw to relax in the shade and sip an ice cold Pepsi. I had never in my life consumed so many soft drinks as I did in Baja. Regardless of their less-than-healthful effects, I'd become addicted to them. It seemed nothing else, including beer, could quench my thirst quite like a Pepsi or Coke.

The only thing I had strength to do was go in search of the Mexican Youth Hostel (CREA) where I planned to meet Eric Ellman. With directions supplied by the waiter at the cafe, I found the hostel a mere 30 minutes away. Much to my surprise it was a huge, walled compound with numerous modern townhouse-like buildings inside, complete with landscaping, and volleyball and basketball courts. All this for only four dollars a night.

I gladly paid up and found myself the sole occupant of a seven-bunk dorm. A Mexican fellow in the dorm next door shared the spacious bath and shower room with me. Once again, the hostel was nearly deserted. Apparently we were the only guests in a hostel that could easily accommodate 100 people. I spent the first hour soaking under a cool shower and the second hour drinking cups if Pepsi and ice. Although there was a small fan in the room , the heat was suffocating. When not flopped on my bed resting, I was padding back and forth to the shower.

With the local ferry rusting away in the harbor and broiling heat making biking suicidal, my only concerns were to stay in the shade and drink cold liquids. By way of encouragement the lad at the front desk informed me that it would "cool off" that night to 90 degrees or so. Maybe down at the ocean, but here in the cement block dorms, absorbing the sun all day like fire bricks in an oven, the temperature plummeted to a frosty 92 degrees, that with the aid of a fan that did lit-tle more than circulate hot air and mosquitos. Looking back, I realize I was on the verge of dehydration and sunstroke. Being a fair-haired and fair-skinned individual I'd taken the precaution of slathering my face each day with sunscreen, but the heat had gotten to me.

Just after dark, Eric appeared and talked me into going out for a cerveza and tacos.

~ ~ ~

Eric Goes Surfing

Next morning Eric and I, feeling like french fries, found ourselves at one of many new pastel-colored hotels, touring time-share condos, lis-tening to endless sales pitches, filling out financial statements, and sidestepping appeals to make "purchasing decisions." All this for a complimentary breakfast and bogus bottle of Tia Maria.

After a sumptuous breakfast, Eric decided we'd go surfing. A native and resident of New York City all of his life he has yearned, since seeing the movie **Gidget**, to mount a surfboard and race down a cresting wave to the delight and edification of bikini-clad young ladies. He was appalled that I, a Californian and former resident of Hawaii, had never been on a surfboard. To redeem myself I agreed to accompany him on a surfing safari to Zipper's, a legendary surfing mecca, just south of San Jose del Cabo and about a 30-minute drive from Cabo San Lucas.

When we arrived the surf looked inviting, but Zipper's was deserted, save for one blond-haired young fellow sanding a surf-board in the shade of a palapa. When learning the daily rental fee for a surfboard was $30, Eric asked if it would be possible to rent one for an hour. The blond chuckled. Eric then informed the blond that he is writing a travel article and asked for a "comp" surfboard, promising to mention Zipper's in the story. The blond howled with laughter.

Secretly, I was glad the rental fee was prohibitive. The last thing I wanted to do that morning, Californian or no, was straddle a surfboard amongst the world class waves crashing onto the nearby beach.

Nonetheless, we retrieved the cooler and beach umbrella from the back of Eric's dust-covered station wagon and trooped down to the beach. While I snoozed in the shade of the umbrella, Eric struck up a conversation with some surfers next to us. Shortly, Eric borrowed one of their boards and sprinted toward the water. I eagerly watched as he attempted to paddle out past the breakers. Three times waves forced him back to the beach. Finally, paddling furiously he succeeded. I watched for a good twenty minutes as he paddled out farther and farther trying to reach a group of surfers sitting on their boards waiting for an ideal wave. But before he reached them a cresting wave carried the surfers on a long ride and in the process moved Eric back half the distance to the beach. Undeterred, he paddled back out to sea again. Finally in an advantageous position he seemed to slump full length on the board and nap. After awhile he sat up, alert to the incoming swells that would transform him from a mere paddler and sitter into a statuesque surfer. Although he paddled furiously, one wave after another passed him by, necessitating more paddling to reposition himself. Hours seemed to go by before I finally saw him rise to his feet in the triumphant surfing position, if only for a few seconds, then slump to the board again as another wave surged swiftly beneath his surf board. At long last he paddled back to the beach where the young surfers pulled him from the board and half carried him to the shade of the umbrella. For good reason, he was utterly exhausted.

"Well, how was it." I asked.

"Great, fantastic...surf...God, it...takes a lot of...energy, whew."

"Sure looked like a lot of fun."

"Yeah, you going to give it a try?"

"Nah, not today. Waves just don't look right to me."

~ ~ ~

The Witches of Candeleria

Next morning at Papi's, a breakfast place in downtown Cabo, Eric made the absurd suggestion that we go for a mountain bike ride.

"Bike ride, in this heat," I exclaimed, "I can hardly walk. A camel wouldn't go out on a day like this and you want to go mountain biking."

I suggested that we go down to the marina and see if I could find a boat to hitch a ride over to the mainland. After coffee, we walked across the street to the newly constructed marina, where to my surprise there were only a half dozen yachts and powerboats berthed there.

When I asked the skipper of one of the sailboats about the possibility of crewing on a boat headed for mainland Mexico, he grinned and shook his head. It was chubasco (hurricane) season, he cautioned. No boats were headed anywhere and wouldn't be going or coming until September. In the meantime, Eric wandered away in search of a charter fishing boat he hoped would give a "comp" trip to a writer of travel articles.

Next to the sailboat I looked over a huge power yacht named "Escape." The name appealed to me so I called to the blonde lady working on the flying bridge. She merely shook her head when I asked if she knew of any boats headed for the mainland, then invited me aboard for a rum and coke and a tour of the air-conditioned interior of the Escape. Afterward, we slumped into comfortable chairs in a carpeted salon next to the galley to sip our drinks, chat, and feel the rejuvenating effects of the cool air pumping out of the air conditioning ducts. I started to come back to life. It was the best I'd felt in weeks. Just as I got comfortable I saw Eric pacing back and forth on the dock. Reluctantly, I told Marti, my hostess, I had to go biking with my buddy. At the door of her frosty sanctuary, I said good-bye. Marti promised to ask around among friends and fellow seamen about boats heading to the mainland, but she cautioned it was chubasco season. She invited me to stop back any time to check with her.

I persuaded Eric to drive up to the mountain village of Candeleria, rather than risk the possibility of sunstroke on our bikes. In the heat of the day we began driving into a cauldron of sand and sagebrush. To call Eric's vehicle a station wagon is generous, for it had little more room than a cramped 2-door economy sedan. What limited space there was, was chock full of biking gear, camping gear, food, bottles, clothes, tools, cameras, spare bike tires and wheels, a case of Pacifico, a huge ice chest, a typewriter, and an eclectic collection of books, manuals, magazines and newspapers. As we bumped along the dirt road leading into the mountains, two mountain bikes on the roof clattered for attention.

Eric drove with his left hand on the steering wheel and his right clutching a tape recorder. In addition to being a frustrated surfer, he had the makings of a frustrated stock car racer. I noticed a paperback on the dashboard. A copy of *Holidays in Hell*, by P.J. O'Rourke.

"A self-help book," I asked.

"Kind of. You want it, it's yours. I'm almost done with it. Got anything to trade."

"*Barchester Towers* by Trollope."

"You read that stuff?"

"Sure, I like Victorian Lit."

"Got anything else."

"*Stick* by Elmore Leonard."

"It's a deal."

We drove through a forest of tall, closely spaced cactus. Suddenly, I got claustrophobic and began to sweat. Eric yelled something into his tape recorder, "Mile 15.6, elevation 800 feet, steep vado, toughest climb on ride."

He shot a look at me. "Hey, what's wrong. You car sick?"

I told him about my cactus phobia. Eric thought I was joking.

The air got noticeably cooler as we climbed into the hills. It was so refreshing I wondered why they didn't build some new hotels up here. I thought it would be a welcome relief.

Candeleria is a small mountain puebla dominated by a cathedral and shed housing a diesel generator that provides electricity for two hours each night to the handful of residents. We parked in front of the church and got out to stretch our legs. As we looked around, the manager of the new Conosupco, a government subsidized grocery store, walked toward us carrying a burlap sack on his shoulder. He recognized Eric who had biked there two days earlier. Eric introduced me to Rito, then asked if there was any truth to the stories and legends about witches in Candeleria. Rito smiled and said the witches were old now and didn't fly around much. They've kind of retired, he smiled. Rito excused himself to deliver the sack still lumped on his shoulder. We walked over to a enormous fig tree growing out of rocks at the edge of a ravine. Its roots branched out over the rocks like steel cables. What was left of a stream trickled by in the depths below us. Three giant, redheaded vultures were perched in the top branches of the tree. They looked well fed. Eric called them nature's garbage men. He assured me they were not dangerous, explaining the lack of muscles in their talons precluded their attack on animals and carrying them off. They lived on carrion and looked like they enjoyed their work.

As we climbed into the lower branches of the tree the vultures leaped lethargically into the air and flew off.

Eric advised me never to let a vulture puke on me. Puke was their only defense, he explained. Eric had a biologist friend involved in vulture research. As vulture puke is as corrosive as battery acid, his friend always wore old clothes whenever studying them. Vultures can digest ball bearings, rivets, and lug nuts, according to Eric. Regardless of their weak talons, I kept a sharp eye out for their return.

On our way down the mountain, Eric told me that in addition to having been a New York bike messenger, he had also been a taxi cab driver. I opened two Pacificos, reluctantly passing one to Eric.

While roaming around the docks later that day, Eric was able to buy a freshly caught Dorado. That night at the Hostel we barbecued thick filets of fish and invited three new arrivals, all Frenchmen, to join us for dinner. Ludovic Monroe and Laurent Guazzone were touring

Mexico, after having completed two years graduate work at a university in Houston, Texas. Their countrymen, Alain Cano was finishing up a third world tour that started in Argentina. All three would be returning to France shortly. Next day, before they caught the afternoon bus, all of us hiked out to El Arco, the massive arch-shaped rock formation at the tip of Baja. In the process my camera met an untimely death by salt water. While wading through the surf on the way to the arch I was caught in a breaking wave, forcing me to consign my Nikon to the trash barrel.

~ ~ ~

Manana Is Good Enough For Me

Two weeks later, I was swinging in a hammock sipping rum and coke. The mercury in the thermometer, as usual, had topped out at 100 degrees. I swear it was stuck there. It appeared that I was stuck in Cabo. I didn't care. I didn't have any energy or ambition to care. Manana was my most ambitious thought. By then I was working on the 58-foot Bertram power yacht helping Marti clean brass and oil teak decks. In a spurt of energy I even changed the oil and filters on the diesel engines. As a respite from our work, I'd accompany Marti to her condo to swim in the pool and dry off in the late afternoon sun. At night we'd barbecue fish, drink rum and coke, and watch the sun set far off in the Pacific. Nights at the beach condo were cool compared to the boiler room dorms of the hostel.

Eric had gone north to check out a few more mountain bike rides before returning to the states. Marti was also gone to the states for a month of visiting family and friends. I was in charge of boats, condos, trailers, and Jeeps.

Most evenings would find me in the hammock beside her house trailer all under the shade of a giant palapa. I'd swing in the hammock, read, and sip cold drinks. I had sunk into a bottomless pit of ennui. There must have been some electrolytes in either the rum or Coke that my body was craving, or why would I drink it morning 'til night.

Before he left, Eric told me that the way to escape the heat was to take the La Paz ferry to Mazatland and head for the mountains where it would be cool, additionally I'd see some of the finest scenery in all Mexico. Manana is soon enough for me. Today, whatever day it was, I would drive into town in Marti's jeep and a trade a paperback at the small library at the Broken SurfBoard Cafe in downtown Cabo. While in town I'd get more Pepsi and ice. Then when it got real hot, I'd take the 12-foot Boston Whaler motor boat out to El Arco to do some snorkeling. It would be a full day, but I'd better not forget to return to the marina by 8 p.m. to shower and have dinner with Jay and his girlfriend Jessica aboard the Crystal Gale. Grilled, marinated Dorado was on the menu.

That was the way I spent June and July. Sure enough there was an occasional Hurricane alert, with accompanying wind and surf, but the storms would always break up far out in the ocean. Occasionally, Jay and I would go deep sea fishing in the Boston Whaler. Though it wasn't the best time of the year for fishing we'd always manage to hook a few fish the charter boats missed.

One hot day late in July I looked up from the hammock in the shade of the palapa and there was Marti carrying her suitcase. I knew it was time to leave. Suddenly, I remembered Eric's advice about taking the ferry to Mazatlan and riding into the mountains.

Chapter 7

Mainland Mexico

Somewhere in the mountains east of Mazatland and west of Durango I stopped pedaling to look around and catch my breath. I was up in the mountains at the 4,000-foot level; it was cool, there had been some rain, and I was feeling great. For the first time in months I wasn't bathed in sweat. Also, I had energy and strength. I felt like I'd escaped the torture chamber of hell.

As Eric Ellman predicted there was heavy truck traffic on the highway south of Mazatland-not so on the road I turned onto leading up into the mountains. This two-laner snaked its way through rolling farm country. I must have passed a dozen roadside stands displaying generous mounds of an exotic type of fruit. At first I didn't know what they were, so I asked the driver of a pickup loaded with the mysterious yellow-orange fruit. After a lengthy explanation in Spanish, most of which I didn't understand, he gave me several ripe mangos, half of which I consumed on the spot. To this day they are one of my favorite tropical fruits.

Coasting down a hill toward a village I saw a vado, but this one had water flowing over it. Mexico has found it much cheaper and more practical to build vados (cement roadways across streambeds) than bridges. I biked across many a bone-dry vado in Baja, but this one was the first to have water in it or on it. Considering most streams and rivers in Baja are dry 80% of the year, bridge construction would not be cost effective. But this wasn't Baja and the vado in front of me had plenty of water from recent rainstorms. I waited by the side of the vado until a pickup drove slowly across the stream, water rising to its wheel hubs but no further. Judging the depth as shallow, I removed my shoes and socks and pushed my bike into the stream, thankful the water didn't soak into my panniers. The stream crossing also gave me an opportunity to wash and cool my hot, sweaty feet.

When I stopped for a jugo de pina (pineapple juice) in the village, I was told there was much rain in the mountains. Farther up the mountain road I learned that vados sometimes don't work, or more accurately, work only too well. I crested a hill to confront a line of traffic parked on the highway. Pedaling to the front of a line of cars and trucks I saw a rain-swollen river nearly cresting its banks. I guessed correctly that the vado was submerged under at least five feet of water, causing traffic to back up on both sides of the river. Drivers and passengers emerged from their vehicles to gather on the riverbank, gauge the depth of the water, and estimate aloud how long it would be before the river dropped to a level safe enough to cross. I estimated one would have to wait a day, maybe two, for the waters to recede to its docile pre-flood stage. Then too, it could rain again, in fact, it could still be raining in the mountains. It was anybody's guess as to when the swollen river would drop and be safe to cross.

"It will go down in an hour, maybe two," a truck driver assured me looking at his watch. With an air of futility, he climbed into the cab of his truck and pulled a straw cowboy hat over his eyes.

Regardless, drivers of the large passenger buses were already busy unloading baggage holds and with the help of passengers piling boxes, bags, and freight in the aisle inside the bus.

In the meantime, a roadside refreshment stand was doing a thriving business. I bought a Pepsi and sat under a palapa to wait and watch people watching the river. Hours later, I heard the roar of a diesel engine. I watched, along with a hundred other people, as a large truck drove cautiously across the vado, water flowing swiftly around its huge tandem wheels. The river had receded only about two feet. Next in line, the bus with empty cargo bays roared across. Cheers and whistles filled the air as people raced to their vehicles. This was not the time to be over-cautious; who knew when the next rainstorm would erupt.

For a few pesos, kids in bathing suits helped guide and push cars and pickups through the thigh-deep water, just in case wet electrical components caused an untimely stall. With my bike and gear in the bed of a pickup, I helped the youngsters push the truck swiftly across the vado. Smaller vehicles, like VWs and Datsuns, wisely remained queued up until the river dropped still further.

High in the mountains the next day I noticed I'd broken the 9,000-mile mark. At last I had renewed momentum and enthusiasm. My goal at the time was Barranca de los Negros, a national park recommended by Eric. Because Mexican highways are not cluttered with directional and informational signage prevalent in the U.S., one has to follow one's map closely.

~ ~ ~

La Familia Sanchez

Cycling through beautiful rolling hills flanked by haciendas and pine forests I got caught in a torrential downpour, forcing me to stop alongside the road and hastily pull on my rain gear. It was raining so hard I could barely see. Riding was impossible and temporary refuge was nowhere to be seen. So what did I do? Deciding that to do nothing is sometimes the best course of action, I draped my ground cloth over the bike and stood there hoping the pounding rain would soon taper off, if not stop completely.

A big Ford four-wheel drive truck went splashing by. I watched as it braked, pulled off the road, then backed up to me. The driver jumped out and hurried over to where I stood. He told me I had to get out of there, it was muy peligroso (very dangerous) where I was standing, adding that he'd help me put the bike in the back of his truck and take me to his restaurant a few miles down the road. There I could dry off and wait out the rain. At least that's what I understood him to say, my Spanish at that point was far from the fluency level. Regardless, I felt reasonably certain I'd gotten the gist of the conversation.

Daniel Sanchez was soaked to the skin by the time we got my bike and gear stowed in the bed of his truck, while I remained warm and dry in my suit of rain gear. As we pulled onto the road, I discovered Daniel's family-owned restaurant was not far down the road and I was welcome to stay there and wait for the rain to stop. I would be warm and there was food to eat. About ten minutes later, the truck slowed and we pulled into a dirt clearing in front of what looked like a ranch house with adjacent horse corrals. We had arrived at Restaurante Sanchez. Although the rain had diminished it had by no means stopped, so the area in front of the restaurant was a quagmire. A young boy and girl ran out to help Daniel and me remove the bike and gear from the truck and shuttle it into the cafe. Daniel's mother, sister, grandmother and grandfather, aunt, and assorted nephews and nieces came out of the kitchen to see what was going on. I waited for his mother to say, "What have you dragged in this time," but before she could open her mouth Daniel explained the situation in rapid-fire Spanish.

With the help of Daniel and the kids, my bike was stowed inside against a wall, partially blocking the entry to the kitchen and my rain gear and assorted clothing strung about chairs and hung from nails on the wall. Heat from the wood-fired cook stoves in the kitchen permeated the small cafe.

Before changing out of his wet clothes, Daniel called to someone in the kitchen to bring me food and coffee. Luxuriating in the warmth and hospitality, I sat at one of the tables eating. In no time at all I was warm and full of victual and the milk of human kindness. There was a considerable language problem on my part, but with the help of Daniel's niece and nephew I was assured that I was their guest and could stay there as long as I wanted. The kids had honed their rudimentary English language skills by watching TV and were eager to practice with me as their captive tutor. Everyone else went about their business in the kitchen, paying little attention to the gringo stranger in the cafe. I even got an opportunity to watch as Daniel sliced up a dried Pig hide, then with the help of his mother and aunt, fashion the chunks into deep fried pig skins to be packaged and sold to customers.

A few patrons came and went, but no one appeared to mind that my gear and bike were scattered around the small dining area. When it began to get dark, I thought I'd overstayed my welcome so I started gathering up my clothes and rain gear, but Daniel suddenly appeared. He told me to leave everything where it was, that he wanted me to return to the nearby town of Llano Grande and be his houseguest. When I approached my bike, thinking that I'd take it with me, Daniel shook his head and said there was "no problema," it could stay where it was. For a second I thought about getting my Kryptonite lock out and locking the bike, but I sensed this might offend Daniel and his family, so I gathered up a few things and followed Daniel and his niece and nephew to the truck. Naturally, I was reluctant to leave my bike, along with my $6,000 bankroll in the seat tube, but instinctively knew everything would be safe.

With thunder clouds scudding across the sky and raindrops spattering the windshield, we arrived in the village, a small, mud-caked settlement of a few hundred people, most of whom worked at a nearby saw mill and box factory.

Inside the spacious, single-story adobe house, Daniel introduced me to his bothers and sisters, all in their early to late teens: David, Esther, Marisela, Alejandrina, and Keila. At first I was under the impression that the oldest female was Daniel's wife, but learned amidst teasing and laughter that he wasn't married, however as the oldest male in the household he was in charge. I never learned what happened, if anything, to Daniel's father and was too reticent to inquire. We gathered in the living room to watch a black and white TV. The program seemed to be a Mexican sitcom much like "All In the Family." After the show was over, I was inundated with questions about myself, my trip, my family, and dozens of questions about life in the U.S. I did my best to satisfy their curiosity, relying on them to help me translate. Then they started pointing to various things in the room and wanted to know the English word for it. To add balance to the situation, I asked them to supply the Spanish word for the object indicated. Along about bedtime I discovered there wasn't any indoor plumbing so with the aid of my tiny pinch light I wandered around out in the courtyard until I found the privy, lacking a toilet bowl. What I observed was merely a hole in the floor of the privy. But accustomed by now to primitive bathroom facilities I quickly took care of business and returned to the house.

Early next morning, Daniel drove me back to the restaurant where I was relieved and reassured to see my bike and miscellaneous gear exactly where I left them. Joining me for a breakfast of scrambled eggs, tortillas, and coffee, Daniel said he hoped I'd enjoyed my stay and wished me "mucho suerte" on the rest of my trip. When I questioned him about Barranca de los Negros I believe he said it was down the highway 50 or 60 miles, "mas o menos".

The driver of a Pepsi truck bought me a pop at a truck stop late that afternoon. With my weather-beaten map laid out on the soft drink cooler, I pointed to a tiny green dot and asked how far it was to Barranca de los Negros. With several pairs of inquisitive eyes looking from the map to me with broad smiles on their faces, the truck driver shook his head and explained as precisely as possible that I'd passed the park 25 miles, "mas o menos", back down the road. How I missed it I'll never know. I will swear up and down that I didn't see one sign making the slightest reference to the park. My only guess is that in Mexico, along with most other Latin American countries, there is so little interest (except on the part of tourists) in national parks there is no need to promote them. Most natives have neither the time nor resources to enjoy a vacation, let alone travel hundreds of miles to camp out and commune with nature. It's not part of their cultural experience. Leisure time, if any, would be spent with their extended family at home or with a nearby family member. There was a time in the U.S. when this was also a tradition.

~ ~ ~

El Centro

After a few weeks of traveling in Mexico, I no longer relied on my South American Handbook. The information was accurate enough, but I came up with a better system, one that allowed for a greater degree of creativity and spontaneity. My system proved reliable throughout Mexico, Central, and South America. Simply stated it was "following my nose."

Upon entering a city or puebla, I'd look for the highest church steeple, knowing it would mark the main plaza or central business district. In lieu of a steeple, I'd watch for a sign pointing the way to "el centro." Opposite the main cathedral one will invariably find a plaza or public park. Flanking the park, or close by, were the hotels, cafes, restaurants, and businesses, generally the least expensive.

Arriving at el centro, I'd pedal around the plaza to see where everything was located, then perhaps stop in the public park to sit on a comfortable bench, sip a cold drink, and possibly nibble on a bag of homemade popcorn, or an ice cream cone. With my energy sufficiently restored, I'd pick out a hotel or posada, push my bike to it, and inquire about prices and accommodations. If I weren't satisfied I'd walk a few doors away to another hotel to make another inquiry about room rates. Generally, I would find adequate accommodations for three or four dollars per night.

With my bike and gear secured in my room, I'd take a shower, usually down the hall, then go in search of a cafe or restaurante. If I didn't find one that caught my eye, I'd walk across to the park to inspect the comestibles of vendors cooking numerous items on braziers or spits on the sidewalk. A taco here, a fruit cup there, a burrito over yonder and soon my stomach would be bursting. In a few instances where more than one vendor sold the same item, e.g. juices or tacos, they would enthusiastically compete for my business by engaging in an impromptu price war. This often proved to be both fun and economical, at least for me. Generally there would be one or more street musicians playing guitars or accordions providing a welcome dinner serenade. With minimal expenditure of time and energy I'd take care of all my needs and wants around the central plaza.

After a leisurely stroll around the plaza to aide digestion, I'd return to my hotel room to read, write in my journal, or plan the next day's bike route. On more than one occasion I found an excellent cafe or pizza parlor by merely "following my nose."

~ ~ ~

Whistling In the Dark

The streets of Puebla Vincente Guerrero were a sea of mud. Nearing the central plaza, the narrow street changed from mud to muddy cobblestones, which made for such a rough, precarious ride I was forced to walk the remaining distance to the plaza. Across the street from Cathedral Santa Elena was the Hotel Santa Elena, a three-story, newly whitewashed adobe building. A complementary whitewashed adobe wall with iron spikes on top segregated the hotel from the street. Between the wall and the entrance to the hotel was a patch of extremely green grass, in the middle of which stood a three-foot high statue of the Virgin of Guadalupe. Arranged neatly about the base of the statue were pots of blue, orange, and white cut flowers.

At first glance I thought I'd stumbled into a convent, but at the registration desk a sweet old woman assured me it was a hotel and assigned me a room on the second floor. With the help of the Senora, I secured my bike in a storage area next to the kitchen-dining room on the ground floor.

My room was spotless. I enjoyed a cold shower in the most elaborately tiled bathroom I'd ever seen. The overall cleanliness and orderliness of the hotel reminded me of an Army barracks before an inspection.

Ironically, during my shower a tremendous downpour had begun outside, so not wanting to walk around in the rain I descended to the hotel dining room for something to eat. The poorly lighted, Spartanly furnished room was empty of people and eerily quiet. Pulling a straight back chair up to an old table covered with oilcloth, I sat down and waited for someone to appear and take my order. Behind the thin wall separating the dining area from the kitchen came the laughter of two women. Some time passed before a girl about 16-years old emerged from the kitchen to present me with a well-used one-page menu, all of this accomplished without saying a word.

While glancing over the menu, I heard a strange tapping noise in the hallway outside the dining room. The tapping got louder and louder. Mixed in with the tapping was the melodic sound of whistling.

I looked up from my menu to observe a white cane exploring the threshold of the room. Shortly, a middle-aged Mexican gentleman dressed in neat blue suit and white shirt entered the room, his cane striking chairs, tables legs, and the wall as he negotiated a path to a table. Alerted by the whistling and cane tapping a youthful waitress emerged from the kitchen.

"Buenos Tardes, Senor Guzman."

"Senorita," he said slowly, his head swiveling around to identify the location of the waitress.

The girl slipped her hand on Senor Guzman's arm. As she guided him past my table his cane tapped my shoe making a soft thunk. Verbally ticking off the items on the dinner menu, the waitress helped Senor Guzman get seated. After a few minutes of reflection, Senor Guzman ordered the "especiale." On her return to the kitchen she took my order as well.

The dining room became uncomfortably quiet. Senor Guzman knew I was there and could probably tell from my accent when ordering that I was an American. I wanted to say "good evening" to him, but wasn't quite sure how to go about it or even if it would be good manners.

Senor Guzman broke the impasse by saying hello and asking where I was traveling. I gave him, as best as I could, a recap of my bike trip. He expressed admiration. Another silence followed, but again Senor Guzman filled the breach by telling me, in broken English, that his favorite music was from the big band era of the 1940's in the U.S. Music, good music, was of luxury, he said. He was especially fond of Benny Goodman, Glen Miller, and Tommy Dorsey. He began whistling a lively tune I quickly identified as "Pennsylvania 65000." Encouraged, he followed it with "Little Brown Jug." Again, I called out the name of the song. Smiling, Senor Guzman tapped his fingers on the table as though he were seated at a piano keyboard.

We passed the time with our version of "Name That Tune," until our dinners were brought in and we could relapse into cliches about our favorite food, drink, and dessert.

After dinner, I ordered a second cup of coffee. With a sigh, Senor Guzman pushed his chair away from the table and abruptly stood up. Turning in my direction, he bowed formally and wished me a "good evening" and "bien viaje."

I listened attentively as he tapped his way out of the dining room and down the hall, the whistled notes of "Route 66" swirling in his wake.

~ ~ ~

The Lucky Traveler

I counted twelve church steeples in Somberete; a picturesque town set in a bowl amidst high mountains. I'd stopped on the hill alongside the highway to catch my breath. My system for finding "el centro" seemed to be on the chopping block as I looked about in confusion. However, one steeple dominated the rest so I made my way towards it. I learned from my *South American Handbook* that Somberete was noted for its silver mines, some still operating in the surrounding mountains. To a lesser extent it was also famous as the location for John Wayne movies.

Narrow streets eventually opened onto a spacious plaza flanking the main cathedral. There in the broad plaza and park, I stopped to get my bearings. A man about 60-years old, dressed in slacks and sweater, was walking past me, so I greeted him and asked if he could direct me to a hotel. As it turned out, Moises Munoz was the Director of Tourism for Somberete. While telling him about my bike tour, he escorted me to a nearby hotel, which he highly recommended. He talked with his friend the owner, who at first didn't seem amenable to my staying there, but Moises persisted and I was finally given a room. Moises insisted on giving me a walking tour of the town, so I quickly stowed my belongings and joined him outside the hotel. Walking across the plaza past shops and stores set back in a protective arcade, Moises explained the "confusion" at the hotel. The President of Mexico, Carlos Salinas de Gortari was scheduled to address the residents of Somborete the next day. He and his staff had reserved the hotel, but Moises persuaded his friend to let me have a room anyway.

In addition to his duties as Director of Tourism, Moises, a photographer by trade, was also founder and director of the local museum. Fortunately, our tour of the town included visits to only three of the 12 churches. Perhaps the highlight of the afternoon was a visit with the Mayor of Somberete, a friend of Moises. Back at the hotel later that afternoon, Moises promised that his son Alejandro, a college student, would call for me at 6 p.m. to escort me to their home for dinner.

Later, at the Munoz home I was introduced to Moises two daughters, both teenagers. With the help of the Munoz children, all of whom were learning English in school, we enjoyed a pleasant conversation. After dinner, Moises showed me his studio and a collection of photographs of movie stars that had stayed in Somberete while filming on location at nearby Los Organos. In addition to John Wayne, there were shots of Kirk Douglas, and Anthony Quinn. (Quinn was Mexican.)

I arrived back at the hotel after dark. To my surprise, there were uniformed police outside and inside the hotel. After brief interrogation by a policeman and a nod of approval from the hotel owner, I was allowed to go to my room. I quickly fell asleep, but was disturbed many times during the night by the interminable flushing of the toilet located next to my room.

I ambled down to the dining room on the first floor next morning rubbing sleep from my eyes and trying to decide on my plan for the day. Fascinated by the little town and the warmth of the Munoz family I was thinking of staying over another day, perhaps to visit one of the silver mines operating in the nearby mountains or join Moises and his family in the plaza to listen to the Presidential address.

The dining room was crowded with men in suits and uniforms. I guessed the President's aides had arrived late the night before. There was much turning of heads and abbreviated conversations as I pulled up a chair to a small table and looked over the menu. The owner of the hotel was summoned to a large table across the room where several men in suits drank coffee and smoked cigarettes. Glancing occasionally in my direction, he talked and smiled at the man seated at the head of the table. As I'd gotten used to being an object of curiosity during my travels, I continued to peruse the menu and sip the excellent coffee supplied by the incredibly efficient waitress.

I looked up to say "good morning" to the hotel owner, who smiled cryptically at me as he passed my table headed to the lobby. What's that all about, I thought, as I visualized a plate of scrambled eggs, tortillas, a fruit cup, and glass of juice.

"Senor Hawkins," a well-modulated voice called from the big table.

I looked over to recognize the Mayor whom I'd met the previous day. All heads were turned in my direction. The Mayor motioned for me to join him. I walked slowly to the table wondering if I was guilty of some untoward indiscretion. With great solemnity and perhaps too many words, he presented me to the man at the head of the table, Presidente Salinas.

"Please, Senor Hawkins, sit down, sit down," Presidente Salinas encouraged good-naturedly as a chair was vacated for me. "I understand that you are riding a bicycle to South America," he continued.

"Yes...sir."

"That's quite a trip. I wish you much luck. And how do you like Mexico?"

I told him the story of being rescued from a rain storm by Daniel Sanchez and staying with him and his family in Llano Grande and how Moises had taken me under his wing here in Somberete. It wasn't until halfway through our brief conversation that I realized we were conversing in English. Suddenly, I remembered reading that El Presidente had been educated at Harvard as an economist. Graciously excusing himself to resume a meeting with local officials, I returned to my table to enjoy an excellent breakfast. I made a mental note to always breakfast with the reigning politico of the country I was cycling through.

Having decided to layover another day, I joined Moises and family in the plaza to listen to Salinas' address. My lack of fluency in Spanish allowed me to learn only the highlights, which covered topics like improved local economy, prosperity, and honest public officials.

When Moises was showing me to the door after dinner with his family that night, he looked at me with a critical eye and exclaimed, "Jorge, you are a lucky traveler."

~ ~ ~

Hans Eugen Redux

The main highway was clogged with heavy truck and car traffic. To make cycling more interesting, there wasn't any shoulder on the busy two-lane road. With the aid of my helmet-mounted rearview mirror, I found it prudent to pull off the road whenever a large truck or bus sped up from behind. To exacerbate the problem, the highway narrowed still further as it made its way through a small village, forcing me to ride only inches away from passing vehicles. The narrowness of the main street, combined with assorted potholes and depressions created lines of slow, bumper-to-bumper traffic entering and exiting the village. The weather had not been cooperative either. Cloudbursts had consorted to shower down on me periodically making it expedient to don my rain parka and keep it on.

Sweaty and overheated, I took advantage of a hiatus in the showers to push my bike onto the sidewalk and remove the rain gear. Besides, the density of the two-way traffic in the street had made me extremely nervous. While pulling off my parka and scanning the street for a cafe or bakery, I heard a loud roar directly behind me. I turned abruptly to see two huge motorcycles pull onto the sidewalk and come to a stop behind me. Both motorcyclists were encased in foul-weather gear and full-face helmets. One of the motorcyclists had quickly parked his bike, removed his helmet, and was pointing at the "Alaska to Tierra Del Fuego" sign on the back of my bicycle. The bearded cyclist smiled at me as he approached.

"We saw your sign a few blocks back. My friend and I are also traveling to fire land."

I looked over at their huge BMW dirt bikes loaded down with boxes, bags and assorted gear. Straddling the other cycle, the second rider finished removing his massive helmet. I stared at him in amazement. He looked at me questioningly, then pointed a finger at me.

"Is it you?"

"Hans-Eugen, I can't believe this. I remember you from Alaska." I blurted.

"This is interesting," Hans-Eugen said dismounting.

We howled with laughter, as Martin stood by puzzled. I explained to Martin Richter that Hans-Eugen Nusser and I had met and camped together in Christochina, Alaska two years previously. Fortunately, for all of us, Martin's English was particularly good.

Figure 8: L-R: Hans-Eugen, author, Martin Richter

I learned that after saying goodbye to Hans-Eugen in Alaska that he had returned to Germany to complete courses in Engineering and earn his degree. During that time he'd met Martin at a BMW motorcycle rally where Martin proposed the tour from Alaska to Tierra Del Fuego. Having at that time graduated from Divinity School, Martin was anxious to undertake a world class adventure before settling down to the life of an assistant vicar in Germany.

As they were headed to the nearby city of Zacatecas, as I was, we made plans to meet there and get together for a reunion. To insure our meeting I gave Hans Eugen one of my business cards, instructing him to leave it at the main tourist office in Zacatecas with the name and address of the hotel where they'd be staying.

Unbelievably, everything went according to plan. I no sooner pulled up to the tourist office in downtown Zacatecas, when a young man hurried outside to give me my business card and directions to the hotel where I'd find Martin and Hans Eugen. About the only downside to finding them was the steep cobblestone street leading up to the hotel and their room on the third floor, requiring four trips to get my bike and gear to the room. Normally the three-bed room would have been cramped, but with the combined gear of two motorcyclists and a bicyclist, the room looked more like the proverbial junk closet.

After settling into my bed and taking a shower, I learned that Martin and Hans-Eugen had been on the road for two months. Originally landing on the east coast of the U.S., they worked their way south and west across the states, eventually entering Mexico at Tijuana. They planned to be in Tierra Del Fuego by Christmas, then ride up the east coast of Argentina, Brazil, and Venezuela, there to hop a plane back to Germany.

Nearly a year after our reunion in Zacatecas, I learned by post that they completed their trek safely and with the exception of minor mechanical difficulty, without incident. Hans Eugen had taken a job in Germany with an environmental firm, while Martin had married and assumed his duties as assistant vicar in the small town of Flossenburg, Germany.

That evening we took to the streets to explore the city. After dinner in an inexpensive taqueria, we wandered through the narrow "calles" of the university quarter where we met two law students who invited us to their apartment to talk and share a bottle of tequila. During the evening, an exuberant "Tomborosa band" (sort of a mobile brass band) stopped in a nearby courtyard to entertain the residents and perform while a group of youthful dancers followed them about.

At 6 a.m. next morning, we began the laborious process of hauling our gear down to the alley on the ground floor to refit our vehicles and continue on our respective ways to Tierra Del Fuego. Thanks to both Hans Eugen and Martin, I was able to get pictures of the three of us before we split up. True to their promise, I received color slides from them upon the completion of my tour and return to California.

Although I was the first one out of the gate and on the road that morning, it wasn't long before my friends caught up with me on the highway out of Zacatecas. Waving and beeping their horns, they soon disappeared over a hill. For a short while I was both jealous and depressed. They could cruise along at 60 to 70 mph sometimes covering 500 miles in a single day, without even getting tired; while I would be lucky to achieve 11 mph and 60 miles in a day. Only then if there wasn't any tough hills or nasty weather between me and my destination. Later that morning, I remembered that while comparing travel notes with Hans Eugen it was I who had colorful stories of adventure and misadventure bursting forth as though from a broken fire hydrant, while their stories were mainly iterations of gas mileage, distance covered, and hassles with the "aduano" (customs) at border crossings. Ah yes, once again I almost succumbed to the mindset gap.

~ ~ ~

I Cried In the House of Diego Rivera

I returned to the museum at 4 p.m. to find I was the only visitor. I'd discovered the museum earlier, but arrived just as they were closing for siesta. Much of the afternoon had been spent tramping up and down the steep cobblestone streets of Guanajuato, birthplace of world famous and controversial muralist Diego Rivera, born there December

8, 1886. Arriving back at the museum promptly at 4 p.m. I found myself unusually tired and gasping for breath, relieved to learn that Guanajuato was situated in the mountains at 6,500 feet. The elevation, I guessed, was taking its toll and my discomfort was not another incipient bout of Montezuma's revenge.

Rivera's childhood home is a well preserved and maintained national historic site; allowing visitors to stroll from room to room, mostly furnished with the original furniture. Displayed on the walls of each room were Rivera's sketches, working drawings, cartoons, and paintings showing the artist's growth and maturation. Unfortunately, one had to travel to Mexico City, New York, or San Francisco to view first hand his celebrated murals. Trying to comprehend Rivera's vision from the excellent selection of works displayed at his birthplace was like trying to grasp the grandeur and magnificence of Yosemite by looking at a postcard.

In a quiet room, surrounded by his working drawings for the controversial mural he did for Rockefeller Center in New York City, I was humbled by his vision of class struggle and the abuses of political power to subject the masses. I wiped away tears to scrutinize his complex, visceral drawings.

~ ~ ~

Carne Asada, Papas Fritas, And A Giant Color TV

There was something happening with annoying regularity. I observed this something in Mexico, Central, and South America. In Guanajuato, for example, I stepped next door from my hotel to a restaurant whose menu and prices would seem to indicate a fairly upscale establishment. Whether I wanted to or not, I was going to watch and listen to, along with the other patrons, a Dodgers-Mets game (Dodgers 3 Mets 2, top of the 6th).

Looking up from my plate of carne asada and papas fritas, I found myself like everyone else, including the waiters, glued to the TV. A behemoth Sony was perched on the cash register counter no more than 25 feet from my table. In that location it would have been difficult not to watch. To make the scene even more bizarre, the commentary was in English.

Chewing on my last French fry, I couldn't tear myself away from the screen. The score remained Dodgers 3, Mets 2, at the top of the ninth. The Mets had the bases loaded. There were two outs. Up came a power hitter. He took a few practice swings. Then out of nowhere, the Senora appeared with the remote control in her hand and changed the channel to some kind of Mexican soap opera. The patrons, including myself, let out a howl of protest. Her sons gathered around their mother to beg that she quickly change back to the baseball game. There was much muttering amongst the clientele, the scrape of chairs, footsteps hurrying to the exit. At last she relented and switched back to the game, but by then it was over with a final score still Dodgers 3, Mets 2. I'll never know what happened with the final hitter. Was it a fly out, a line drive to short, or maybe he just went down swinging.

Regardless of how vehement my protestations regarding the presence of color televisions in restaurants and bars, I'll be the first to admit they seduce me every time.

~ ~ ~

The Witch of Irapauto

I couldn't get enough sleep in Guanajuato and kept blaming it on the elevation, but the next day, about 20 miles SW of Guanajuato, I discovered what was really bothering me—another bout of "turistas." This one more virulent than the premiere event in Baja.

Somehow I managed to pedal to the small town of Irapauto, barely 32 miles south of Guanajuato. There I had little strength or energy to do anything, but flop on a bench in a little park and take a nap. Upon waking I knew I'd have to find a place to stay, hopefully one not far away. In my agitated state I made the mistake of asking a woman for directions to a hotel. Some thirty minutes later, I thanked her and went back to my park bench more confused than ever. Feeling another "attack" brewing I leaped on my bike and headed for the train station where I was sure of finding a posada or hotel nearby. Cycling down the street near the train station I spotted a building that looked like a hotel with a cervezeria on the ground floor.

In the street in front of the hotel, an old man on a bicycle stopped alongside me. Pointing at the hotel, he kept saying, "putta, putta" and shaking his head. Motioning for me to follow him, he pedaled away with me close behind. Two blocks further along, he stopped in front of another hotel and pointed at it. "Muy bueno, senor," he said with a smile of approval, then was on his way. Later that day, I found out he'd stopped me from checking into a brothel. In my condition that could have been embarrassing to both me and the ladies working there.

The Senora at the "nice" hotel quickly checked me into a ground floor room, and none too soon. Unfortunately, the bathroom was "down the hall." Now I know why my "condition" is called the "trots" as I spent most of the afternoon "trotting" back and forth to the bathroom. When not so engaged, I lay on my bed writhing in pain with stomach cramps. Naturally, I didn't have an appetite, but did have an unquenchable thirst. Sometime that evening I fell asleep and didn't wake up until 9 a.m. the next day. Still groggy and weak, it was all I could do to sit up on the side of my bed and gulp water. There was no point in thinking about traveling that day.

Later that afternoon, I managed to stumble to the lobby in search of a cold Pepsi or Coke, but the Senora talked me out of the soft drink, promising to bring a cup of herbal tea to my room. Quickly gulping the tea down I fell back on the bed and slept for three hours, waking up about 4 p.m. Needing some air and exercise, besides the hasty trips to the banos, I got dressed and walked around the block. Finding myself outside the train station I decided to go in and inquire about a train to Mexico City. I was having difficulty communicating with the ticket agent, until a young fellow, Rodrigo, who had lived in San Diego, came to my assistance. By taking the night train, departing Irapauto at midnight, I could connect with a sleeper in Mexico City at 8 a.m. that would take me to Oaxaca. I knew I wouldn't be healthy enough to ride for a few days, so I made plans to return later that night to book passage.

Back at the hotel, I paid my bill and thanked the Senora for her kindness, then went to my room to sleep until 11 p.m. when I planned to leave for the train station.

The night desk clerk knocked on my door at exactly 11 p.m. to make sure I was awake. After a precautionary trip to the bathroom, I pushed my loaded bike through the lobby and out into the dark street. Minutes later I arrived at the train station. I was surprised to see the benches and most of the floor filled with sleeping bodies. Must be a popular train ride, I thought while finding a place to settle down next to my bike and wait for the ticket window to open.

While looking over the mass of bodies in all sorts of positions and states of rest, a creature walked slowly into the lobby from the platform where the trains arrived and departed. It was difficult to determine what gender the individual was as it was wrapped from head to foot in blankets and shawls. In one hand the creature carried a broom. As it moved closer to the middle of the lobby, the overhead lights more fully illuminated it. For a second I thought I was looking at the wicked witch of the East. I half-expected it to point an accusing finger at me and croak, "I'll fix you my pretty." It was then that I noticed it had a sack hanging around its neck with a live chicken inside. On its left shoulder was perched a cat. Long shoulder-length, disheveled hair and the contour of the face confirmed my suspicions that the creature was a woman possibly 35-45 years old. The exceedingly dirty blankets and shawls notwithstanding, I could tell the body beneath was fairly slim, if not emaciated. Her movements were not those of an old person, but had the quickness and suppleness of youth. Whenever anyone came within five feet of her, she would take her broom in both hands and start sweeping toward the person until they retreated. Not that many people came close to her, for I suspected she must have smelled much worse than she looked. Then too, who would want to get close to a person with a live chicken dangling from her neck and a cat perched on her shoulder.

When the ticket window finally opened I was told the train for Mexico City didn't leave until 3 a.m. Though my timing was a bit off, I was able to purchase a ticket anyway. With a three-hour wait ahead of me I went back to the hotel. There I persuaded the night desk clerk to let me use my vacated room to nap until the train departed.

Returning to the station at 2:45 a.m. I was amazed to see still more people crowded into the lobby sleeping. It was then I found out from Antonio, a university student from Mexico City, that most of the people sleeping in the railroad station were homeless. Only a few would be taking the train.

With his help I got my bike squared away in the baggage car and got a receipt for the few pesos I paid as a freight charge. Although both of us had first class tickets, the passenger car, even at that hour, was almost full. So I took a seat next to an old gentleman, who seemed a bit put out when I asked him to remove his bag from the window seat. Soon after the train was underway, the old fellow began removing layers of clothing in what could easily have been a Charlie Chaplin routine. Off came two sports coats, off came two sweaters, off came a shirt, and off came a pair of trousers. At last satisfied with his wardrobe, he carefully folded the garments and placed them in the overhead luggage rack. I dozed off to the steady, rhythmic cadence of the train wheels on the track. When I awoke I was surprised to see the old fellow of many garments had detrained along with most of the other passengers. I immediately slumped over into the vacated seat next to me and fell asleep again.

~ ~ ~

The Good Samaritan

The train pulled into Mexico City at 11 a.m., four hours late. The connecting train to Oaxaca had long since departed. After I woke up enough to get my bearings, I determined I was feeling better. I even had an appetite. Though intimidated by the crowds and reputation of the Capital city, I retrieved my bike from the baggage car, pleased to find everything in order, then rolled it along the platform and down into the main lobby. There with the help of a bilingual computerized information system I was directed to a short line where I was able to purchase a reserved ticket on a sleeping coach, or privado, on the next train for Oaxaca, departing in seven hours.

Good, I thought, this would give me a chance to see a little bit of the city and get something to eat along the way. I was able to roll my bike to a storage area where I paid a few pesos to store it. For all the reports I'd heard about pickpockets, muggers, white slavers, and such, I found the people I circulated amongst to be rather pleasant and non-aggressive.

Standing on the steps outside the train station, I got to chatting with a taxi driver who used to live in Oakland, where his favorite pastime was attending prize fights at local boxing arenas. When learning of my recent lower G.I. problems he told me he had a guaranteed method of avoiding the "turistas." According to Manuel, the secret was to drink 2 straight shots of tequila before eating. Works every time, he said. I never followed his advice to the letter, preferring to take a shot of tequila with salt and lime after dinner. Manuel directed me to a nearby cafe where I was able to order pie and coffee, both quite tasty.

I tired quickly during my short trek, so made my way back to the station to wait. I found a seat on a bench outside the luggage area where my bike was secured. That's where I met Nigel, a British chap of about 20-years old. Over 6-feet tall and dressed all in black, to include leather jacket, vest (no shirt), shorts, combat boots with heel taps and black horn rimmed glasses, Nigel made a striking appearance. Although one could hear Nigel coming a hundred yards away because of his noisy heels, there was little chance of his escaping attention. First of all he was a gringo, a tall one at that, secondly because of his eye-catching outfit, and thirdly because of bright red hair done up in dreadlocks. Nigel loped into the waiting room with all eyes riveted on him, looked about for a second, then took a seat next to me. I couldn't resist engaging this gentlemen in conversation and was glad I did. Nigel had just returned from Costa Rica. When first arriving in the U.S. from England, he bussed across the states, then south through Mexico to Central America. He gave me interesting, practical information regarding travel in Central America, recommending places like Guatemala and Costa Rica, but cautioning me about El Salvador and Nicaragua. Finally, I got around to asking him if he had a paperback to trade.

"Yes, yes, believe I do," Nigel said rummaging through his huge Army duffel bag.

Out comes *In Patagonia*, by Bruce Chatwin. Coyly, I handed over the Captain Gringo adventure novella I recently finished. I was surprised that Nigel was delighted with the trade. Checking my watch, I saw it was 6:30 p.m. I asked Nigel if he knew when the Oaxaca train would be boarding. He didn't know, but a gringo across from us told me it was boarding that very moment and I must hurry or I'd miss it.

I quickly checked my bike out of the baggage room and began pushing it quickly and carefully through the lobby looking for track 7, which I learned was upstairs. Not wanting to take the time to find the baggage cart ramp going upstairs, I managed to push my loaded bike up two flights of stairs. When at last I arrived at gate 7, the ticket taker merely shook his head and motioned for me to go away. I showed him my reserved ticket for the sleeper, but he was unimpressed. He pointed repeatedly at my bike and seemed to say something about the baggage car or freight car.

I felt a painful cramp in my stomach. Sweat beaded on my forehead. I kept pointing at the train. "Oaxaca, si?"

"Si senor, pero no bicicleta," the attendant iterated.

My stomach began to boil. I looked around in desperation. An armed guard blocked the entrance to the train platform. Beyond the iron picket fence I could see steam or smoke hissing from the exhaust vents of the Oaxaca train.

Out of nowhere like a true Greek "deus ex machina" a Mexican fellow appeared at my side. He looked at the ticket taker, then asked what the "problema" was. The good Samaritan asked to see my ticket, which he scanned quickly then said, "We must hurry." He led the way up a ramp, thankfully avoiding another flight of stairs. Once on the platform, I followed him, half-sprinting, past a long queue, past ticket takers, past armed guards, through steel gates down a platform next to a waiting train, eventually to the baggage car at the end of the train. All of this with my bike in tow.

The baggage man was about to close the door when the Samaritan yelled something in Spanish I didn't understand. Whatever he said, the man in the baggage car smiled ingratiatingly and swung the doors open. I rolled my bike into the car, there to bungee if off securely. I gladly paid a $2 freight charge while the Samaritan oversaw the transaction, insuring that I received a valid receipt. My amigo took my ticket and led me quickly to the other end of the train, where a conductor punched the ticket and motioned for me to hurry aboard. The Samaritan said something to the conductor, then he turned to me and said, bien viaje. I offered him some money, but he merely smiled and nodded his head. I felt like I owed this man my sanity, if not my life, but

before I could think of the appropriate words the conductor motioned
to hurry on the train, so I shook the Samaritan's hand and said muchas
gracias. Seconds later, the train began pulling away. To this day I have
no idea who the Samaritan was or where he came from. Sometimes
traveling is a mysterious blend of magic and mysticism.

~ ~ ~

Foreign Intrigue

I was escorted to my "privado", a small compartment with a large
window. Amenities included a comfortable velour-covered seat, overhead storage rack, and a stainless steel sink that pulled out of the wall
exposing a mirror. There was also a small toilet, thank god, that proved
convenient on more than one occasion. Strangely, all of the instructional signs scattered about the compartment were in English. During
the trip, I learned the coach was one of many Pullman passenger cars
purchased from the United States during the thirties when U.S.
Railroad companies were upgrading their rolling stock. Thanks to the
genius of George M. Pullman, the car's designer, a bed folded out of the
wall. Although it occupied much of the space in the compartment, I
couldn't resist sprawling upon it to enjoy a luxurious siesta.

Later, a knock on the door woke me up enough to hear a porter
announce that dinner was being served in the dining car. I carefully
pushed the bed back into its wall enclosure, then pulled out the sink
and washed my face. Refreshed and nursing an appetite, I stepped
into the aisle-way, where an attendant dressed in starched white
jacket and black pants waited to escort me. Entering the dining car
was like stepping back in time, to the United States of the 1920's and
30's. All of the appointments and decor were original art deco. There

was much ornamental etched glass and chrome. Everything that was-n't painted purple or gray was nickel-plated. A waiter showed me to a small pedestal table for two, where I slipped into a leather-uphol-stered, curved bench seat. A place setting, glass of water, and menu materialized on the table as my eyes wandered around the dining car admiring the appointments. The cost of this episode in time travel was a mere $34.

Suddenly, the waiter was at my elbow again to ask if I'd like a cocktail. Laying the menu aside, I realized I hadn't eaten anything for the past 24 hours, except the pie and coffee in Mexico City. I ordered a cerveza. Smiling his approval, the waiter disappeared. I could easily imagine Senor Guzman tapping down the aisle whistling "Chattanooga Choo-Choo."

While sipping my glass of cerveza, the porter escorted an elegantly dressed woman in her mid-forties into the dining car. She had the demeanor of a woman used to being waited on. By now all of the tables were occupied. She walked slowly down the aisle, paused next to my table, then slid onto the bench seat at my side. For a second I thought I'd usurped a reserved table. She leaned over and placed a hand of slender, red-tipped fingers on my forearm. "Do you mind, Senor," she asked with a trace of a Spanish accent. Her alert eyes were like obsidian marbles. Thick raven hair cascaded over bare shoulders to the small of her back. Other than vermilion lipstick, her shapely, aristocratic face showed no evidence of cosmetics.

"No, not at all," I said relieved to have a dinner companion.

The waiters clamored to her side, setting out silverware and glasses, menu, and wine list. The headwaiter appeared to ask if the lady would like a cocktail. She ordered a gin and vermouth.

I introduced myself. Josephine told me she lived in Washington, D.C. What she did exactly, I never found out, but guessed she was a spy, an attractive one at that. From her metallic purse she withdrew a gold cigarette holder and fitted a Galoise cigarette to it. Out of nowhere, the headwaiter materialized to light her cigarette. She tilted her head back to exhale smoke toward the ceiling, then raising her drink in her left hand, she looked at me and whispered, "Salud." Then she winked. I was almost sure she winked. I raised my glass of beer and took a sip. If she had said "bottoms up" or "here's mud in your eye," I would have been less unnerved, but a wink. I looked quickly around the dining car to see if perhaps I was involved in some kind of subtle practical joke, but the other diners were busy with their food, or looking out the window at the sunset. She lighted another cigarette with an elegant silver lighter from her purse.

Josephine was on her way to Oaxaca to visit her family on part of her holiday. She had never traveled alone before, she confided. I'm sorry, I replied. Arching, thick black eyebrows, she laughed and patted my arm.

Soon the waiter brought us fruit cups and a bottle of wine. A small amount of wine was poured carefully into my glass. I sipped it and nodded approvingly. Josephine smiled, exhaling smoke from her nostrils as our glasses were filled. We clinked our glasses together, then drank deeply. I knew she must be a spy or at least the mistress of some high ranking official or military leader. I must be discreet, I cautioned myself, just in case someone was watching us. Shortly, the waiter brought our orders to the table. I had the chateau briand. Josephine ordered fish. While I wolfed down my steak and fried potatoes, Josephine toyed with her food, occasionally filling our wineglasses. For dessert we ordered fresh coffee served in a silver pot, along with dishes of pineapple ice cream.

Sipping her coffee and smoking another cigarette, Josephine patted my arm and asked where my family was. I wasn't married, I explained, so I was traveling alone. This saddened her, she said. I casually asked about her family in Oaxaca. When I looked up from my coffee cup, I was surprised to see she was crying. She excused herself and hurried from the dining car. Extinguishing her cigarette smoldering in the ashtray, I wondered what could have provoked such an emotional outburst.

Learning from the waiter that my dinner and the next day's breakfast were included in my fare, I returned to my compartment contented, but continued to speculate about my mysterious dinner companion. Once there, my attention was turned to more pressing matters. My dinner made a hasty, untimely exit. Afterward, stretched out on my bed, I thanked Mr. Pullman for the ingenuity and foresight of designing a railroad car with private compartments fitted out with toilets. With a thoroughly empty stomach and large intestine, I was soon rocked gently to sleep by the train.

About 6 a.m., I awoke to watch a tropical landscape emerge from the gray dawn. I was rather amazed to see corn fields, flowers, palm trees, banana trees, and a myriad of lush green vines and plants all form before my eyes and become slowly saturated with a collage of greens, yellows, blues, and reds..

In the dining car seated at the same table as the night before, shafts of golden light from the rising sun made the art deco furnishings look richer and a bit surreal. I sipped my orange juice and waited for the thick black coffee I knew I shouldn't have. When I looked up Josephine was walking slowly toward me. She was wearing a tight, black dress and smiling radiantly. I found it difficult not to stare at her. She slid in beside me, patted my arm, and asked how I slept. Rather than bore her with the grim details, I said I'd slept like a baby. And you, I asked. She blotted her red lips on a napkin, then smiling confessed she hadn't slept well. As her smile dissolved into a bit of a frown, she quickly pulled a cigarette from her purse, stuck it in the filter, then handed her ornate lighter to me to do the honors.

Over poached eggs, bacon, toast, and jelly, she informed me that she had recently left her husband. I set my coffee cup down and quickly looked around the dining car. Forget the spy business I told myself, she's a woman on the run, probably the wife of a high ranking official, one with a quick temper, perhaps a streak of sadism, and on top of that he was probably insanely jealous. Why any minute the train might come to a jolting stop and be boarded by Army officers. Who knows what kind of trouble I could be in just sitting by her.

"My husband has been seeing another woman. I should have expected it. It is a common thing."

Good, I thought, maybe he doesn't care who his wife dines with. He's probably too busy with diplomacy and girlfriends to even think about his estranged wife.

During my second cup of coffee, the porter passed through the car announcing that the train would be arriving in Oaxaca in 30 minutes. I set my cup down, leaned over and told Josephine that I had to return to my compartment to pack.

She patted my arm firmly a final time and said goodbye through a haze of cigarette smoke.

~ ~ ~

Jorge Quickly

I couldn't resist putting my hiking boots on and rushing out to explore the beautiful, charming town of Oaxaca. About the size of a football field, the main square was a hive of activity; with strolling musicians and vendors selling their wares beneath giant shade trees. Surrounding the plaza were numerous shops, cafes, and restaurants set back in porticoes beneath massive stone buildings. After a reconnaissance of the plaza and surrounding streets, I'd expended the little strength I had so I took a chair outside one of the cafes facing the plaza. There, like many other gringo tourists, I studied my *South American Handbook*. While reading, I came across the name of a small restaurant, Cafe Quickly, I walked by earlier. As it was highly recommended I decided to return there to check the menu and prices. Thanks to the **SAH** recommendation it had become part of the gringo trail establishing itself as a place to network, talk English, and perhaps swap a book. The menu had an interesting combination of "world food" ranging from California smoothies to Swiss Muesli.

While eating a bowl of corn flakes, I started reading a local English language tourist handout. The one article that immediately caught my eye was headlined "Turista Sickness." It warned against taking Keopectate, Milk of Magnesia, and other anti-diuretics, describing them as "corks" or temporary solutions. The writer strongly recommended a local herbal tea brewed from Ixtafiate. I vowed then and there that I would procure some of this magical herb and once and for all cure the "turistas" that were still plaguing me. No sooner had I exited the Cafe Quickly, then I began feeling an eruption building in the lower regions. So Jorge hustled quickly back to the Aurora Hotel for emergency servicing.

After an hour of bedrest I decided I would purchase at least a bushel basket of Ixtafiate and cure my GI problem once and for all or I'd never build up enough strength to ever bike again. Consulting my **SAH** once more, I discovered the public market was but a few blocks away from the hotel. But first I had to visit a bank to change some travelers checks. In any bank this can be a time consuming, frustrating experience, but in a Mexican bank it's the ultimate test of patience and tenacity.

After a wait of ten or fifteen minutes, I was face-to-face with a cashier and was ready to countersign the travelers checks when the clerk shook her head and informed me I had to get a signature from one of the officers of the bank. An hour later, with the required signature I took a position at the end of the single queue allocated for cashing traveler's checks. As the line inched its way slowly to the cashier's cage, I struck up a conversation with the person in front of me. By the time I got to the counter we were old friends. Ed Bergman a 69-year old retired builder and contractor from Texas was currently living in Oaxaca with his 27-year old Mexican wife Lucy. He owned a house on the outskirts of the city. A large house, he assured me. After telling him about my running battle (literally) with the "turistas" and my pending search for the miracle herb Ixtafiate, Ed suggested that I be their houseguest for a few days. Lucy would join us for a trip to the public market to insure that I purchased the correct herb, warning that a miscue on my part might compound the problem rather than cure it. Finally when our money transactions were completed we drove in Ed's truck to my hotel where I checked out.

Driving into a rundown barrio I began to have misgivings, but was reassured when we pulled up to a walled fortress. With a beep of the horn the iron gate rolled back to admit us into a broad, cobblestone plaza half the size of a basketball court. Ten-foot high adobe walls were made even more intimidating by mounds of broken, jagged glass projecting from the top of the wall. Ed's villa reminded me of something out of the dark ages; it looked like a walled city built to withstand a siege of Visigoths.

The two-story L-shaped house had galleries on the second floor with doors opening into bedrooms. The kitchen, living room, bathrooms and various storage rooms occupied the ground floor.

In the kitchen, Ed introduced me to his wife Lucy and her numerous relatives. After a tour of the villa, Ed and Lucy escorted me to the public market where Lucy's brother and cousins operated vendor stalls. Our first stop, however, was at a juice bar where Lucy ordered me a concoction she promised would help stabilize my condition. She told me it was a drink made from Guayaba fruit, among other ingredients. Afterward she lead us through a narrow labyrinth of booths and stalls offering everything from fresh cuts of meat to live chickens to sunglasses and cassette tapes. At length we came to a stall selling herbs, spices, and various organic medicines, including Ixtafiate. When Lucy held the bag of Ixtafiate up for my inspection I rolled my eyes and guessed it was merely a handful of discarded weeds. But Lucy vouched for the efficacy of the herb, promising to brew a pot for me as soon as we returned to the villa. God only knows what I would have purchased if left to my own devices.

I spent the afternoon sipping copious amounts of Ixtafiate tea and talking with Ed about his life in Mexico. He and Lucy divided their time between their villa in Oaxaca and another home in Texas. Ed had designed plans for a low cost, energy efficient house that looked something like a modified dome. Instead of wood, he planned to use rebar and stucco-cement. He calculated the cost of materials at about $15,000. Complete house plans and construction notes would be offered to interested individuals and groups at cost through "Mother Earth News" magazine. That Fall, Ed said with enthusiasm, he would begin construction of the first house when he and Lucy returned to Texas.

As the hours rolled by, several of Lucy's relatives dropped in to visit. Eventually the small kitchen was crowded. With most of the pot of herbal tea gone, I was beginning to feel sleepy, plus the need to make a trip to the toilet. It wasn't a crisis situation, but I knew sooner or later I'd have to go. My problem was the toilet was off the kitchen. There wasn't any door, just a curtain that pulled across the doorway. With my stomach cramping slightly, I weighed the benefits of not going to the bathroom as opposed to the humiliation of having a dozen people, almost all total strangers, listen to the malodorous discharge of my bowels. My eyes kept getting heavier and heavier, so I excused myself from the table to wander into the living room and flop on a couch where I fell asleep instantly. Sometime around midnight, I woke up to the sounds of Ed locking me in the living room, where I would spend the night. He had snapped at least three locks the size of paperback novels on the iron grillwork behind the living room door. With all the locks in place, doors barred, windows shuttered, Ed turned the dogs loose in the courtyard, then locked himself and Lucy into their bedroom. As peace and quiet descended on Villa Bergman, I took the opportunity for a leisurely visit to the bathroom.

Over coffee next morning, Ed told me that despite all the security precautions his place had been burglarized last winter while he and Lucy were in Texas. Before they departed for a trip north later that day, Ed drove me back to the Hotel Aurora where I checked into my old room.

That night on the way to Cafe Quickly, I passed a street person who was eating glass. Eating it on the sidewalk outside the cafe where patrons could look on either in disgust or amusement. My stomach gurgled briefly as I hurried by the glass eater.

Next day I toured Monte Alban (500 BC-AD 1469), the temple city of the Zapotec Indians whose people once numbered about 40,000. The Monte Alban of today looks down from its flattened mountaintop onto Oaxaca, some 5.5 miles below. It is interesting to note that descendants of the Zapotecs, primarily women, still produce and sell their highly colorful, and intricate blankets and clothing at one of the plazas in Oaxaca.

After two more days in Oaxaca, I felt sufficiently recuperated to get on my bike again and do some pedaling. On the bright, sunny morning of August 25th I headed south for Mitla, another important archaeo-logical site.

In the days that followed, I climbed through some of the most mountainous parts of Mexico. One of my descents, possibly the longest one on my trip, totaled nearly 16 miles. At the bottom of this descent I could feel an incredible difference in temperature. It had warmed up significantly.

I definitely knew I was out of the mountains and back into tropical heat when I cycled into Tehuantepec. During my brief stay there I met Canadian, Fritz Renger, who together with two other bikers had toured the Yucatan, Guatemala and Belize. Part of their route in Guatemala on dirt roads and trails took them into Tikal the back way. Over a beer at our hotel, Fritz warned me that Tehuantepec was the last town of any size before the Guatemala border and advised me to stock up on food before leaving.

Part Three

Middle Of the Americas

Chapter 8

Central America

I cycled to Tapachula, Mexico to get a visa at the Guatemalan Embassy. This side trip was a classic example of the importance of timing in life. I arrived at the embassy precisely at 2 p.m. when they were reopening after lunch/siesta. There was only one other person, another gringo, waiting to get a visa. Twenty minutes after the door opened, I had my visa and was on my way.

Exiting Mexico was as uncomplicated as entering; a perfunctory stamp in the passport, adios, and away I go. The Guatemalan border on the other hand was a different story. To complicate a complicated situation, for the first time I had to deal with exchanging two foreign currencies, that is I had to change my pesos for quetzals. Before I could even get to the immigration office to fill out a visa form I was besieged by a half dozen money changers flashing calculators in my face and screaming, "dolares, dolares," plus nine or ten kids clamoring to "watch" my bike while I took care of business with the "aduano." All this while the drivers of trucks, buses, and cars fumed and snorted around their vehicles watching armed guards and unarmed customs officials open boxes and bags, peer into engine compartments, and run their hands up inside fenders and wheel housings. Rounding out the cast of this comic opera were beggars and vendors selling sunglasses, watches, ice cream, soft drinks, baskets, and blankets. For a minute I thought I was the only person in the world with money.

After filling out the necessary forms and presenting them to the appropriate official, I was escorted outside to show another "appropriate" official my bicycle, which however was surrounded by several curious "appropriate" officials and a few soldiers. For the third time in an hour I told them, as best I could in Spanish, how I had biked from Alaska to Guatemala on my way to Tierra Del Fuego. I'm not sure how all this came out, but I was surprised when the officer in charge asked if I knew Rambo. Rambo is a very popular fellow in Central and South America. Every other truck and bus has Rambo's name painted on it in bold, bright letters.

Showing the customs official a bill of sale for the bike, my American Youth Hostel membership card, my California driver's license, and my American Red Cross CPR card, then and only then was my visa signed and passport stamped. I needn't have worried about anyone walking or pedaling off with my bike. Who in their right mind would have attempted it with the squad of gun-toting soldiers surrounding it? I wasn't at all sure I wanted to disturb them, knowing that I'd probably have to recount my story about biking from Alaska, etc. etc.

It was from the frying pan into the fire, as they say. No sooner had I wheeled my bike away from the soldiers, then the vendors, money-changers, and kids swarmed down on me again. Regardless, I had to change my pesos for quetzals or I'd be out approximately $60. The phalanx of sunglass-wearing, attaché-toting moneychangers struck me as the Latino version of "The Blues Brothers." They trooped down on me like clones flashing their calculators and yelling about dollars and travelers checks. Two hundred eyes watched as I pulled my wallet from my fanny pack. I counted up my pesos, turned to the least intimidating "Blues Brother" and handed over the fistful of pesos. In a flourish of professionalism, he unsnapped his attaché case, withdrew a banded pile of brightly colored paper, wetted his thumb and forefinger, and then counted off 308 quetzals. I was so happy playing with my new fistful of money it never entered my head to count it to insure that I hadn't been shortchanged. Besides the numbering system on many of the bills didn't make sense. One corner was stamped "1/2" while the face of the bill was imprinted with a "QO 50." Also imprinted on the face of the currency was "cincuenta centavos de quetzal." So who's to know. Besides the beauty of the currency wasn't the numbers stamped on them, but the colorful inks and artwork. They had these neat little quetzal birds, green and rust colored, with long plumed tails in the upper left hand corner and a line drawing of the Aztec God Tecunuman in the right corner, plus all kinds of fancy signatures of Presidentes, Jefes, and Gerentes (whatever they are). What the heck I thought, I probably had the collector's edition of Guatemala's paper money. Besides, my calculator had been trashed long ago.

Once I extricated myself from the hordes, I mounted my bike and pedaled into the lush green Guatemalan countryside. Thus I made my entrance into Central America. Days passed quickly and uneventfully as I biked through rolling farm country, where cool, clear streams flowed down from the mountains and under the bridges along the Pan Am Highway. On the banks of most of the rivers and streams, women washed clothes while children swam and played in the water. At mid afternoon, I usually stopped to take a swim and cool off in the shade along a riverbank, while the kids and women watched me curiously. It was warm, both day and night, but not the oppressive, interminable heat of Baja. Then too, if I didn't stop for a swim, a late afternoon shower would usually accomplish the same result. Gradually, the highway rose from tropical lowlands, passing volcanic mountains enroute, climbing gradually to mountain pine forests shared by Guatemala and Honduras.

~ ~ ~

Managua

The coolness of the mountains eventually gave way to the hot, semi-arid lowlands of Nicaragua. Once again I longed for the coolness of the higher elevations. But not for long. Just as I cycled into Managua, the sky opened up with a torrential downpour that forced me to take refuge in a cervezeria, where I sipped a beer and watched insane rush hour traffic race by. Soon the sun set, the traffic eased, but the rain continued to come down in buckets.

With the help of my S.A. Handbook, I wrote down directions to a few hospedajes in a nearby barrio. Then I donned full rain gear, mounted my bike, and proceeded in the pitch black, rain still pouring down, to search for a place to stay. The main stumbling block in this quest was the complete lack of street signs in downtown Managua. After a fruitless and frustrating tour through dark, deserted streets, I pulled onto the sidewalk to hail two young kids looking in a store window crammed with radios and TVs. Realizing my Spanish was inadequate they motioned for me to follow them as they jogged through the rain eventually leading me to a hotel. They seemed pleased to split the dollar tip I gave them for their trouble.

Later in the hotel cafe, I met Danielle, a young German lady, who was staying next door at Hospedaje Norma, where rooms were only $2 per night. As my room tab was $12 I checked in the next morning, but had to pay $4 because I wanted to keep my bike in the room with me. My main reason for stopping over in Managua was to find the Bikes Not Bombs facility and meet with the director Shannon O'Reilly. As this was my first mail drop since crossing the Mexican border I was anxious to see if I had a letter or two waiting for me. Again I was stymied by the lack of street signs and the fact that Bikes Not Bombs had recently moved to a new location, this information was gathered at the local post office.

By way of diversion, Danielle suggested we ride out to Lago Xiloa a few miles outside Managua for a swim. After she rented an ancient three-speed at Hospedaje Norma we began our expedition. Needless to say the swimming beach at the lake was nearly deserted, so we were able to enjoy a refreshing swim by ourselves.

Armed with the few scraps of information gathered from the post office and the Senora at the hospedaje, I cycled off in search of Bikes Not Bombs. Hours later when I finally caught up with Shannon at the spacious Bikes Not Bombs shop, he handed me a package containing three letters and a book. Shannon took the time to give me a tour of the facility and explain their goals. Briefly, bikes and parts are collected in the United States and shipped in containers to Managua, where Nicaraguans assemble or repair the bikes before selling them at reasonable prices to local people. As many bikes as possible are routed to rural areas so that teachers and health workers can facilitate access to small villages in remote areas. Other than Shannon, the shop in Managua was staffed by Nicaraguans.

Back at Hospedaje Norma I settled into a rocking chair made of rebar to read my mail, but my mind was a kaleidoscope of images provoked by a city and country in turmoil, both politically and economically. Every place I turned I was confronted by the black and red murals of Daniel Ortega and the recently departed FLN. At that time the country was run by the democratically elected Violetta Chamoro who represented a coalition of 14 political parties, each seemed diametrically opposed to the others. Somehow they had toppled the Ortega regime which had held the reigns of power for about ten years. With a new crisis surfacing weekly, it seemed the Chamarro government would crumble any day, perhaps any hour. Tension and uncertainty were written on everyone's face, except the charismatic, smiling face of Daniel Ortega painted on every other door and wall in the city. One had only to stand on a street corner to be accosted by the roving cambio people to get a feel for the deteriorating economy. On my first day in Managua the exchange rate was one million cordobas to the dollar, the next day it was a million and a half to one and rising. The exchange rate was so out of control most travelers would only exchange ten or twenty dollars at a time. In fact, the Senora at Hospedaje Norma would only accept U.S.

dollars in payment for rooms. Though the official economy was in a tailspin, the black market was thriving. It seemed to be the focal point of energy and activity in the country. While the shelves of all the state supported supermarkets were empty or filled with hundreds of boxes of powdered milk or hundreds of cans of plum pudding, the black market offered such a comprehensive selection of goods one could buy a new Japanese motorbike, a tin of Russian caviar, a new Sony color TV, a pair of Reeboks, or Jordach jeans.

The black market area was the size of ten football fields. Every square inch was crammed with hard goods, soft goods, produce, crafts and every kind of plastic, metal, or wooden gimcrack and bauble known to man. It was a circus, a shopping mall, a den of thieves, a public forum, and farmer's market all rolled, tangled and mashed into one giant sordid, immensely intriguing venue. I emerged from my first trip disoriented, confused, and weary.

~ ~ ~

Casa de Plywood

A piece of black electrical tape fashioned into the number 1 was peeling from the plywood door or my 8'x10' plywood room. Numero uno. From the depths of this warren of wood, rebar, and electrical wiring, Senora Gabriella, a matron of about 60-years old, emerged to ease her bulky frame into one of the chairs made of reinforced iron rods or rebar. She set her small blue plastic radio on the communal table, then pulled a newspaper from her apron. While the Beatles sang about a hard day's night, she read her paper. A group of German brigade workers surrounded the other table, busy preparing reports and position papers on collectivized farms, public health clinics, and numerous other volunteer programs they were involved in.

The only thing of substance at the hospedaje was the ten-foot high steel and chain link fence that sealed it off from the street, making one feel like an unwilling resident of a prison camp. To reinforce the image, the fence was topped off with steel spikes and curlicues of concertina barbed wire. The Senora was a benign warden: collecting tariffs, meting out criticisms and insults, and generally keeping a wary eye on everyone and everything happening in her plywood hacienda.

Inside the barrier there were about 30 plywood rooms, most were grimly outfitted with two single plywood beds, a wire clothesline running from corner to corner and a single 50 watt bulb suspended from electrical cord dangling from the ceiling. In the center of the compound were three plywood enclosed shower stalls that belched cold water, and two toilets, also framed by plywood. Flushing the commodes was accomplished, sporadically, with the help of an empty gallon paint can which one filled from either of two 50-gallon water drums blocking most of the narrow aisle in front of the showers. That is one would pour the contents of the paint can into the commode causing the toilet to flush. Sometimes this method didn't work; the resulting mess is something I'd rather not go into.

Each section of plywood had it's own special paint scheme, some were green, some red, some black, some orange; all were faded and peeling. The roof of the casa de plywood served two purposes. Firstly, it provided some protection against the rain that poured down every afternoon for an hour or two, and secondly, it served as a storage area for all manner of objects, a partial list of which would include: discarded automobile tires, odd pieces of pipe and wood, cannibalized bicycles, cases of empty pop and beer bottles, chunks of cement curbing and sidewalk, and various and sundry pieces of broken furniture and household appliances.

Because afternoon rain showers were more predictable than the city water system, a 250-gallon water tank perched on a 20-foot tower of steel pipes just outside my room. The Senora's muttering husband made sure it was full everyday by running a hose from the sink to the water storage tank.

I guessed it has taken the Senora and Senor at least 30 to 40 years of cobbling to whip together their plywood shrine.

Managua was the only Latin American city where my "el centro" navigating system failed. The central part of the city was once nearly leveled by an earthquake and never completely rebuilt. Instead of rebuilding from the rubble, the ruling politicos decided or were persuaded to build a lasting monument to the people, so they constructed a multi-million dollar soccer stadium. Rather than the steeples of Spanish colonial churches dominating the skyline soaring steel light towers, hulking over the stadium like spindly-legged gargoyles, catches one's eye. I cannot help but feel that some of my paltry tax dollars found their circuitous way into the cement and rebar that forms the bulk of that structure. Oddly enough, the stadium was never used during my week-long stay in Managua.

Perhaps inspired by the absurd size and cost of the soccer stadium, some other politico decided that what Managua really needed was a multi-storied, luxury hotel. Again the logic of such an enterprise escaped me because only 10% of the population could barely afford to stay at the Hospedaje Norma, let alone the grandiose International Hotel.

Another American, Maryann, also staying at the Hospedaje Norma persuaded me to accompany her to the public market. Early on a Saturday morning we boarded one of the overcrowded buses to make our way there. Two gringos entering the black market immediately caught the attention of the "cambios" or moneychangers working in the area. We were set upon by a half dozen calculator-waving fellows before we were ten feet into the market area, but succeeded in breaking through their ranks, like star running backs, to escape into aisles and tunnels of jeans, athletic shoes, and clothing of all sizes, shapes, and colors. At length we stumbled onto a section specializing in food and drink. I started off with my old standby of guayaba juice with a quail's egg, while Maryann ordered the "especiale" a combination juice drink of oranges, pineapple, and guava. Our drinks were followed by something resembling a Caesar salad, but on a bed of noodles. With Maryann ordering I simply relaxed and consumed the dishes set in front of me.

Wanting to "share the wealth" with as many vendors as possible we walked another 10-feet to order fruit cups for dessert. As we elbowed and shouldered our way through narrow aisles, watching as hogs and chickens were butchered before our eyes and beneath our feet, smelling pots of steaming tripe, brains, tongue, and looking at the picture tubes of hundreds of TVs all displaying the same dismal pictures of querulous politicians, we were struck by the many similarities between this public bazaar and the infamous American shopping mall. In short, it was an obscene display of consumerism. After hours of wandering, looking, haggling, eating, and drinking we reached a new level of ennui similar to those feelings of disgust and desperation one succumbs to at 10 p.m. Christmas Eve at a Macys department store.

Almost in a state of panic we found our way out of the market in search of a small park where we could sit on the grass or lean against a tree, listen to the chirping of birds, and see a clear blue sky.

Early next morning I said goodbye to Maryann who was on her way to a rural village to do volunteer work at a health clinic. Soon after she departed I rolled my loaded bike through the front gate of Hospedaje Norma for the last time and headed south to Lago Nicaragua. It was a great relief to escape the traffic-choked streets of Managua where buses, trucks, collectivos, and automobiles challenged each other in a mock death race from corner to corner, alternately beeping horns, stomping accelerators, and jamming on brakes-all in a acrid haze of diesel exhaust.

After a long slow climb out of the dismal city, I topped out and began a descent along a nearly deserted highway through rolling hills where adobe houses flanked fields of crops. The 58-mile trip to the northern shore of Lago Nicaragua was one of my most enjoyable cycling experiences in Central America. No matter the place, cycling amongst rolling hills through peaceful farm country always buoyed my spirits.

The small town of Granada on the northern lakeshore was pleasing to both eye and ear. Its cobbled streets may have been narrow, but then there was little vehicular traffic to crowd them. Adobe houses with tiled roofs looked orderly and well maintained. The traditional main plaza was flanked on the south side by a large cathedral.

From the plaza I could look down the main street to the quay and the vast panorama of Lake Nicaragua, an inland sea or huge fresh water lake approximately 90-miles long and 35-miles wide at points. From Granada I planned to take a 5-hour boat ride to the island of Ometepe somewhere out on the vastness of the lake. A few hundred yards from the quay I found a hospedaje where I rented a room facing out on a flower garden located in the interior courtyard. According to the owner I'd be able to purchase a ticket on the quay for the boat leaving early the next day for the island. After a shower and a nap, I walked down to the pier and found the ticket office open. I understood the ticket seller to say that the boat would leave at 2 p.m. the next afternoon. Additionally, I paid 25 cents extra as a freight charge for my bicycle.

On my way back to the hospedaje I stopped at a small cafe with the unlikely name of "Drive In," recommended in the South American Handbook. A blatant misnomer as "Drive In" was only accessible by pedestrians. Regardless, as their only patron I naturally received prompt and attentive service. While the staff and management devoured their dinner at a nearby table, I enjoyed a hamburger with papas fritas and two cups of excellent coffee.

One of the most pleasant features of Granada, for good reason, was the scarcity of tourists and all that tourism brings to small, quaint villages on the shores of eye-catching lakes. Judging from my walks about the nearly deserted plaza I was the only gringo in town.

~ ~ ~

Lago Nicaragua

Having had some experience with third world schedules and time tables, I loaded my bike early next morning and pedaled down to the quay, but to my surprise the huge boat sat idling and from all appearances ready to depart. Cycling quickly onto the pier, I pulled up to the loading ramp and presented my ticket to the person in charge. In a volley of Spanish, I was exhorted to get my bike and myself aboard as preparations had already begun to cast off. Here things got complicated further or perhaps they just got more interesting. In order to get onto the boat I would have to cross a narrow, swaying plank about two-feet wide spanning a distance of eight feet between the pier and boat. This would have been only mildly disconcerting had it not been for a 20-foot drop from the swaying plank to the water. A number of passengers had gathered about the railing of the boat to speculate amongst themselves about my predicament. The stumbling block here as I saw it was the necessity of walking across the gangplank while pushing my heavily laden bike. Motivated by another volley of encouragement from the ticket taker, I grabbed the bike by the handlebars and walked, as best I could, across the plank to the safety of the deck. Not a performance rating a standing ovation, I expected at least a few smiles of approval from the passengers observing my balancing act, but was greeted with grim silence bordering on apathy. No sooner had I gained purchase on the deck then the plank was hauled back onto the pier, thick hawsers flung onto the decks, and with a toot from a whistle the boat was under way. Later, I learned from a steward that I had misunderstood the boat's departure time, instead of 2 p.m. it departed at 12 p.m., thus I learned the two-hour difference between "dos" and "dose."

The wooden gangplank notwithstanding, the 70-foot steel-hulled boat was quite shipshape. Generous seating arrangements were available indoors, but as the weather was warm and sunny, most passengers, including me, preferred to lounge about the deck. Unlike other modes of third world public transport I've experienced there were few passengers on board. The main purpose of the vessel was transporting goods and supplies and to a lesser extent people to various communities around the lakeshore and to the islands.

As the boat chugged its way onto the smooth lake surface, I managed to curl up under a life raft and take a siesta. Some time later a fellow passenger who wanted to make sure I didn't miss the view of the smoking volcano on the Island of Ometepe, which we were fast approaching, awakened me. I followed this gentleman to the ship's railing where he pointed excitedly at Volcan Concepcion which was belching smoke from its apex. I estimated we were about five miles from the island. As I watched, the wind blew the smoke clouds away, revealing the top of the volcano. The scene was made more memorable thanks to a clear blue sky as a backdrop and the fast approaching island.

Our first stop at the island was at the village of Alta Garcia. The throbbing engine eased to a slow rumble as the ship drifted alongside an ancient wooden pier where waiting stevedores secured the boat with hawsers. Once secured, a squad of shoeless, shirtless men, none of them young, trooped onboard to begin the back breaking job of off-loading 25 and 50-pound sacks of rice, beans, flower, and other staples. With decks partially cleared, the boat continued on its way to the village of Mayagalpa, my destination. We drifted to the dock at Mayagalpa as the sun was going down. As most of the other passengers had disembarked at Alta Garcia, I thought I'd be able to roll my bike off quickly, but was stymied as the dock at Mayagalpa was much lower than the one at Granada, which meant I had to strip my bike and carry it and my gear down a flight of stairs and onto the pier.

While refitting the bike under the scrutiny of a half dozen young boys I smiled and said, "Muchas carga, si?" They smiled back nodding their heads approvingly.

Within minutes I found the pensione recommended in the *South American Handbook*. After checking in the owner escorted me to a secluded room in the back of a garden occupying most of the inner courtyard. He did this with the air of a famous maitre d' groveling before one of his best customers. That not being the case I wondered if perhaps he thought I was someone else. While going through the usual routine of stripping gear of my bike I heard a bit of a commotion at the entrance of the pensione. When I looked up the owner was rushing towards me with a dozen small boys on his heels.

"They want to see the bicycle, senior, please accept my apologies," the owner said.

Even before he finished his apology the kids were swarming over the bike, poking and prodding and scrutinizing the decals I'd collected on my trip thus far. I tried to explain to them how I'd started in Alaska cycling south along the west coast of North and Central America until I'd arrived at their island on Lago Nicaragua. Judging from their confused facial expressions world geography was beyond their grasp. When they were satisfied with the vagaries of bicycle touring and the enormous load on my bike they drifted away.

It was dark when I took a shower in the outside, cold water shower. Afterward, I put on the few bits of clean clothes I had and lay down on my cot to read, but when I pulled the little chain on the lamp beside my bed nothing happened. Suddenly I came back to reality—I was on an island in the middle of Lake Nicaragua. The only electricity available to the people on the Island of Ometepe, and for most rural villages in Central America, was produced by a huge, greasy, old diesel engine and that would be limited to the hours of 7 to 10 p.m., except for fiestas and religious holidays. Opening my door, I looked down into the courtyard to see a dozen or so kerosene lamps on tables, so I hurried down to dinner before it was too late.

As most of the tables were full, I worked my way amongst the other guests until I saw a young woman seated by herself. She looked up from making notes in a journal. I introduced myself and asked if she would mind if I joined her.

Sabina, an attractive German woman, was traveling alone. She'd taken a leave of absence from her job as a nurse and was on her way to Bluefelds on the Caribbean coast of Nicaragua to work as a visiting nurse for a few months. I was surprised she didn't mind traveling by herself in such a troubled country, but she seemed to be taking it in her stride. She thought I was the adventurous one what with biking throughout Central and South America. I told her I was more impressed with her adventure than mine, knowing the risks involved for a lone female traveling in a third world country. Based on my observations thus far on my trip it seemed that Germans had a lot more of the explorer in them than any other nationality. Many of the Germans I'd met in out of the way places had been traveling alone.

I felt sluggish next morning when I got up. After a trip to the toilet I knew I had lower GI problems again. So I spent most of the day reading and talking with Sabina who invited me to take a stroll around town with her. During our 30-minute walking tour of the greater Mayagalpa area we wandered down to the dock where I inquired about the boat departure schedule for the following day. I learned a boat would be departing for San Jorge at 1 p.m. From San Jorge, located on the western lakeshore, I would be able to reconnect with the Pan Am Highway, some 10 miles west of the village. I spent the remainder of the afternoon talking with Sabina in the pensione garden. She planned to take the early bus to Alta Garcia, the first stop for the boat I'd taken the previous day.

Curious as to why my stomach/bowel problems were recurring, I thought back to my first day at the pensione. I'd asked the owner about filling my water bottles, emphasizing the need for "agua filtrata" or filtered water. The Senor pointed to a water tap near the garden entrance. "Esta aqua filtrata, senor," he said pointing at the chrome filtering mechanism attached to the water spigot. Reassured, I filled my bottles, consuming most of the water that day. Only later did I learn from a seasoned third world traveler at the pensione never to trust filtering mechanisms in the third world. More than likely, he explained, the filter element had clogged up years ago and been thrown away, never to be replaced.

Not the best of news for me. Ever since my last bout of "turistas" in Mexico I religiously purified drinking water with my Katadyn filter, but getting lazy and complacent I neglected to use it at the pensione, relying instead on the word of the owner, who was immune to various microbes residing in his water supply.

Next morning I was again surprised when arriving at the pier. Time-wise I was a half-hour early and had my ticket and freight receipt in hand. The surprise was the size of the boat. No 70-foot, diesel-powered, steel-hulled ship, this craft looked remarkably like the African Queen. And from the looks of her this was not her maiden voyage. Instead of a quirky steam boiler to provide power, this ancient wooden boat was powered by a Chevy V-8. When the engine started, the resulting valve clatter sounded suspiciously like my old truck. This was my introduction to the Princess Anna. I stood at the end of the pier watching brown-skinned youngsters leap from the roof of the boat into the lake and wondering where I was going to stow my bike and gear, as the cargo area in back of the engine compartment was already piled high with an assortment of boxes, bags, suitcases, burlap sacks, and cages of live chickens. Already, a dozen or so passengers were seated on the benches fixed to the gunwales. When I made an attempt to push my bike down the narrow gangplank forming a tenuous link between pier and boat, one of the crew yelled at me and pointed to the roof. After a minute of consideration, I guessed the roof was as good a place as any for the bike, so I began stripping off the panniers. After lifting the bike onto the roof I climbed up after it and tied it down with rope and bungees. Satisfied it would survive the two-hour cruise to San Jorge; I jumped down and began shuttling the remainder of my gear aboard the Princess Anna. With my gear secured, I sat back to watch the members of the crew, dressed only in shorts, crawl in and out of the engine compartment carrying greasy wrenches, hammers, and other tools. Then to my amazement, I saw one of the crew assist the owner of a Japanese motorcycle aboard and park it in the middle of the aisle. I was convinced that if I'd have greased some palms my bicycle would have been stowed there as well.

The other passengers, numbering about 20 by now, seemed to be a rather grim lot. As departure time neared a few more passengers, mainly women in plain dresses or in jeans, boarded carrying the ubiquitous chicken by its tethered legs. Without doubt the most interesting passengers were two hogs, each weighing in the neighborhood of 300 lbs. More to the point, the way they boarded the boat was of special interest. In all it took the owners, most of the crew, and a few fellow passengers to coax, cajole, and threaten the behemoth porkers to cross the narrow gangplank to the boat. I had no idea how stubborn or how bellicose hogs could be. Perhaps, I thought, the reluctance on the hogs' part was due not to the anticipation of a potentially rough voyage, but to the realization this would be a one-way trip as they were headed to market. At last the two rotund traveling companions were beaten and threatened sufficiently to coax them across the gangplank onto the bow of the boat in front of the wheelhouse where they settled down alongside each other for a well earned siesta.

About this time I wouldn't have been surprised to see the unshaven, cigarette-smoking Charlie Alnut emerge from the depths of the engine compartment and yell to the crew to make ready to cast off. However, the only thing that emerged from the engine compartment was the "thunking" sound of a Chevy V-8 accompanied by a cloud of exhaust that stained the ceiling with a black scum.

At last, with all human and animal cargo aboard we cast-off and chugged slowly out onto the vastness of Lake Nicaragua. Behind us emerged the still smoking cone of Conception Volcano. Though the lake got a bit choppy, the Princess Anna chugged slowly and unfalteringly toward San Jorge. Some two hours later we snubbed up to the pier. Anxious passengers were already shoving and elbowing each other to be first to disembark even before the gangplank was secured. Their impatience worked in my favor, for by the time I had my gear in order and ready to transfer to the dock the small vessel was deserted except for the hogs. After piling my gear on the quay, I climbed onto the roof of the boat and untied my bike and with the help of one passenger transferred it to the safety of the dock. All the while the hogs were creating a pandemonium signaling their approaching disembarkation.

Feeling a bit nauseous, I began the ritual of refitting the gear to my bike. In the midst of the process I looked up to discover I was being silently watched by several men, none of whom seemed particularly happy about anything. Anxious to get back on my bike and pedal to the nearby town of Rivas, where I planned to spend the night, I tried to ignore them. But soon one grim looking chap stepped closer and said something unpleasant, then rubbed his thumb and forefinger together-the universal sign for money. I couldn't figure out what he was demanding money for. Growing pains in my stomach and bowels did not enhance the situation. Shortly thereafter his comrades closed ranks about him echoing his demand for money. Feeling vulnerable I pulled out my freight receipt and showed it to the ringleader, who pushed it aside and reiterated his appeal for money.

All the while I continued loading gear on my bike the demands for money grew more belligerent. In addition to being confused, now I was damned scared. I knew I couldn't make a run for it, under the circumstances that would be foolhardy, so I pulled a million cordobas from my fanny pack (worth about one U.S. dollar) and thrust it at the rogue. This didn't seem to pacify him or his cohorts in the least; in fact I thought any second they would overpower me and take my wallet and any gear that caught their fancy. I knew I had to do something and do it quick, so I got on my bike and began pedaling away, figuring they would do one of two things: either overpower me or let me go. Luckily they broke ranks and let me cycle away, hurling much verbal abuse in my wake. I pedaled as fast as I could until their vehement threats were inaudible.

~ ~ ~

Sanctuary

Rolling into the village of Rivas an hour later I was weak and shaking like a leaf, more attributable to growing GI problems than from my recent confrontation. I was convinced I was in for another siege of hydraulic bowels. At the edge of the village a young fellow on a ancient three-speed bicycle pulled alongside me and smiled. I said hello and asked if he knew where a hospedaje was. Instead of stopping to give me directions, he motioned for me to follow him. Down the main street into Rivas we pedaled at last coming to a stop in front of a clean, albeit nondescript house.

"Hospedaje esta aqui," he said still smiling then pedaled away.

I propped my bike up against the four-foot high retaining wall supporting the sidewalk then wearily climbed up five steps to the sidewalk and approached the front door.

There was a room available, the senora assured me and only $3 a night. She also served dinner if I cared to eat there. In no condition, mentally or physically, to price shop I told her I would take a room.

Out on the street again, I grabbed my bike and tried to horse it up the steps to the sidewalk. This proved my undoing. Halfway up the steps I felt a sharp pain in my lower back. I let the bike go and watched helplessly as it crashed down the steps into the street where it lay like an expired plow horse. I tried to straighten up, but it was impossible. My temper flared as I cursed myself for flagrant stupidity. After a few minutes of rest and recrimination, I laboriously and painfully stripped panniers and gear off the bike and began the arduous job of moving them up to the sidewalk. From there I made five agonizing trips to my room where I secured everything before collapsing on the cot in spasms of pain and nausea. While gulping down a handful of aspirin I guessed my riding days were over. I wondered how I could pedal a bike loaded with 75 lbs. of equipment when I could barely stand up and walk. Moreover, I felt weak, sick, depressed, and alienated, among other things. About the only thing I was thankful for was my recent escape from the desperados back at San Jorge. That and the bicyclist who guided me to the hospedaje and getting a room on the ground floor.

Somehow I managed to extricate myself from my cot. Feeling painful muscle spasms I rolled onto the floor, then clutching a chair in one hand and the edge of the cot in the other, managed to push and pull myself to my feet. After a cold shower and another fistful of aspirin I hobbled to the dining area in the courtyard, 98 steps from my room. I poked at my rice and beans, but enthusiastically drank a bottle of cold beer. That night, after experimenting with a dozen or so sleeping positions, I finally found one that allowed me to twist into a semi-fetal position and thus sleep fitfully for a few hours.

The spirit was willing, but the flesh was definitely weak, but not weak enough to prevent me from getting out of Nicaragua that day. The frontier, I calculated, was only 50-miles south of Rivas. Nothing would keep me here another day, except total collapse, I vowed. So, slowly and painfully, I loaded my bike. The major problem was "how" to get on it. Lifting my leg carefully over the top tube I eased it down until I was standing flat-footed. With beads of sweat on my forehead I lowered my butt onto the saddle, stuck my right foot in the toe clip, and then pushed off with my left foot. I applied pressure slowly to the pedals until I was rolling along smartly. Thankfully, the road south was relatively flat. After 15-minutes of cycling the pain tapered off and I started feeling better.

I was in such good spirits I reluctantly stopped for a cold drink just before crossing the Nicaraguan border. Dismounting was more of a chore than I figured. First of all, I couldn't find anything to prop my bike against to help with the dismount procedure. It was impossible to lift my leg without triggering a spasm of pain in my lower back, so coasting up to a the steps in front of a cafe I grabbed hold of the wooden banister with one hand and the handlebars with the other. Carefully, I swung my right leg over the top tube. Once off the bike I propped it against the fence next to the banister. Despite the pain I had to laugh at myself and what I must have looked like to the two women inside the cafe. Though they didn't say anything when I finally opened the screen door and hobbled inside, they did look at me with questioning eyes when I ordered a soft drink.

My only reward for this painful expedition was I'd soon be out of Nicaragua and in Costa Rica. This was accomplished with another half dozen reruns of my getting-on-and-off-the-bike routine before finally cycling into Costa Rica.

~ ~ ~

Sick Bay

Four days later I arrived in Quepos, Costa Rica, not only with a sore back, but also with a virulent case of dysentery. I reached the end of my rope at the beach resort of Manuel Antonio south of Quepos. There I was able to rent a room at Cabinas Ramirez right on the beach. Thank God my room had a toilet, as I spent the next five days either on my back or hurrying from my bed to the toilet. Food and drink went right through me, so naturally I lost my appetite, as well as some weight. Even the copious amounts of water I drank were unpleasantly purged from my body. Depressed and scared after five days of this routine, I knew I had to do something or I'd wind up in the hospital. I was so weak and dehydrated I could barely muster enough mental energy to think straight. Then I remembered fellow biker Dr. Sam Walker of Palo Alto had given me two types of antibiotics before I started my trip. So I found my first aid kit and rummaged around until I found the antibiotics. My dilemma now was there were two sizes: big pills and small pills. Almost two years had passed since he'd given me the antibiotics so I couldn't decide which pill to take. The cryptic pharmaceutical labeling on the packaging was of no help either; rather it merely confused matters. Realizing I had to do something, I chose the smaller of the pills, figuring it would do the least damage if I made the wrong choice. I popped the little capsule in my mouth and chugged down a half-quart of filtered water.

Just before I fell asleep I vowed I'd never drink unfiltered water or lift my loaded bike again.

My trips to the toilet were dramatically reduced allowing me to sleep and gain strength. As the day progressed I consumed more and more water to counteract dehydration.

Next day, I felt strong enough to stagger down to the beach cafe behind the cabinas for a glass of juice and bowl of cornflakes, which to my surprise stayed with me. After a few hours of rest in my room I went out for a short walk on the beach, then repaired to the cafe to sip coffee and watch the surf. At the very least I commiserated, I had a beautiful place to recuperate. It would have been a far different story if I'd gotten stuck in Managua.

In the days that followed my bowels stabilized, my appetite improved, and I began feeling like my old self again. Sufficiently ambulatory, I began planning a trek to San Jose, about 150-miles inland. Every morning, after my bowl of cornflakes and bananas, I'd walk down the beach two miles to the entrance of Manuel Antonio National park then turn around and head back to the cafe where I'd sip coffee and watch other travelers come and go. As the days passed I experienced a substantial increase in strength and energy. My breakfast fare of cornflakes was supplanted with eggs, toast, and coffee. Short beach walks were supplemented with short bike rides in and around Manuel Antonio and a longer ride into Quepos, about five miles north of the beach.

During my convalescence I began to appreciate the natural beauty of Costa Rica. Everywhere I looked I saw something new and beautiful: palm trees, banana trees, orchids, bromeliads, bougainvillea, hyacinth—a veritable riot of colors and smells attacked my re-energized senses.

~ ~ ~

Poru Vida

One morning while breakfasting and studying a map, I was distracted by music issuing from someone's tape player. Once again I recognized a favorite instrumental by Dire Straits. I called over to three chaps at a nearby table to turn up the volume. One of them called back to come and join them. Grabbing my map and coffee, I pulled up a chair at their table and introduced myself to three total strangers. Axel Grubock and Christoph Gerhold, both Austrians, were on a month-long holiday. The third person, Fernando, a Tico, lived in San Jose, but spent his days off at Manuel Antonio.

While Mark Knofler sang about industrial disease and MTV we got acquainted. Noticing my map, Christoph asked what my travel plans were. I brought them up to date on my trip thus far, then outlined my plan to trek up to San Jose then over to Limon on the Caribbean coast. Both Austrians expressed interest in joining me. With Fernando's help we drew up a tentative itinerary agreeing to depart the next morning.

As our trek around the country would take at least two weeks, I had to find a secure place to store my bike and most of my gear. The dilemma was solved expeditiously by Louis, the manager of the cabinas where I was staying. He generously volunteered to allocate space in his small office where he and his wife would be able to keep an eye on my bike. I felt a bit reluctant about stowing my bike and gear in his office, as it not only took up a lot of space, but effectively blocked the aisle to the small bathroom near his desk. Luis repeatedly assured me with a smile and shrug that there was "no problema."

The three of us boarded a bus early next morning. Smiling and waving from the open-air cafe nearby, Fernando yelled, "poru vida." A saying I'd hear frequently in Costa Rica during the month I spent there, it loosely means that life is for living. After a scenic ride through mountains and coffee fincas we arrived in San Jose. With only a bit of trouble we located the hotel recommended by Fernando.

Here we secured inexpensive rooms at the Gran Centro Americano in downtown San Jose.

After a quick shower we rushed into the streets in search of a Chinese restaurant, also on Fernando's recommendation. But it was dark and having newly arrived in the city, we were disoriented. So we rushed around like cub scouts without a compass. At last on a side street deep in the bowels of the city we saw a sign advertising a "Chino Restaurante," embellished with Chinese script. Inside, we eagerly pointed at the menu while a Tico waitress scribbled on a pad. Not long after we gulped half of our beers, the table was piled with platters, plates, and bowls of rice, shrimp, sweet and sour pork, cashew chicken, soup, and one small pot of tea. Our plan had been to order two or three entrees and split them between us, but due to a slight miscalculation or communication problem on our part we wound up with nine entrees, plus three huge bowls of rice. In all there was enough food to feed half the population on San Jose. Regardless, we did it justice, carrying away only a carton of food apiece to be snacked on during the next two days. Thankfully in my post-dysentery state I was ravenous.

After our oriental feast, we hurried into the streets in search of some nightlife, but within the hour we found ourselves, not unwillingly, standing in line at "Pop's" ice cream shop, a popular creamery with stores throughout the city.

At about 11 p.m. we found ourselves outside San Jose's most notorious bar. Reputedly once a high-class brothel, Key Largo, was housed in a splendid colonial mansion and had the look of an extremely expensive watering hole. Feeling somewhat underdressed, undercapitalized, and bit self-conscious toting cartons of leftover Chinese food; we walked across the street to a less intimidating bar named Nashville South. Enjoying cold beer and country and western music we passed the time flirting with the pretty Tico barmaids.

Next day we explored daytime San Jose. Our primary mission was to change money, as the most attractive rates of exchange or "cambio" were to be had in the capital city. Not far from the main square, we met

Mike an American motorcyclist, currently working for a Tico river rafting company. Under his guidance, we soon arrived at the small upstairs office of a helicopter rental company that, according to Mike, had one of the most generous exchange rates in all of Costa Rica. Although I never really understood the connection between helicopters and money exchange I followed Mike's lead.

We waited in the outer-office until Ricardo, the English-speaking principal summoned us, one by one, to his inner-sanctum. With walls plastered with photographs and prints of various sizes and shapes of helicopters, Ricardo exchanged piles of colorful colones for smaller piles of colorful dollars and traveler's checks. Of course all cambios outside of the banking institutions approved by the state were totally illegal. And yet a gringo tourist could not walk more than a dozen paces in downtown San Jose without being solicited by one or more of these black market cambios. There must be a lot of money to be had in changing money, but for the life of me I could never figure it out.

~ ~ ~

Diablo Brown and the Machete Brothers

At 4 p.m. the train jerked to a stop in the jungle. A rain-swollen Reventazon River raced past, white spume marked the rapids like whipped cream on chocolate pudding. Up ahead I could see the narrow gauge tracks, two pieces of shimmering silver, disappear into a green wall of vines, banana trees, sugar cane, and palm trees. The sky had clouded over threatening rain. San Jose, Costa Rica was six hours behind us. We waited.

The two Austrians sitting across from me with Walkman earphones on their heads looked like pilot and co-pilot experiencing extreme turbulence. Axel looked over at me, "Poru Vida," he said. I looked out the open window and watched people start to get off the train and gather alongside the tracks in groups of three and four. They waited.

Thirty minutes later, still with no idea why we'd stopped, Christoph, Axel, and I climbed down out of the passenger compartment to have a look around and stretch our legs. A vendor strolled among the knots of people selling soft drinks, popcorn, salted banana chips, and coconut ice cream. We watched from the riverbank as a tree trunk plunged into the rapids then split in half as it smashed against a rock. Suddenly, the train lurched backwards. We hurried onboard hoping whatever the problem was it had been solved as mysteriously as it occurred.

Minutes later the train came to a jolting stop on a spur line. We'd left San Jose that morning at 10 a.m. for what the guidebook described as a "leisurely seven-hour ride to Limon, on the Atlantic coast." It was now 5 p.m., getting dark and the train was stuck in the middle of nowhere. No one seemed to mind, except the three of us. We stared at a passing work crew clad in yellow rain slickers, clutching tools and smoking cigarettes. Shortly afterward, the diesel locomotive pulling our train uncoupled and followed after the work crew like a dutiful cow policing up her wandering calves. The five wooden passenger cars sat in the gathering dusk like refugees waiting hopefully, but not understanding where they were or what was going to happen to them.

Again, everyone disembarked to stand in clusters beside the cars. The Austrians unsheathed new machetes from tooled leather scabbards. Advancing anxiously into the vines and banana plants, they slashed and chopped aggressively, though with little purpose. The Spanish speaking "Ticos" smoked in amused silence. Unsure of the Austrians expertise with the long, sharp blades, I backpedaled and watched as a narrow clearing to the river emerged in the wake of their flailing machetes.

Figure 9: The machete brothers-Axel, author, Christoph.

With the suddenness of a door slamming it was pitch black. Everyone climbed back into the dark of the passenger cars, none of which was equipped with lights. Three small children across the aisle from us whined with impatience and hunger. Sitting in the dark listening to the jungle sounds and roaring river, I pulled a Mini-Mag flashlight from my pack and tied it to the rail of an overhead baggage tray. With two new batteries provided by Axel, we sat and talked in the narrow cone of light. Somewhere in the back of the car someone began strumming a guitar. Someone else started singing in Spanish; a melancholy ditty, we guessed, about floods, train wrecks, and jungle spirits.

From a rucksack on the floor, Christoph retrieved a half-bottle of Jim Beam. My porcelain coffee cup was filled with whiskey and Coke, then passed around amongst the three of us. The guitar music ended with a thunderous riff followed by scattered applause, then the melancholy sounds of a harmonica filled the void. Identifying the song as "Me and Bobby McGee" I started singing along. Shortly, Christoph and Axel joined in. When the song ended there was more applause, this time louder. Christoph refilled the cup with more whiskey and Coke. Axel handed me a set of earphones connected to the Walkman. As I peered out into the pitch-black jungle, the guitar music of Dire Straits filled my head. Shortly after "Telegraph Road" ended the train jolted forward. Soon we were racing along the riverbank headed for Limon. The rain had stopped. A brilliant moon reflected off the river. As we were only five cars behind the locomotive we could see the massive headlight bore a hole of illumination into the wall of black ahead of us. The train snaked its way along the riverbank, passenger cars rocking gently from side to side, eventually turning away from the river and entering the coastal lowlands. Lights and hearth fires blazed as we lumbered past small villages.

When the train stopped at a small nameless village, disgorging many passengers, we began to feel the humidity of the Caribbean. At 10:15 p.m. the train pulled into Limon, a large port servicing the banana industry.

"Hey mon, you need Taxi? I carry you now, mon," a black face called to us on the platform.

I followed in the wake of the long-legged Austrians as they hurried to the hotel recommended in their German travel guide. We were drenched in sweat when we entered the crumbling hotel. Seconds after a behemoth black man disappeared into a back room with our passports, Christoph whispered, "I don't feel this to be acceptable. George, do you feel this way?" I shrugged, feeling only the need for a cold beer and a shower.

When the man returned with our passports Christoph snatched them up and said something in Spanish, then turned on his heel and headed for the door. Axel and I took his cue and followed with our backpacks. The black man's nostrils flared, his jaws clamped shut like a dungeon door. "Okay, mon," he snarled as we retreated. Regardless of their expertise, I was glad to be tagging along with the machete brothers. The humid night was filled with the sounds of Reggae music and mosquitos. Tired, hungry, and feeling the weight of our backpacks we spotted a lighted sign on the side of a two-story building—Hotel Fung. A room on the second floor overlooking the main square cost two dollars apiece. Although a half dozen cockroaches occupied the shower in the bathroom they graciously disappeared into the woodwork as soon as I turned on the water faucet.

We were famished. Our last meal had been a breakfast of egg McMuffins at the McDonald's in San Jose early that morning. After a quick shower we hurried down to the street in search of a restaurant. Fortunately, there was a Chinese restaurant on the street level around the corner—Restaurant Fung. We ordered beer and chop suey. Three heaping plates arrived before our first beer was finished. Gulping the food down like prisoners, we watched a color TV above the bar. At a table nearby, five fleshy Costa Rican women drank beer and puffed cigarettes. The girls night out. They watched covertly as we guzzled beer and wolfed down chop suey. After another round of beer, Christoph called for the check. Our waitress appeared with a slip of paper with a conglomeration of figures scrawled on it. I thought we'd lay a pile of paper currency on the table and stroll back to our room for a well-earned night's sleep. But no.

"This is absolutely wrong," Christoph spat out looking at the bill clenched in his hand.

The waitress snarled something in Spanish.

"No, no, this is absolutely incorrect," Christoph flared back jabbing at the paper with his index finger.

The waitress retreated to the bar, returning shortly with a menu and a calculator. We watched with incredulity as she totaled our bills separately arriving at three different figures. An enigma since we'd consumed the exact same items. She did her calculations again; the results were equally disparate.

Christoph was beside himself. "This is totally wrong," he said shaking his head. "This is stupido!"

The waitress frowned. An explosion of Spanish erupted from her mouth. Again she reworked the figures, arriving at new sets of totals, none of which pleased Christoph. Pushing some currency to the center of the table, I suggested that perhaps we should graciously, but quickly slip away.

"Stupido, stupido, stupido." Christoph shouted.

The ladies at the next table next stared at us over their bottles of beer. I was glad the Austrians' machetes were safely stowed back in our hotel room. Pulling a calculator from his tote bag, Christoph grabbed the slip of paper from the waitress and began calculating the figures. Several men at the bar watched us intensely. Two Chinese men clad in equally stained aprons appeared at the table. A heated discussion ensued, partly Spanish, partly Chinese, with the waitress.

Christoph finished his calculations, then thrust the calculator at the waitress. "That is the correct total. You have made an absolute error."

Except for a rap song blaring on the TV, Restaurante Fung was silent. The Chinese scowled at the waitress. The waitress scowled at us. The five Tico ladies waited for something to happen.

Suddenly, the waitress slapped her forehead, grabbed Christoph's calculator, once again orchestrating a flurry of computation. This time her total matched those of Christoph's. She smiled sheepishly as the two Chinese men showered her with verbal abuse. The younger of the Chinese men grabbed her calculator and flung it out the door into the deserted street.

Christoph beamed. All attention turned back to the color TV. The waitress collected the money in silence as we pushed back our chairs. The two Chinese men hurried back to the kitchen.

On the way back to the hotel, Christoph said, "Batteries, the batteries were almost dead, kaput."

"Yeah, but that sure was good chop suey," I commented, glad to be on my way to the hotel and not to the local medical clinic or jail.

At 6 a.m. next morning, we quietly and expeditiously departed Hotel Fung for the bus station, there to catch a ride to Cahuita, 30 kilometers (18.6 miles) south of Limon. Typically the bus was jammed with human bodies, bags, boxes, even a few chickens. Everyone was bathed in perspiration. The humidity was suffocating. We found ourselves jammed tightly into the stairwell, cheek to jowl, at the back of the bus. Our backpacks squeezed in at our feet made it impossible to move. Securing a seat was out of the question. Even with all the bus windows wide open, there was a foul odor which would have been uncomfortable had it not been for the clouds of cigarette smoke neutralizing it.

Somehow a black man, introducing himself as Jonathan, managed to squeeze in amongst us. Our faces were only inches apart. Jonathan reeked of Rum and cigarette smoke. He was on his way home to Puerto Viejo, just south of Cahuita.

"A lovely, lovely beach, very lovely," he said with obnoxious frequency.

With a smile, he told us his wife was going to be "very, very angry, mon," when (and if) he ever returned. He walked away from his home awhile ago without telling his wife. He wasn't sure if it had been two, three, perhaps four weeks since his departure. Before Jonathan disembarked at a roadside tavern long before the Cahuita stop, he asked the Austrians if they would "carry me back to Austria, mon."

When the bus turned off the pavement onto a dirt road and headed east I knew we were getting close to Cahuita. Though many passengers had gotten off along the main road to disappear into the jungle, the machete brothers and I remained crammed into the well of the rear exit. We were amazed at the agility and equanimity of the Ticos who had to scale the barrier of backpacks and duffel we had created.

In Cahuita, the bus pulled alongside a two-story woodframe building of faded green paint, serving as both general store and disco. Music, mostly Reggae, pounded from the back half of the building housing the disco. As we walked past on the street we found we had to raise our voices to be heard over the bass-dominant music. In a way Cahuita reminded me of the Costa Rican version of Faulkner's Yaknapatapha County. Dust hung in the air like fog with each passing bus or horse drawn wagon. Everyone moved with loose-limbed sluggishness. The humidity was nearly palpable and tasted of salt. Perspiration dripped from the brow like a leaky faucet.

Local swains lounged on the open porch outside the general store smoking cigarettes and watching tourists like little children mesmerized by a tank of tropical fish. An old black man, aged and withered like a prune, descended the creaking board steps of the store with the aid of a wooden cane, stopping in the dirt at the bottom to expectorate a gob of varnish-colored liquid into the street. Every other young black who bebopped by had his hair trussed in the cable-like strands of the Rastafarians.

When the bus stopped we barely had time to clear our packs and ourselves out of the exit door before the passengers descended to the street. Bob Marley impersonators, idling on the porch of the store, sighted in on the new arrivals with the cunning and anticipation of bird dogs.

Shouldering our packs we walked down the dirt street toward the beach and national park. Close to the beach we wandered into the courtyard of a Hotel with adjoining bar and cafe.

At the hotel reception desk, Marcella, a Swiss expatriate, looked up sleepily from his desk, taking a long pull on a beer. He lit a cigarette and tried to push himself up from his chair but was too drunk to manage it. With a sigh he fell back into the chair and smiled.

"Do you have any accommodations." Christoph asked.

"I think so," Marcella replied, scratching his long unruly hair.

After rummaging around in a drawer he withdrew a key the size of a hammer and pushed it carefully across the desk.

"Go upstairs and take a look," he said nonchalantly, then lowered his head onto his arms and promptly fell asleep, the cigarette still burning in the nicotine-stained fingers of his right hand.

We pushed the door to room 215 open without the aid of the key and walked tentatively inside. The floor sagged under our weight. Humid heat rushed past us into the cool, dark hallway. Three unmade beds greeted us like derelicts from a Charles Bukowski novel. Sodden ceiling tiles hung tenuously from exposed rafters, victims of recent rainstorms. As we tiptoed to the center of the room I had visions of plummeting through the floor to a subterranean pit filled with rats and crocodiles.

Christoph kept shaking his head and muttering, "No, no this is not acceptable. George, give me your opinion."

I merely rolled my eyes and started a slow retreat to the hall. Not wanting to wake Marcella from his siesta, Christoph placed the key on the desk as we made our way back to the sunbaked street. With Christoph's seal of approval, we moved into an airy, second story room with shower in a new hotel just across the street. I crawled onto a bed made up with designer sheets and pillowcase to match. I suspected foreign investors, joint ventures, Yen. After a cold shower, I lay sprawled on my bed reading the last chapter of my Chatwin book.

The machete brothers hurried from the room towards, I guessed, a cold beer and hot ambiance of the nearby disco. I contented myself with the book and cool breeze created by the ceiling fan.

Around dinnertime Axel and Christoph returned with smiles on their faces. A good sign I thought. At the disco, they had met Tico Rico. One of the locals. He invited them to go lobster fishing with him in the morning.

"I know all the fishes in Cahuita, mon," he had assured them.

I begged off going on the lobster expedition, explaining I needed to update my journal, go for a swim, and investigate the town. But motivated by the prospect of fresh lobster, I volunteered to make arrangements with the cook at the restaurant next door to prepare the lobster feast for us.

Next morning, after breakfast, they hurried down to the beach where Tico Rico and his boat waited. Not more than an hour later, Axel and Christoph returned. Excitedly, Christoph dug into his knapsack. They needed 2500 colones to pay for Tico Rico's fuel. As they rushed from the room, I calculated that 2500 colones would buy enough fuel to get them to Limon and back and then some. I wondered if it was necessary to go that far for lobster? During my early morning swim I watched as small children plucked the succulent, clawed specimens from the ocean floor not 50-yards from shore.

About three hours later, sitting on the veranda sipping a cold beer and scribbling in my journal, I looked up surprised to see the machete brothers plodding down the dusty road toward me. Gone were the perky smiles and joie de vivre that permeated their faces earlier that day. Before they opened their mouths, I guessed correctly, that Tico Rico had disappeared with the "gas money." In all probability he was on his way to Limon, but not for lobsters or fuel. (It takes cojones to steal my colones.)

After a beer and cheap advice, we went to the Guardia Civil, the local version of the Sheriff's office. Inside the windowless shed, Axel and Christoph poured out their tale of deceit and felony to a strapping, athletic black who reminded me of my Army First Sergeant.

He pushed back his San Francisco Giants baseball cap and mopped his forehead with a bandana. "I know dat boy. He steal. He sell weed. His mother can do nothing wit him," the Chief growled.

Shortly, he dispatched one of his minions to track down Rico or his mother. With his administrative duties taken care of, the Chief resumed his inspection of the newspaper spread out before him. Leaving Axel and Christoph at the Guardia Civil hut to await further developments, I returned to the hotel. Two hours later the Austrians returned and with them the news that Tico Rico's mother appeared before the chief, handed over 2500 colones and profusely apologized for her wayward son, still to be accounted for.

Later that afternoon we boarded another bus to head still further south to the small beach town of Puerto Viejo. For the first and last time in our journey we got seats on the bus.

The surf rolled up lazily over a corral reef onto a white sandy beach across the street from the general store and Cervezeria that also served as the last stop on the bus line. Once again we trudged the empty dirt streets in search of a Cabina or hospedaje. But stop. Axel spotted a sign for a Pizzeria with a directional arrow pointing due west. The Pizzeria boasted of homemade dough and a dozen or so toppings, including pineapple. Specialty desserts like Key Lime pie, chocolate decadence cake, and homemade ice cream were offered. Unfortunately the place was closed, but according to the owner and head pizza maker, she would open at 6 p.m. Sympathetic to our housing dilemma she recommended a new hostel only fifteen minutes away by trail in the jungle hills overlooking the town. At the edge of the town soccer field, we found a handcarved sign for Kiskadee Lodge beside a worn dirt path. Crossing a footbridge over a small stream we soon found ourselves in the coolness of triple canopy jungle.

Maracoya fruit, tasting much like a cross between a plum and guava, lay scattered on and beside the trail meandering by a gurgling stream. Decaying fruit filled the moist air with a bittersweet fetidness. Butterflies splashed with blues, oranges, greens, and blacks glided amongst the vine-wrapped trees along the trail. Stopping to catch our breath on a hill we peered down into a clearing 50 yards below us to see a two-story hostel constructed of dark hardwoods native to the area. Small clusters of papaya and banana trees dotted the front yard showing evidence of a gardener with a keen eye and uncanny sense of proportion.

For once no dogs barked as we approached. Red, purple, and pink flowers and plants overflowed a porch furnished with handcrafted chairs and tables. A serene silence enveloped the hostel like a shroud, disturbed only by the sounds of birds and insects. We helloed from the trail to signal our approach, but no one seemed to be at home. Walking noisily across the broad planked veranda of the first floor, we called out again, but without response. Gladly dropping our heavy backpacks, we ensconced ourselves in hammocks strung from thick beams.

Sometime later, a gringa padded across the plank floor in bare feet. Alice, the owner, welcomed us to Kiskadee Lodge. While brewing a fresh pot of coffee, she regaled us with a brief history of the lodge and herself, then asked shyly if we thought $3 a night was too much to ask. We looked at each other, barely containing our laughter, then allowed that considering the location and amenities $3 a head was a fair tariff. While entering our names and passport numbers on the first page of her registry, she told us we were guest numbers 21, 22, and 23. Kiskadee Lodge had been opened a mere three weeks.

After settling in the men's dormitory on the second floor, Alice gave us a guided tour of the lodge. She beamed as she briefed us on the open air shower located a few steps from the lodge and overlooking the jungle below it. Hardby was a rustic wood outhouse affording occupants pleasant jungle vistas. Other amenities included nature trails, a bathing stream, and a well-stocked paperback exchange library. Encouraging us to make ourselves at home and help ourselves to any food or drink in the kitchen, Alice asked that we keep track of our board in the notebook provided. She wondered aloud if 5 cents for a banana and 10 cents for a cup of coffee seemed equitable? Biting her lower lip she quickly added that bananas could be had gratis if we were willing to walk a few yards into the jungle and pluck them ourselves. Also, one free refill of coffee was acceptable.

Sitting around the hardwood table on the veranda, Alice apologized for not having a refrigerator or television. We encouraged her to eschew those items in favor of tranquility. Electricity, however, was available from 7 p.m. to 10 p.m. thanks to a small gasoline generator.

While chatting, I looked up the hill where the trail topped out to see a giant black man, slim but big-boned, come lumbering down toward the hostel, a machete swinging from his right hand. We looked at Alice with questioning eyes.

"Oh, that's my boyfriend, Diablo Brown," she whispered.

Hardly a boy, I guessed Diablo Brown was in his early 60's. His muscular physique evidenced a life of hard physical labor. Over coffee, he told us about growing up in Limon, working in the jungles as a teenager harvesting wood, and of his favorite past time—baseball. A pitcher of some local fame, he had traveled all over Central America playing ball, more often than not for the championship team. Married five times, he'd produced or fielded a complete team of his own progeny. He thought at least two of his wives were still living, but scattered somewhere between Limon and Panama.

"But what of your name," Christoph asked, "Diablo means Devil in Spanish, is this not right?"

Testing the edge of his ancient machete with a callused thumb, he said quietly, "We don't talk about that, mon."

I quickly changed the subject by enthusiastically calling everyone's attention to an egg-sized spider crawling up my right leg. With the skill of a surgeon, Mr. Brown flicked the intruder from my calf with the machete, backhanding it over the railing to its rightful home. Other than a few closely shaven hairs, my calf was unscathed. Axel and Christoph looked at each other approvingly. They'd found a hero.

In the days that followed, we learned Diablo was a man of many talents, besides those he shared only with Alice. He had superintended the clearing of the jungle site and built most of the lodge with his own hands, without the aide of power tools. He had cut the hardwood trees, dragged them to the construction site and with the help of local carpenters and joiners had split the trees into planks.

"We have the laurel, the teak, the mahogany…" he ticked off the various native hardwoods incorporated into the showcase lodge, "they will last many hundred years."

Additionally, he cooked, tended the garden, and made a daily trip to town for seafood and other supplies. Whenever they could, the machete brothers grilled Diablo Brown about his jungle experiences, especially those involving snakes. My ears perked up one afternoon when I heard him admonishing the Austrians to be on the alert for the insidious "Mata Buey."

"Precisely what is a mata buey," I asked from behind my paperback.

"Ha mon, de mata buey, he have de poison to kill de ox. Ho, he have plenty poison, mon. You kill his wife, he come after you, mon. You call him bushmaster."

"And just how big is this snake?"

"Ho mon," Diablo smiled, "I kill one maybe twenty feet. Don't worry, mon, dat long, long time ago. I see de small one now, maybe ten feet."

"Ten feet," I said with a note of alarm in my voice. "Then there could be one or more small bushmasters out there," I said nodding toward the jungle.

"Don't you worry, mon. I ain't seen one in long time."

Stretched out in my favorite hammock one afternoon, I watched as Diablo showed Axel and Christoph the proper method of honing a sharp edge on their machetes using banana oil and a sharpening stone. As proof of his expertise he took his own blade and proceeded to mow the lawn below the veranda. Not satisfied with such a pedestrian display, the Austrians hacked away a quarter acre of jungle to test their blades, then called to me to join them on a bushwhacking jaunt into the jungle. Diablo Brown looked up from his lawn mowing.

"Watch for de mata buey, mon!" A deep, ominous laugh followed us into the jungle.

Looking over my shoulder, I watched as he made serpentine swishes in the air with his machete.

Following Christoph and Axel, for me at least, was like riding behind a harvesting machine. Vegetation started disappearing at such an alarming rate, I wondered if a representative of the Costa Rican government might not site the Austrians for some type of environmental depredation.

Upon returning after our last jungle foray, Diablo Brown informed us he had prepared a special dinner. In the morning we would be leaving Kiskadee Lodge. He encouraged us to lay our machetes aside, shower, and change clothes. Sensing the formality of the occasion, we all put on clean shorts, though held firm on going barefoot.

Seated at the head of the table, Alice reminded me of a dowager Queen holding court. From Diablo's kitchen appeared endless courses of fresh lobster, carrots, crab, squash, french fries, baked red snapper; all washed down with beer. Cradling our distended bellies in both hands and groaning with pleasure, Mr. Brown served us a dessert of baked banana bread and a pot of fresh coffee. Later, swinging in our hammocks and smoking cigars we lavished outrageous compliments on the head of the mysterious, but talented Mr. Brown. His superb culinary accomplishment cost us $4 each.

Silence and grimness presided at the breakfast table the next morning, rather than the usual high-spirited horseplay. Adding to the dismal mood was the unexplained absence of Mr. Brown, who we wanted to thank personally for his patience and kindness during our stay. The three of us had chipped in a few thousand colones apiece with the intention of presenting it to him at breakfast. We left the gratuity with Alice who assured us he would get it immediately upon his return. No slouch at the stove herself, she whipped up some spicy omelets with toast and opened a jar of her homemade Guava jam.

Shouldering our packs, we shuffled dully down the trail to Puerto Viejo to catch the afternoon bus to Limon. Crossing the soccer field, I looked up to see Diablo Brown approaching with his sack of supplies in one hand and machete in the other. In faded bib overalls he looked seven feet tall. We stopped in the middle of the field to say goodbye. Abruptly, he pointed his machete at our feet, twirling the blade back and forth in an S-pattern. Shaking his gray head and laughing, he started up the trail to Alice, Kiskadee Lodge, and the jungle.

The bus back to San Jose from Limon took only two and a half hours compared to the 11-hour train ordeal it took to get there. Later that night, after an Italian dinner, we found our way back to Nashville South only to discover it had moved, or better yet the bar had changed its name, while Nashville South reopened in a new location. Looking across the street at the posh colonial mansion housing Key Largo we couldn't help but speculate on the bacchanalian life surging within.

Strolling nonchalantly inside we were immediately aware that women outnumbered men two to one. The ladies were scattered about the premises on chairs, settled in overstuffed sofas as though a floral designer had arranged them.

We found room at the crowded horseshoe-shaped bar just inside the front door and listened to piano music coming from one of the many rooms within. No sooner had our bottles of beer been placed before us than we found ourselves hemmed in on all sides by a bevy of

Tico women anxious to socialize. The place reminded me of the many "body shop" watering holes in San Francisco, California, but with one important difference-these ladies charged for socializing. I was stunned when the beauty at my elbow informed me how much the "socialization" cost. But since the majority of the clientele seemed to be Texans I guessed the prices were not out of order. With our beers finished we made haste to leave and renew our search for the new Nashville South and some vintage Jimmy Buffet music.

When arriving back at Cabinas Ramirez a few days later, I was relieved to find my bike in Louis's office exactly where I'd left it. From all indications it hadn't been touched. After securing our old rooms, the three of us changed into shorts and flip flops and walked down to the beach cafe to find Fernando planted at his favorite table drinking beer, smoking cigarettes, and watching life pass by.

Next day, after a drenching morning rain, I bid farewell to the "machete brothers," Louis, and Fernando and pedaled down the road headed southwest into the mountains. After a scenic ride amongst date palm and banana plantations I began a slow climb into lush green mountains to the provincial town of San Isidro, not far from the main highway leading to Panama.

~ ~ ~

Eddie and The Natives

The road south of San Isidro descended through rolling hills to the coastal plain, but the closer I got to Panama the more the road deteriorated, with occasional gaps in the pavement caused by mudslides and landslides. While negotiating my way through one of the slide areas a sharp rock punctured my rear tire. Not long after I'd begun repair work, it started to rain. Shortly thereafter the rain shower turned into a full-scale tropical downpour forcing me to pull on all my raingear and stand helplessly beside my upended bike with gear piled alongside. Out of the rain, just like in the mountains east of Durango, Mexico, a truck pulled off the road and stopped alongside me. The window came down and the driver yelled at me in English. "Come on amigo that's nowhere to work on your bike."

At the side of the truck I told the driver my predicament. Eddie, the driver, jumped out and helped me load bike and gear into the back of his truck. When Eddie finally pulled himself behind the steering wheel he was soaking wet, while I, encased in my rain parka, was warm and dry.

"This is the wettest I've been since my own bike trip around South America." Eddie laughed.

We drove away into a dark and stormy night.

Eddie was from Peru. Years ago, in the 60's as a teenager, Eddie got on his dilapidated three-speed bicycle to begin a multi-year circumnavigation of South America, during which time he learned to speak Portuguese, English, and some German. Somewhere along the way he teamed up with a Native American Indian, who was also riding a bike and traveling around South America. Eddie drove like a stock car racer through potholes and mudslides, through wind and rain—talking a mile-a-minute in English and Spanish. Just as Eddie and the American Indian began a trek into the mysterious Darien Gap between Colombia and Panama, a right rear tire blew out on the truck.

"You got a flat tire, now I got one too," Eddie laughed stopping in the middle of the highway to replace the flat with a spare. I kept a wary eye out for traffic as Eddie wrestled the replacement tire on, whistling and chuckling to himself.

Once again soaked to the skin, Eddie pulled himself back into the cab. Off we sped into the rain and pitch black. "I have many flat tires on this road, so don pay attention."

Fair enough, I thought.

Eddie and the Native had to get rid of their bikes somewhere in the Darien. No big thing according to Eddie because they could barely hike the snaking, sometimes intermittent path through dense jungle and swamp. They ran out of food and for all practical purposes, water. On the tenth day Eddie threw up his hands and told the Native they were hopelessly lost. The Native shrugged his shoulders and told him not to worry. Next day they stumbled into a Choco Native village. After four days of rest and recuperation, Eddie suggested they continue on. The Native shrugged his shoulders again and told him he'd just as soon stay put as he was fascinated by his hosts, who by primitive hunter gatherer techniques were able to survive in what appeared to be an uninhabitable place. With his pack full of provisions and with a Choco guide, Eddie said goodbye to his American Native friend and his hosts and struck out for Panama. After another ten days of hiking and slashing, the trail Eddie was following intersected a river. The trail bifurcated on the other side. Eddie took a left and his guide took a right. A few hours later Eddie arrived at another Native village, but this one had canoe-like boats with outboard engines. Next day Eddie rode in one of the boats to a mission settlement upriver where he saw a dirt road that eventually got him to Panama City. Eddie lighted a cigarette and shrugged his shoulders,"And then I met this woman…"

Eddie steered the truck into a combination Texaco station-Chinese restaurant. The rain poured off the angled tin roof like a waterfall. Several large trucks were parked outside; their drivers inside slumped over cups of coffee or glasses of beer smoking cigarettes. We pulled up chairs to a table and drank beer while Eddie's flat tire was being repaired. About five minutes later a Chinese lady stopped at our table to unload a metal tray of plates and bowls of food. A multi-course dinner compliments of Eddie. While working on a second beer, a grease-smeared teenager came into the restaurant and informed Eddie his tire was repaired. Eddie glanced at his watch, slapped his forehead, and said,"My woman will not be patient, I must go."

For the hundredth time Eddie wished me good luck and warned me about the Darien Gap. A minute later he was gone. I pulled on my rain gear and trudged outside to repair my own flat tire.

Next day I rode south under sunny skies. About ten miles south of Palmer Norte, I stopped to watch an alligator cross the highway. Two days later I was in Panama.

Chapter 9

Panama

Alonzo the Banana King

Panama is a city of banks not churches. There are churches, of course, but they are not as visible as they are in most Central and South American cities. Nor is Panama a city of charred tanks and bullet-riddled buildings, at least when I was there, one year after the U.S. invasion and the kidnapping of its most notorious citizen-warrior, Manuel Noriega.

What is Panama? It is a city of banks and medical clinics and athletic shoe stores. The most visibly noticeable buildings in Panama City are its modern, soaring multi-national banks.

"Nowadays, the international banking center of Panama consists of 110 banking institutions, which total assets amount to 16 thousand million dollars," the Panama tourist magazine, *Panama 2000*, boasts.

Then too, there's the Panama Canal that rakes in $1.2 billion a year. In 1999 the U.S. will turn over full control, at least that's the plan, to the Panamanians. It's only money.

Before the "political" crisis in 1989, there were 122 international banks in Panama City. Justifiably nervous about security, a few banks closed their doors and moved out. Bank of America, Swiss Bank, Bank of China, Bank of Colombia, and many more are still there. By all outward appearances they are flourishing.

The main question is—why so many banks in such a small, third world country? For one thing Panama, like its colleague in Switzerland, allows depositors to maintain numbered accounts. Sounds suspicious, but if the Swiss can do it, why can't they. No need to send couriers off by jet to Switzerland with suitcases full of currency.

The tourist magazine further states, "The national government...will prevent, through all possible ways, the use of the banking system to hide criminal activities." Numbered bank accounts notwithstanding. This defensive rhetoric seems to intimate that Panama will not allow the billions of dollars in illegal drug trafficking on their doorstop to be deposited there. Numbered bank accounts notwithstanding. I guess this means that all the money in the Bank of Colombia is profits from say, the sale of coffee. Or maybe from the sale of souvenirs to the millions of tourists not flocking to that country. We'll never know. *

All outward appearances seem to indicate that Panama City is a thriving world trade business center. Many of the plate glass, banking monoliths are scattered along the Via Espana—the Rodeo Drive of Panama City. For the first time since leaving California I saw a Porsche. I even saw a Synagogue, a first in all Central America.

Along the Via Espana we have the fashionable shops, the boutiques, the salons that bristle with the cachet of international purveyors of luxury—Rolex, Cartier, Gucci, Pucci, and Lucci. For more pedestrian offerings we have Florsheim, L.A. Gear, even a Victoria's Secret. All these emporiums have young, nervous security guards posted at the front door. These clean-centurions are armed either with sawed-off shotguns or machine guns. I kept wondering why they looked so nervous. I would hate to be caught shoplifting in one of those establishments. No mere lecture and slap on the wrist here, obscene torture would be meted out with a heavy hand.

*This is offshore banking used to both launder dirty money & hide from taxation.

Most numerous and visible amongst these boutiques were those offering trendy athletic shoes-Adidas to Reebok. I counted nine stores alone selling exclusively athletic shoes. As most Panamanians went barefoot or wore flip-flops I wondered who was buying all the Nikes, New Balance and British Knights. At one such store I counted 20 brands of what used to be called "sneakers." Prices ranged from $25 to $75. This in a country where the annual income is about $1500. Numbered bank accounts notwithstanding. With all of these high tech athletic shoes available I never saw a jogger.

Along the fringes of the Via Espana are scattered numerous medical clinics all with a different specialty, e.g. ophthalmologists, surgeons, gynecologists, dentists, skin doctors, even a hair doctor.

Armed guards are everywhere, at banks, hotels, athletic shoe stores, even at McDonalds. One morning while eating an egg McMuffin I watched the uniformed guard at the door pace back and forth patting a holstered .38 revolver. All the armed guards wear sunglasses making them appear more sinister or perhaps more professional. Sipping my cafe con leche, the guard suddenly snapped to attention as a huge armored car pulled up out front. Three uniformed guards leaped out the back door. Two of them sporting revolvers, pump shotguns and sunglasses took up positions at the entrance. The third guard rushed inside, leaving his colleagues to posture and prance outside like modern dancers performing an impromptu "Ode to Armaments."

Seconds later the guard inside rushed through the revolving door with two bulging satchels and into the back of the truck, followed shortly by the shotgun dance duo. The armored car sped away. All of this took less than sixty seconds. McDonalds in Panama City, like everywhere else in the world, does a thriving business.

My introduction to the bustling city of Panama was as a passenger on top of a truck sunk to its axles with 24,000 lbs. of bananas. The truck was owned and driven by Alonzo Flores, entrepreneur and self-styled "banana king" of Panama City. Once a week Alonzo and his crew drive north to the Costa Rican border in his Ford diesel truck, stopping along the way at various plantations to buy bananas. When the truck is dangerously loaded with its yellow cargo they turn around and head back to Panama City where Alonzo brokers his cargo. Most of the bananas wind up in North American supermarkets. Simple: buy low, sell high. But one must take into account the vagaries of high finance-dead batteries, flat tires, burnt out alternators and such. From my perspective I can only say that bananas do not make for comfortable seats.

During most of the journey I was perched high atop the cargo enjoying the sights, when it wasn't raining. But during the breakdowns along the way I climbed down to talk with Alonzo who recounted the experiences of his family during the U.S. invasion. I think this is what he told me in broken, garbled English.

About Manuel Noriega. "I hit'em, I hit'em, the (blankity, blank) pina cabeza. Wore hoppy dot (blankity blank) ees in U.S. Now jew got de problem."

Alonzo and his crew were unanimous in their vilification of Noriega. In fact my running survey showed that 98% of Panamanians were glad to get rid of him. I guessed the 2% sorry to see him go were his lawyers, accountants and uniform makers. Oddly though, in a follow-up survey the same 98% said they were sorry he was gone. Oh well, people frequently change their minds.

Not surprisingly, Alonzo has experienced a new surge of business since Noriega's departure. Life is good; he and his family have a home, a car, and plenty to eat, especially bananas. He even bought his wife and two young boys new athletic shoes. Alonzo's dream is to go to the United States, buy a Peterbilt tractor, and become a long haul truck driver, preferably hauling something other than bananas. He is a bit tired of bananas. He, like most other Central and South Americans, thinks the U.S. is the land of milk and honey. Comparatively, it is.

During my sojourn in Panama City I had a nightmare reminiscent of the movie **Marathon Man,** starring Dustin Hoffman and Laurence Olivier. I believe the freshly painted walls of my room and a few cervezas had a lot to do with it. The Senora at the Pensione Flamingo had the "no frills" hotel repainted pink during my stay. It was hot and humid in Panama and Pensione Flamingo was not air-conditioned.

Paint fumes hung in the air like fog in San Francisco. Drinking beer didn't help. One night in my sweltering 10' X 10' room I dreamed I was an unwilling patient in one of the many medical clinics along the Via Espana. Nurses dressed like Carmen Miranda were holding me down on a table. At length they succeeded in strapping me to it. Everything: walls, ceiling, furniture, was painted Day-Glo pink. Wouldn't you know, there was a chrome ceiling fan that didn't work. A door opened. A doctor dressed in Levis and Reeboks came toward me holding a tray of syringes. Big syringes, the size of toothpaste tubes. His face was horribly pockmarked. His hair was black and close cropped. The doctor and Carmen Miranda nurses wore high top athletic shoes. I struggled weakly as the nurses held me down. Grapes, avocados, oranges and bananas fell from the heads of the nurses during the struggle.

The doctor picked up a foot-long syringe.

"Is it safe," he asked in a soothing voice.

"Safe, sure it's safe," I spat back.

He held the syringe up and pumped it. A stream of pink liquid shot from the needle.

"Is it safe?" This time his voice had a hard edge.

"What's safe? Traffic, air quality, your Swiss bank accounts."

He jammed the needle deep into my jaw.

"Is it safe?"

My mouth tasted of copper, my eyes strobed. The nurses formed a conga line and danced around the table.

"No, it's not safe, not safe at all," I yelled.

I finally woke up drenched in sweat. Two hours later I was on an airplane bound for Cali, Colombia. Goodbye Alonzo the banana king. Goodbye Carmen Miranda. Hello Medellin cartel.

Part Four

Bottom Of The Americas

Chapter 10

South America

"Do you know there's a road that goes down Mexico and all the way to Panama? And maybe all the way to the bottom of South America where the Indians are 7 feet tall and eat cocaine on the mountain side."

-Jack Kerouac

On The Road

Assembling my bike and gear in the deserted baggage claim area at the Cali airport kindled the curiosity of a young policeman, who after a few minutes of observation helped me make final modifications. A small circle of baggage handlers and taxi drivers formed about us, many asking questions or wishing me luck.

When the bike was finally fitted out I was persuaded to roll it to a nearby scale where with the help of the police officer I muscled it onto the platform where it weighed in at 60 kilos or 120 lbs. To satisfy a few skeptical kibitzers I encouraged them to step forward and heft the bike for themselves. The few that did smiled and slapped their forehead with the palm of a hand.

With the young policeman clearing the way I rolled my bike outside where he stopped traffic in the street so I could pedal away safely. Not far south of the airport I was cruising along a flat road when a cyclist on a Vitus road bike pulled alongside me and gave me a high five. As we pedaled along I did the best I could to explain my bike trip. Afterwards he passed over his water bottle, encouraging me to take a sip. I did and knew instantly it wasn't water. The cyclist explained it was a blend of raw sugar cane and pineapple juice. Quite tasty. When I asked directions to the nearest town, he motioned for me to follow him. About six miles down the highway we turned into the small town of Palmira where he left me in front of the Hotel El Dorado. Carrying my gear to the second floor it suddenly dawned on me: contrary to everything I'd expected, Colombianos were helpful and friendly. Once again the "reality" of travel stood in sharp contrast to the "illusion" of travel.

The Senora at the front desk described the geography south of Palmira as "muy plano." For days I cycled through a flat landscape of sugar cane and pineapple fields stopping about every six miles at a road junction, many times occupied by a military checkpoint. Always there were about a half dozen kids selling juice, pop, homemade ice cream, and slices of pineapple. After a rest and some refreshment I'd cycle on to the next road junction.

~ ~ ~

Don Juan On A Canondale

It was late afternoon when I came to a stop in the town of Popayan. A quick check of my cyclometer showed I'd pedaled 11,460 miles. I estimated I had roughly 6,000 miles to go. Sipping water from my bottle and looking around I saw a another cyclist headed toward me on a new Canondale bike. He stopped alongside me.

"That's the first touring bike I've seen in Popayan. Where are you going?" the Colombiano said in English.

"I'm headed for Tiera Del Fuego. Say, your English is very good."

"I just got back from Cordova, Alaska where I worked in a cannery."

"I started my trip in Anchorage, not far from there."

"Welcome to Popayan. My name is Fabiano Jaramillo. Where are you going right now?"

"Just looking for a pensione where I can get a room."

"Why don't you stay with me at my apartment, it's just a few blocks from here. There's plenty of room and later I'll take you on a tour of my city. You'll like it here; there are many beautiful women. Come on, follow me."

Fabiano explained he'd recently returned to his home in Popayan, but planned to return to the United States to marry his girlfriend who lived in Wisconsin.

Fabiano's apartment could easily be characterized as the ultimate "bachelor's pad." A spacious living room had comfortable chairs, a couch, and a huge stereo system. In the middle of the first floor, off the living room was a kitchen with bar facing out on the living room. Upstairs was a bedroom and a loft that Fabiano used as a den and guest bedroom.

Later that day I accompanied Fabiano and his friends, Juan and Maria, to an open-air market in downtown Popayan where we had a lunch of empanadas and chica. Chica is a traditional Colombian drink made of corn and pineapple. After lunch Fabiano and I walked through town ending up at a motorcycle shop where Fabiano picked up his repaired motorbike. Needing to change more dollars into pesos while in Popayan, Fabiano offered to take me to a friend of his who owned a trucking company, but changed money on the side. So amidst a warehouse jammed with bales of cotton and hemp, Fabiano led me into a cluttered office where Senor Malusco took my "dolares" and from a dented metal box withdrew a wad of pesos, counting out 20,000 to make the exchange. We spent most of the afternoon riding around town on Fabiano's motorbike, but had to stop numerous times while passing a boutique or tienda where an attractive woman would rush to the door and call to Fabiano. "Mi caro, where have you been, why have you not come to see me."

Figure 10: Fabiano, the Don Juan of Popayan, Colombia.

Fabiano would stop, flash one of his big smiles, yell something to the lady, and then we'd speed off down the street. A few blocks further on Fabiano would come to a stop in front of a shop and beep his horn. Seconds later another young lady would run out of a tienda, throw her arms around Fabiano's neck and kiss him.

"Why have you not called me, you bad boy."

And so went the afternoon. But the highlight of my tour was a visit to the Mayor's office in the beautifully designed municipal buildings. Here Fabiano led me through corridors and up stairs until we were finally at the door of the Mayor himself. Fabiano knocked on the outer door, then waited with a big smile on his face. Seconds later the door opened. Once again we stood facing a beautiful lady, this one however was the Mayor's personal secretary.

"You devil, you have been back a week and you have not come to see me," the lady spat with pursed lips. Then a big smile broke across her face and she threw her arms about Fabiano's neck. "Let me kiss you before you run away and I don't see you."

At last when they broke apart, Fabiano introduced me to his "friend" Carmen and told her about my bicycle trip to the tip of South America. I could tell by the expression on her face that she had other things on her mind, the least of which was bicycle touring. However, she did give me a cordial peck on the cheek before escorting Fabiano and me into the Mayor's private office. Lucky for me the Mayor was out of town, as the highlight of my visit to his office was sitting in his chair with Carmen on my lap while Fabiano snapped my picture.

The day ended at a restaurant in downtown Popayan where, as usual, Fabiano knew the female owner who took extra care in serving us a dinner of soup composed of corn, vegetables, yucca, and avocado, followed by grilled beefsteak, fried potatoes and rice. All washed down with fruit smoothies. For once dessert was out of the question for me.

After-dinner activities found us walking around downtown Popayan sipping coffee or an aperitif at bistros and cafes, talking with attractive women, and listening to guitar music or salsa combos. Sometime about midnight I crawled into my sleeping bag in Fabiano's loft exhausted. Just before falling asleep I remember hearing Fabiano open the front door and the silky voice of Carmen greeting him.

~ ~ ~

Jairo's Juice Stand

Plano y abajo, that's the way the Colombianos described every road I cycled on and for the most part they were correct, except that some roads were more abajo than others, especially the roads in southern Colombia. But the long ascents were usually rewarded at the top with a juice stand, often they were the only sign of civilization on the top of an 8,000' or 9,000' pass.

A mustachioed man in his early forties hurried out of the wooden shack where I propped my bike. He smiled and beckoned me to sit down in a lawn chair next to his fruit stand, the centerpiece of which was a handcranked blender.

"I have an excellent drink for you my friend, please sit and rest while I prepare it especially for you," insisted Jairo.

I watched as he sliced oranges and bananas then packed them in his handcranked blender, adding honey, a shot of brandy, a quail's egg and a splash of something he called Radiomalto. This last ingredient he assured me would cure impotence and any number of other things I'd never heard of. Also, Jairo said with a wink and a tight fist, it would promote virility.

Figure 11: Public transportation in Colombia, near Popayan.

With all the ingredients stuffed into the blender, Jairo grasped the huge handle, similar to the handle on an old fashioned ice cream making machine, and began cranking. He served me a tall glass of his "jugo especial" while I lounged in the lawn chair. I drank it quickly and immediately ordered another one. I can't vouch for the efficacy of his juice drink, nor of any of the singular ingredients, but they were tasty and quenched my thirst. Then again, I can only report that I biked another 12,000 miles without a health problem of any kind, so maybe there was something to his elixir.

~ ~ ~

The Brotherhood of Caffeine

It was midday and I was cycling along a curvy, two-lane road high in the lush mountains when I came around a corner and saw a small cafe. A single red pickup truck was parked outside. From the road I could see a shaded veranda with a half dozen tables. As I walked up the steps to the veranda I noticed two men eating at one of the tables. I greeted them as I slipped into a chair at one of the tables nearby. While I ate and sipped a Pepsi, one of the two men at the adjoining table asked where I was riding. In the midst of my story, the second fellow motioned for me to join them at their table, where he poured me a glass of Agua Diente and encouraged me to finish my story. Soon the bottle was empty and another was ordered. Our glasses were filled again, one of the men proposed a toast to a successful bicycle trip. How could I refuse.

Silvio and Antonio talked rapidly to each other so rapidly I couldn't follow them. As the second bottle of Agua Diente was drained, Silvio asked if I'd ever visited a coffee finca. Although a coffee lover most of my life, I admitted I never had the opportunity, but would be honored to do so.

"Well then," Antonio said, "You must be our guest. We have a small coffee plantation not far from here. It is a beautiful finca, you will like it."

We headed higher into the mountains crowded in the front cab of their pickup, with my bike and gear in the back. A bottle of Agua Diente was passed back and forth between us. I was quite relaxed by now and never gave a second thought about jumping in a truck with two Colombianos I'd never seen before. The red pickup raced up and down the mountain road with what I thought was alarming speed. At the small mountain village of Rosas, Antonio pulled off the road and came to a stop outside the local bank. Silvio rushed inside. Minutes later he returned with the president of the bank. Both men were smiling. Silvio had told his banker friend, an avid recreational cyclist, about my bike tour. Renaldo wanted to buy me a drink and hear the story himself, so the four of us repaired to a nearby open-air cafe where I rehashed my story while quaffing the obligatory Agua Diente. By now I'd become extremely loquacious and for some reason my Spanish improved considerably.

Renaldo, the banker, kept exclaiming, "Muy fuerte, muy fuerte, senior." Meaning I was a strong rider. For some reason, Renaldo was extremely interested in Alaska, so I told him, in my best Spanish, about my singular bear encounter on the Yellowhead Highway in Canada. He was enthralled and captivated like a child listening to "Goldilocks and the Three Bears" for the first time. He'd only seen pictures of bears, which he described as, gigantic furry beasts as big as a pickup.

"How can people live in a land where such a dangerous animal as the bear roamed around in the wild," Renaldo marveled. "I will never go there until these bears are subjugated," Renaldo vowed while waving at the waiter to bring another bottle of Agua Diente. I somehow steered Renaldo off the subject of bears back to cycling. Finally, he excused himself to return to work.

Minutes later, the three of us got back in the truck and headed still higher into the mountains. Every so often Antonio would pull off the road at a small clearing where a handful of compesinos would materialize out of the bush. Antonio would give each man a handful of pesos, then make an entry in his notebook. After repeating this process four times in a distance of six miles I began to wonder what was going on. Silvio explained the men worked on their finca in remote locations, so on a certain day each month they would come down to the highway to get paid.

Antonio pulled off onto a roadside clearing at a vista point high above a valley. We got out of the truck and walked to the edge of the overlook. Silvio pointed down to the lush green valley stretching southward for miles. I could barely see cattle grazing on the hillsides far below.

"That is our finca," Antonio said nonchalantly.

"You mean down there," I said pointing to a reddish speck in the valley floor.

Antonio waved his arm from left to right, "All that you see is the finca."

The red truck plunged down a steep dirt road toward the valley floor. At the bottom of the descent, I saw a huge brick chalet-style structure in the final stages of construction. Nearby was a sprawling ranch house with red tile roof, corrals, and fishponds. But what really caught my eye was a new swimming pool.

As we piled from the truck and headed for the pool a weather beaten, slender Colombiano approached us from the main ranch house. He was dressed in jeans and faded workshirt, but was shoeless. A shy smile revealed more space than teeth.

"Eduardo, mi amigo, como esta." Antonio said shaking the man's hand.

Eduardo was the ranch foreman, overseer, and Major-domo. Without being asked he dispatched one of his kids to the ranch house to procure the ubiquitous bottle of Agua Diente. Without a second's hesitation we walked to poolside, stripped to our shorts, and leaped into the water like three kids on the first day of summer vacation.

Later, while sipping Agua Diente by the side of the pool, Silvio looked over a me. "Jorge, you must stay and be our guest. You stay as long as you want. Unfortunately, Antonio and I must return to Popayan to our families. You will stay, yes?"

"Yes, I appreciate the hospitality."

"And tonight, you will have a special dinner," Silvio said while motioning to Eduardo. "Send one of the muchachos to catch some fish at the ponds."

Instantly, one of the small boys who had been swimming dashed to the side of the pool, grasped a fishing pole and ran toward the upper pasture. Not more than 30 minutes later, the boy returned with a fish still quivering in his hands. He held it up proudly before Silvio and Antonio. I guessed the fish weighed about two or three pounds and looked similar to a big mouth bass.

"Well, what do you think Jorge, will you eat this fish?"

"Sure, it looks good to me."

With a nod of approval from Silvio, the young lad sped off to the kitchen to give my dinner to the cook.

At breakfast next morning, Eduardo asked if I'd like some milk. Assuming a pitcher was kept handy in a refrigerator, I said yes. Eduardo disappeared. I finished breakfast, had a second cup of coffee and waited for the milk. Finally, with my cup of coffee in hand I went off to investigate. Not far from the ranch house I found Eduardo and a ranch hand at the corral. Up closer, I was surprised to see Eduardo in the process of milking a cow. With the task completed, he came over to where I watched from the fence and offered me a bowl of milk, still warm from the cow. I took a big drink, then handed the bowl back to him and told him to pass it around.

At noon, I loaded my bike, said goodbye to Eduardo then began the long haul up the dirt road to the main highway. Halfway up I was forced to dismount and push my bike. At last on the main road, I gave one last look down at the ranch house and heaved a sigh, before getting back on my bike and starting a long descent.

~ ~ ~

Pasto es Frio

No matter who I asked how far it was to Pasto, I'd always get the same reply-Pasto es frio. No one seemed capable of calculating the distance either in kilometers or time. It was always Pasto es frio or Pasto is cold. At the top of the 8,000' pass above Pasto I stopped at the military checkpoint to pull on my gloves, windpants, and balaclava and to zipper up my windbreaker. No doubt about it, it certainly was cold on top of the pass. After a swift descent at 35 mph I cycled into Pasto. My first thought was, yes indeed Pasto es frio.

In downtown Pasto I found a room at the Residencia Los Cerros for $1.50 per night. Nevermind that I had to carry my bike and gear to the second floor, that there were no locks on the door, or there wasn't any hot water in the bathroom down the hall; it was cheap, it was centrally located, and it was across the street from a police station.

That night I found a great little place that served pizza and beer no more than six blocks from the residencia. With a full belly and smile on my face, I walked out of the restaurant and took a right turn. It was dark, but no matter I knew I was only a few minutes away from my hotel. The streets suddenly filled with people like a flash flood. Children were dressed like witches, ghosts, and all manner of evil spirits. I guessed they were celebrating a fiesta or Saints day, then it suddenly dawned on me it was Halloween night. Parents and children surged in and out of shops, the children laughing, screaming, and blowing toy horns. I suddenly looked at my watch and realized I'd

*1.52 miles.

been walking around for almost an hour and the residencia was nowhere in sight. So I backtracked for awhile, but still nothing looked familiar. Confused, I turned around again hoping to spot a familiar shop or building, until finally I stopped and admitted to myself that I was hopelessly lost. On top of that, I couldn't remember the name of the residencia, nor did I have a room key with a name and address on it, nor did I have a receipt with that information. After another 30-minutes of walking hither and yon, I threw up my hands and jumped in a nearby taxi. I'd had a long, hard day of climbing steep roads and was in no mood to be lost.

"Where would you like to go," the driver asked politely.

"To my hotel."

"And where is your hotel, senor?"

"Sorry, I don't know."

My Spanish language skills were not much help in this situation.

"What is the name of your hotel, senor?"

"I'm sorry, I don't know."

" Senor, you are lost, no?"

"No, I am."

"Si, you have all the indications of one who is lost."

"Si."

"Perhaps you have a telephone number, an address?"

"Sorry. The only thing I know is that the hotel is across the street from the police station."

"Senor, there are four police stations in Pasto."

The driver was a patient fellow. He kept driving and asking questions, pointing at buildings and asking if I recognized any of them. I felt like a hopeless idiot. The driver had a perfect right to drop me off at the nearest police station and let them handle matters. And that's exactly what he did. He pulled up in front of a police station and low and behold I looked across the street and there was the Residencia Los Cerros. First thing back in my room I wrote the name, address, and telephone number of the residencia in my pocket notebook. Then in a wave of relief and exhaustion I crawled into bed.

I was summoned rudely from a deep sleep early next morning by the local high school marching band taking advantage of the deserted streets for their weekly practice session. I checked my watch to discover it was a few minutes past 6 a.m. It is impossible to ignore a high school marching band, especially one that circles the block several times pounding out the same tune over and over. At 7:15 a.m. I reluctantly crawled out of bed.

After a 12-mile climb out of Pasto, I finally topped out on a pass rising from the southern side of the volcanic bowl encompassing the town. After pulling on my gloves and windpants I pushed off on what was one of the longest and most exhilarating descents on my trip, all 16.62 miles. I pedaled and coasted down the twisting mountain road at speeds ranging from 25 to 40 mph, finally bottoming out in a lush river valley. I immediately removed my multiple layers of clothing to enjoy the sun and warmth. Looking south I could see a river, like a blue ribbon, twist its way through a green floodplain dotted with orchards and cultivated fields, many of the fields brimming with ripe tomatoes.

~ ~ ~

Hot Rod Heaven

Not far from the Ecuadorean frontier is the small Colombian town of Ipiales, a typical unattractive, bustling border town, with one exception. The town appeared to be caught in an automotive time warp. As I cycled around the central plaza my eyes were immediately drawn to the taxis and automobiles parked along the street. All were vintage 50's and 60's Fords, Mercurys, and Dodges, with sweeping tailfins and yards of sparkling chrome. Despite their age all appeared to be in excellent condition. Having had some experience with vintage cars, I couldn't help wonder where they got their spare parts. But why so many Fords, Mercs, and Dodges of the same era?

These boats are not known for their miserly fuel consumption. Maybe in another misguided attempt to reduce a foreign trade balance the U.S. government shipped a few boatloads of vintage Fords, Mercs, and Dodges to our South American neighbor. And just maybe because of some bureaucratic bungle on the part of the Colombian government, all the aged Detroit iron wound up in Ipiales. Local politicians, being what they are, decided to keep the windfall hush-hush. Instead of notifying the central government in Bogota about their latest boondoggle, they rationed the cars out to all eligible voters and potential voters. The vintage automobiles I saw parked around the main plaza had achieved a near state of deification.

Getting lost was no problem here in Ipiales as my pensione was directly across from the main plaza. But once upstairs in my room I was faced with a unique challenge. Thanks to a semi-inebriated Senor I was ensconced in a large room with five beds. My job was to discover which bed was the most comfortable. I seemed to have special talents for this kind of task, so went about sprawling and lounging on each bed until I was satisfied I'd culled out the least satisfactory and cast my deciding vote for the winner-a slightly saggy double bed with a red chintz bedspread. But why so many beds in a single room? Typically, most pensiones are set up to accommodate the average family, which in South America runs between 8 to 15 persons. Before retiring to my chosen bed I realized it was Friday night, so I took the normal precaution of inserting my earplugs which have served me well in numerous "Friday night" situations. Then I fell asleep.

Next morning I wheeled down the street at 7 a.m. to the Galaxia Cafe and Panaderia. I joined a local cyclist at a small table near the front window so we could keep an eye on our bikes outside. Apparently of the same early morning temperament as me, Alfredo sat quietly across the table, sipping his cafe cortado and chewing listlessly on a sweet roll. After breakfast Alfredo volunteered to guide me out of town to the road leading to the frontier, which I guesstimated was 6 to 8 miles south of town.

I cleared both Colombian and Ecuadorean customs in record time, perhaps because it was a bit after 8 a.m., which in South America is equivalent to 5 a.m. in the U.S.A. Even the few moneychangers in residence put in a lackluster performance trying to separate me from dolares. They were focussed on gulping their cafe and taking long drags on their first cigarette of the day. However, one ambitious cambio, perhaps sniffing the enticing aroma of American dollars, stirred to life to exchange my $53 in pesos for 53,000 sucre. As a consolation prize I gave him a handful of Colombian coin.

In what had become a typical frontier crossing, I pedaled across a bridge over a river and entered Ecuador.

Chapter 11

Ecuador

$\mathbf{I}$ swear, right across the bridge I started climbing my first hill. By the time I reached the top of it I knew it wasn't going to be my day. My legs felt like lead and I had to stop many times to eat and drink. Even relatively flat stretches seemed difficult. At one of my rest stops I dug into a pannier to find a can of tuna and some year-old granola, which weren't much help even discounting the age. What helped was a long descent into a small village just off the main road. I couldn't find it on my map, nor were there any road signs signaling its existence. Road signs in Central and South America are few and far between, because, all things considered, they are an extravagance. If people didn't know the name of the town why would they go there? Que lastima!

Pedaling into the village I was instantly aware that it was market day. In addition to produce; cattle, hogs, and chickens were on sale in the main square.

I stopped at the edge of the plaza to watch a footrace. When the crowds cleared away, I pedaled around the square searching for a pensione. The weather had turned cool and rainy, so I didn't much care where I stayed as long as it was dry and inexpensive. That's what I found, your basic third world, no frills pensione. My room, facing out on a narrow interior courtyard, measured 8' long by 8' wide, with an 8' ceiling. There were no windows, which lead me to speculate that the pensione had once been a jail or perhaps designed and built by a contractor specializing in jails. The only ventilation came from a crack at the bottom and top of the wooden door. A narrow cot with a straw mattress took up much of the space and with my bike inside against the wall, I was forced to climb over the front of the bed. The single amenity in the room was a naked light bulb hanging from a piece of black electrical wire protruding from the center of the ceiling. It was definitely dry, though cold, so once again I resorted to the warmth of my down sleeping bag.

An open-air bathroom with shower was located at the far end of the courtyard, about 20-feet from my room. A swinging french door allowed access to the shower. This feature allowed shower takers to look out into the courtyard while performing their ablutions. Though this arrangement allowed bathers maximum ventilation, it also allowed for maximum exposure, in more ways than one, to the elements while doing so.

Soon after moving into my cell I pulled on my sweats, a wool shirt, grabbed my soap and towel and headed for the shower. Earlier, the Senor at the pensione assured me that "hot" water was available in the shower, "mas o menos." My favorite Spanish expression. He seemed downright proud of the hot water as though he was the owner of the first and only color TV in the village. Besides, how could I doubt the veracity of a man dressed in a blue pinstripe suit, wool poncho, and black sombrero? As the room cost a measly $2, I wasn't about to quibble.

The cement floor in the shower room was exceedingly cold, forcing me to hop from one foot to the other, whilst trying to figure out how to turn on or in some manner activate the hot water. Here was the situation. Sure there was a showerhead poking out of the wall and sure there was a faucet, but there also were two thick black electrical cables snaked around the showerhead. I traced the black snakes back to a wall breaker switch reminiscent of Dr. Frankenstein.

With no written instructions available, I turned on the water faucet, threw the switch and stepped back. My feet at this point were numb with cold. To make matters more interesting my shower room antics were being monitored by four aged Senoras seated on a bench at the other end of the courtyard. Trying to maintain what little dignity remained, I smiled and went about my business.

After testing the icy cold water spewing from the shower head several times, I concluded either I was not doing something right or the village electrical plant was closed for the day. Nervously fiddling with the breaker switch and praying for divine intervention, I finally gave up. By this time I was mostly wet anyway, so with clenched teeth I leaped under the frigid torrents coming from the showerhead. When my teeth started clattering uncontrollably, I decided I was clean enough. Stepping out of the shower stall, I was less than pleased to notice my towel lying on the cold, wet cement floor. Anxiously drying myself with my wool shirt, I turned to see steam billowing up from the shower stall. Just as the water reached scalding temperature, I reached over and threw back the breaker switch. By this time clouds of steam were frothing up from the shower room into the courtyard like giant clouds, causing the cronies to point and cluck at me, the hapless gringo. I returned to my room fairly clean and totally awake.

~ ~ ~

The Colonel Would Not Approve

A quick stroll around the plaza led me to the only restaurant in town. More precisely, my nose led me to the restaurant. Just outside the front door was a barbecue made from half of a 50-gallon drum. Spitted chickens were roasting over the coals of a wood fire. The aromas wafting from the barbecue could be sniffed from any part of the village. What with market day, the place was doing a brisk business.

Though no signs or menus touted their rustic fare, a look inside vouched for its popularity.

The interior of the restaurant was dim due to lack of lighting and dusty windows. Smoke covered the walls and ceilings as though a fire had once gutted the place, but truth be known, it was probably because the chickens were roasted inside the restaurant during inclement weather. Knots of men and families sat around wood picnic-style tables, eating pollo and drinking from liter-size beer bottles. I was not surprised to find that I was the only gringo in the place, quite possibly in town.

Pulling a chair up to a small table along the far wall, I waited nervously for a waiter or waitress to descend on me, but none did, so I walked to the counter where a cashier took bills and made change. There I placed an order for the "pollo especiale" and a bottle of cerveza.

Before I finished half my beer, a wooden platter, overflowing with a whole chicken, new potatoes, rolls, and a small salad, was placed in front of me. I thought the server had forgotten to give me silverware and a napkin, but a quick glance around alerted me to the local etiquette of eating with one's fingers. In lieu of a napkin, the Senora ripped a piece of butcher paper from a roll kept handy at the side of the counter and handed it to me.

Apparently, business was better than usual because the cook at the brazier outside called for more chickens. Stuffing my mouth with large strips of chicken I silently watched as the cashier and another woman dragged a large wooden box from the back room and set it in front of the counter. The box contained a dozen or so defeathered chickens. Brandishing long, sharp knives the two women set about the task of butchering the naked birds, this while patrons stepped over and around them when entering or exiting the establishment. None of these proceedings had any effect on my appetite, but for the first time in years I was unable to finish a bottle of beer.

My hunger assuaged, I stepped up to the cashier to pay my bill. After making a few notes and figures on a piece of butcher paper with a stubby pencil, she showed me the total. Forget cash registers and calculators, this was a mountain village of pencil and paper and fingers and toes. Withdrawing a handful of sucre from my fanny pack, I watched as the Senora took my fistful of colored paper and opened a drawer behind the counter. To my amazement, the drawer was over-flowing with paper currency. Apparently, Ecuadorean business people do not have to account to a bureaucracy like the IRS. She dropped my wad of bills in the drawer, withdrew a half-dozen pieces of paper currency and handed them over to me. Making no attempt to reconcile my bill or count my change, I pushed the money into my fanny pack and strolled back to the pensione satisfied that if a mistake had been made it was in my favor; if not, I was none the wiser. I'll bet you've never seen anything like that at your local Kentucky Fried Chicken.

Odd thing is I entered Ecuador earlier that day with 50,000 sucre. That evening I totaled up 50,890 sucre. Somewhere along the way, possibly at the restaurant, I made a few hundred sucre. Go figure.

Figure 12: Ecuadorean border crossing.

The next few days of cycling proved scenic, but the people were on the whole a grim lot. They didn't come close to the Colombianos for warmth, vivacity, or energy. The few cyclists I saw on the road in Ecuador passed me by without so much as a nod, while in Colombia every cyclist smiled, waved and said hello or pulled up alongside for a chat. It amazed me how two countries could share a border and yet be so dissimilar when it came to personality.

~ ~ ~

Otavalo,Ecuador

I woke up around 5 p.m. by the Senor showing someone the room next to mine. Stepping outside onto the patio to get some air I said hello to the Senor and the young lady he was talking to. She seemed quite hysterical. Seeing that I was a gringo, she asked if I spoke English. As her Spanish wasn't too good, I helped translate for the Senor. I told her what the room rates were, adding that the Residencia Herradura was the nicest place I'd looked at in Otavalo.

Agnes Van Zeyl, from Rotterdam, Holland, had been in Ecuador only two days. She'd arrived in Quito the day before and spent a frustrating, hectic day hassling with customs, finding a room and generally trying to cope with a different culture in a big city. This was her first visit to South America. In desperation, she hopped on the first bus to Otavalo. I thought she was going to burst into tears any second. Taking my advice she took the adjoining room.

Over dinner that night, I told her I thought she was suffering from a combined case of jet lag, culture shock, and elevation (Quito is over 9,000', Otavalo is 7,500'), adding that after a few days around a quiet town like Otavalo she'd be in great shape. Following dinner we strolled

1.7 miles   1.42 miles

through nearly deserted streets, only the occasional sound of a door closing or a dog barking disturbed the tranquility. Before returning to the residencia we walked to the Cafe Shanandoah, where I had a good cup of coffee and piece of homemade apple pie with ice cream, an unusual menu item for a small Ecuadorean town. Over her cup of tea, Agnes smiled with delight and awe as I wolfed down the dessert as though I hadn't eaten for days.

After a early morning visit to the local market where vendors and artisans refused to be photographed unless paid, we began a trek up and over the steep hills south of town to Lago San Pablo. The sky was crystal clear. Sounds from the village followed us up the steep track to the hilltop. Working our way up through a grove of eucalyptus trees, we stopped to catch our breath and watch a boy of about 10-years old herd a bunch of recalcitrant goats. At about 8,000' altitude, we gladly stopped along the track to catch our breath, snap a picture, and enjoy the view overlooking the tiled roofs and church towers of Otavalo below us. Topping out, we could look straight down on the placid, blue waters of San Pablo Lake.

After a short and welcome walk down to the lakeshore, we continued following the dirt track southeast through a cluster of adobe huts with thatched roofs. Characteristically, a few chickens, a pig, and a dog scratched in the dirt outside each house. The more prosperous mini-ranches also had a cow tethered in a grassy paddock nearby.

The only visible activity in the village was a handful of women washing clothes in the stream feeding the lake and a some children playing and swimming in the water nearby.

On the south side of the village we met Mercedes, a local artisan who invited us to her home to see her work and perhaps buy something. Dressed in traditional Indio clothes of blue and white skirt, hand-stitched mess jacket, and blue and gold turban-like hat, she carried her 10-month old daughter in a sheet on her back. Necklaces of stamped brass were set off by the brilliant white of her tunic. And like most of the villagers she was barefoot.

Figure 13: Weaver in Otavalo public market.

At a small adobe hut near the main dirt track, Mercedes introduced us to her husband or brother (we were never sure which) who was busy at his loom fashioning some type of multi-colored garment, but stopped to greet us. He took charge of the little girl, while Mercedes showed us some of her colorful belts, sashes, and ponchos.

Agnes was taken with a multi-colored belt Mercedes was working on and agreed to pay 1,000 sucre ($1.40) to purchase it. Mercedes told us to return in an hour for the finished belt. Agnes and I walked down to the lake to find a place to eat some snacks we had in our fanny packs, there to amuse ourselves by watching a young boy and girl shepherd a dozen pigs in a marshy area at lake side. Although one or two of the pigs weighed about 200 lbs. the kids showed no fear of thrashing them with sticks forcing them to move in the desired direction, which was diametrically opposed to the direction the pigs had in mind. Eventually the kids willed out.

As promised, Agnes' handcrafted belt was ready when we returned to Mercedes' hut. I purchased a blue, red, black, and gold hatband for 500 sucre or about 70 cents.

Passing through the village on our way back to Otavalo we couldn't help but notice a number of villagers lying alongside the road dead drunk or weaving their way precariously along the dirt road. Men and women, staggered and stumbled through the streets, or seated themselves alongside the road or in the street and fell into a drunken sleep. All the men were dressed immaculately in traditional garb of black fedora, blue poncho, white calf length trousers and sandals. We watched in amazement as children pushed and shoved the adults in an effort, we assumed, to guide them safely and expeditiously back to their homes. It appeared to us the entire adult population of the village was inebriated and guessed they were celebrating a fiesta. Regardless, I've never seen so many intoxicated people in one place at one time.

After a brisk hike back to Otavalo, Agnes and I made our way directly to the Shanandoah Cafe. David, the owner, sat down with us. He and his younger sister and brother owned and operated the cafe. This was only one of his business endeavors, David told us confidentially. He was also an exclusive vendor of safes. With the cat out of the bag, so to speak, David flipped open a glossy color catalog featuring his company's safes. He showed us small safes, medium-size safes, and large safes, describing the features of each product as though we were potential buyers. The commercial safes were monstrous steel monoliths 5' high and 4' wide and reminded me of the steel monsters one would see in the American West in the 1800's. As my eyes scanned the color images I couldn't help wonder where the safe market, if any, was in Ecuador.

"This one is indestructible," David said jabbing a finger at the picture of a safe the size of a small battle ship and regurgitating a list of data recently memorized.

When I asked David about the size of his sales territory, figuring it would surely encompass the northern half of South America, he tilted his head and smiled, "I have the entire area in and around Otavalo. It is my goal to sell three safes per week." he said slamming his catalog closed.

I got the feeling that David had succumbed to the hyperbole of a magazine or newspaper advertisement promising untold wealth and success for just a few minutes of work each week. A motivational tape had undoubtedly accompanied the catalogs and sales brochures. It became clear that David was using us to practice his sales pitch.

I wasn't about to tell David that he'd be lucky to sell three safes per year in all of Ecuador, let alone the small, remote town of Otavalo. Nor was I going to remind David that most Ecuadorean business people, including him, didn't have cash registers, preferring to operate out of cigar boxes or empty coffee cans. I also guessed the cost of one of the commercial safes would run 2,000 to 3,000 American dollars. The reality was that the commercial safe market was but a handful of large businesses in Quito.

With his sales pitch completed, I fully expected David to flip open an order book and ask how much I'd like to put down. I finished my coffee, smiled at him politely, and wished him the best of luck.

On a deserted stretch of highway south of Otavalo I stopped to scrutinize a large stone monument only to discover I'd just crossed the Equator into the southern hemisphere. My odometer registered 11,891 miles from Anchorage. A faded yellow stripe of paint ran across the road bearing silent witness to this point on the globe that was equidistant from the north and south poles. Instead of the wild, pagan initiation rituals associated with mariners crossing the equator for the first time, I took out my camera to record this singular moment of my life on film. Then after a rest and sip of water I pedaled into the southern hemisphere.

~ ~ ~

Mean Streets

I hadn't planned on reaching Quito that day, mainly because the last 14 miles was a steep climb from a river valley to the high plateau, at 9,349", on which Quito is situated. Starting at a bridge crossing the river I began my slow, tenacious assault on the mountain, made doubly hard and unpleasant by the continuous line of diesel trucks and buses plodding up the highway next to me. Diesel exhaust from passing vehicles spewed over me as they inched their way past at 6 to 7 mph. That's steep.

When finally achieving the high plateau and Quito the sun was setting. My legs felt like wet noodles and my stomach was growling like a rabid Baja dog.

I stopped at the first restaurant I saw and gobbled up a cheeseburger. While eating and recuperating from the ascent, I studied my map only to discover the pensione I wanted to stay at was on the opposite side of the city. This meant I'd have to cycle in the dark through a labyrinth of streets and deal with the hectic and dangerous vehicular traffic swarming there. My route to Pensione Ramirez was made even more unpleasant because the pensione was located in the depths of the steep, cobblestone streets of Old Quito, where serpentine alleys, no more than 10-feet wide, were choked with both pedestrians and motor vehicles. When I finally found the address I

* 1.77 miles.

was looking for I was chagrined to learn that the Pensione Ramirez had changed hands and was now Pensione La Luz. In no mood to cycle any further, I took a room, carried my bike and gear to the second floor and collapsed on a narrow cot.

Next morning I walked to the South American Explorers Club in central Quito intending to pick up a resupply of freeze dried food, clothes, and a new journal I'd sent ahead to Quito before leaving the States. I also hoped to find a letter or two waiting for me there. After searching high and low, clubhouse manager Betsy Wagenhausen reported she couldn't find anything for me.

Tired and depressed I sat down on a couch to gather my thoughts.

After another search of the storage room, Betsy confirmed her first report. Perhaps, she suggested, the missing suitcase containing the items was mistakenly forwarded to the Lima, Peru clubhouse. When next she phoned them or received a call from them she would inquire about the missing luggage.

The long hard ride, 62 miles worth, the previous day, plus Quito's elevation of 9,348' had taken its toll. A bit down at the heels, I made my way back to the La Luz. While crossing a street not far from the S.A.E. clubhouse a shiny black sedan with smoked glass windows sped out of the parking lot of a government building into the street almost running me down in the process.

My temper, dangerously hair-trigger, snapped. I shouted a loud litany of expletives at the rampaging motorist, to some effect I soon discovered. The car braked to a stop and backed up to me. The driver's window slowly opened, revealing a black-haired, mustachioed man dressed in an elegant military uniform. Judging from the multi-colored epaulets on his shoulders and glittering brass on his collar he was an officer of considerable rank.

"What did you say, senor?"

"I said, 'you're driving like a goddamn maniac.' You almost hit me."

Looking steadily at me from behind dark glasses, he said in a calm, controlled voice, "I'm sorry."

The window zipped closed and the car raced away. Thank God, I whispered. I cautioned myself to control my temper at all costs, regardless of the circumstances or I could easily end up in a jail cell or worse.

Taking Betsy Wagenhausen's advice I moved from the La Luz to the Residencia Marsella which was much closer to the S.A.E.C. and within easy walking distance of the central business district where I usually took my meals.

As the streets of Quito were jammed with vehicular traffic, most spewing thick, pungent exhaust into the air, bicycling was out of the question, so I became a reluctant pedestrian. But even as a pedestrian I felt like a moving target. I was reminded of the almost suicidal nature of traffic in Panama City, where I fully expected taxi drivers to speed onto the sidewalk to run down defenseless tourists.

Considering more than 2/3 of the populace was afoot, I found it hard to believe the city was so blatantly lacking basic pedestrian amenities, like crosswalks. It became clear that one became a high-risk taker when attempting to cross any city street.

Two days after my initial visit to the S.A.E. clubhouse, I returned to learn that through the efforts of the secretary, Sharise, my belongings were found wrapped securely in a plastic bag under a small mountain of baggage in the infamous storage room. In addition to warm clothes, 20 freeze-dried meals, and a new journal, I was in receipt of two letters and a book sent by my biking pals in San Diego. I was considerably relieved to get the supplies before heading into the high Andes and deserts of Peru.

While walking that evening to my favorite cafe in the crowded streets of Quito Viejo I suddenly felt someone move quickly to my side and point at my back, while speaking rapidly in Spanish. The young lady who was doing the pointing and talking was also trying to persuade me to remove my fanny pack, which contained my wallet and passport. Ignoring her persistent entreaties, I pulled the fanny pack around to my stomach to discover it covered with a splattered egg. Whereupon, the lady pulled some paper towels from her purse and again encouraged me to remove the pack so she could clean it. Somewhat confused as to what was going on, I looked around to find I was outside the cafe I was enroute to, so I pushed her aside and retreated to the cafe. Still not realizing what was going on, I hurried to my usual table with the towel lady at my heels. But one look and a shout from the Senora at the counter sent the towel lady scurrying back to the street.

Later, I learned from another traveler at the residencia that I was the near victim of street crime. The young lady so eager to help me, he explained, was undoubtedly in league with one or more accomplices whose objective was to snatch my fanny pack as soon as it was removed for cleaning.

So it was with no regret that I departed Quito into the countryside and less predacious folk.

~ ~ ~

I Visit A Hog Farm

Somewhere south of Ambato I stopped at a deserted cafe alongside the road to eat breakfast and put on more warm clothing. The weather had turned cold and clouds filled the valley blocking views of the snowcapped volcanos nearby. I was eating a breakfast of boiled eggs, tortillas, and instant coffee when a pickup truck stopped outside. Moments later a well-dressed man entered the cafe. Without hesitating, he joined me for breakfast. Between bites of food and sips of coffee, I tried to answer his copious questions about my bike trip. His English was about as good as my Spanish, so there were a few gaps in our conversation, but I understood most of his questions and my answers seemed to delight him.

Jose Yanez Quintano was a veterinarian working for a company named Agripac. He lived in Ambato, but traveled all over Ecuador visiting fincas to inspect, inoculate, and minister to the health needs of livestock.

Over a second cup of coffee, Jose suggested that I accompany him to a hog farm, not just any hog farm, mind you, but the largest one in Ecuador. Since it was located in the direction I was going I gladly accepted his offer and looked forward to chatting with him further. Jose explained he was going to the hog farm to make some observations. This intrigued me. What kind of observations does one make at a hog farm? As we drove higher into the mountains, Jose told me there were 3,000 porkers or more at the farm, depending on how prolific the maternity ward had been.

3.92 miles

Along the way we passed Chimborazo (20,702') but as in the case of Cotopaxi (19,347') which I cycled past a few days earlier, clouds obscured most of the mountain. During the next few hours we climbed high into the clouds, then descended steep roads until we were rolling through lush subtropical jungle. After the bleak earth-tones of the altiplano, it was a relief to feast my eyes on the riot of colors sweeping by us.

At last we reached the hog farm sequestered in an area of jungle-covered rolling hills. Emerging from the truck, I was instantly aware of the pressing heat and humidity. We had dropped at least 5,000' in elevation. Layers of clothing were stripped away until once again I was dressed in shorts and singlet.

I followed Jose to the ranch house where he introduced me to Enrique the foreman. From the back of the house Jose pointed uphill. I could see the shiny tin roofs of a dozen or more pig barns, all of necessity open sided. Each barn was about 50 yards long and 20 yards wide.

Pulling on rubber boots provided by the foreman, I followed in Jose's footsteps as he lead the way up a track to the various sheds. The stench even from a distance was almost palpable, forcing me to breathe through my mouth.

* 3.68 miles.

The first barn we entered, after first stepping into a footbath of germicide, was the maternity ward. With clipboard in hand, Jose questioned the foreman about the care and feeding of the mothers-to-be, making copious notes as they talked.

I stared in amazement at 20-odd sows weighing in at 500—600 lbs. each sprawled on their side nursing as many as a dozen piglets each. Most of the behemoth mothers made Lucy of Ventura look like an anorexic.

Next, I followed Jose and Enrique to the stud barn where several boars lay napping and contemplating their virility. These gentlemen, I guessed, must have weighed about 800 lbs. They looked so big, fat, and lethargic I wondered if they were capable of standing on their four hooves, let alone performing the mission they'd been singled out to do. Absurd political metaphors danced in my mind as I observed these "heads of state" slumber and grunt, but they are so obvious I'll let the reader fill in the details. Although they looked indolent and somewhat vulnerable, I held my breath for reasons other than fear, until we passed into another barn that was the pig version of kindergarten.

My two-hour tour afforded me the opportunity of seeing pigs in every stage of life, from birth to maturity. Of course representatives of the final stage of maturity were absent for obvious reasons, i.e. at some point in the life cycle they were converted into sausage, bacon, and chops.

Here are my "observations" of a hog farm, which I'm sure differ substantially from Jose's.

- Pigs, regardless of gender, do a lot of lying about and sleeping. The stench of pigs and pig excrement is not as bad as one would think, especially with a favorable breeze. All things considered there weren't many flies.
- Mature pigs are so big and lazy (no offense Lucy) they can barely get to their hooves, except at mealtime when they miraculously transform into Olympians.
- Piglets are cute.

- Teenage pigs are as obnoxious as their human counterparts. There was much posturing, bullying, yelling, whining, and general bedlam.
- Young stud porkers eat, sleep, shit, and piss on each other with abandon and seem to enjoy the hell out of it. True male bonding.
- None of the pigs seemed to realize the end result of all the good food and leisure time, and just as well.

Admittedly, a tour of a hog farm can be educational and somewhat interesting, but it's not quite the same as visiting, say, an Arabian horse farm, or better yet, a nudist colony.

After the hog farm, Jose and I drove down the road to a small village for a late lunch where customers and staff alike were watching American pro wrestling on a color TV. What a bizarre experience it was to be an American in a third world country, in a remote village where indoor plumbing and potable water were still 20 years in the future, only to see Hulk Hogan menacing Andre the Giant with a 2x4. Narration in Spanish, of course, blended with the Hulk's verbal abuse of Andre. What have we done to the world?

While eating our "pollo y arroz" Jose and I talked about the rumors of war in the Persian Gulf. He had been following the war news more closely than I. For one thing, he can read Spanish language newspapers. I, on the other hand, had to be content with headlines. He had access to his own TV, while I had to be satisfied with TV's in restaurants, which typically were tuned to soccer matches, soap operas, or wrestling matches.

After dinner, I thanked Jose for the tour of the pig farm and said adios. Once again, I mounted my bicycle and headed south.

~ ~ ~

Restaurante Nuevo Al Pago

At 5 p.m. I arrived in the small puebla of Naranjal after what seemed to be miles of effortless pedaling—muy plano. Now in southwest Ecuador I was rolling along coastal plains enjoying warm, sunny weather, riding once again in shorts and T-shirt. I felt exceptionally fit, optimistic, and glad to be out of the cold, high Andes. For hours I'd been cycling through hundreds, perhaps thousands, of acres of banana plantations, the road divided the green, evenly spaced plants down the middle like the slash of a machete.

In the puebla of Naranjal, a misnomer perhaps, I had trouble finding a place to stay. For one thing there were only a few pensiones and they were full, but somewhere in my circumlocution of the dirt streets a bicyclist came to my assistance. I followed him to the Residencia Lupe where I secured the last available room. The Lupe was fairly new and resembled a small, American-style motel.

Unfortunately, my room had a few design flaws. There weren't any windows, vents, or exhaust fans to provide much needed ventilation. Although the room had a bathroom complete with toilet, sink and shower, there was no plumbing in the shower stall. So after a thorough sponge bath in the sink, I headed into the dark night in search of a place to eat. This was an easy task as the cafes and restaurants were lined up side by side along the Pan Am highway, the one and only transportation corridor linking Ecuador with Colombia to the north and Peru to the south.

Walking north on the dirt path along the highway I saw the welcoming lights of a cafe about 100 yards ahead of me. The half dozen trucks and cars parked outside seemed to indicate, if not quality fare, at least popularity. The sign above the entrance read Restaurante Nuevo Al Pago.

Seated at a small table, I ordered a beef steak, papas, and a beer. Although pork was on the menu, I felt more than a tinge of guilt even thinking about ordering it. Halfway through dinner, an attractive Caucasian woman entered the cafe and took a table across from me.

"Do you speak English," I asked.

"Yes, yes, I know English."

"Well, would you like to join me?"

"Yes, thank you I would like that."

Hilde was a blond Norwegian about 5' 2". She was the manager of a nearby cocoa plantation owned by a Danish firm. She'd been managing the plantation for the past two years. Although she had what I considered an unusual and interesting job, she was more interested in hearing about my travels than telling me about herself.

"Chocolate is chocolate. Besides work, and there's a lot of that, there isn't much to do around here," she sighed over her beer.

As we started in on a second beer, a tall, blond, athletic fellow bounded into the cafe and headed straight for Hilde. Uh oh, I thought to myself. Hilde immediately introduced me to Bo David Blomberg, a Swede and husband of the Ecuadorean lady who owned the restaurant. Additionally, he was an engineer for a Swedish manufacturing firm. While Bo David ate a late dinner served by his wife, Hilde excused herself explaining she had to return to the cocoa finca to prepare for an early morning meeting with representatives from the Danish firm that owned the finca.

While he ate, I told Bo David about my bike tour to Tierra Del Fuego. A year ago, he said, four British women came through Naranjal also headed for TDF. They too had started in Alaska.

"Well, you know, they came to this town and looked so tired and hungry my wife and I let them stay here with us. They were quite some women."

After complimenting Bo David on his wife's excellent food I prepared to pay my bill, but he insisted that I be his guest.

~ ~ ~

A Mercedes Benz

I pushed my bike over a rickety bridge apparently damaged by a recent flood. On the south side of the bridge I stopped to take a drink from my water bottle. Behind me a typically gaudy, battered bus creaked and groaned its way across the one-lane span, then beeped as it passed by. Out of nowhere a huge Mercedes sedan came to a stop alongside me. Front and rear windows swooshed down revealing a quartet of men all swathed in silk shirts, sunglasses, gold jewelry, and Rolex watches. They stared at my bike and me.

"Where are you going?" The man in the front seat asked.

"Tierra Del Fuego," I answered, maneuvering my bike so they could see the Alaska to Tierra Del Fuego placard.

"You are an Alaskan?"

"No, no, I started in Alaska."

"But how did you get here?"

"I...I rode my bicycle."

There was a pause. Four heads converged in consultation. A flurry of Spanish.

"And you passed through Germany and Italy." Front seat inquired.

"No. Canada, U.S., Mexico, Central America, then Colombia..." I explained wondering what Germany and Italy had to do with anything, but suspecting something was getting lost in the translation.

Again the four men conferenced.

"Senor," Front seat began, "surely you have passed through Spain. That is correct, yes."

I shook my head slowly trying to be cooperative and trying not to offend four sociable gentlemen in an elegant motorcar.

"No. Spain is in Europe." Adding hastily, "So are Germany and Italy."

"Ah, senor, you are a world traveler, yes, but my friend, you must have been traveling for many years to reach Ecuador on a bicycle. Are you not tired?"

"Actually, I've been traveling about two and a half years, but yes I'm a bit tired."

More consultation. Front seat pushed his hand out the window.

"Here senor, we want you to have this, it will help you on your journey."

I smiled, taking the handful of currency he offered. Then a hand thrust out of the back window. I took the objects offered-two cans of Del Monte fruit salad.

"Bien Viaje," they called as the windows closed and the huge sedan sped off. I stood there alone by the side of the road watching the car disappear. With 5,000 sucre in one hand and two cans of fruit salad in the other I wondered how four obviously rich and powerful men could have such a faulty understanding of world geography.

~ ~ ~

Las Vegas Night in Machala

After two uneventful stops at military checkpoints, I pedaled into the city of Machala, which according to my map was approximately 50 miles from the Peruvian border. Somewhere between Naranjal and Machala I'd broken the 12,000-mile mark.

A fair-sized town with spacious streets and broad boulevards, Machala showed signs of prosperity, at least by third world standards. Feeling naively flush with my 5,000-sucre stipend, I cycled about in search of the Hotel Rizzo, about the only recommendation listed for Machala in the South American Handbook. Wheeling up in front of it, I was overwhelmed. Amongst a meticulously clean, landscaped court-yard, was a three-story, sparkling modern hotel, the likes of which I hadn't seen for what seemed like years. My body seemed to surge toward it like a piece of metal drawn to a magnet. A bit intimidated by its formidable appearance and my contrasting shabbiness, I nonetheless decided to inquire about room rates. What with my recent windfall and two cans of fruit cocktail I was a man of unlimited potential.

The attractive Senorita at the registration desk informed me with a bright smile that a "privado" or single room would cost 14,000 sucre or about $17. Feeling like a rich gringo I decided to spend the night in luxury and sloth, before facing the privations of the Peruvian desert, next on my travel agenda.

In addition to an immaculately clean, tile bathroom with gleaming chrome plumbing, my carpeted, draped room had a king size bed, color TV with satellite hookup, small refrigerator stocked with beer and soft drinks, and, low and behold, it was air conditioned.

After a long, rejuvenating hot shower, I sprawled on the bed and took a siesta. Sometime during my nap I rolled over on the TV remote control, turning the television set on. I woke reluctantly to the sights and sounds of an international soccer match, then stabbed the button to silence the TV. I rose slowly to dress for an elegant dinner in the hotel restaurant.

A large serving of spaghetti and meatballs went far in quenching my rioting appetite, but not far enough to preclude a dessert of ice cream and fruit followed by an espresso.

Earlier, while reviewing the menu I noticed a message on the back cover announcing that gambling was available to hotel guests in the casino attached to the hotel. Feeling the seductive hand of lady luck massaging my ego and imagination I strolled next door to investigate what seemed like an incongruous business considering I was in the backwaters of Ecuador. Regardless, lady luck was smiling on me. I mean, earlier that day hadn't I received a windfall of 5,000 sucre and two cans of fruit cocktail. Wasn't this some karmic sign that I was riding a wave of pure, undeniable good fortune?

Entering the casino reminded me of entering the side door of a high school gymnasium. There was a complete lack of pulsating neon and doormen swathed in Arabian-like pajamas and plumed turbans.

None of your Las Vegas gaudiness or frivolousness here, no sir. The entrance door was just a plain door with a functional, but plain door handle. On the plain door was an equally innocuous placard announcing "Casino Entrance."

Inside the dimly lit, but spacious hall the size of a basketball court, I expected to hear the jangle of slot machines, whoops of joy, the rattle of dice, or the snap and riff of cards being shuffled, but the only sound I heard was the whir of fan blades knifing the air overhead. I looked slowly around at the slot machines lined up against the walls and the dice, twenty-one, and roulette tables forming an oblong ring in the center of the room. Staring back at me, as though caught in freeze frame, were the card dealers, croupiers, and pit bosses standing behind, leaning on, or seated at their tables. I was the only potential gambler in the house.

I felt like a schoolboy who having been sent to the principal's office for a well deserved dressing down regarding habitual truancy, instead finds the principal and his homely secretary naked and writhing on the floor.

As if cued by a signal from the pit boss, the dealers shuffled their decks of cards, spun their roulette wheels, or stacked and unstacked small towers of multi-colored chips on the green felt before them. I walked quickly to the closest twenty-one table and sat on the middle stool in a semi-circle of six. The dealer, not looking at me, collapsed the fanned out deck of cards in front of him, cut the deck into two equal stacks, and proceeded to shuffle them together.

"Hello." The dealer finally said.

I pulled my 5,000-sucre gift from my fanny pack and laid it on the green felt in front of me to purchase chips. In the blink of an eye a cocktail waitress was at my side to take an order. I requested a Pepsi. Before my drink arrived not more than two minutes later, carbonation still fizzing, I'd lost 10,000 sucre in five straight hands. The dealer looked at me with a frown. I'd blown $12.50. I was about to leave when the door was flung open and four stylishly dressed men hurried into the casino laughing and calling out to the dealers. All of a sudden the place came alive.

"Ola Senor bicyclist, how are you," one of them called.

I spun around on my stool. I couldn't believe my eyes, it was the four guys in the Mercedes I'd met earlier that day.

"Buenos noches," I said.

They were still outfitted in expensive slacks and shirts; gold necklaces and bracelets sparkling on tanned necks and wrists. They gathered around me at the twenty-one table. Front seat with a cigar the size of a jumbo hot dog in his teeth slid onto a stool beside me.

"How's your luck, amigo?" he asked.

"Not so good, I just lost all the money you gave and more. Sorry."

"That's not so funny," he said laughing.

As we talked, two cocktail waitresses swooped down on the men with trays of bottles and glasses, greeting the men like long lost cousins, which they may well have been. For all I knew they owned the place. Front seat took a long drag on his cigar, washed it down with some beer, and then drew closer.

"Listen, my friend, you must be my guest here. You will surely bring us luck. You have the luck coming here all the way from Alaska, no. That is a very big sign, verdad."

I was about to politely thank him for his generosity and make my exit, but he was in the process of introducing me to his friends and proclaiming that I was going to bring them much luck. As I was shaking hands with his friends the cocktail waitresses returned with more refreshments. Two of the men wandered off to the crap table. Carlos, who I recognized as the driver of the Mercedes, sat down next to "front seat" who had introduced himself as Julio.

"Here, you drink your beer and I will take care of things." Julio said pushing a bottle of beer in front of me.

He turned to the stoic dealer and said something rapidly in Spanish and with what sounded like authority. Instantaneously, the dealer pushed large stacks of chips in front of the three of us. The only thing I knew was the color of the chips in front of me was not the same as the chips I'd recently lost.

Tentatively, I pushed a single chip onto the betting circle in front of me. Seeing this, Julio laughed, reached over, and pushed a handful of chips into the circle. While the dealer completed his shuffle, Julio snapped his fingers at the cocktail waitress stationed nearby and said something to her. While inspecting our first hand of cards, a box of cigars was placed on the table in front of Julio, who removed one from its protective tube, sniffed the length of it, then satisfied, handed it to me. The way he thrust it at me I knew I had little choice in the matter. Soon all three of us card players were discharging a curtain of pungent smoke in the air around us.

"Muy fuerte, amigo, play strong." Julio coaxed.

I noticed that Julio and Carlos had ten chips each in the betting circle in front of them. I silently thanked God for a pair of Jacks, placing them face down to indicate I would stay with that hand. Both Julio and Carlos busted. I turned my cards over to beat the dealer's hand of 19. I heaved a sigh of relief.

"Si, si, you got the luck, amigo, just as I said," Julio boasted with a broad smile, smoking cigar waving about in his hand like an emergency flare.

Then he reached over and pushed 20 chips into the betting circle in front of me, this in addition to the stack already there. After winning that hand too I was convinced that Julio was right about my luck. And in no time, perhaps three beers and a cigar later our side of the table was covered with mounds of colored chips. By God, I told myself, I'm on one helluva incredible roll. Julio was making outrageous bets, pushing stacks and stacks into the betting circle and laughing like a fool when they fell over. If he lost a hand he would double or triple the bet to get even. At some point, the pit boss pushed a small cart loaded with racks of chips to the side of the table to reinforce the house bank. While doing so, he smiled ingratiatingly at Julio.

It was just after a new dealer was rotated to our table that I began to lose; once the streak started, it was like a sinking ship. Likewise, Julio's castles of chips melted away to a few decrepit shacks. Carlos had long since cashed out and visited with our cocktail waitress.

Declining a new supply of chips I thanked Julio and told him my luck had played out and it was time to go to my room as I planned to cross the frontier into Peru the next morning. Having no idea of the amount of money I'd lost it did, however, occur to me that Julio might expect some kind of reimbursement, like a year as an indentured servant on his banana plantation or perhaps a harsher settlement like the ritualistic amputation of one or more of my fingers. I was prepared for at least a trifling amount of verbal recrimination, but Julio merely smiled and waved his cigar.

"My lucky amigo from Alaska, you must continue your journey. Bien viaje, amigo."

"Thanks again, Julio." I said gripping his hand with my sweaty palm.

"Jorge, can I send some women to your room, yes, let me do that."

"Thank you , no, I must get my rest, its been a long day," I said diplomatically, working my way slowly, but persistently to the door.

On my way back to the room, I suspected a tap on the shoulder and a muffled cough, quite possibly a vice-like hand would grip my arm. One of Julio's lieutenants would begin a speech that would go something like "Perdone Senor, but in the matter of the half-million sucre."

~ ~ ~

Devious Eggs

The hotel staff was unanimous in their disagreement about how many kilometers the frontier was from Machala. Not a single person would commit to a specific figure, rather, their answers were couched in evasiveness, e.g. "not far," very close." The only common thread of agreement was their insistence that the frontier or border was only an hour from Machala. This, of course, was the time it took a bus or collectivo traveling at 80 mph to reach the border.

Sipping coffee and studying the menu in the hotel cafe, my eye stopped on an item labeled "Huevos Devios" which I mistakenly translated into "devious eggs." How could eggs be devious, I mumbled to myself. Ever the gambler, recent experiences notwithstanding, I ordered "Huevos Devios." To my delight and surprise I enjoyed a breakfast of softboiled eggs, toast, and a fruit cup. Fortified with "devious eggs" and a double cappuccino, I exited Machala bound for the frontier which I calculated to be a few hours ride. By mid-afternoon, I guessed, I'd be in Peru.

About every six miles I had to stop at a military checkpoint to show my passport and give them my spiel about riding a bicycle from Alaska to Tierra Del Fuego. When finally arriving at the frontier town of Huaquillas, I was disappointed to learn the customs office or "Aduano" where I needed to get my passport stamped was closed for lunch but would reopen at 2 p.m. In the meantime, I decided to search for a place to stay, rather than cycle into the unknown wastes of Peru late in the afternoon.

Stepping into the dirt streets of Huaquillas, I was reminded of one of those infamous towns that sprung up near the gold and silver mines in the American West in the 1800's. The very air seemed charged with the scent of corruption and debauchery. The three-block area closest to the border crossing was lined with a gauntlet of vending stalls covered with faded canopies. My ears vibrated with the din of vendors hawking their wares, of sharp-tongued haggling, of numerous radios blaring a mixture of salsa and rock, of dogs barking and snapping at each other and unwary pedestrians, of babies crying, of battered trucks and cars, most missing mufflers, inching their way through the street. The smell of human sweat, of diesel exhaust, of urine and feces, of frying linguisa and pork and fish and tortillas, of cigarette smoke and whiskey all commingled in this malevolent, seething patch of dirt.

The variety and volume of merchandise piled and hung about the stalls was mind boggling: watches, athletic shoes, shirts, jeans, underwear, soap, shampoo, plastic toys, Christmas lights, Norwegian cookies, Russian caviar, candy bars, tape recorders, radios, televisions, cigarettes, and every size, shape, and color of knickknack extant, most made in China.

Strolling and gawking as I pushed my bike down the gauntlet of vendors, some selling food and drink from two-wheeled carts pushed or pedaled by the proprietor, I was solicited for cold drinks, popsicles, empanadas, watermelon, ice cream, and pineapple and orange juice.

The last block before the border, the ground zero of Huaquillas, amongst the throng of vendors was a group of cambios or moneychangers seated in a row of folding chairs. With few exceptions they looked like an orderly group of businessmen waiting to meet with their lawyer. All the cambios wore sunglasses, all wore clean trousers and white shortsleeve shirts, all displayed a gold or silver watch on their wrist, all had an attaché case perched on their lap. If one cambio reached up to scratch his nose or cross his legs, I expected his colleagues to instantly follow suit. And they had an air about them of professionals, not to be confused with the rabble hawking soft drinks and popsicles, these chaps were captains of the currency market, financial counselors, investment bankers, or possibly charlatans

To my surprise, none of the cambios came racing toward me flashing a calculator and shouting "dolares, dolares, dolares." With some reticence I approached one of the seated moneychangers knowing I'd have to change my Ecuadorean sucres to Peruvian intis and cash a few traveler's checks to boot before entering Peru. A random poll of three cambios produced the same exchange rate, verified by their handheld calculators. With a sigh of resignation I handed over my 2,000 sucres and three $20 traveler's checks. In exchange I received 27,400,000 Peruvian intis and change. As the cambio counted out stack upon stack of intis I realized that once again I was a multi-millionaire, on paper at least. The only downside to all this money changing was the current exchange rate of 440,000 intis for one American dollar.

But the real question was "how much" an inti would buy. Because of the shear volume of the colorful Peruvian currency now in my possession I was forced to buy a new fanny pack to accommodate it. To my chagrin the new fanny pack I bought from one of the vendors cost 2,500,000 intis. I began to see the light. With my new, spacious fanny pack stuffed to the seams with intis I set off for the Ecuadorean customs house to get my exit stamp, arriving there a few minutes before the office reopened.

To my displeasure the hallway outside the office was packed with people of all genders and ages. Some smoked cigarettes, some clutched one or more children on their hips, and some even held a live chicken. At least the chickens were well behaved, which I can't say for the slobbering, whining kids. There were boxes and bags strewn all over the floor, radios blaring, even a few stray dogs maneuvered in and around people and baggage.

Into this maw of sweating, agitated humanity I thrust myself. It was like being caught in a ferocious ocean undertow that drew me steadily, inexorably into the depths. To form an orderly queue that would impose a modicum of order and efficiency was totally out of the question; chaos, boiling tempers, pushing, shoving, and an elbow in the ribs was the order of the day.

When at last the Aduano's door squeaked open a tidal wave of flesh and sweat surged toward it and would have inundated the office were it not for the stern-faced uniformed soldier blocking the entrance. Like a piece of flotsam I was pitched hither and yon, one second about to be regurgitated out of the building, the next spun on my heels and pushed uncomfortably close to the armed soldier. I tried in my best Spanish to convince the soldier I wasn't jumping ahead of the other jetsam. Instead of a tongue-lashing he grabbed my passport and thrust it at the customs official in back of him. Seconds later I was summoned, with a nod of the head, into his office. In the cramped room I scanned the Aduano's desk overflowing with forms, correspondence, newspapers, coffee cups, and soda pop cans. While flipping through my passport, he engaged himself in a running bout of verbal abuse on those clerks and secretaries attending him. Not looking up from his desk, the Aduano asked a few routine questions, then with whirling arms, stamped and initialed my exit visa and passport like a machine. Before I could blink I was out on the dusty street again trying to cram my passport into my bulging fanny pack.

That night in my hotel room, primed with a few rum and cokes I made a list of things I'd learned during the 12,000 miles accumulated since departing Anchorage, Alaska in 1988.

- Don't put things off. Delaying becomes a habit.
- Learn to deal with failure. The ratio of success to failure is about 60/40.
- Don't put much faith in what people tell you: 80% is misinformation,10% is truth, and 20% is lies,
- Money, especially the American dollar, is mutlilingual.
- Material things are not intrinsically good. They only serve to divert us from important things.
- If there's no risk, there's no satisfaction.
- Never sleep with your mouth open.

Next morning when trying to exit Ecuador I was detained briefly at the border. The soldier inspecting my passport couldn't understand why I hadn't entered Peru the previous day, when my Ecuadorean exit visa was stamped. Another soldier, for reasons unknown to me, came to my defense explaining to his colleague that I was traveling on a bicycle, therefore I wasn't in any hurry to enter Peru, preferring to spend the night, like any sensible person, in Huaquillas. After a bit of eyebrow twitching and finger popping, the first soldier returned my passport and waved me through the border.

Chapter 12

Peru

Once past the Peruvian military checkpoint I cycled down the highway marveling at the utter desolation of the landscape and wondering why two countries would kill each other over such worthless real estate. Passing within a few yards of fortified bunkers, burned out tanks, and other charred evidence of territorial disputes accrued over the years it seemed such a waste of time and human resources.

South of Tumbes, an oasis town, the highway maneuvered out to the coast where once again I met up with my old traveling companion the Pacific Ocean. Here it was cooler. Here also I began a leg of my journey that would spool out thousands of miles of desert with only brief intermissions at oasis villages blessed by rivers coursing down from the Andes.

At this point, the terrain appeared, if not hospitable, at least not unfriendly. I was stocked up with 20 freeze-dried meals, five water bottles, and water filter to help navigate this arid, sparsely populated region.

At a beach south of Zorritus I made my first camp in Peru. After pushing my bike down a sandy road to the beach, about 100 yards from the highway, I pitched my tent. Along the shore as far as the eye could see were countless fish camps, constructed of bits of board, canvas, and cardboard. The pescaderos strung nets in the shallows close to shore or plied the offshore waters in small boats. My neighbor explained that shrimp and small lobster were the most popular catches along the beach, but lately only shrimp were being harvested.

Ocean breezes cooled the air. As the sun began dropping toward the horizon far out on the ocean, I cooked up a dinner of freeze-dried chili, with almond crunch and coffee for dessert. Later with the sun down and brisk ocean breezes freshening the night air I crawled into my tent for an evening of total solitude, infringed upon slightly by the gently rolling surf.

~ ~ ~

The Man Who Saw Too Much

A few days and a few hundred miles south along the Peruvian coast the highway cut inland through burning hills and desert. Temperatures increased to near boiling. I was careful to top off my water bottles at every opportunity, but those opportunities got fewer and farther between.

Good pavement stopped abruptly in the small village of Los Organos and what remained wasn't so much a road, but a battered and broken collection of asphalt chunks. Los Organos, an eyesore of oil pipes, derricks, wells, and drilling equipment, had a thin veneer of black crude staining and permeating everything and everyone in the village. In addition to shacks and shanties cobbled together from wood and tin, there were several abandoned adobe foundations used as corrals by scavenging pigs and goats.

The mangled road climbed up into the surrounding hills, baked brown under thousands of years of unrelenting sun and parched from lack of precipitation, before making a direct assault on the desert. On and on I pedaled into the heat and desolation where the geography hadn't altered significantly for hundreds, perhaps thousands of years. Here, time wasn't measured in days, months, or even years but falls more easily under the jurisdiction of some imperceptible geologic clock.

As Gerald Hawkins wrote in *Beyond Stonehenge*, *"Long-term for geologists means a hundred thousand years. When one picks up a red-bellied stone in the sand (at Nazca, Peru) it has not been disturbed for millennia."*

And yet every so often I passed a solitary hut or cluster of hovels constructed of skeletal tree limbs, straw mats, tin cans, a plank of wood, perhaps topped off with a purloined sheet of metal; the roof functioning solely as a sunshade, rain being the anomaly here.

Naked children played in the dirt in front of those doorless, windowless dwellings, while cadaverous dogs pawed through piles of trash and garbage nearby. A few goats might be seen chewing or cropping some type of nourishment sprouting from the hardpan, or more likely, I guessed, they were just chewing out of habit. I could not believe even a goat could find anything to sustain life in that wasteland, let alone a human being.

And what of the human inhabitants? Or were they subhuman, throwbacks to prehistoric time, which was what that place reminded me of. I could just as easily believe they were extra-terrestrials who needed no life sustaining sustenance. But there were real people out there, however precarious their existence. Then I began wondering if I was really seeing people; mightn't I just as easily be experiencing a mirage or hallucination? Why not? I was dehydrated from the relentless sun and heat. I was bleary-eyed. Maybe I was in the initial stages of sunstroke? Mile after mile, day after day, I pedaled and sweated, but kept seeing the same brown and gray hills with the road forever reaching toward them, but never getting there.

The only thing I was reasonably sure of was that I was traveling back in time physically and mentally—and it was all confusing, frustrating, and incredibly scary.

I felt like the Reverend Hubert Diana in Wilbur Daniel Steele's short story, "The Man Who Saw Through Heaven."

"...he was aware of his own eye passing vividly through unpartitioned emptiness, eight hundred and fifty centuries at the speed of light!"

"That's right Mr. Diana, you may well stare at it: between now and now ten thousand histories may have come and gone down there..."

I would have believed a camel caravan or space ship as readily as those scattered pockets of human life. Perhaps that is the key to travel. The mysteries of Nazca, Easter Island, Stonehenge-they are all the more believable to the traveler. Extra-terrestrials, lost civilizations: their explanations seemed as plausible as the mysterious equation that brought me there. Are we not all part of some experimental process, a tad diabolical, the compete comprehension of which we are still groping for?

I kept penetrating the wasteland layer by layer. Every hundred miles or so an oasis would break the monotonous brown and gray horizon. More hovels, more half-finished adobe walls. Yet another stream turned river had escaped the clutches of the Andes to wind its circuitous way to the Pacific Ocean, the same ocean I'd observed with indifference along the western coasts of North and Central America. Now as a time traveler it had new significance. It was the glue, the substance, just like our bodily fluids, that held the parts of the world together in the unified mass called planet earth.

Somewhere during my journey through time and space I lost the capacity to assimilate. My senses shut down temporarily. I cried, I laughed, I was humbled, I was both elated and depressed. I'd seen too damn much just like the Reverend Diana.

Hours, days, light years later I came back to life in Arequipa. Still dazed, I found a residencia named Casa de Mi Abuela (My Grandmother's House). It was behind a high wall of faded ochre, near the end of a street rising out of el centro. Inside were flower gardens—reds, pinks, and yellows against a backdrop of green grass. Shade trees rustled in the breeze. After a thousand miles of brown and gray I was almost blinded by the variety and intensity of the colors.

On the first floor was grandmother's room, the white-haired matriarch who has lived there over a hundred years. She sat in a wheelchair near the window looking out at her flowers. The day of my arrival I celebrated my 49th birthday. Grandmother raised a claw-like hand and waved to me as I passed. I waved back. I went to my room and slept for 16 hours, waking at dawn not knowing where I was, but feeling refreshed and happy. Happy that my journey through the wasteland was over and happy I'd found grandmother's house. Sunlight poured through the bedroom window. Later, I went down to the garden to eat breakfast and drink numerous cups of thick, black coffee. Not having eaten a full meal in weeks, I was famished. Birds sang in the trees as I wolfed down my food. Like a jolt of electricity I could feel my strength return. During the previous weeks my body and mind had been stretched beyond their normal limits. For the first time, perhaps the last, in my life I'd been transported to other worlds, other times-past, present, and future.

I was satiated with knowledge, experience, metaphysics, and spiritualism—all those things that conjure up diverse, incongruous images. One thing I knew for sure was I'd never again doubt the existence of other worlds, other civilizations. Unaccountably, my only concern was how long our present civilization would last. I wondered if we were at the end of an epoch or at the threshold of something bigger, grander.

On the day after my arrival in Arequipa I found myself walking behind a tall, lanky fellow with blond hair. His pace matched mind so precisely I couldn't pass him without breaking into a jog. As I was searching for a tourist office to get information about a trip to the Colca Canyon I didn't want to slow down or speed up, so I followed in this chap's footsteps as though in a race walk, until he stopped abruptly. I almost collided with him.

"Say, do you speak English," I asked a bit embarrassed.

"Yes, a little."

"I'm looking for this address," I said showing him my notebook. "Would you have any idea where it might be?"

After looking at the notebook briefly, he turned around. "I believe you have passed it. Go back one block. The tourist office is on that corner."

"Thanks for your help. Do you live here in Arequipa?"

"No, no, actually I live in Puno, at Lake Titicaca. Have you been there?"

"Not yet, but I'll be going there on my way to Machu Picchu. Say, would you know of a good pensione in Puno? I want to find a place to store my bike while I take the train to Cuzco and Machu Picchu." I said, telling him about my trip from Alaska to Tierra Del Fuego.

"Well, you know Puno is a small town. About the hotels I don't know much," he said with a thick Scandinavian accent, "but let me think, yes, I have a spare room at my home where you can leave your bike, that will be no problem. By the way my name is Jan Olsen."

Taking my notebook and pen, Jan wrote his name, address, and telephone number down. He smiled while assuring me that Puno was so small I could walk or ride the few short blocks from the train station to his home.

"One thing to consider is the elevation at Puno. It is over 6,000 meters (12,500') you should stay over a day or two to acclimate." He cautioned.

Jan was married and living in Puno with his Peruvian wife Betsy and their two young children. I thanked him again before shaking hands and retracing my steps back down the street where, just as Jan said, I found Maje Tours office and the congenial manager, Mario Silva.

At 2:30 a.m. the next morning I was awakened by the night desk clerk at Casa de Mi Abuela. In a fuzzy, dreamy state I pulled on my hiking boots and warm clothes, then stumbled downstairs to the lobby where two couples, also half-asleep, waited silently by the door. We soon discovered we were all scheduled for the same bus trip to the Colca Canyon, Peru's bigger, deeper version of the USA's Grand Canyon. By 3 a.m. we were all on a bus rumbling through the narrow, cobbled, empty streets of Arequipa picking up other people scheduled for the tour. With that mission completed and headed out of town,

* 2.37 miles.

everyone except our tour guide and the bus driver was snoozing in their seats.

Upon negotiating a rough stretch of road, we came to life, some with more enthusiasm than others. I zipped my heavy jacket up, plunged my hands in deep pockets to ward off the sharp chill that attacks just before dawn. Under a diaphanous sky to the east we could see the soaring peaks of the Andes, many snow-capped volcanic cones. Our bus stopped at a viewing point while the sun rose higher. All of us stepped into the chill air to survey the horizon of red-tinted volcanoes, made more dramatic by an intense blue sky. I held my small binoculars up to watch a black smoke cloud curl from the tip of one of the volcanoes. I guessed the elevation at approximately 13,000'.

The bus continued across the altiplano, beeping at an occasional herd of llama or vicuna grazing close to the road. Just about the time my stomach was sending up warning signals reminding me it was time for breakfast, the bus pulled into a small adobe building; a singular, lonely structure amidst the stark, barren landscape. Here we were served a breakfast of coffee, bread, and soup.

Later that morning we stopped at an overlook at the edge of the Colca Canyon, a sunny rock ledge high above the Rio Colca, still cutting a path in the lower depths of the canyon, as it had for millions of years. Then in the sky above us, as if on cue, a lone condor glided out over the canyon, wheeling higher and higher in the thermals. With my binoculars, I followed its flight until my arms began to ache and I had to lower them.

~ ~ ~

Night Train to Puno

With Mario's help at Majes Tours I booked a reservation on the night train to Puno. Although it was a first class car where meals and refreshments were served, sleeping compartments were unavailable.

At 6 p.m. one evening I wheeled my bike through the beautiful gardens of Casa de Mi Abuela and through the locked gate to the street. It was with more than a little sadness that I left this beautiful residencia. A few blocks away I met Mario at his office where he gave me the train ticket and a card with the name of his friend and colleague in Puno who, Mario assured me, would meet me at the train station.

In addition to advising me to keep a sharp eye out for pickpockets and thieves, Mario volunteered to escort me to the Arequipa station. As it would be dark when I arrived there, he wanted to insure that my bike was properly checked and stored in the baggage car and that I met with no misfortune before boarding the train. So with Mario on my left side and my bike on my right, I walked the several blocks to the station.

As I should have anticipated, the baggage freight check area at the station was total chaos. Stacks of produce boxes, bales and cases of every size and shape formed small mountains outside the freight office, which had just opened. Already, there was a horde of people collected outside the door pushing and shoving each other to get inside. Forming a line to these people is as alien as a Fourth of July barbecue. Mario suggested that I wait outside with my bike while he squeezed his way through the crowd to enlist the help of his "friend" who worked there. Armed with 100,000 intis, a negligible sum amounting to a few American dollars, he disappeared in the throng while I stood by my bike on the freight dock watching trucks pull up and unload their cargo.

Perhaps five minutes later, Mario returned with his friend, who surveyed my loaded bike with mild amusement. He turned to Mario and said something sharp, then both men hoisted the bike onto their shoulders and miraculously made their way through the milling crowd, like twin Moses parting the waters of the Red Sea. Justifiably, I watched with concern as my bike, with most of my gear and stash of $5,000 in cash and traveler's checks disappeared. I waited outside in the dark with my backpack containing my rain gear, sleeping bag, and tent, wondering if I'd ever see my bike again.

This time when Mario reappeared perspiration beaded his brow, his hair was disheveled, and his shirt open to his chest, but he was smiling nonetheless.

"Your bike is in good hands," he assured me, "now Jorge, come with me I'll take you to the Pullman car."

Accepting my train ticket and freight receipt, I followed in the furrow he created as he plowed his way through the crowd in the station waiting room. After whispering something to the guard at the platform door, we hurried down a line of waiting railroad cars to the first class coach.

Shaking my hand and wishing me a good trip, he said, "Keep an eye on your luggage and whatever you do don't get off the train at Juliaca, that is the most dangerous city in all Peru. And remember, Pasqualli will meet you in Puno."

When Mario left I realized how lucky I'd been. I'd avoided hours of frustration checking my bike at the freight office, queuing up at the ticket window, and possibly being robbed or assaulted. In just the few days I'd been in Arequipa I met many a traveler who told me about slashed pockets, stolen cameras, wallets, purses, and missing luggage. It seemed that of all the countries I'd traveled in so far Peru was the one with the highest risk factor.

Shortly after storing my luggage in the overhead rack and settling in my seat with a copy of *Moby Dick*, secured from the lending library at Casa de Mi Abuela, four Italian women in their early 40's came chattering noisily into the car and settled in seats across from me. They too were on their way to Machu Picchu. Unfortunately their flight from Lima had been cancelled forcing them to bus and train to Cusco.

"But so what." One of the ladies offered accompanied by a symphony of gesticulation. "What's a the big hurry. We like a trains, yes. We have a many trains in Italy. Right."

The other women pumped their heads in agreement.

"Come on a you Machu Picchu," she concluded.

Though I'd prepared myself for a cold ride through the Andes, donning layers of pants, shirts, and jackets, I was pleasantly surprised after the train departed Arequipa to find the Pullman car heated. Additionally, woolen blankets were distributed as the train rattled its way up the western slope of the mountain.

Enjoying the luxury of not sharing the seat with another passenger, I stretched out and fell asleep about 9 p.m. and woke up at 5:30 a.m. next morning to witness spectacular sunrise views of the eastern face of the mountain and the blue expanse of Lake Titicaca. All this while the train made its way through the dreaded Juliaca to Puno farther south on the western shore of what guidebooks credit as the world's highest navigable lake. The key word here is "navigable." I wondered how any lake could not be navigable. By dictionary definition a navigable lake is deep and wide enough to allow passage of ships and boats.

At the Puno train station, I suspected I was being followed as soon as I got off the train. I stopped abruptly, turned around and found myself looking into a clean-shaven face with a black moustache that accented a gold tooth punctuating an enormous smile.

"Pasqualli?"

"Yes, yes. Senor Hawkins I believe. Mario has telephoned me. Come to my office just a few short blocks. You must have a cup of matte de coca,* it will help you adjust to the elevation. Come, my son Renaldo will claim your fabulous bicycle. Yes, yes, my friend Mario has told me about your absolutely fabulous adventure."

I handed over my freight claim check to Pasqualli's son, a lad of about 14-years old who hadn't said a word, but I could tell my bike would be fetched up properly. While sipping my cup of matte de coca in his office, Pasqualli informed me he could arrange a tour of the Inca trail for me that would include train fares, a guide, llama pack train,

*Coca is the plant cocaine is derived from. Peruvians have long chewed it's leaves to help against high altitude affects.

and a cook. This four-day deluxe excursion, including one night's hotel accommodation in Cusco, would cost a mere $130.

Without even thinking about shopping around or asking for something in writing, I plunked down the money and made a reservation. It may be extravagant, I told myself, but I'd been looking forward to visiting Machu Picchu for over ten years, besides this would be my Christmas present to myself. I looked up from my coca tea to see Renaldo push my bike up in front of the office. After a quick inspection I was relieved to find it was in good shape with nothing broken or missing.

A few minutes later, using Pasqualli's telephone, I dialed Jan Olsen, the Swede I'd met a few days earlier. Not only did Jan confirm that he had a storage spot for my bike, additionally he told me I was welcome to stay at his home. Pasqualli insisted that Renaldo escort me to Jan's house, located but a few blocks away. Those few blocks however, were uphill, so Renaldo's help with the bike was greatly appreciated. Although I was only carrying my backpack I quickly felt the effects of walking up the steep, cobblestone streets at 12,500' to Jan's place. In fact, I was breathless when at last I climbed the two sets of stairs to his second story apartment. With Jan and Renaldo's help we carried bike and gear upstairs. Before leaving, Renaldo promised to meet me at 6 a.m. at Jan's and escort me to the station to catch the early train to Cusco.

Jan's wife Betsy, who worked at the local bank, would be home at 2 p.m. to join us for an early dinner. In the meantime Jan kept busy with work on his computer and minding their two children, 1 1/2-year old Christian and 1-month old Fleming. While Jan was occupied I stowed my bike in the spare room and gathered together all the clothes and equipment I planned to take with me to Machu Picchu.

Afterward, Jan and I sat at the kitchen table drinking tea and talking. Jan brought me up to date on the Gulf crisis, which he'd been following with BBC reports on his short wave radio.

Jan, a doctoral candidate in environmental resource management was working on various community projects to improve health standards in rural Peruvian villages. Later that year, he would have to return to Sweden to complete requirements for his dissertation. Betsy, his wife of three years arrived home from work in mid-after-noon. After meeting me, she checked on the children, then served us a hearty soup of meat, corn, vegetables, and rice. That night I slept soundly on a mattress in the front room.

I awoke at 5 a.m. groggy from too much sleep and too much ele-vation. In the dark I scrambled about as quietly as possible, rolling up my sleeping bag and cramming gear into my backpack until it was near bursting. Emerging from the bathroom off the kitchen, I found Jan heating water for coffee. He sent me across the street to the neighborhood baker for a dozen rolls fresh from the oven. He wanted me to take half of the rolls on my trip to Machu Picchu.

At 6 a.m. I opened the front door, looked down in the street just filling with early morning sunlight and there was Renaldo waiting at the foot of the stairs. I shook hands with Jan and told him I'd be back in about seven days, if all went smoothly. Walking down the steep cobbled street, with Renaldo leading the way, we headed for the train depot. Without the usual crowd of seething, boiling humanity, Renaldo led me through the station waiting room directly to the railroad car, showed me to my assigned seat, then handed me my ticket and a letter of introduction to Victor Herrera of Gold Tours in Cusco. Victor, Renaldo explained before leaving, would meet the train in Cusco.

~ ~ ~

The Inca Trail

Sitting half-comatose by the window I heard the familiar gay ban-tering of the Italian women I'd met on the train from Arequipa. Their vivaciousness was a welcome tonic after the grimness of the locals. By a stroke of good luck, the train departed only one hour late. As soon as we began rocking and rolling north to Cusco, a waiter staggered skillfully down the aisle with a tray on his shoulder, looking more like a professional tightrope walker than a waiter. Acknowledging my signal for a cup of coffee with a raised eyebrow, he adroitly placed a cup and saucer on a rickety table in front of me then miraculously filled my cup to the rim without spilling a drop. During his ministrations, the car bucked and heaved as though trying to go airborne, and for all I knew it just might have any second.

Attempting to lift the cup to my mouth was a bit like playing pin-the-tail-on-the-donkey during an earthquake. The quantity of liquid spilled was greater than that which reached my mouth, much to the detriment of my shirt and pants. Undaunted and hungering for my morning caffeine I grasped the cup in two hands, lowered my head to just inches above the table, then with some clumsiness managed to capture a mouthful of coffee. During all of this elaborate juggling a Swiss couple seated across from me watched with interest and no little amusement. While a trickle of coffee ran down my chin I smiled back at them and shrugged my shoulders. Uttering a sigh of resignation I decided to forego my customary second cup.

The train had steadily chugged its way across the high plateau up into the terraced valleys north of Titicaca, wending its way beside the turbulent Rio Vilcabamba. Dense columns of Eucalyptus trees lined the river near several villages we passed. Along the way we dropped a few thousand feet in elevation, this signaled by the raging river and the emergence of lush semi-tropical vegetation. At every new vista the Italian women would point and squeal with glee and shout superlatives while clapping. "Bellesima," "Que Bella," they chortled.

How we arrived punctually at 7 p.m. in Cusco I'll never know. Unlike Ishmael who I'd been following from New Bedford, Massachusetts to the rolling decks of the Pequod, I paced the aisle desperate to plant my feet on terra firma. The train eased into the Cusco station with a load of fidgeting passengers. At the head of the line I searched the darkened trackside area for Victor Herrera without the slightest idea of what he looked like. Out of the shadows stepped a well-dressed Latino who grabbed my arm.

"Senor Hawkins," he inquired.

"Si," I stammered, "You must be Victor."

"Come we must hurry onto the bus."

Which we did promptly, but not promptly enough to get a seat. The Italians clamored on behind me laughing like High School freshmen on a field trip.

At the Plaza des Armas in the center of Cusco most of the passengers, including Victor and I, disembarked and scurried off to claim rooms at various hotels nearby. Entering the Hotel Conquistador, Victor pulled me aside to a table in the lobby and ordered a cup of matte de coca with the usual endorsement, "for the elevation."

Although I'd have preferred a bottle of beer I sipped the matte and asked, "I thought I had a room reserved at the Hotel Suecia?"

"No, there are no rooms available there," he said pushing a hotel registration form in front of me. "You will like the accommodations here much better."

"But Pasquilli assured me I'd have a room at the Hotel Suecia."

"Yes, yes, but they are booked. It happens all the time. Please, I will take care of everything."

A few sips of matte later, Victor took my completed form and ushered me upstairs where the Senora showed us to a room that was obviously occupied by the Italian women from the train, who were in the midst of showering and changing clothes. They laughed uproariously while pushing Victor and me back into the hallway. The Senora, with eyes downcast, told Victor to wait while she opened another room with her passkey only to find it occupied as well. She dragged us back and forth, up and down, until a single room was discovered and I was wearily ensconced there. But before I could even use the toilet for a much-needed bath, Victor herded me back to the lobby for another matte de coca. Limp from hunger and fatigue I sipped the matte and looked over at Victor who seemed preoccupied and kept glancing around and clearing his throat.

"Senor, ah, Hawkins, about the Inca trail tour…"

"Yes."

"I regret…it has been cancelled."

I almost spit the matte on the table. "Cancelled! But I paid in advance, here's my voucher."

"Unfortunately, due to the sickness of the other 'personas' the tour has been cancelled. There is no need to get upset."

It took a few minutes for his news brief to sink in. Rather than pound my fists on the table and throw my cup of matte across the room, I pushed myself slowly away from the table and stood up.

"I'm going to my room to take a shower. Then I'm going to a restaurant for dinner."

"Senor Hawkins, I assure you I will arrange everything. Yes, you will have your Inca Trail tour."

"Fine, fine. I'll meet you back here at 11 p.m. and we will discuss your arrangements. But, either I get my Inca Trail tour or I want a refund."

"As you wish, I will guarantee that I will arrange everything to your absolute satisfaction."

I turned to go up to my room when the Italian women came skipping down the stairs, singing and laughing. They waved with disgusting cheerfulness as they raced past me out into the street catching up Victor in their wake.

Just around the corner from the hotel I almost fell into an Italian restaurant located in an arched portico facing the Plaza des Armas. While inhaling a beer and munching bread a seven-piece Peruvian folk band assembled next to my table. Instead of candlelight and silence my head was soon throbbing with the melodic sounds and rhythms of zamponas, guitars, drums, and flutes. In all a none-too-subtle reminder of the botched plans for the Inca trail. I wondered if Hiram Bingham, credited with rediscovering Machu Picchu in 1911, experienced similar problems in his quest for the fabled Inca redoubt.

Native folk music or no, I fell to my meal of lasagna with gusto. Afterward, numbed by a second bottle of Cuscuenia beer (brewed

locally, but owned by German brewmeisters) I sat back to enjoy the
music just as the concert ended.

Walking back to the hotel I girded myself for a confrontation with
Victor of what I'd come to call "No Tours, Ltd." The way I envisioned
it our brief but heated meeting would end with my demand for a full
refund. I was so frustrated I even entertained a fleeting thought of
returning to Puno without my trip to Machu Picchu. But deep inside I
knew I would have to overcome my ambivalence and muster all latent
forces of tenacity and determination to achieve my long sought after
goal, knowing full well I'd probably never get another chance to visit
Machu Picchu again.

Back in the lobby of the Hotel Conquistador I pondered the irony of
my situation, i.e. wasn't I like one of the naive peasants bilked and
subdued by a handful of Spanish equestrians a few hundred years in
the past? Surely, Victor had some of that exploitive Spanish blood
coursing through his entrepreneurial veins.

Fifteen minutes late, Victor pushed his way into the lobby. He
slipped silently into a chair across from me determined not to make
eye contact.

"Senor Hawkins, I have good news."

"You mean the tour is on?"

"Yes, but…"

"But what!"

"There will be no llamas."

"Okay."

"…and there will be no cook."

"Uh-huh."

"And it will not be a complete tour."

"Please Victor, exactly what will the tour include?"

"I have arranged for a guide. He will accompany you to Machu
Picchu. You will have the partial tour."

"But I paid $130 for a complete tour with llamas, cook, porters, and
a guide"

"For an additional $50 I can arrange that."

"No, if you can't provide what I paid for I want a full refund."

"I've already arranged for a guide. Also, you will have two nights accommodations at Machu Picchu and your train tickets are included."

"And I want one night's accommodation at the Hotel Suecia when I return to Cusco," I bargained.

"Yes, I will arrange that."

"OK. When do I leave for Machu Picchu?"

"I will meet you here at 6 a.m. tomorrow with your guide."

"Alright, it's a deal. I'll see you a 6 a.m. Goodnight Victor."

"Perhaps a matte de coca before you retire?"

"No thanks, I'm exhausted. I'll see you in the morning, here, 6 a.m. Correct?"

"As you wish. Buenos Noches."

I awoke promptly at 5 a.m., took a shower, then arranged my backpack. Pacing back and forth in the lobby, the nightclerk snoring behind a newspaper, I wished to hell I could get a cup of real coffee. The endless cups of matte de coca if anything had soured my stomach. "Matte,mate,matte. Jesus," I muttered. At precisely 6 a.m. I pushed my way through the lobby door into the dark, narrow street. Not ten feet away sat the dark hulking silhouette of a Peruvian Army personnel carrier looking for all the world like it had run out of gas or been abandoned. Two not unreasonable possibilities.

The street was silent and empty of people. With no Victor in sight, I returned to the lobby. By now, accustomed to the tardiness of Latin Americans, I glanced at my watch, estimating that Victor would arrive closer to 6:30 a.m. As things usually went that would be considered prompt.

At 6:45 a.m. I stormed into the street fuming. Five more minutes and I'd go up to my room and go back to bed, I swore. Then out of the shadows two men approached at a lively pace. One of them I recognized as Victor.

"Senor, where have you been," he asked excitedly.

"Where have I been? We agreed to meet right here at 6 a.m. It's nearly 7 a.m."

"But Senor we were supposed to meet at my office and now it is late. The train leaves at 7 a.m."

"Victor, it's now 7:05 a.m."

"Yes, all the more reason to hurry, please get your backpack. And where is the taxi?"

"Taxi, what the hell do you mean taxi."

"Hurry Senor Hawkins we haven't a moment to spare. I don't understand why you didn't have the taxi waiting as we agreed."

I ran into the lobby seething and grabbed my pack inside the door. Jesus, I needed a good cup of coffee. Outside I was about to ask Victor why he hadn't hailed a cab, when one screeched to a halt beside us. A female tour guide bustled inside where I could hear her tongue-lashing the desk clerk. Victor grabbed me and pushed me into the cab along with his companion. He pressed a handful of intis into the driver's outstretched palm as the tires squealed and we raced off, presumably, to the train station.

Careering through the streets it suddenly occurred to me that I hadn't the slightest idea who the other person was, or why he accompanied us. At length, Victor piped up.

"Excuse me , Senor Hawkins, permit me to introduce you to your guide, Cosme Guiterrez."

Cosme, dressed in running shoes, slacks, and sweater looked like he was on his way to school rather than a three-day trek in the mountains. We rode in silence. My nerves were stretched to the breaking point. I couldn't help wonder if I was really setting out on a trek to Machu Picchu or being taken hostage by the Sendero Luminoso. Who cared, I lamented silently, as long as I could get a cafe cortado I'd be content. The narrow gauge train, stained and disfigured with years of use and abuse was sitting beside the station, the throbbing diesel engine filling the air with smoke and fumes.

Victor lead us through the packed lobby waving tickets at guards who stepped aside to allow us access to the loading platform. Cosme and I scrambled at his heels, until at last Victor found the first class Pullman car. Pushing us up the steps, as though we were distant relatives who outstayed their welcome, he handed the train tickets and itinerary to Cosme and slipped away. Sensing the train would not depart for another hour, I persuaded Cosme to accompany me to the nearest snack bar where I purchased cafe cortados for both of us. When the caffeine finally percolated to my brain I began to relax and question Cosme regarding the particulars of our forthcoming trek. I was pleasantly surprised to learn he was both a University student steeped in the lore of the Inca civilization and a leader of dozens of tours to Machu Picchu. Also, he was part Quechua, speaking both Spanish and Quechua fluently. His English was near fluent as well.

Back in our reserved seats in the Pullman car he outlined our trek plans while the car filled with other tourists. The train groaned its way up the steep tracks out of the bowl in which Cusco is situated. Once over the ridge we descended at a rapid pace into the Vilcanotta/ Urubamba Valley where we enjoyed spectacular views of the Urubamba River and a feast of semi-tropical plants and flowers surpassing anything I'd seen in Peru so far. When the train came to a stop a few hours later in Aguas Caliente we descended to a dirt path beside the tracks, surrounded on both sides with cafes and mercados catering to tourists. We immediately repaired to a small cafe where I ordered up coffee and a breakfast of pancakes and eggs. Cosme ordered a cup of tea and watched with amusement as I dispatched a plate-sized pancake.

"I never saw pancakes before, they were unknown here until so many American tourists started coming here in the '60's. Now there are few Americans and many Europeans. But, still there are pancakes. I wonder about this." Cosme philosophized as I ate.

I didn't feel like burdening Cosme with the negative travel advisories disseminated by the State Department warning Americans about the real dangers of rebel terrorists calling themselves the Sendero Luminoso or Shining Path; nevermind drug traffickers, and cholera epidemics. Then too there was the volatile state of Peruvian politics, not to mention a depressed economy. Yes Cosme, contemplate pancakes, these other matters are not for chaps like us.

After purchasing bread, fruit, and canned foods at a railside mercado, we began a pleasant hike up the railroad tracks along the Urubamba River. I wondered if the river could be rafted, but doubted it. At least at this time of year the river raged through narrow stone canyons and around towering boulders. From my viewpoint, any navigation would be classed as attempted suicide.

We stopped to rest a few minutes before crossing the iron bridge spanning the Urubamba. A few hundred yards on the other side of the bridge Cosme and I began a steep climb up a narrow trail, some 2,000' to Machu Picchu. Halfway up the trail, Cosme volunteered to shoulder my pack, leaving me to carry my oversized fanny pack crammed with camera, binoculars, and rain gear. Leap-frogging up the trail we were forced to grab onto rocks and roots to pull ourselves along. At half my size, Cosme scrambled and leaped upward with undiminished enthusiasm, giving not a thought to the 40-lb backpack weighing him down. Suddenly the trail spilled out onto a curving dirt road named after Yale professor and Machu Picchu discoverer Hiram Bingham, which would be used later that morning by the tour buses ferrying visitors to the world renown Inca site. Until then we shared trail and road with only a handful of other hardy trekkers. When finally achieving the plateau we stopped to fill our water bottles outside the visitor's center, which at that hour was deserted.

At the stone arched entrance gate to the ruins, Cosme advised me to go ahead of him while he took care of the tickets, for some odd reason he didn't want me around during the transaction, which I guessed had something to do with a discount. I was more than agreeable to his request because it enabled me to be the first and only visitor to the ruins that morning. What a beautiful morning it was-sunny, warm, with cotton-candy clouds forming on distant peaks.

I strolled down the stone pathway awestruck and mesmerized. Ahead I could see the high-peaked, thatch-roofed stone houses, brilliant green swaths of lawn lining the narrow alleys between houses, and massive stone walls surrounding them. All was silent. Second only to a visit to Notre Dame cathedral in Paris, this historic and mysterious mountain peak emitted an aura of spiritualism. In the background loomed the precipitous peak of Huayna Picchu (Young Mountain), a mighty sentinel standing watch over its kin, flat-topped Machu Picchu (Old Mountain) 1000' below. On either steep side of the Inca ruins the mountain fell away to the tumultuous Riobamba—approximately 2,000' below.

It was everything I'd ever read about (Hiram Bingham to Paul Theroux) and more. I sat down on a rock on a hill overlooking the ruins to drink in this visual feast and absorb the ambiance. My first impressions were of incredible spiritual power, tranquility, and of unequaled natural beauty. It was the most powerful place I'd visited in my life. At last I saw Cosme trudging slowly up the path with my backpack. Now I understood why he'd sent me ahead, while he secured our entrance passes. He had allowed me a singular first impression of the most personal, unencumbered kind. When he reached my observation point I motioned for him to put the pack down and rest. Handing him my bottle of water, he took a long swig then passed it back.

"Do you ever get tired of coming here?"

Cosme looked around a bit then turned to look directly at me, his eyes like black marbles.

"This is my home. It always welcomes me. You have felt it, no."

I shook my head. I knew exactly what he meant.

"Come," he said,"I want to explain a few important things before the tourist buses arrive. When they come we will begin our trek up there," he said pointing at Huayna Picchu.

I looked up at the steep, green peak in the background and winced. From my vantagepoint it looked near vertical and promised to be a challenge.

Standing beside the Hitching Post of the Sun, a massive flat-topped boulder approximately 20' x 20' with a squared-off column nearly centered in the mass of granite, Cosme explained how Inca priests had used it as a sundial for calculating the appropriate time to plant and harvest crops on the terraced hillsides, where every inch of soil was used to cultivate corn, potatoes and other crops, many of which are now extinct.

As the sun beat down on us from a sky partially filled with billowing clouds, I realized that even though I'd done a fair bit of research on Machu Picchu it was inadequate compared to the information Cos had presented. When the tourist buses started arriving, Cos suggested it was time to stretch our legs by climbing Huayna Picchu the steep, green-mantled peak looming above us on the north side of the ruins. Still shouldering my pack, Cos lead the way up the step narrow trail. Occasionally we'd have to climb up rope or bamboo ladders to advance. Every few hundred feet we'd stop to look down at the ruins below us which seemed to shrink as we climbed higher and higher.

At last achieving the summit, after precarious scrambles up a shear rock face to the pinnacle of Huayna Picchu, we sat down to enjoy one of the most spectacular views I've ever witnessed. Below us, perhaps 1,000 feet, lay the sparkling granite structures of Machu Picchu, the jewel in the crown of the Inca civilization. Silently, I thanked God the Conquistadors hadn't discovered the Inca redoubt; if they had I'd probably be looking down on soaring church steeples and red tile roofs.

Also, we could look down and observe the roaring Rio Urubamba speed its way through a horseshoe curve at the base of Huayna Picchu then like a giant boa constrictor head southwest into steep, jungle-covered mountains. When I looked over at Cosme he was shaking his head.

"What's wrong," I asked

"Oh, I was just thinking what a shame it is that the Incas did not have a written language. Of course they had a rich oral history, but that has been lost."

Cosme was silent a moment, then he pointed down at Machu Picchu.

"You know, we may never know for sure what the ruins really are."

After a meager lunch conjured up from the depths of my backpack, Cos suggested that we backtrack halfway down the trail and strike out on a secondary trail leading to the infrequently visited Temple of the Moon in the jungle depths west of Huayna Picchu.

"One hour of hiking, maybe two and you'll see a fascinating Inca ruin few tourists visit. There is much jungle and possibly a few snakes," Cos said.

"Why isn't it visited much," I asked snapping on my fanny pack.

"A difficult trail. Only experienced hikers should attempt it. When we return to Machu Picchu the tourists will be gone and I will conclude the historical perspective I began earlier," Cos said like a university professor.

The trail, narrow and steep, dropped almost straight into the jungle, cool and shady, but not before we encountered more bamboo and rope ladders slowing our descent.

Another Inca ceremonial site, the Temple of the Moon is fashioned from the bowels of an enormous cave. As Cos predicted we were the only visitors. In the cool interior of the cave, Cos pointed out wall niches where mummified bodies or sacrificial offerings had been displayed during religious ceremonies. Not in any way comparable to the ruins above us, Temple of the Moon provided a peaceful setting in which to rest and mull over the things I'd seen and digest the copious information provided by Cosme. At this time I wanted to take full advantage of this stop, knowing the trek back up to Machu Picchu, being mostly uphill, would be arduous. Regardless of the elevation and amount of hiking I'd done in the past two days I was feeling quite strong. My feet were in excellent shape thanks to the pair of lightweight hiking boots I'd been carrying since Alaska.

Though my gastrointestinal system had been subjected to a broad spectrum of new parasites and foreign microorganisms it was functioning perfectly. I guessed that by this late date I'd achieved a true road-tested stomach comparable to that of a vulture. Just as I was about to snooze in my carved rock seat in the cave, Cos shook my shoulder. With the backpack strapped on his wiry body he coaxed me back on the trail.

Figure 14: The incomparable Machu Picchu.

After an intensive historical overview delivered nonstop by Cosme, covering the Temple of the Condor, Inca religious training and ceremonies, art, athletics, and a dozen other subjects, we prepared to head down the stone trail to Winay Wayna, a restored tambo on the Inca trail six miles south of Machu Picchu. Halfway up the trail leading to a small Inca guard station, under restoration, in a saddle above Machu Picchu Cosme again motioned me to proceed while he stopped to talk with an amiable security guard patrolling the perimeter of the ruins.

From my observation point at the restoration site I looked back at the ruins spread out before me like an impressionistic chess set. I removed my binoculars and scanned the plateau watching the sun reflect off dressed granite boulders, many weighing over a ton.* I could also look down at the ever-raging Urubamba River. Hearing a noise

* The heaviest boulders weigh 9 tons (18,000 lbs). How these were moved up 2000' cliffs & into position is still not known anymore than how they were shaped into perfect mortarless joints.

behind me I turned to see a lone backpacker climb slowly up the last stone steps to the saddle.

"Hello," I said when he stopped nearby to rest and enjoy the view.

"Why that's bloody handsome," he said looking down at Machu Picchu.

"Did you hike in from Winay Wayna?"

"Yeah, camped near the ruins, but would a kipped up at the hostel had I known it was there. You headed there?"

"You bet. Me and my guide will stay there tonight. How was the trail?"

"Not as bad as I expected. Rain made it a bit dicey in spots, otherwise it was glorious," the Brit said with a huge smile.

For a brief moment my mind conjured up images of llamas, cooks, and porters.

"Any trouble on the trail?"

"If ya mean robbers, no. Hardly saw another soul, 'cept two other trekkers. Only thing you gotta keep watch for is the vipers. Give'em enough advanced warning and they clear out fast enough." The Brit said cinching down the straps of his pack and pushing himself to his feet.

"Have a good day," I said as he began his descent to the ruins.

Shortly, Cosme appeared and immediately launched into a history lesson regarding the frequent appearance of tambos, about every six miles, along the Inca Trail. These way stations, according to Cosme, were used by sojourner and soldier alike to rest, obtain food and water, also as relay points for Inca runners carrying messages throughout the far-flung Inca empire, whose northern capital, at one time, was Quito, Ecuador some 1500 miles away.

Descending the saddle onto the trail we followed the narrow winding path across the eastern flank of the jungle-covered mountain on our way to Winay Wayna. The trail navigated through thick foliage affording cool, pleasant hiking. Occasionally, we'd pass a wide spot in the trail fortified with slabs of rock similar to those used when the Incas first constructed the trail. Cosme explained Inca travelers used these wide spots to allow llama pack trains easy passage on the trail, which in many areas along the steep mountainside narrowed to as much as two feet. I could understand how these "turnouts" would be helpful. In a few spots where landslides had washed out sections of the track small bridges of cut bamboo or slender trees spanned the gap. In other places crude ladders were placed to assist trekkers in negotiating steep ascents and descents.

Generally, we were able to maintain consistent elevation along the mountainside and at many places I could look out across the valley to the high peaks to the east or straight down into the wild Urubamba River. At mid-afternoon after many rest stops to sightsee we rounded a bend in the trail and there was the roof of the hostel. Only accessible by the Inca trail to guests, the hostel was a welcome relief to many a hiker who'd spent a day or two on the rainy, muddy trail. Not only was it spacious and designed to fit into the jungle surrounding it, but hot meals and beverages were available.

After stowing our gear in a dorm-style room, we walked out onto the terrace to see thunderclouds descend from the peaks towering above us to unleash torrents of rain. With leg muscles tingling I followed Cosme into our dorm for a welcome siesta. When I woke up one hour later, Cosme was snoring enthusiastically.

Sitting in the lounge writing in my journal I began to smell the subtle aromas of food being cooked somewhere in the Hostel. Checking my watch to discover it was past 6 p.m. I wondered what had become of Cosme, so I returned to our room to find him curled up in his blankets fast asleep. Knowing he needed a hot meal more than I did, I finally succeeded in waking him up and report dinner was being served. Soon enough he joined me in the empty dining room. We were served steaming bowls of pasta, vegetables, potatoes, and chunks of meat, plus the traditional cups of matte de coca. After mopping up our bowls with chunks of bread, we persuaded the Senora to supply us with a second helping, which was dispatched with the same speed and relish as the first.

Cosme woke me up next morning at 6 a.m. with assurances of fresh coffee in the dining room. After breakfast and three cups of real coffee, we made our way down to the ruins a few hundred yards from the hostel. Early morning mists cleared the peaks surrounding the ruins allowing brilliant sunlight to lash down at the orderly, symmetrically positioned stone buildings of Winay Wayna. Only half the size of Machu Picchu it was, nevertheless, an impressive edifice, particularly since it was built on a steep jungle-covered mountainside. Hundreds of tons of expertly dressed rocks and boulders had somehow been moved and fitted together to form a compound of a dozen buildings. They sparkled in the sun like diamonds, a thick growth of vines, assorted trees, and bushes, having been recently cleared from the walkways around the buildings.

Now stripped of their high pitched thatched roofs, they were nevertheless monuments to a civilization whose enterprise and skill were dispersed throughout much of South America.

Down at the lower border of the ruins I looked up the steep stone walkway to see a half-dozen young Peruvians advancing toward me with machetes. Alarmed, I turned to ask Cos for guidance, concerned I was being ambushed by a band of Sendero Luminoso, the guerrilla army that had been terrorizing Peru for years. Fearing I was about to lose my wallet or perhaps my life, I was poised to make a run for it when Cos appeared out of nowhere smiling and waving at the machete-wielders.

"They are government workers," he said, "they clear away the jungle from the ruins and make improvements on the trails. If they didn't it would be covered again in a few months."

I felt the muscles in my chest and shoulders relax, barely avoiding a sigh of relief.

Winay Wayna, according to Cos, was a major tambo along the Inca trail, stretching from Cusco to Quito, Ecuador. Travelers, traders, and soldiers as well as their beasts of burden, llamas, found temporary shelter, plus food and water at tambos like Winay Wayna. Usually spaced at six-mile intervals, the tambos were also convenient resupply points and rest stops for the runners who traversed the Inca trail delivering messages throughout the empire.

On the trail back to Machu Picchu I saw a snake draped across the path. Giving it plenty of warning in the form of rock kicking and whistling I was more than a little disappointed when it refused to give me the right of way. Approaching the 3-foot long green and yellow body, with my hiking staff at the ready, I wondered why it refused to move. A closer inspection revealed a sharp slash below its head, apparently delivered by one of the machete-wielders now hacking away at the ever-encroaching jungle at the ruins. What irony I thought, instead of interlopers lusting after my dollars and Casio watch, one of those men may have saved my life by dispatching this potentially lethal snake.

Arriving back at Machu Picchu at 9 a.m. we again had the ruins to ourselves, save for a few security guards patrolling the area. Starting at the Temple of the Sun we began another walking tour and history lesson of the Inca civilization. Cosme footnoted his lecture with comments regarding the inability of the Spanish to find Machu Picchu, as well as speculation about El Dorado, the fabled lost City of Gold, which Cos believed was located somewhere in the depths of the eastern cordillera waiting to be discovered.

We stopped for a rest at the Temple of the Condor, a stone monolith fashioned from a gigantic granite slab, which with a little imagination could be recognized as the outstretched wings of a condor, one of the world's largest birds. About 1 p.m. my head throbbing with facts and speculation we began a weary descent on the trail back to Aquas Caliente where a soft bed, hot meal, and soak in the hot springs awaited.

Upon our arrival there the first item on our agenda was a couple of 1/2-liter bottles of Cuscuena beer at a cafe near our pensione. A few doors up the calle, Cos had secured rooms for us at the newly refurbished Pensione Imasumac (what beautiful in Quechua) owned by friends of his. After a shower we repaired to our room for a well-deserved siesta. Much later, we grabbed our towels and soap and hiked a few blocks further up the Calle to the public hot springs for a bath and soak.

Under a clear sky sparkling with constellations, I submerged my body up to the neck and began to feel the tightness and soreness of muscles dissipate. Soaking and watching heads bobbing in the water like so many apples in a barrel of water I looked up to see three Japanese fellows lower themselves into the steaming water. As they passed me one of the trio looked at me with surprise. I stared back thinking this can't be.

"George, is that you?" the Japanese fellow called.

Instantly I recognized Yugi Ataka, a motorcyclist I'd shared a room with in Chachabui, Colombia. In short order I learned Yugi made it safely to Quito, couldn't find the residencia I'd recommended, but did contact the South American Explorer's Club and later made a successful climb of Cotopaxi. To my surprise Yuji liked Quito. Before rejoining his friends we made plans to meet for pizza and beer later that evening at a small restaurant a few doors from the Imasumac pensione. Minutes later, Cos motioned to me from the side of the pool.

"It is time Jorge. You must not stay in too long."

"You're right of course, but it does feel great."

"Come along we'll get dressed."

"Hey, Yuji and his friends are going to meet us for dinner."

Next morning, knotted calve muscles still protesting, I followed Cos down the calle to the train tracks.

"Cos please slow down." I petitioned.

"If you want a seat we must hurry."

"The only thing we must absolutely do is stop for coffee."

"Jorge, you drink much coffee."

"It helps me adjust to the altitude, avoid the dreaded soroche."

"Ah, you sound suspiciously humorous."

"You mean like I'm putting you on?"

"Si. When you joke you are feeling good. Verdad?"

"Si, muy verdad."

"Jorge that of course is not correct, but again you have suspicions of humor."

"Verdad, verdad."

As I drank my second cup of thick Peruvian coffee Cos tugged at my sleeve and pointed to the locals and tourists swarming onto the train.

"I told you we should have left the hotel earlier." I joked.

"In that case Jorge, you would have been sleepwalking."

As Cos predicted we did not get seats, so were forced to stand crammed in the aisle like sardines amongst locals holding boxes, sacks and assorted bundles. Despite the congestion in the aisle vendors with trays or baskets of fruit, empanadas, candy, soft drinks and other items managed to miraculously negotiate the aisle, all the while hawking their goods, making change, and generally looking like this was a normal way to conduct business. Oddly, I suppose it was.

Cosme cautioned me to keep my eyes open and stay close to him just in case a pickpocket lurked nearby. As an added precaution I kept my two fanny packs secured about my stomach with one hand on them at all times, the rocking and rolling of the train and the coming and going of vendors notwithstanding.

We detrained along with many locals at Ollantaytambo, the former Inca administrative and municipal center of the Urubamba Valley. Cos immediately set off for the ruins at the edge of town with me in tow. Perhaps larger than Machu Picchu, but less magnificent, it was impressive nonetheless. Cos pointed out some castle like stone structures on the hillside southeast of the village where, he commented, Incas stored a five-year supply of food as a hedge against natural disasters and the vagaries of war. Just as a light rain started, my stomach reminded me not so gently that I hadn't supplied it with breakfast. I listened inattentively to a continuation of Cosme's epic history lesson, taking every opportunity to sit down and massage my throbbing calves. Balking at another chance to climb a ladder-like stone staircase, I wondered aloud what one might find by way of food and drink in the sleepy village below us.

With a sigh reminiscent of one of my college professors, Cos concluded his history lecture then stomped down the path to the village. Along the way he pointed out that the stone houses we were passing, laid out with the symmetry and precision of a California housing tract, were originally the residences of chief Inca administrators.

In a small cafe on the main square I gobbled up a plate of eggs and vegetables suspiciously similar to a Denver omelet, served with bread and coffee. I was thinking of informing Cos, as politely as possible, that I could not absorb another fact or piece of information when he pushed his cup of tea aside and looked at me.

"Now we will board a collectivo and return to Cusco, unless you would rather visit another tambo just south of here."

"I think you're right, it's time to head back to Cusco."

~ ~ ~

In Cusco at the Chez Maggy restaurant later that night I met Cosme for a celebration pizza dinner and a few liters of beer. Eating like a prisoner concluding a hunger strike I expressed my gratitude for his rich, informative interpretation of the ruins we visited and for his fellowship along the way, adding that my visit to Machu Picchu had been one of the highlights of my bike tour, perhaps of my life.

"Now you can die a happy man. Verdad?" Cos smiled.

"Muy verdad." I grinned.

~ ~ ~

The Island of Taquile

The womb of mankind. That's what the native Aymara Indians believe Lake Titicaca to be. If it's not the highest lake in the world at 12,500' it's damn close. It measures 110 miles long and 40 miles wide at the widest point and there are many islands in the lake. One of them is the island of Taquile, the island of weavers. From Puno it's 21-miles out in the vastness of Lake Titicaca. Today it's home to about 200 Quechua Indians, descendants of the Incas, who support themselves mainly by weaving incredibly complex, colorful pieces of clothing on antiquated hand looms.

They believe, as did their ancestors, that the Sun God Inti created the first Incas, Manco Capac and his sister, Mama Ocllo. Inti instructed them to wander the land and show man how to live off the fruits of the earth. According to legend Inti came to life on the Island of the Sun, some 100 miles south, in Bolivia.

Figure 15: Island of Taquile on Lake Titcaca.

There are a few Inca ruins on the Island of Taquile. In addition to weaving, Inca descendants make a living by farming and fishing, and by letting a few tourists rent adobe huts from them. There are no telephones, no automobiles, no television, no fast food restaurants, no shopping malls—the list of "no's" is almost endless. What does Taquile have a lot off? Peace and quiet. If you've ever wanted to live for a few days in an environment fairly comparable to a sensory deprivation tank then Taquile is the ticket.

The motor launch that brought me and a dozen other tourists and locals to the island took three and a half hours to navigate the cobalt blue waters of the lake. When the boat hove to at the stone pier, I could see the path, built with flat stepping stones, wind its way 300 yards to the top of the cliff where the main village was located. There the village elder met and welcomed us to the island, then directed us to the small stone and adobe farmhouses where we would stay.

At an elevation of 12, 507' hiking the trail up to the village was a slow, tortuous affair filled with frequent stops to catch my breath and allow the blood to circulate, ever so slowly, to my protesting limbs. Which, I might add, were still feeling the effects of my three-day hike on the Inca trail.

When I arrived at a small farmhouse a middle-aged man showed me to an even smaller adobe cottage with a thatched roof. Dressed in traditional clothes of hat with drooping sash, cotton shirt with colorful woven vest, white pantaloons secured with a woven purple waist sash, and feet clad in sandals, he vanished without a word when we arrived at the cottage. The silence was palpable and not at all displeasing. Inside the cottage I dropped my backpack on the hard-packed dirt floor then eased my body onto a straw mattress secured to an adobe platform that was part of the wall. Supplied with three wool blankets the bed proved extremely comfortable. As there were no windows, the open wooden entrance door supplied the only light. Situated far out on the lake at over 12,000' I knew the nights would be cool, more so because among one of many things Taquile didn't have, it didn't have conventional heating appliances. The few stands of Eucalyptus trees on the island would have been decimated thousands of years ago had the natives resorted to burning the wood in hearth fires, rather than relying on wool blankets and hearty constitutions. Cooking had been done for many years on propane stoves.

Though Spartan my small bungalow, with adobe walls two or three feet thick and a ceiling height of barely seven feet, was homey. I pulled my Mini-Mag flashlight from my pack and tied it off on one of the poles supporting the thatched roof. With these domestic chores accomplished I stretched out for a siesta. My eyes were barely closed when I heard shuffling and muffled voices outside the cottage. Thinking perhaps Frank and Mike, two other Americans I shared the boat ride with, had come by to visit, I pulled on my boots and clomped to the doorway. Squinting into the bright sunlight I saw what looked like two shoeless, grinning, dark-skinned Smurfs, faces smudged with dirt and black hair falling to their shoulders. They stared at me with dark saucer-like eyes. I said hello, but they remained silent and immobile. Suddenly I remembered the bag of hard rock candy Jan advised me to bring along for occasions just like this. Begging was forbidden, but who was to say that a five or six-year old with a sweet tooth and a little patience couldn't accept one or two pieces of candy.

As soon as the barefoot little girl in faded cotton dress heard the crinkle of cellophane her doughy dark mouth spread into a crooked smile. The Smurfs accepted two pieces of candy each but stood their ground until I sat down on a flat rock just outside the cottage and popped a piece of candy in my mouth. Instantly a piece of candy was stuffed into their mouths. I watched ballooning cheeks palpitate and splayed toes dig into the rocky soil of the yard. And then as if responding to a distant call of pipes, heard only by Smurf ears, they tumbled over the rock wall and disappeared.

Figure 16: The candy monster of Taquile Island.

I stood up to discover the cottage door had blown shut, which ordinarily would not have been a problem, except this cottage door was equipped with a handcarved wooden draw bolt and lock with a wooden key suspended from the lock. In addition to feeling tired and sluggish my nose was running and my throat was sore. When I finally figured out how to operate the lock and open the door, I gulped some Aspirin and fell back into the wool blankets for a nap. After what seemed like hours I opened my eyes. Forcing my legs over the side of the bed into my boots, I shuffled outside to sit on the flat rock and tie my laces. When I looked up I saw one of the little Smurf girls observing me from behind a rock wall. I couldn't help but smile while reaching in my pocket for more candy. Instantly , she was standing in front of me. I handed over two more pieces of candy, then unwrapped a third which I put in my mouth hoping to relieve the soreness at the back of my throat. Hearing the heavy thump of approaching footsteps she vanished. With cameras swinging from their neck Mike and Frank walked into my mini-courtyard. Both chaps just finished two-year Peace Corps assignments in Paraguay, but before returning to the U.S. they were making a trek to Peru, Bolivia, Chile, and Argentina.

"How's the digs?" Mike asked sitting down across from me.

"Great. Just took a nap. How's your place."

"We're sharing a little place like this just over the hill," Mike said.

"You hungry?" Frank asked.

"Sure. Haven't had anything since breakfast in Puno, except for a couple pieces of candy."

"There's a small place in the plaza where we were this afternoon. Want to join us?" Mike added.

"Give me a second I'll get my jacket."

Halfway to the village, about 500 yards from my cottage, we stopped on a hilltop to enjoy magnificent riparian views. Shafts of sunlight were cutting down through clouds and shimmering like copper plates on the nearly calm lake surface. To the southeast we could see the snow-capped mountains of Bolivia, approximately 100 miles away. Following the long-legged former Peace Corps workers across the plaza to the restaurant I was suddenly aware of someone approaching from the side. I stopped in confusion as an old Quechua man dressed in traditional garb grasped my right hand in his and shook it heartily. Grinning but silent he backpedaled across the plaza.

In the empty but spacious cafe, which once might have been an assembly hall, we sat down at a heavy wooden table that could easily have seated 50 people. Not surprisingly the "especiale" of the day was a tortilla Taquilena, which when eventually served to all three of us looked and tasted quite like an omelet.

Another something the island didn't have was dogs. For the first and last time in almost two years I fell asleep and awoke without the usual "anvil chorus" of barking, yelping dogs.

On my way down to the pier the next morning I stopped in the doorway for one last look around and was a bit disappointed at not seeing the usual Smurf kiddos waiting patiently behind the wall. I was about to stride off when I looked down on the flat rock just outside the door. Kneeling down for a closer observation I discovered a small handwoven reed boat about 10 inches long. After carefully placing it in my backpack, I scattered a dozen or so pieces of candy on the rock, then headed down to the harbor.

On the return passage to Puno a storm came up forcing the skipper of the motor launch to put in at another island for a few hours where we watched rain clouds race down the lake to Bolivia. With whitecaps still breaking over the bow we forged ahead in the gathering darkness. Soon enough the distant lights of Puno were seen and used to guide us safely ashore. Strangely, upon entering the estuary at Puno all the lights were suddenly extinguished, as if someone flipped a switch. As the moon hadn't risen yet it was pitch black. Using the headlights of the buses waiting to pick us up at the pier, the skipper steered our boat carefully through the narrow channel until at last the launch bumped against huge truck tires secured to the pier.

~ ~ ~

Fiesta in Juli

Arriving at Jan and Betsy's apartment late that night I was relieved to see a lantern burning in the front window. As I reached the top of the steps Jan opened the door and ushered me into the kitchen where he brewed us a cup of coffee and we talked about my Taquile odyssey.

The warm glow of a brass kerosene lantern, actually a Chinese knockoff of a Coleman, threw an abbreviated circle of light on the table as we talked and listened to BBC updates on the Gulf war. Bush's ultimatum regarding the release of U.S. hostages had not been met. U.S. troops and aircraft carriers were heading for the middle East.

I slept fitfully that night, waking up every hour to gulp Aspirin in hopes of easing the throbbing in the back of my throat. I figured my tonsils, ancient tonsils according to my doctor, were inflamed. My throat was engorged with copious amounts of saliva which I was forced to expectorate every few minutes into my multipurpose coffee cup. Next morning , Jan took me to the Farmacia to purchase medicine recommended by his wife Betsy.

By mid-day the swelling in my throat eased, but now my sinuses were draining a prodigious stream of mucus. I spent most of the day sitting around the kitchen table swilling matte de coca and gulping medication.

Under a brilliant sky next morning, Jan pointed me to the road south to La Paz, Bolivia, which thankfully wound its way along the lakeshore. Being mostly flat with a few rollers, I made steady, if not speedy, progress. Fifty three miles south of Puno I arrived at Juli, Peru a small Puebla in the midst of a five-day fiesta. Marching bands and colorfully costumed dancers made endless circles around the main plaza, whilst I pushed my bike along the sidewalk looking for a pensione.

Hour-after-hour the bands and dancers circumnavigated the main plaza, their dissonant, repetitive music bouncing off the walls of adobe buildings facing the park, while mobs of people gathered at the curb to call to friends and cheer, again and again, for their favorite dance team. Gradually the musicians strayed off key with increased frequency. The dancers at the head of each band slowed to a point of a walk, giving the impression, from at least one observer, that he was watching a slow motion version of a parade. The tempo slowed to an inverse proportion of Chica and beer consumption. The women dancing in front of the bands were doing what looked like a modified two-step rock and roll, dressed in frilly multicolored mini-skirts, accented with sequins, ribbons, sashes, and leather belts with giant buckles.

Men dressed in bird-like costumes of feathers and carved wooden masks cavorted amongst the crowds gathered on the sidewalk. Amongst all of this riotous activity a small army of vendors scurried amongst the crowd. I sampled portions of carne asada and roasted potatoes with hot sauce, then continued my search for a room. A discouraging proposition due to the influx of people from miles around attending the fiesta. But at last I found accommodations in a hospedaje just off the main plaza at a cost of $1.60. Succumbing to growing waves of exhaustion, I took some medication, fell onto my cot, and barely managed to open *Moby Dick* before falling asleep.

Awake early next morning to the familiar sounds of crowing roosters, I discovered I'd fallen asleep fully dressed. I eased my legs over the side of the cot and plunged my feet into my cycling shoes. After splashing my face with water and brushing my teeth in the banos nearby, I returned to my room to begin the laborious process of transferring bike and gear down the rickety staircase to the ground floor. At last, my sinuses seemed to have run dry and my throat, though a bit scratchy, wasn't sore. I no longer cringed at the thought of swallowing. My timing here was perfect for the streets would be deserted for at least three hours while people recuperated from last night's revelry. In the peaceful, litter-strewn plaza I mounted my bike and cycled quietly out of town.

Halfway to Copacabana, Bolivia I stopped alongside the road to brew a cup of tea and eat a peanut butter and jelly sandwich. The altitude and ravages of my head cold had taken their toll, particularly of strength and endurance, now seriously depleted. As I sat their sipping tea and looking out at Lake Titicaca, a goat snuck around the adobe wall unseen and devoured my sandwich. Before I could even reach for a stone to pelt it with the goat disappeared.

~ ~ ~

Chapter 13

Bolivia and Chile

The descent into La Paz, Bolivia was long and precipitous. From the road high above the city it looked like a scooped out open pit mine. Below me was an enormous basin filled with rickety adobe houses dropping down from terrace to terrace to the bottom where central La Paz, with its ancient churches and government buildings, was located.

Founded by the Spaniards in 1548, the population today is well over 1 million. A tad over 12,000' La Paz claims the singular, if somewhat dubious distinction, of being the world's highest capital. Much to the discomfort of tourists from around the world life at 12,000' requires a set of lungs the size of scuba tanks.

Everything about my stay in La Paz was diametrically opposed to my visit to Quito, Ecuador, even my entrance. If you remember, I had one long, hellacious climb up to Quito, while my arrival in La Paz was prefaced by a lengthy, steep descent. Somewhere during my downhill race the speedometer clocked 42 mph. Without any hitches, I located the Hotel Torino, recommended in the *South American Handbook*. The hardest part of my arrival was hauling my bike and gear up a flight a stairs to the registration desk, then another flight of stairs to my room, a small windowless cell, but conveniently located next to the banos.

Friendly people and a slow pace of life were another striking contrast to Quito. Though there was a goodly amount of street traffic it didn't have that hard, felonious edge like the kamikazes of Quito. Or maybe it was just the altitude that forced people to slow down and take a more gracious approach to life. More than likely, it was just another inscrutable cultural anomaly.

Just lugging bike and gear up two flights of stairs put a serious drain on my energy. Once settled in, I lay down for a siesta wondering all the while how I could introduce this "cultural anomaly" into the hard driving, beat-yer-brains out pace of life in the U.S.

I awoke with a headache, but paid little attention to it as I hurried to shower, dress, and hit the streets in search of food and drink.

Later that evening the mild headache escalated to a raging migraine in my forehead above the right eye. I quickly and expertly diagnosed the symptoms as a malignant brain tumor. Having done this, I rushed out to the nearest store for a bottle of Napoleon Brandy figuring, although not a wonder drug, it would at least dull the sharp pain to a mild throb. In the morning I awoke to observe a half bottle of brandy and a half read *Moby Dick* on my nightstand. Despite a handful of Aspirin and another shot of brandy the brain tumor, which I expected to explode any second, continued to throb with such intensity my eye started twitching involuntarily. Securing a second handful of aspirin, I decided to rush to the nearest farmacia in search of a more reliable diagnosis and more efficacious medicine.

The white-smocked, attractive lady at the farmacia listened to my story of head pain, melon-sized tumors, Aspirin, and brandy as I recited and acted out my problem, much to the edification and entertainment of her patrons. Following my dog and pony show, she coolly and professionally wrote a prescription and handed it to a white-smocked assistant who promptly filled a bag with brightly colored capsules and charged me about $1.75. I was directed, if I understood correctly, to take two capsules every 4-5 hours. During the next three days I stayed in bed. I had little energy for anything more taxing than sipping brandy, reading *MOBY DICK*, swallowing a pill now an then, and blowing my nose.

~ ~ ~

The Senora and Moby Dick

After two and a half days of convalescence I finished, to my chagrin, the prodigious *Moby Dick*. And still the headaches continued, if only intermittently. So what was I to do? I'd scheduled myself for one more day of sick leave, but without anything to read how could I justify remaining in bed? I suddenly remembered there was a small, well-stocked exchange library downstairs next to the Senora's registration desk. Working up enough energy and ambition later that morning I hobbled down to her desk, where I scanned the titles of over 100 paperbacks crowded on the shelves. The spine of a paperback caught my eye. I stopped and read the title, *Blue Highways*. Yes, that was the book I needed. Although I'd already read it, it was my first choice to finish up my sick leave. There was only one slight glitch, the glass sliding doors protecting the books were locked. I soon discovered the Senora had the only key. It was a straightforward deal, I'd get my copy of *Moby Dick* bring it down to the Senora, exchange it for *Blue Highways*, then return to my room and hunker down for another day of reading. Though there was a slight pressure above my right eye, I hurried to my room grabbed *Moby Dick* and rushed downstairs to find the Senora, a bulky matron in her 60's with a fondness for black dresses, absorbed in an oversized ledger on her desk. I pushed my copy of *Moby Dick* across the counter.

"Senora, I'd like to exchange this book for one in the library," I said pointing to the *Blue Highways* paperback behind the locked glass door.

She looked at me as though I were asking her for sexual favors, then put her ledger aside. The red index fingernail of her right hand tapped the cover of the book. She turned it over as though checking for fleas, then pushed it back to my side of the counter.

"No Senor, it is too dirty, too broken down."

I was shocked and speechless. I had to get back to my sick bed and I had to have *Blue Highways* and the only person in the world separating me from the book was this dowdy old woman who had appointed herself critic and literature censor of the Hotel Torino. My right eye began to twitch.

"Senora, this is one of the classics of world literature. Okay, it's a used book, but all the pages are here and it's certainly in just as good condition as some of the other books and…"

"No Senor, please take that book away from me."

My eye twitched uncontrollably.

"I can't believe it. This is a great book, one of the best examples of American literature," I droned on until the Senora finally slammed her ledger shut and disappeared into some rear chamber smelling suspiciously of burning cabbage.

In the silence that ensued, the tingling above my eye matured to a dull ache. By the time I reached my room and slammed the door violently, the ache had ripened to a intense, shooting pain. I drank a half-glass of brandy while I fumed and tried to think of some scheme or caper that would enable me to liberate the book I wanted. I was prepared to go to any length short of bombing the lobby or hog-tying the Senora. Swallowing the last of my pills, I laid down for a fitful nap.

Waking some hours later, the pain above my eye had reached an untenable stage. I pulled on my jacket and made my way back to the farmacia. When I presented my prescription to another white-smocked pill dispenser I was met with raised eyebrows and pursed lips.

"Una momento, Senor," she said disappearing amongst the shelves of medicines behind the counter.

Momentarily, a man about my age emerged from the back room. I correctly assumed he was the chief pharmacist. Luckily, he spoke good English.

"Senor, there has been a terrible mistake. I hope you will not think badly of us."

"Mistake, what mistake. I have a prescription written by one of your own pharmacists."

"You see, that is part of the problem. The Senorita who wrote this is not a pharmacist."

"But after hearing my symptoms, this is the prescription she wrote," I said pointing at the paper he held in his hand.

"I'm so sorry to inform you Senor, but this is a medication normally prescribed for pregnant women. I can only suspect that my employee thought you were getting the medication for your wife."

"But, I'm not even married. Jesus, I could have died or worse I could have ruined my insides."

"No, no, Senor," he laughed," there was no danger of that. The worst that could have happened would have been acute diarrhea or vomiting."

"Well, what I really need is something for the pain over my right eye."

The pharmacist listened attentively as I described my symptoms in elaborate detail.

"Now I see that you are suffering from soroche. Senor, it is the altitude that has given you this pain." He said pulling a pen from his breast pocket and scribbling on a piece of paper. "Give this to Rosa. This will relieve the pain and once again, Senor, I apologize for the confusion."

I got another little bag of pills and hurried back to the hotel wondering if the new pills would override whatever chemical imbalance was created by the first pills or if they'd provoke some type of unpleasant chemical reaction. Not arriving at any definitive conclusion, I bought another bottle of brandy on the way back to my room. I realized, somewhere en route, that it was dark and it was after 8 p.m. and I hadn't eaten that day. With my bag of pills and bottle of brandy, I stopped by a cafe I'd discovered my first day in La Paz. It was well after 10 p.m. by the time I got back to the hotel. When passing the registration desk, instead of the Senora, I saw a young fellow seated at the Senora's desk listening to rock music and reading a comic book. As my foot reached the third step of the staircase leading to my room, I got a brilliant idea.

In my room I retrieved the Melville book, pulled a few hundred bolivianos from my wallet and placed them within the pages so that an inch or so was visible. With a smile on my face, I marched downstairs to the front desk. I approached the registration desk with an air of authority and laid the book on the counter so the lad reading the comic wouldn't fail to see the money. It took a few minutes to get his attention, but when I did he was at the counter in a flash. I pointed at the bookcase and explained what I wanted, pushing the Melville tome closer to him. He smiled like a Cheshire cat all the time. Without hesitation he went back to the desk, opened a side drawer and removed a key. His movements were so quick and practiced I suspected he'd been through the same routine before. Within a space of maybe 60 seconds, the exchange was made and I was on my way to my room with **Blue Highways**, laughing all the way.

Next day I felt good enough to join my neighbor across the hall. Mark, a Brit from the U.K., was just as eager as I was for an expedition to the public market which would accomplish the dual goals of getting exercise and food. Within easy walking distance from the hotel, the market was a fairly orderly, by third world standards anyway, market with half the stalls under temporary canopies and the other half inside a maze of permanent booths.

"Now look at that," Mark said pointing at a row of five juice vendors lined up side-by-side. "Let's have a little fun."

Walking close to the stands, each piled high with fresh cut oranges, bananas, pineapple, guavas and other assorted tropical fruit, we listened to the husky Senoras tending the stalls begin a litany of self-stroking hyperbole that would do homage to P.T. Barnum. Mark shuffled from stall to stall asking the price of a jugo grande. Soon he had a price war going that eventually netted us ḁ large fruit drinks with an egg for a mere fifty cents. Afterward, we shopped for sliced turkey, roast beef, rolls, tomatoes and assorted garnishings which we took back to the hotel for a luncheon in the courtyard.

Still unable to fully appreciate the taste of food and drink, I retired to my room to take some pills and enjoy a nap. Dozing in my window-less cubicle, it finally dawned on me that the only way to really cure my migraine headache, symptomatic of high altitude sickness, was simply to descend to a lower altitude. I would do that the very next day I decided.

~ ~ ~

The Little People

Three Chileano backpackers, Fernando, Luis, and Marco helped me check my bike on the train that would carry us across the Bolivian alti-plano, eventually down to the oasis town of Calama in the Atacama desert of Chile. I felt reassured when I was allowed to push a bike into the baggage car next to our own passenger coach where we had reserved seats. When at last the crowded train lumbered out across the flat, desolate landscape, I took my seat which was directly across from a couple with two small children, ages perhaps four and five. In the seats directly in back of me, the Chileanos played cards. Across the aisle, a young Israeli couple, Ricci and Ronny, read books. I settled down to a reread *Blue Highways*, occasionally looking over at Ricci who thumbed disconsolately through a fat paperback, while Ronny was glued to their *South American Handbook*.

When the opportunity presented itself, I asked Ricci if she'd be interested in trading books. She willingly passed over *The Name of The Rose*, by Umberto Ecco, which I'd already read, but as I was nearly finished with a reread of my book I was open to a deal.

The train chugged into a desert sunset like a stone dropped into a bottomless well. The next thing I knew, Ricci was pummeling my shoulder energetically.

"George, you've been talking in your sleep, loudly."

"Huh," I retorted running my fingers through my hair and trying to come to life.

Ricci leaned closer . "You were calling out, something about leprechauns and Carmen Miranda and about being safe."

"Nonsense," I said defensively. "I never talk in my sleep. Now what's this about leprechauns?"

She smiled. "The little people, that's what I thought you called them and then you yelled, 'yes, yes it's safe.' "

I stood up to see the Chileanos smiling up at me from their seats. Their amused silence confirmed Ricci's statement, but before I could say anything else Ricci grabbed my arm.

"Come with Ronny and me, we're going up to the dining car."

Pulling my jacket on I looked down at the couple seated across from me huddled under blankets with their kids, all fast asleep.

A harried waiter slammed plates of chicken and rice in front of us as we looked out the window at a moonrise. With a bottle cap opener tied on his belt, the waiter pried the caps off three cokes. The caps landed on the tablecloth in front of us. We watched as the foam from each bottle surged out and down the side of the bottles onto the tablecloth, once a perfect example of starched while linen, but now an impressionist's canvas of food and drink.

After my first few mouthfuls of the chicken I was pleasantly surprised. At last my taste buds had been resurrected, not only that, I was feeling much better. Looking over Ronny's shoulder I watched our waiter take a long pull from a beer bottle, followed by a deep puff on a cigarette, before making another round of the tables.

Much later, back in our car, in a sitting position with my head on a pillow fashioned from my rolled up jacket, I slept through the night. According to Ricci, as we drank coffee in the dining car next morning, I hadn't talked in my sleep. She assured me this was the case as she had been up all night reading and being serenaded by nocturnal woodcutters felling the forests of Morpheus.

About noon the train stopped at the Bolivian frontier, which happened to be located in the middle of nowhere, but reasonably close to the Chilean border. When we detrained to get our passports stamped the desert heat hit me like a blast furnace. Immediately, I began shedding layer after layer of clothes until I was down to a T-shirt and pair of jeans. Miraculously, for the first time in weeks I was able to inhale and exhale without wheezing or dislodging hidden chambers of mucus and phlegm. My head was clear and I felt surprisingly energetic. Emerging from the Bolivian aduano with my exit stamp I noticed people were now seeking the narrow strips of shade alongside the depot, rather than planting themselves on the ground in the brilliant sunlight.

"George, please hurry we must exchange our bolis, the train will leave any minute." Ricci advised.

Oh God, I thought, here we go again. As usual I'd given little thought to my finances while in La Paz. I remembered cashing a few traveler's checks and a $20 bill or two, but had no idea of how much I'd spent or how much Bolivian currency was left. Queued up behind Ricci and Ronny, I rummaged in my fanny pack to find some colorful paper money. Along with a fistful of Bolivianos, I discovered an equally fat, but nearly worthless collection of Peruvian intis.

As I waited, I was able to gain valuable insight into the art and science of "haggling" as Ricci and Ronny verbally grappled with a shriveled up, toothless old hag who had a cache of Chilean pesos hidden in the folds of her tattered cloak. When at last the money changed hands, I stepped up like a child handing over his piggy bank to a total stranger. With Ricci and Ronny watching like hawks at my shoulder, I handed my "bolis" to the hooded crone who counted them out in a high shrill voice before reaching into the recesses of her skirt. Slowly, she withdrew a packet of new bills, broke the band, and then began carefully counting off a goodly number. Finally, looking at Ricci and Ronny with disgust, she handed them over to me. When I offered her my Peruvian intis for exchange, she spat on the ground and motioned me aside. I would have to be content with several 100,000 inti bills to paste in my journal as souvenirs, all incredibly valued at less than one U.S. dollar.

My main interest in the Chilean currency was its colored inks and a new gallery of mustachioed, balding statesman or overdressed military leaders decorating the bills. The subtleties of international finance and currency rates were completely lost on me.

Steam hissing from the undercarriage of the train, we raced up the steps and returned to our seats anxious to get on with the trip. A mere five kilometers from the Bolivian border the train came to a halt again, in another section of treeless, lifeless wasteland. Fifty yards from the train we could see a large, nondescript adobe building. Underneath a mirror-like tin roof, the faded lettering painted on the side told us it was the Chilean aduano.

"Why are we stopping here," I asked of no one in particular.

"This is Chile," Fernando said as we looked out at the baking desert. "Everyone must go through customs over there. Everything must be unloaded from the baggage car and brought to the aduano."

"Even my bike?"

"Even your bike."

Following the three Chileanos and Ricci and Ronny, I watched as baggage and boxes were handed out the side of the baggage car and set on the ground alongside the tracks to be claimed by their owners. My Chileano friends helped me unload and assemble my bike and gear before claiming their backpacks and hiking over to the customs building where a ragged line of humanity had already commenced.

When the last of my gear was secured to my bike I pedaled across the hardpan to the shade on the western side of the building. The queue snaked back from the open shed about 30-yards. As each person had to hand over everything they were bringing into the country they were generally surrounded by boxes, bags, family members, and luggage. The line moved with glacial speed, so I contented myself with sitting down beside my bike and reading my new book, booty from my recent trade with Ricci.

About three hours later, bringing up the rear of the line I gratefully pushed my bike into the shade of the inspection shed where a dozen idle officials looked up from their tables. The inspector facing me smiled and called over his supervisor. They looked me over for a moment then waved me through, without even a routine thumb through my passport.

Back at the side of the luggage car I joined the others handing up their possessions to be stored inside once more. Fernando and Luis helped me muscle my bike back into the car.

"Jorge, welcome to Chile. Cheer up, amigo. Now it is downhill to Calama."

"Does this happen all the time?"

"Yes."

"What are they looking for?"

"Everything, nothing. You don't have any contraband do you?"

"Not that I know of. Just a lot of dirty clothes."

"Yes, it is the same with us." He laughed.

I pushed my bike to the rear of the baggage car to a secure space inside a chain link cage, then bungeed it off to the wall insuring that it wouldn't fall over if the train suddenly stopped or, God forbid, derailed.

All the baggage was loaded. All the passengers had returned to their seats. And still the train had not moved.

Fernando and I sat on boxes looking out the baggage door at the desert. I told him about my experiences crossing the desert in Baja, California.

"You will have much desert here in Chile too," he commented. "But once you get to Santiago the land changes, there will be many farms and many vineyards."

"Yes, I've heard the wine is good here."

"Verdad, but right now I'd like a cold glass of schop."

"What's that?"

"Cerveza, beer. You like beer, Jorge?"

"God, I love it. I'd pay five dollars for a cold beer right now."

We both stared out at the desert visualizing tall glasses of cold beer. The train lurched forward almost knocking us off the crate. We closed the door of the baggage car and returned to our seats in the next car where a conductor passed through the aisle collecting passports in a basket.

Upon our arrival in Calama, I was lucky enough to get at the head of the line to claim my passport. Unfortunately, the customs inspector had forgotten to bring entrance visas with him. It was 4 a.m. The news didn't cheer us up. Everyone was as stressed as a group of prisoners getting ready for a jailbreak.

If everyone would be patient, he explained, more tourist cards would be secured from the local customs office. Once the cards were filled out, stamped, and countersigned with his signature, he explained, our passports would be returned. Patience was all that was required, he said to the sleepy, cranky, muttering, cursing, slovenly passengers packed in the aisle outside his compartment. After a 30-hour train ride, mediocre food, and lack of sleep, patience was a rare commodity. It was one of those situations where the wrong word or tone of voice could start a riot. Reluctantly, we returned to our seats.

As for me, I had nowhere in particular to go. I would have to search the streets with Ricci and Ronny and a the other tourists in search of a room. Regardless, I was extremely anxious to get the hell off that train. At last the tourist cards arrived, the line reformed and passports were returned. As luck would have it, my passport was lost and was not found until everyone else had detrained. But this worked to my advantage. When I arrived at the baggage car it was completely empty save for my bike and gear. I'd missed the usual confusion, pushing-and-shoving, and general chaos of detraining. Without delay, I rolled my loaded bike onto the platform and joined ranks with Ricci and Ronny to navigate the dark, deserted streets of the small desert town in search of a hotel or pensione. From the darkness of the platform a voice called out.

"Jorge, bien viaje. Ride safely, amigo," Fernando shouted.

~ ~ ~

A Schop Shop

I would have slept longer than 10 a.m., but for the noise of a vacuum cleaner working its way noisily toward my room. No more than an hour later I was standing in the sunshine outside the hotel waiting for three Brits. I was relishing my new found health and anxious to explore Calama. The Brits came down from Bolivia with me on the train and coincidentally had taken rooms in the same hotel.

Calama was from all appearances a small, clean, friendly oasis town set in the Atacama desert. You'd never guess at its extreme isolation from the rest of Chile. It seemed more like a beach town, but for one important missing ingredient.

When the Brits showed up we lost no time in finding a good cafe on the main plaza. Trying to make up for food deprivation during the last three days, we all ordered large breakfasts of bacon, eggs, toast, and cafe cortados-the Chileano version of cappuccino. As they were headed off on a bus trip to San Pedro de Atacama and wouldn't be back until next day, I volunteered to stow their backpacks in my room. I welcomed the chance to spend another day in Calama before striking out into the desert heading west for coastal Chile and the town of Antofagasta, a distance of about 150 miles. To a lesser degree the additional time would allow me to familiarize myself with the local schop parlors where, over a glass of beer I'd be able to investigate the cultural nuances of Calama, as well as bring my journal up to date. That evening I went out on a self-styled culinary tour of the town, consuming carne asada, papas fritas, salads, fruits, and multiple servings of schop.

~ ~ ~

Mirage

Departing Calama two days later, I pedaled down the main street to my favorite cafe for breakfast and a cafe cortado before heading southwest into the desert hoping to reach Antofagasta in two or three days.

My first day out, with flat straight road and a tail wind I'd pedaled 50 miles by noon and looked forward to my first 100-mile day since Baja. But, just as I reached the 60-mile mark the rear axle seized up. A bit disappointed but also curious about the cause of the seizure I got my toolkit out and prepared to operate. Oddly enough, the day before I'd done extensive maintenance on the bike. It didn't take long to discover the retaining bolt in the free hub had loosened up causing the seizure. The problem was how to tighten it. A large hex-head nut inside the freewheel was the culprit, but as far as I knew I didn't have a big enough allen wrench to make the adjustment. Then I got to thinking about John Powell's bicycle maintenance class in Ventura, California. I dug to the bottom of my tool kit and there it was—the correct size allen wrench compliments of John Powell. I fitted the wrench into the bolt and tightened it down. In another 15 minutes I was pedaling down the road again, enjoying a vigorous tail wind. Later that afternoon, about 1 p.m., my stomach started grumbling and to make things interesting my water supply was nearly exhausted with no sign of replenishment in sight.

Perhaps a mile or so ahead on the straight, flat road I spotted a single tree and a small structure that looked like an old-timey telephone booth. Cycling closer and closer, I began to make out some kind of graphic painted on the side of the structure. Sure enough it was a painting of an ice cream cone. Above the two-tone illustration was the word "helados" which is one of the first Spanish words I learned. I suspected I was seeing a mirage. As there were no cars parked nearby, I figured the little booth had been abandoned. What an unlikely spot for an ice cream vendor, I thought. Coasting slowly up to the wood structure, I planned to take advantage of the shade on the side to make a couple of sandwiches for lunch, but to my astonishment there inside the booth was a man sitting on an ice cooler reading a newspaper. He looked at me as if I was from outer space.

"Ayee, Senor, I didn't hear you ride up. What are you doing out in the desert on a bicycle. This is dangerous."

I was about to ask him the same question, when he jumped up, opened the lid of the cooler and withdrew an ice cold, homemade pineapple ice cream cone.

"Please Senor, eat this and cool down."

Figure 17: Only ice cream vendor in the entire Atacama Desert.

No argument there. I bit into the cold, creamy pineapple cone wondering if perhaps I was hallucinating. My taste buds told me otherwise. Noticing my prodigious appetite, the vendor had a chocolate cone ready when the pineapple disappeared. After a strawberry cone, Raymondo lead me to a pipe in back of his ice cream parlor where I was able to fill my empty bottles. Enough seepage water from the pipe kept a solitary tree alive. As I rested in the shade a few cars and trucks pulled off the road to buy ice cream. I began to wonder how Raymondo got to and from his remote ice cream parlor. Unless he had a vehicle hidden away under the desert sand, he was on foot. The mystery was solved just before I departed, when a bus, headed for Calama, stopped on the other side of the highway. Raymondo quickly gathered up his newspaper and cooler, said adios to me, then scurried across the road to the waiting bus. I would almost bet he paid for his ride with an ice cream cone. I bet he sold his few remaining cones to a captive, but agreeable, clientele on his way back to Calama.

A change in the direction of the wind forced me to slow down to 6 mph that day, but with a little over 100 miles on the odometer I wasn't unhappy to pull over at a gasoline station and cafe.

After dinner, I got permission to pitch my tent in back of the gas station. Opting for a generous slice of shade on the leeward side of a shed, I pitched my tent and prepared to go to sleep. Just after the sun went down I heard footsteps pass my tent, tweaking my curiosity. Seconds later, I heard the squeak of rusty hinges as the door to the shed was pulled open. Momentarily, a diesel engine throbbed to life filling the once quiet desert night. As I was a mere ten feet away from the shed I felt the full impact of the mechanical din, plus a low-grade vibration that passed though the hardpan beneath me.

Too sore and too tired from a long day of cycling to relocate my tent site, I pulled my earplugs from the handlebar bag, secured them in my ears and gradually drifted off to sleep. Needless to say I got an unusually early start next morning. Into a windless, cloudless morning, with the first rays of the sun on my back I headed west for the Chilean coast. Once again, I rolled off 50 miles before noon. That day the temperature promised to be hotter, probably reaching the high 90's.

~ ~ ~

Christmas in Antofagasta

There wasn't any white-bearded Santa Claus on the corner ringing a bell, nor was there any snow or cold weather or the obnoxious sentimental Christmas music that people are subjected to at this time of the year back in the U.S. But there were plenty of Christmas Eve shoppers filling the streets. A city of over 200,000 residents, Antofagasta lays claim to the largest population in northern Chile.

Earlier, when pedaling out of the desert I was surprised to look up and see my old friend the Pacific Ocean spread out like one vast blue welcoming mat. Only a few hours and a few miles earlier an arid desert stretched to the horizon, soon to be replaced by millions of square miles of water.

The mood in the streets was one of happiness, which I found to be the case throughout Chile regardless of time or place. This was a pleasant surprise after so many frenzied Christmas eve shopping sprees on my own behalf. I'd concluded years ago that Christmas was a conspiracy amongst the business community to separate shoppers from most of their dollars in a single month, rather than over a period of a year.

Far from being depressed in a foreign country far from home during Christmas, I felt relief and contentment. I was exempted from the annual obligatory chore of mailing dozens of smarmy cards preprinted with my name and buying presents for relatives I disliked.

Besides, it was pleasant to walk about in shirtsleeves and shorts, stopping now and again to enjoy a glass of cold schop, a lomita burger, or even an helados. Who needs or wants sub-zero temperatures, ice-caked windshields, or extravagant credit card bills.

~ ~ ~

Farm Country

Temuco, south of Santiago, reminded me of what small farming towns in mid-America are like. Clean, spacious streets, tidy storefronts where one can buy farm supplies, get a saddle repaired, a tractor fixed or buy a pair of boots and jeans-all on the same street. The pace of life was slow, the temperament of the people friendly. For the most part they seemed satisfied with life, enjoyed simple pleasures, and were oblivious of the stress and pressure of the world outside.

The small, but attractive hotel I stayed at had the original polished oak plank floors laid down about 1930. Overstuffed chairs with cro-cheted doilies on the armrests overwhelmed the small lobby, but attracted the eye of the weary traveler. In the dining room off the lobby a large table with a seating capacity of about 30 people served guests family-style meals. If you arrived late you got leftovers.

Large brass skeleton keys to each room were tucked in numbered wooden slots behind registration desk in the lobby. A polished mahogany banister could be gripped for support when climbing car-peted stairs to the second floor rooms. Here elevators were still a thing of the future. Sunset, viewed from the window of my second floor room, overlooking trees and hay fields was a rich, slow motion process. When darkness finally came I could hear swallows swooping down through cool air gobbling up clouds of recently hatched mayflies. Cicadas unlimbered their back legs filling the night air with unfinished symphonies.

Next morning after breakfast, I passed a travel agency with a poster of a ship plying the waters between Puerto Montt to Puerto Natales, the jumping off point for Tierra Del Fuego and the world famous Torres Del Paine National Park. Inside, an attractive female travel agent told me that if I planned to take the ferry to Puerto Natales I'd better make advanced reservations or I'd be out of luck. This being the high tourist season, passage was at a premium and booked months ahead as there were only three boats per month making the roundtrip. After a few minutes deliberation I made a reservation for the January 15th departure from Puerto Montt. The three-day trip, including meals, cost about $90 US.

In the heart of the Chilean lake district southeast of Temuco I found my first real campsite in months. This on the shores of Lago Villarrica. The hectic city streets of Santiago, some 400-plus miles to the north, were all but forgotten. I pitched my tent in a grove of shade trees and sat in the warm sun enjoying a view of the lake, inwardly relishing the peace and quiet.

During the past few days I'd enjoyed excellent cycling along a two-lane country road that snaked its way through wheat and barley fields, past grazing dairy herds, and beside crystal clear streams. In all, some of the prettiest farm country I'd ever seen. An added bonus was a lack of traffic.

Deeper into the lake district, cycling under blue skies, I got my first glimpse of the snow-capped volcano, Villarrica, a wisp of smoke spewing from its snow-capped cone. Enjoying bucolic scenery, camping on lakeshores, and exploring small towns, I worked my way slowly south to Puerto Montt anticipating the boat trip south to Puerto Natales.

~ ~ ~

There Are No showers In Animal Class

I was pacing back and forth outside the passenger shed watching cars and trucks drive slowly down a cement ramp into the cavernous hull of the "Ro Ro" Tierra Del Fuego. The boat that would take me to Tierra Del Fuego and the final leg of my 3-year odyssey.

A Chileano with a video camera did a slow pan of the ship, then turned to me and smiled.

"You've come a long way my friend," he said pointing his camera at my bike and then at me. As I looked over my bicycle, loaded down with the usual gear strapped here, bungeed there, it suddenly dawned on me how much the bike had been through. It was starting to show its age. In terms of mileage, it had over 16,000 not-so-easy miles on it. Yet, to date it had never given me a second's trouble. I only wished that I was built as sturdily as my bike.

I paced back and forth trying to deal with the latest dilemma. When I checked in at the ticket office earlier, the clerk informed me I'd have to pay a 23,000-peso freight charge on my bike, which at the current exchange rate amounted to $28 US. Which wasn't exorbitant, but the travel agent in Temuco assured me my bike was considered baggage and would be taken at no extra charge. After thinking it over I returned to the ticket office to be told by another agent that my bike was not considered freight, so there was no extra freight fee. I couldn't decide whether to pay the extra freight charge or gamble on getting my bike on board without paying the fee.

As I paced and pondered, another cyclist from the U.S. rolled up to the shed and secured his bike next to mine. Sunburned, with a salt and pepper beard, he took his time inspecting my bike and gear.

"Looks like you've done some traveling he said pointing to the colorful national flag decals stuck on various parts of the frame.

"Over two years on the road now. Started in Alaska. Where are you headed?"

"South to Ushuaia. Been traveling off and on now for nine years. Been to China, Australia, New Zealand, New Guinea. This is my second time around in South America. Came back to see my girlfriend in Santiago. I love Chile. The women are great, the wine's great, and everything is cheap."

"You cycled in China?"

"Some. Had to backpack most of the Great Wall though. There's a lot of places the Wall stops you know, but some beautiful country."

So says Millard Farmer, a fortyish U.S. citizen from the state of Delaware. If memory serves me right Millard is the only Delawarian I'd ever met in my entire life. To this day I'm not sure which piece Delaware accounts for in the jigsaw puzzle of North American geography. I think its somewhere on the East coast north of Maryland.

Millard had a leering smile that reminded me of a mischievous Jack Nicholson. His mountain bike had panniers and camera case he'd made himself. Also attached to the rear rack was another oblong black bag which I found out later housed a churanga, a Chilean musical instrument about the size and shape of a mandolin but with guitar strings. Other musical devices found among Farmer's kit bag were a jaw harp from Papua, New Guinea, a harmonica, and a kazoo.

After exchanging travel small talk with Millard, I asked him if he thought we'd have to pay the extra freight charge for our bikes.

"Who knows, depends on who's in charge of loading and how much they had to drink last night. See the guy over there with the yellow hardhat. I bet he's the main man," the world traveler said pointing at a small, wiry man about 60-years old.

"I'll go talk with him," I said removing a 1,000-peso bill from my wallet. Minutes later I returned to report to Farmer.

"I think he said to roll the bikes on as soon as passengers are allowed to board. You know, I took a boat like this from La Paz to Mazatlan in Mexico. I was able to roll my bike into a little space next to the cars and trucks. It worked out real good. By the way you owe me a beer."

Millard shot me one of his Jack Nicholson smiles, opened one of his rear panniers and pulled out a liter box of Chileano wine.

"Will this do?"

I nodded my head with approval, noticing also there were at least two more boxes of wine among Millard's gear. While we compared notes, another gringo shouldering a huge backpack strolled up followed closely by an attractive gringa. When he got closer I recognized him. It was Charlie, a guy I met at the S.A.E.C. in Quito. He bought some of my extra gear. After introducing him to Millard and meeting his wife Sherry we all sat down on the grass to talk over our travel plans. We discovered we all had seats in what the navigation company referred to as "pioneer class" but what most traveler's called "animal class."

Waiting the interminable wait, Charlie opened up a bag Sherry was carrying and pulled out a churanga. Millard's eyes lighted up when he saw the instrument. Immediately, he removed his and began strumming it, explaining while tuning the strings that he was learning to play. Charlie showed him some basic chords.

An hour later with tickets stamped and seats assigned, we queued up at the gate. Millard and I were at the front of the line with our bikes, eyes fixed on the gaping cargo bay of the ship. When the gate opened we rode or bikes to the lip of the ramp leading into the boat. Showing our tickets to a roly-poly Chileano, our names were checked off his passenger manifest. We then pushed our bikes up the ramp into the hull and secured them in a small pie-shaped space next to the stairwell leading to the upper decks. After removing the gear we'd need during the 3-day voyage we locked the bikes together. Fears about the security of our bikes vanished when a half-dozen other cyclists rolled aboard and stacked their bikes around ours.

With backpack, tent bag, and handlebar bag in hand, I followed Millard up the narrow, steel staircase. Progress was temporarily halted when a woman in front of Millard got her huge suitcase stuck in the stairwell. Once the logjam was cleared, we worked our way slowly up to the passenger deck, where we negotiated our way amongst diesel tractors and trailers chained down to the steel plate deck.

Following a line of passengers staggering under the weight of backpacks and baggage we arrived at the cafeteria through which we gained entrance to "pioneer class." Our home for the next three days was a large doublewide trailer secured to the ship's deck. The 60-odd seats in this billet looked suspiciously like old Greyhound Bus seats; half faced port and half-faced starboard.

In the process of negotiating our way to our seats, Millard bumped into an old woman weighed down with cardboard boxes and a burlap sack that emitted a strange noise when jostled. Our curiosity whetted we watched her waddle to a front row seat directly under a TV suspended from the ceiling then settled into our own seats, conveniently located next to the storage closet, already half-full of backpacks and assorted luggage.

There were private cabins available in another part of the ship, but they had been reserved months in advance. We soon got bored and restless and began an exploration of the ship from bow to stern. A warm, sunny day promised at least an enjoyable first day's voyage.

The Ro Ro Tierra Del Fuego was approximately 436' long and 63' wide. It had a capacity of 150 passengers, distributed amongst 95 butacas or seats and 34 cabins. The ship had a maximum speed of 14 knots or about 14 nautical miles per hour. Statistics aside it was a clean, apparently ship shape boat. As well, the crew looked competent and experienced. Which is no small consideration in light of where we were bound and the type of weather and oceans we might encounter. Although we'd face only one small patch of open sea, some of the descriptions of storms, seasonal or no, in Tierra Del Fuego were frightening.

This is what Charles Darwin wrote in his journal , December 17, 1832 when he and the crew of the H.M.S. Beagle first dropped anchor there.

"A single glance at the landscape was sufficient to show me how wildly different it was from anything I had ever beheld. At night it blew a gale of wind; and heavy squalls from the mountains swept past us...Tierra Del Fuego may be described as a mountainous land, partly submerged in sea, so that deep inlets and bays occupy the place where valleys should exist. The mountainous sides, except on

the exposed western coast, are covered from the water's edge upwards by one great forest."

Halfway up a ladder to the upper deck, we discovered Charlie, Sherry, and another gringo had pitched their tents in a small companionway between decks. As they had overhead cover and were only exposed to the elements on two sides, their camp was quite private and comfortable except for the traffic of passengers like us clambering up and down the steel stairway.

Charlie and Sherry, Peace Corps workers from Ecuador, were on a month's leave heading for Torres Del Paine and Fitzroy Park in Argentina for some trekking and climbing. Avid birders, they were constantly peering over the side of the ship testing their new binoculars. As we chatted, the ship slipped away from the dock almost imperceptibly, swung out in the channel to begin the long voyage south. All of us watched from the upper deck as Puerto Montt grew smaller and smaller in our wake. To leeward we passed silently by Chiloe Island.

With the limited boundaries of the ship soon explored I returned to my seat in "animal class" to do some reading before dinner. Momentarily distracted by the thought of food, I began to wonder how all 150 passengers would get served in a cafeteria that seated only 45 people. I envisioned the usual melee of pushing and shoving, but hoped the ship's crew had devised a method of serving, quickly and equitably, their hungry charges.

I read and snoozed, but some strange noise or sound began to tweak my consciousness. I eliminated the rumbling of the ship's diesel engines and the murmur of a half-dozen foreign languages. As crazy as the thought may have been it sounded like something usually associated with barnyards. The sound was so out of context I should have identified it handily. A bit later, when making my way to the head located near the front row of seats I discovered the source of the noise. The old Chileano woman mentioned earlier had a live chicken in a cardboard box at her feet, into it she dropped a handful of feed to the clucking approval of the chicken.

Much later, I was shaken awake by Millard who told me we'd better get in line if we wanted to be seated at the first dinner serving. This was easy to do as the line of people had already wrapped itself around the cafeteria entrance ending conveniently next to our seats. We were joined soon by an enormous Australian named Mike Semken and his friend, Andy Grey from New Zealand. As the wait turned into a siege, Millard opened one of his apparently endless supply of wine boxes and passed it around. By the time we finally commandeered a table we were all relaxed but incredibly hungry.

The dining room was in chaos. Waiters were literally running amongst the tables throwing plates of food in front of diners, much like the person in a zoo who hurls heads of lettuce and chunks of raw meat into the cages of wild beasts. One and all, they looked like they'd been recently paroled from a penal colony for heinous crimes or escaped from the infamous Devil's Island. Adding to the general atmosphere of discomfiture were legions of hungry, impatient passengers skulking around the perimeter of the room looking like malnourished condors and acting like spoiled children.

In a gesture of international peace, Millard opened another box of wine. We were trying to find out what was on the menu only to discover there was no menu, when four plates of exceptionally unappetizing food landed on the table in front of us. Already, bread and butter had been eaten. We sipped our wine and looked at each other apprehensively, each waiting for some brave soul to dig into the oddly textured, colorful food. With some reluctance the Aussie grabbed his spoon like a framing hammer and proceeded. He grimaced and snorted, but quickly dispatched his serving, then emitted a voluminous belch that turned heads at surrounding tables.

I looked down at my plate and couldn't help conjuring up images of Linda Blair in the movie, **The Exorcist.** I pushed my plate aside and refilled my wine glass. Thank God, I told myself, I'd thought ahead to buy a generous supply of meats, cheeses, bread and assorted food items before leaving Puerto Montt. With our unanimous approval, Mike consumed the contents of our plates.

Feeling the pleading, dagger-like stares of those still waiting in line we returned to our seats where we enthusiastically broke into our caches of food. By now the ship had taken to rolling from side to side with unpredictable timing, sending dozens of passengers scurrying to the heads where long lines had already formed or sent them racing outside to the ship's railings. After eating a healthy sandwich or two we watched in awe and disbelief as Mike made his way back to the dining room to scrounge another serving of the Linda Blair special.

Later that night we migrated to Charlie and Sherry's camp where an impromptu sing-a-long got started. Millard fetched his churanga and loaned me the kazoo. With the help of a guitar-playing gringo and voices of a mixed crowd of music lovers we entertained ourselves, kibitzing passengers, and crew with a medley of tunes ranging from 50's oldies to 60's protest songs.

With a chorus of voices, somewhat melodic, wafting into a sky sparkling with clearly defined constellations the good ship Ro Ro TDF rumbled and chugged ever southward.

In the morning, the facetious sobriquet "animal class" was less amusing. The odors proliferating from the 70-odd bodies curled up, flopped over, and stretched out on seats and floor were only surpassed, in degree of pungency, by the toilets servicing those people. To add insult to injury, there were no shower facilities in animal class.

To exacerbate the problem the chicken woman had moved her feathered friend into one of the heads where the pungent smells of chicken shit mixed none to agreeably with the wastes of a higher species.

To clear my head I took an early morning stroll on deck. The sea air was a tonic after a night in our crowded chamber of horrors. While strolling the decks my finely tuned nose detected the familiar and welcome aroma of breakfast.

Seated at one of the cafeteria tables along with a few other early risers or insomniacs, as the case may be, I was joined by an extremely vivacious British lady about 30-years old, who looked as if she'd just stepped out of a hot shower, instead of the Dantesque barracks I'd emerged from. She smelled, unmistakably of lavender bathsoap. Sue

Pritchard smiled so radiantly and chirped with laughter so animatedly that she forced me to crack a smile on the otherwise blank wall of my early morning face.

"I can't believe how lively you are. My first guess, if I didn't know better, is that you have a cabin with a private shower and unlimited hot water."

"Not a'tall, but I have done a bit of investigating."

"And…"

"Well, promise you won't blab this about, you must promise."

"I swear on my mother's grave."

"Well, there are commodious shower facilities in the forward deck where the first class cabins are located. Come I'll show you."

I quickly fetched my towel and toilet kit then followed Sue as she climbed stairs, scurried down corridors with signs saying "Privado." At last Sue stopped at a vented door, looked both ways then pulled it open and pushed me inside. Gleaming brass, stainless steel, polished mahogany and best of all a shower stall where I could soak and steam under scalding water surrounded me. My only concerns, as I stripped off my clothes, were that a ship's officer would batter the door down and banish me to animal class forever or that the supply of hot water would stop before I had a chance to jump in the shower. As a precaution I bolted the door. Considering it was not quite 6 a.m. I was allowed to complete my toilet leisurely, relishing every ounce of hot water washing over me. After the shower caper, I made a clean getaway and met Sue back in the cafeteria.

As an added bonus, she had a cup of coffee waiting for me. This was a woman of unlimited resources, I told myself. A bit later, Millard, Mike, and Andy drifted in and along with them rumors that the Gulf war had started. No details were available, so we hoped the rumors did not prove up. Over coffee and rolls Millard entertained us with stories of native fishermen in the Philippines who caught sharks by lassoing them, then beat them unconscious with clubs.

By this late date my stomach was so impervious to assorted depravities Millard's tales of atrocities had no effect and I was able to eat my breakfast with gusto. So did Sue.

A native of Queen's Park, Chester, England and more recently of Hong Kong where she dropped out of a career in International Banking, Sue was traveling throughout South America. Her most recent excursion was exploring the Pantanal in Brazil, where she joined natives for a night of crocodile hunting. Now she was headed, like the rest of us, for Torres Del Paine.

Soon, with little in the way of diversion, except speculation about the Gulf crisis and the depraved offerings of the subhumans inhabiting the galley, life aboard ship fell into a routine of eating, talking, reading, drinking, sleeping, and walking the deck, until foul weather forced the curtailment of the last activity. Most of the passengers began to resemble underfed over-rested zombies as we shuffled our way between dining room, seats, head, and clandestine trips to the shower. The night before our arrival in Puerto Natales we heard a BBC radio news report that the Gulf war had commenced when Iranian missiles were fired on Israel. Those of us from the U.S. felt self-conscious. As for Millard and me, both Vietnam vets, we thought here we go again.

Within minutes after the loading ramp was lashed down to the pier at Puerto Natales, Millard and I cycled off ahead of everyone else and sped down the main street in search of the Hospedaje Dickson, recommended highly by Paul De Schepper, a Dutch cyclist I met in Puerto Montt. This tactic was necessary as we knew that the small village with limited accommodations would fill in a matter of minutes after the ship docked.

Upon arriving there we learned from the sole occupant, a German climber, that the Senora was down at the pier soliciting clients. Fortunately, the Senor was available to assign us rooms. Shortly, we were on our way to investigate the town. In Puerto Natales this took no time at all. Within an hour we'd sniffed out the best cafe cortado and dessert place in town. The weather here was cooler and windier, but with the sun out it was a pleasant climate.

~ ~ ~

A Dinner Party

What better way to celebrate the end of a 3-day sea voyage and reunification with terra firma than a quiet dinner with friends at the Bahia Restaurante.

At one end of the room was a large, wood-fired, brick rotisserie. On it was a whole lamb or asada. A 20′ long communal table filled up most of the low-ceilinged room. The walls were decorated with stuffed muskrats and beaver, the skins of llama, and one large bobcat. This along with assorted pieces of equipment used by gauchos, South American cowboys.

Rico our waiter brought us three pitchers of red wine. We drank a toast to the Ro Ro Tierra Del Fuego and the fact that we were off it. Millard slipped his cassette of blues music in a nearby tape player. Instantly the twangy riffs of Johnny Lee Hooker guitar music filled the room.

There were at least ten survivors of the 3-day voyage gathered around the table salivating over a menu featuring fresh salmon and a carne asada roasting on the spit nearby. Amidst a conglomeration of conversations, blues music, the three pitchers of wine were drained, as were three huge bowls of fresh salad. Soon enough we were all plunging large chunks of salmon into our eager mouths, while Rico hustled around the table refilling wine pitchers, bringing more salad, and generally making sure everyone was accommodated. I looked up to see Mike the Aussie standing admiringly beside the asada turning slowly on the spit. From his pocket his withdrew a large knife, sliced off a piece of meat and popped it in his mouth. He chewed for a second, then loudly exclaimed, "Jesus, this is bloody fucking great." Instantly, his knife plunged into the meat again. A line quickly formed behind Mike, who volunteered to be our asada master of ceremonies.

B.B. King serenaded us. Rico eyed us nervously. Ernesto, the five-foot, corpulent cook and owner appeared in the doorway at the far end of the room with a huge butcher knife in his hand. He stomped down the length of the room, his apron discolored with various portions of blood, wine, and grease.

"You want asada, si, it is the finest in Tierra Del Fuego," he bellowed slicing off chunks of meat and placing them on waiting plates.

Rico relaxed and smiled, then Ernesto yelled something at him. He disappeared, but returned promptly with three large bottles of wine compliments of the Ernesto, who was now seated next to Millard and exclaiming animatedly about his virility which, he sighed, resulted in the premature death of two wives. His current wife was some 20-years younger than him, he boasted.

Mike the Aussie was engrossed in his third plate of asada. Charlie found a guitar and strummed it meditatively, while Sherry his wife was dancing with one of the stuffed muskrats. Sue and I were simultaneously feeding each other and dancing. Andy the Kiwi dabbled at his salad while reading a month-old copy of *Time Magazine*. On a bet instigated by Millard and Mike I consumed a heaping bowl of Ernesto's "salsa especiale" and won 500 pesos. Oddly enough, the salsa tasted as innocuous as vanilla pudding.

When next I looked up from an empty wine glass, Mike was arm wrestling with Ernesto and Rico had removed his shirt revealing a hairy chest festooned with nautical tattoos. As Sue and I whirled about the room in a half-waltz, half-polka, two kayakers from the states, Bob and wife Francis, were inspecting a cantaloupe-size rock held by Ernesto's geologist son, Juan, who was discoursing on its composition, particularly its high gold content.

"Hey mate, come take a picture," Mike yelled from across the room.

I looked over to see the Aussie giant decked out in rawhide cowboy hat and the llama skin draped across his shoulders like a poncho. Under one arm he clutched a stuffed beaver, under the other a stuffed otter. No sooner had I snapped the picture, then all the stuffed animals, skins, and assorted memorabilia were snatched from the walls for an ad hoc group photo, to include our host Ernesto who served as a capstone supporting the tilting entourage.

Somewhere around midnight, it came time to settle the bill. Ernesto sat at the head of the stable head-to-head with Rico printing figures on a long sheet of butcher paper. Wallets were withdrawn from fanny packs, like six-shooters from holsters. When the tally was completed, Millard translated for those who cared, into U.S. dollars. Stacks of colorful currency were piled on the table. Slowly people began pushing back their chairs.

"Hey everybody, there's a disco in town. Let's go dancing." Sherry yelled.

"Disco es muerte, long live rock and roll," Millard yelled back. We all echoed his statement like a battle cry.

"Where the hell's the disco," Mike yelled.

"Mis amigos, let me escort you there," Rico called out.

Various voices piped in, "Viva la Disco," "Baille, baille," "Elvis Lives."

Looking across the table over a battlefield of glasses, pitchers and plates, I saw Andy punching the keys of a pocket calculator. At last he announced to no one in particular, "With a gratuity of approximately 30%, the individual share of the bill comes to $6 US per person." But by this time the mound of Chilean currency on the table came closer to $15 US per person. No one, not even Ernesto, bothered to count it as he scooped it up, laughing maniacally while pushing it into his apron.

With our pointman Rico leading the way we poured into the dark night from the restaurant in search of La disco. In response to the cool night air Rico was wearing a Mickey Mouse T-shirt. Except for us the streets were dark and empty, with only the occasional bark of a dog being heard. Soon enough we were piled up behind Rico who was pounding on the door of a what appeared to be an empty, nondescript building. At last the door was flung open, allowing incredibly loud disco music and strobe lights to batter us.

After paying a few pesos apiece for the cover charge we tripped our way into the cavernous void pulsating with music and blinding lights.

Someone pulled a bottle of beer out of my hand and dragged me to the dance floor seething with gyrating bodies and engulfed in a cloud of cigarette smoke. When my eyes adjusted to the murky interior I discovered I was dancing with Sherry and a half-dozen other people. Never a keen dancer, I found myself nonetheless swaying and stomping, occasionally holding someone's hand, and passing to and fro in some kind of musical ensemble, part bebop, part polka, and part African tribal dance. Sweating and breathless I finally escaped the dance floor to join Millard, Sue, Rico, Mike, and Andy. Next thing, I was outside with Sue gulping great draughts of fresh air trying to resuscitate my lungs. Having had enough excitement for the night, Sue returned to the hospedaje with Andy.

Turning to go back into the club I was almost bowled over by Rico, Mike, Millard, and Juan coming out.

"We're going to a club for a beer, you must join us," Rico said marching down the street with his squad of disco dancers.

Not far from the disco we entered what appeared to be your basic neighborhood house, but instead of a living room there was a bar with three or four women seated there. Reddish lights glowed from the walls and tables while salsa music throbbed on a stereo behind the bar. The women at the bar stubbed out their cigarettes and slithered over to our table. One in a mini-skirt exposing husky thighs encased in black fishnet stockings, started massaging my shoulders and suggested I buy her a drink. At least that was what I thought she said, but before I could answer she signaled the female bartender to bring us drinks.

"Is this a private club," I asked Rico.

He and Juan smiled coyly. Millard jabbed my arm.

"This is a genuine Chilean cathouse," he laughed.

A case of beer was spread out on the table in front of us and I was presented with a bill for 35,000 pesos.

Jesus, I muttered, but before I could reach for my wallet, my new lady friend pulled me onto the small dance floor next to our table. Dancing was too generous a word for it, more closely it resembled semi-pro wrestling. When the music ended and I returned to the table Millard was negotiating with one of the other mini-skirted hostesses. Rico was fast asleep with his head on the table and Mike was working on either his fourth or fifth beer. When my friendly hostess suggested I buy another drink, I yawned and told her it was time to leave. Gathering money from those around me, I paid the bill and headed for the door with the others slowly bringing up the rear. It was 5 a.m. when Millard and I finally crossed the threshold of the Hospedaje Dickson. A bit tired, I nonetheless felt clear headed. Millard suggested we catch a few hours sleep before starting out on a trek to Torres Del Paine National Park.

"Sure, no problema," I said falling into my bed fully clothed and fast asleep in under two minutes.

Next thing I knew the Senora was knocking on our door asking if we'd like to eat lunch. It was 1 p.m. and Millard was snoring so loud it was rattling the small panes of glass in our bedroom door. Too late to leave today, I told myself as I rolled over and went back to sleep.

~ ~ ~

The Towers of Paine
(Torres del Paine)

We left for the Torres two days later. It was mid-morning when we finally got our bikes and gear in order. There remained only one problem, the Senora's pet chicken Fred wouldn't get off my bike. During the past few days she had gotten accustomed to sleeping on my rear pannier. I guessed it was some type of nesting ritual or territorial claim. She was so protective about her spot the Senora had to be called to extricate her.

Finally about noon we cycled northeast along the quay and soon found ourselves the only travelers on a broad dirt road. I began to see the first of many road signs I'd come to despise—ripio. Loosely translated it means unusually rough dirt road with potholes and washboards with an occasional rockslide thrown in. At least that was my loose translation. Slight gusty wind and clear blue skies made cycling exhilarating. Far away across the pampas we could see the snowcapped peaks and glacial ice fields of Torres Del Paine National Park. An occasional tour bus or pickup truck would kick up a rooster tail of dust in passing but otherwise we cycled along at a good clip enjoying the views. After three days of forced inactivity on the boat and two more days of revelry in Puerto Natales, we were eager to put some miles behind us. A slight tail wind and gently rolling hills did much to make our first day of biking more than pleasant.

We arrived at a crossroads sheep station late that afternoon and decided to look for a place to stay. The only hosteria, an elegant old estancia converted to a hotel offered rooms at $25 to $40 per night. Having never paid more than $4 during my travels I was shocked. After a bottle of beer in the hosteria bar, Millard and I went back to the sheep station to see if we could find cheaper accommodations or a place to camp.

Alex Teneb, the director of the local electrification project called one of the local sheep herders who agreed to let us sleep in his bunkhouse, which was currently vacant, at no charge. Alex then invited us to a communal dinner at the barracks where he and his crew lived. Afterward we had only to pedal a few hundred yards to the bunkhouse. Though Spartan it had a few basic amenities, like a wood stove and shower room with a half dozen shower stalls, but none with hot water. However, the price was right so we spread out our sleeping bags and enjoyed a quiet night's rest.

Halfway out to the park next day we had to pull off to the side of the road and stop biking to avoid being engulfed in a herd of sheep being driven in from the range. A little further north we got our first glimpse of the Torres. With the help of my sport binoculars I was able to get a closer view of the three main granite towers, like sabre teeth, they lured experienced climbers from all over the world. Wishing to prolong our enjoyment of the superb vista, we put our bikes aside and prepared lunch. We Felt particularly blessed that day because of all the warnings we'd gotten about the vigorous winds that swept relentlessly across Tierra Del Fuego. So far we'd enjoyed only warm sunshine and a slight tailwind too boot.

After a few gratuitous hills, we pedaled around Lago Amarga and uphill to a refugio where we planned to spend the night, before trekking up to the Torres the next morning. As required, we signed the register and showed our passports at the park station a few yards uphill from the refugio. The refugio was no more than a small cabin of ancient plank boards through which the wind had easy access. It was empty save for a couple of backpacks that were stowed there. Millard and I staked out a corner with our sleeping bags and assorted gear. Directly below the cabin, a river, swollen with glacial melt off, flowed swiftly past into Lago Amarga. Exploring around we discovered a foot bridge that spanned the river enabling hikers to gain access to the trail leading up to the Torres. Not far from the bridge I found a grassy bank on the lake. In my shorts I waded into the icy water up to my knees before retreating to the bank, my ankles throbbing with cold. Sponging myself off good at the edge of the lake I dried off quickly thanks to the bright sun.

Cooking our dinner in the cabin, Millard and I talked over our planned assault on the Torres, a 10-mile hike from the refugio. In the meantime, several other hikers arrived at the cabin planning to cook dinner. The inside of the cabin quickly filled to capacity, forcing new arrivals to set up their tents outside.

The main problem with our trek was Millard's lack of a backpack, but with true pioneer spirit , some ineptitude, and a lot of determination, he was able to cobble together a pack from his panniers. Though unsightly, at least it looked serviceable. Once again, my own midsize backpack was ideal to carry my own gear and some of his. I also discovered Millard did not have a tent, cookstove, or even a mess kit.

"How could I carry all that stuff in this makeshift pack," he argued logically.

I argued back that a more equitable distribution of the essential gear, mostly mine, would be achieved if we drank at least one of his boxes of wine. Realizing the strength of my negotiating position he relented with only mild protest.

"Hey pal, who thought to bring all the wine."

"A backpack might have been more practicable," I shot back.

"Not only that Pal, but who brought extra film and two dozen candy bars."

"Candy bars?"

"Yeah, well...besides why do I have to do all the planning."

"Yeah, well you might have planned on a stove of your own. Just remember who has all the freeze dried meals and who will be carrying them up to the Torres."

"Okay, okay. Have some more wine."

"Thanks. What else are you ratholing on me, pal?"

"You accusing me of ratholing. Well maybe you don't want any of this brandy, huh." Millard said pulling a pint bottle from his camera bag and smiling lasciviously.

"Just remember who has the tent!"

"Don't think I was holding out on you, 'cause I wasn't. I was saving this for our absolute best moment, like a celebration."

There was a noticeable frown on his whiskered face as I tilted back the bottle for a drink. In the morning, while boiling coffee water I noticed an accumulation of candy wrappers scattered around the wood box, but paid no attention to them as there were numerous trekkers in and out of the cabin.

We stopped many times along the trail to the Torres, me to study our route up to the Towers of Paine; Millard to swear and thrash about with his cobbled pack, which when fitted on his shoulders looked like he was giving a piggy-back ride to a small gorilla.

Millard's approach to problem solving was both straightforward and entertaining, involving much profanity, generous amounts of kicking, and a liberal beating with his hiking staff.

"Hey Farmer," I'd bark in a moment of impatience,"you'll crush the candy bars."

"Hell I will."

"Whaddaya mean."

"I mean, maybe you don't have to worry about any candy bars."

"I'll bet that was you who threw all those candy wrappers in the kitchen."

"Not all of them. The rest are in my camera case."

"I want my share now, before you scarf up the rest."

"Sure Pal, here take your lousy candy bar. I was just saving it for you."

"Yeah, I bet."

"You callin' me a liar, pal."

Such is the nature of great expeditions.

Out of nowhere, a young American couple came hiking up the trail. We both felt extremely foolish knowing they'd witnessed most of our little chat. I remembered the lady from the night before at the refugio. She was dressed in running shorts, T-shirt, and jogging shoes. He shouldered a large backpack, wore jeans, solid hiking boots, and longsleeve flannel shirt. His nose was thoughtfully covered with zinc oxide. They looked as though they met by accident on the trail; she out for a stroll, he on his way into the wilderness for weeks.

As soon as they left Millard resumed the feeble overhaul of his pack. I reasserted my claim to the candy bar.

Ascending the steep flank of the mountain guarding the Torres like a high wall the infamous winds began. The trail meandered up a steep canyon that resembled a natural wind tunnel. To stay upright even under the weight of my pack, I was forced to lean forward until I could actually touch the ground with my hands. About this time Millard's sunglasses broke in two under the pressure of a particularly treacherous gust of wind and went flying into space like twin tennis balls.

We forged on during a respite in the wind velocity, only to be buffeted about like cardboard cutouts in a gale force wind I guesstimated was blowing at 90 mph. Unable to advance and afraid of turning back we lay down beside the trail, shielding our faces with our arms and waiting for the wind to taper off. When it came we scrambled higher enabling us to find shelter behind a rock ledge. There also were Brett and Gwen huddled together. We settled down beside them glad to find relief from the dust and pebble laden winds. From our protected viewpoint it looked like an airborne landslide. Gwen shivered noticeably.

"Wow, this is scary," she said deadpan.

Brett smiled desultorily.

"Let's turn back it's getting worse," Gwen suggested.

About 20 yards in front of us a car-size boulder broke loose from the mountainside and bounced across the trail like a beach ball, disappearing into the canyon below.

"Whoooaa!" we all whispered.

When at last, 30 to 40 minutes later, the wind slacked off I peeked around the ledge to reconnoiter the trail, noticing that it snaked precipitously across the scree slope that had just upchucked the large boulder. Millard was grousing about how his girlfriend in Santiago had bought his dearly departed sunglasses for his birthday, yadada-yadada.

I looked at Millard and he looked a me.

"Go for it pal."

We scrambled over the exposed trail, making our way as quickly as possible to a grove of trees about 200-yards ahead. Now the wind had slacked off to 50-60 mph, but It was relatively calm in the pine trees. We found a comfortable spot, shucked our packs and made lunch. I got out my binoculars and scanned the trail but saw no sign of Brett and Gwen. Above the trees the wind continued to carry clouds of dust and dirt eastward at great velocity.

We ate lunch and snoozed. Finally, with renewed strength and determination we shouldered our packs and climbed back up to the trail. We made our way swiftly to the forested slopes near the river, glacial fed, in the canyon. The trail began a steep ascent up through the trees until we came to a stream crossing. A single log, elevated about 10-feet above the torrents, offered the only route across the stream, raging and battering itself amongst rocks and boulders. The "stream" was probably running at twice its normal flow due to warm days that intensified glacial melt-off in the upper valleys.

"Damn," we both spat out simultaneously.

At the most, the stream was only 20-feet wide, but too swift and deep to ford. Crossing the log was our only choice, but one miscue and we'd be swept to kingdom come.

"Can't turn back now, pal." Millard said.

We dropped our packs to study the situation. To complicate the log-crossing route, we'd have to wear our packs while tightrope-walking across. Even without the packs balancing, at least for me, would be a difficult matter. Millard explored the stream above and below the log to confirm our suspicions. If anything, he offered, things were worse in either direction. We could camp overnight and wait until the water dropped as melt off decreased later that night, but with only three miles to go to the Torres basecamp we were impatient to move on. As the sky was incredibly clear blue we wanted to reach the Torres for sunset pictures, an opportunity that might not present itself for days or weeks if a front moved in. Millard handed me two candy bars.

"Might as well eat'em now, just in case." he said.

I declined to follow up on his logic, instead I shouldered my pack and moved thoughtfully toward the log. With a balancing staff in one hand, I stepped onto the log to begin my slow, careful one-foot-ahead-of-the-other crossing, which took all of two minutes, but seemed like two hours. Next up, Millard stepped onto the log and all but jogged to midpoint, where he stopped to catch his balance and in doing so dropped his hiking staff. It hit the water and shot downstream like a guided missile. Looking as though he was practicing some teenage dance Millard did everything but click his heels. I averted my eyes. Next thing I knew he was standing next to me.

"Piece of cake, huh," he said smiling.

Not more than 20-yards beyond this crossing we came to a larger, swifter stream. Here again a single log bridged the gap, but this log was half submerged in the raging water. With equal skill and dexterity we managed to cross this one safely as well.

We arrived at the climber's base camp around 4 p.m. Set in a wooded bowl below the Torres, it reminded me of something out of a ghost story, I expected to see a unicorn or perhaps a mammoth lumber through the woods. Various international climbing parties had over the years built cozy little huts, with each new occupant improving and embellishing until they had the looks of vacation cabins.

Also spread amongst the trees, like multi-colored mushrooms, were tents of various shapes and sizes.

Millard and I stopped by one of the elaborate cottages to inspect the interior. Two German climbers were sitting inside at a handmade table sipping tea. Neat rows of shelves housed food staples and a small library. A rock fireplace provided heat and a cooking oven. Everything was neat and clean, even the dirt floor. Stowed orderly about the two men were piles of climbing ropes, carabiners, and assorted mountaineering equipment.

One of the Germans was whittling away on a massive tree root, resembling the tooth of a sabre tiger. Noticing my interest in the carving , he beckoned me closer. I could then see it was a three-foot long carving of the central torre. He and his partner had just completed a successful ascent the previous day. Remembering the extremely vicious winds we'd dealt with earlier I asked what it was like descending the central tower early that morning. The torre had been relatively calm, he explained, making for a quick and safe descent. He quickly added he and his climbing partner had waited two months for the optimum conditions to make their ascent. Hence, he smiled, plenty of time to work on his wood carving.

We pitched camp downhill from the cabins, close to a gushing stream. In the gathering darkness, I cooked up a meal of freeze-dried chicken primavera with tea to drink. For desert, we polished off the last two candy bars.

In the morning the winds had subsided, the sun was streaming down through thickly clustered pines, promising a good climb up to the base of the Torres and ideal photography conditions. After a breakfast of tea and hardrolls we gathered up our camera equipment, a few water bottles, and began the slow steep climb to the three massive spires, still hiding in back of the bouldered slope above basecamp. Up the trail about a mile we began to see the jagged tips of the central Torre, gilded by early morning sun, rise above the rocky canyons around us. The two flanking towers slowly presented themselves like modest siblings crowding an older, wiser big brother.

Finally reaching the crest of the rock pile, we had an unobstructed view of the three Torres and the small glacial lake at their feet. Here we stopped to feast our eyes on the majestic view before us: towering granite spires with a small wreath of clouds forming at the tips of the three towers and a blue sky as a background. Even for non-climbers it's a humbling experience.

While Millard scrambled down closer to the lake, in which huge chunks of ice floated, I pulled my binoculars from my fanny pack. Sitting cross-legged on a flat rock I studied the shear rock face of the central tower, trying to guess which route the German climbing team had taken. In all, it looked like an extremely challenging and rewarding climb. One of the most feared parts of the climbing equation, according to one of the Germans, was the unpredictability of the weather. The treacherous winds alone could turn the towers into a nightmare.

Figure 18: Your author below the Torres.

I took several pictures of the towers with my small, Canon automatic camera. After a hike down to the lake shore, I climbed back up to the relatively flat rock I'd found to sit in the sun and meditate. I'd accomplished two major goals in South America: visiting Machu Picchu and Torres Del Paine. Now, I had one more major goal to accomplish, biking into Ushuaia, Argentina, the bottom of the Americas.

After an hour of bouldering around the base of the Torres, I returned to the flat rock to find Millard eating, once again, the "last" candy bar. Where he was secreting away the booty I couldn't figure out.

Late that afternoon, we gathered our gear and began the descent under fair skies and a slight breeze. The only impediment to our rapid descent was the two stream crossings. What with even warmer weather, both streams were higher and raging with increased vehemence. Now, however, with rest and renewed strength, we took the time to add a second log to our first crossing point, which facilitated a safer crossing.

Figure 19: Cuernos del Paine (Horns of Paine) at Torres del Paine National Park, Chile.

So rapid was our decent, we were back at the footbridge across from the refugio within two and a half hours, but because of accelerated glacial melt off, the footbridge was marooned in the midst of the river its only purpose was to span. Plowing through the knee-high water with boots strung around our necks, we gritted our teeth against the frigid water, but like bosom buddies yelled encouragement to each other.

"Come on, pal, keep moving, for chrissake."

"You wanna lead, go ahead, otherwise zip it up."

"Hey keep that pack up, my film's in there."

With repeated and persistent displays of such fellowship we eventually achieved the gaping lip of the dirt road below the refugio, soaked to our waists, but otherwise unscathed.

~ ~ ~

Chapter 14

Argentina

Theft on the High Seas

Porpoises rose in steady cadence alongside the ferry, while icy winds raked across the exposed gangway in the cargo hold jammed with vehicles. Both Millard and I had multiple layers of clothing on to assuage the chilly passage from Punta Arenas, Chile to Porvenir, Argentina, a three-hour boat ride across the Straights of Magellan.

In addition to my layers, I had on wool gloves and wool hat. Multiple layers notwithstanding, I retreated to the relative comfort of the enclosed passenger compartment. With the boat honing in on the pier at Porvenir, Millard burst into the steamy, crowded passenger cabin where I sat reading my book.

"We've been ripped off!"

I looked at him stunned. We had purposely secured our bikes in the least accessible, most hidden corner of the ferry to avoid theft. On the way to our bikes, Millard ticked off a list of things he was missing, including: camera, film, and rain jacket. After a quick inventory of my own equipment, I determined I'd been robbed of binoculars, sewing kit, MSR stove, and windpants. Luckily, my rain gear had been overlooked even though it had been stored in the same pannier compartment with the binoculars. A brief feeling of relief was quickly replaced with a stunned feeling of loss, then rage. I suddenly retrenched to my Peruvian travel mode of caution, suspicion, and mild paranoia.

With clear skies overhead and a slight tailwind we pedaled down the dirt road to Porvenir and the vast, treeless, windswept pampas beyond. A few days later, after constant battles with headwinds and the "ripio" we charted a course due south through Rio Grande, where a five-mile stretch of pavement buoyed our spirits, then frustrated us when it suddenly disappeared, to be replaced with miles of quagmire.

Now with barely one hundred miles to Ushuaia, the days, months, and years of traveling began to take their toll. I became uncommonly morose. Millard and I pedaled for mile-upon-mile without exchanging a word, or even more unusual, without sniping at each other with the poison-tipped arrows of sarcasm.

Heading up the pass to Mt. Garibaldi in the rain, I stopped for about the tenth time that day. But this time I felt reasonably justified as it was pouring and I had to put on my rain gear. Rain or no rain, I was still eager to reach Hosteria Heruwan, about seven miles south of Garibaldi. Millard, without a rain parka, had sped on trying to reach the hosteria before getting soaked to the skin.

~ ~ ~

Don't Cry For Me Argentina

By the time I reached Hosteria Heruwan I felt like a zombie. I stomped inside and down the hallway to the communal living-dining room. Seated around a large woodburning stove were Millard, a swarthy Argentinean man, and an attractive woman. They barely noticed me their conversation was so animated. I pulled off my rain suit and slumped into an easy chair near the stove. My hands were numb with cold. It took a few minutes before I started coming back to life. Suddenly, I realized Millard was introducing me to our hosts, Jose and his wife Samantha.

After a mug of piping hot coffee was handed to me, we listened to Jose's diatribe on the destruction of the surrounding forests by beavers inadvertently introduced by Juan Peron, the legendary former President of Argentina who held office from 1946-55. With Millard doing the translating, Jose described how the Prime Minister of Canada, on a state visit to Argentina, gave a mated pair of beavers to Peron as a gift. Having no idea of what to do with the beavers, Peron shipped them off to Tierra Del Fuego, the Siberia of Argentina. Without any natural predators the beavers thrived. As the population of beavers increased exponentially, the forests suffered their onslaught. Even with a profitable market for beaver pelts the problem has only worsened. Jose threw up his hands, assuring us he was doing everything possible to reduce the beaver population, including trapping them and shooting them with his .22 rifle. Yet beavers continue to outnumber humans in Tierra Del Fuego. What is to be done with these creatures, Jose lamented. Secretly, I was glad that for once the problem wasn't in some diabolical way related to the United States.

On a fishing trip next day in the woods nearby I witnessed the prolific activity of the beavers in felling timber. As Jose foretold it was a debacle. Considering their appetite for native trout in the numerous streams, I still came away with a stringer of fish.

~ ~ ~

The Road less Traveled

On the road to Ushuaia, Millard perhaps in revenge stopped to take pictures more times than my extremely low threshold of patience would tolerate. Soon, I was way out ahead pedaling furiously through forest and mountain, enjoying sun and warm temperatures. At last the dirt road dropped down out of the mountains rewarding me with a broad, unobstructed view of the Beagle channel, named after the ship on which Charles Darwin made his historic cruise. Within the hour I could see the harbor fronting the small town of Ushuaia. A welcome relief was the pavement that began a few miles outside town. Woodframe houses and cabins climbed the steep hillside north of town.

Figure 20: Author with Japanese friends, Ushuaia, Argentina. End of a memorable bicycle tour.

After one last foray with a pack of mongrel dogs on the edge of Ushuaia, I wheeled eagerly into the city center feeling triumphant. Stopping on the main street outside the Cafe Real, a group of young Japanese tourists surrounded me. Whether they understood me I'll never know, but I told them passionately about my three-year cycling odyssey. One of the girls took my camera, backed up a few feet and said something in Japanese to her friends. I think it was something like "cheese." Her comrades pressed closer, putting their arms around me and hugging me like a long lost uncle. We smiled.

"Aaahso," she exclaimed snapping the picture.

Aaaahhhssoooo!

The End

Aaaahhhssoooo!

0-595-13238-3